Famous and Curious Cemeteries

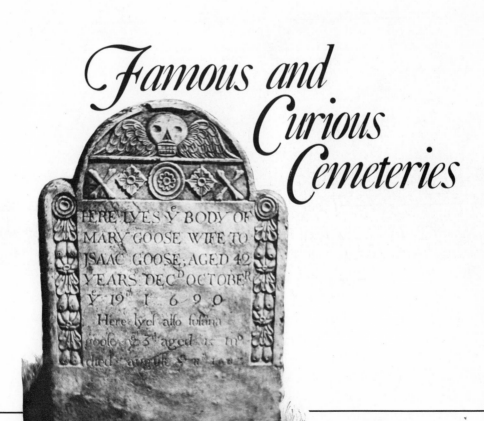

Famous and Curious Cemeteries

A Pictorial, Historical, and Anecdotal
View of American and European
Cemeteries and the Famous and
Infamous People Who Are
Buried There

by JOHN FRANCIS MARION

with 256 monumental photographs

CROWN PUBLISHERS, INC. NEW YORK

ALSO BY THE AUTHOR

Lucrezia Bori of the Metropolitan Opera
Bicentennial City
Philadelphia Medica

Inquiries should be addressed to Crown Publishers, Inc., One Park Avenue,
New York, N.Y. 10016

Printed in the United States of America

Published simultaneously in Canada by
General Publishing Company Limited

Book Design: Shari de Miskey

Library of Congress Cataloging in Publication Data

Marion, John Francis.
 Famous and curious cemeteries.

 Bibliography: p.
 Includes index.
 1. Cemeteries—United States. 2. Cemeteries—Europe.
I. Title.
GT3203.M3 1977   940   77-5530
ISBN 0-517-52955-6

For
Edna Eipper Baum
with love
and in memory of
Albert Crofton Baum
and
Pfc. Albert Crofton Baum, Jr.

C. 1

12/20/77 B*J

Contents

III. AMERICAN MILITARY CEMETERIES OVERSEAS   170

World War I Cemeteries

World War II Cemeteries

Acknowledgments

THIS book would not have been written without the confidence shown in it from its inception, or the constant encouragement of my editor, Brandt Aymar. It would have been an even more difficult undertaking without the assistance of a number of others.

Doris Langley Moore made valuable initial suggestions from London when the book was in its germinal stage. John Morrison, long associated with the Iona Community in the past, supplied me with data concerning the Relig Odhrain. His brother, T. J. Morrison, gave me invaluable information concerning Scottish churchyards. Their sister, N. Brysson Morrison, was untiring in sending me her own researches into ancient graveyards and epitaphs, and she also read my manuscript where it concerned the cemeteries in Edinburgh and Glasgow.

Joseph E. and Ruth Branning Molloy supplied me with old and rare books and informative articles and pictures. Adrianne Onderdonk Dudden, with unerring taste, brought a scholar's and artist's eye to the Central Cemetery in Vienna, and evoked it for me as if I had been there. Ruth and S. Alexander Smith in their researches accomplished wonders in Dublin, and photographed every aspect of Glasnevin Cemetery.

Clive E. Driver, who has made an in-depth study of Green-Wood Cemetery in Brooklyn, generously placed his notes at my disposal. Florence and Robert W. Cabaniss and Betty Christian drove me through the Virginia countryside one autumn to visit the cemeteries of Richmond, Petersburg, Williamsburg, and Jamestown. If a cemetery can be said to be brought to life, then Mary Wingfield Scott performed that feat of necromancy in Hollywood Cemetery in Richmond. And William Schneider, in guiding me through The Woodlawn Cemetery, gave me a liberal education in the subject.

The Honorable Francis X. Connell, associate judge of the Circuit Court of Cook County, Illinois, took time from his judicial duties to gather material for me on the Chicago cemeteries; and Mary Capouya, Robert Hendrickson, and Priscilla Sawyer Lord were constant sources of information. Charles Seeger located for me the grave of his brother, Alan Seeger, the poet, and C. O. Kates granted me permission to quote extensively from the article on the Albany Rural Cemetery that appeared in *American Cemetery*. To all I am extremely grateful.

I also express my appreciation to a number of people at various institutions who searched out obscure or little-known facts for me, or provided me with basic research material. They are: American Battle Monuments Commission, Colonel William E. Ryan, Jr., and Vera C. Winkler; Library of the American Philosophical Society, Whitfield J. Bell, Jr., Roy E. Goodman, Carl F. Miller, Murphy D. Smith, and Hildegard G. Stephans; The First Church of Christ, Scientist, R. Ross Collins and A. W. Phinney; Historic American Buildings

Survey, John Poppeliers and Nancy B. Schwartz; Lancaster County Historical Society, Lancaster, Pennsylvania, John W. Aungst, Jr.; Library Company of Philadelphia, Lillian Tonkin and Edwin Wolf 2nd; Library of Congress, Mary Ison; Newport Historical Society, Newport, Rhode Island, Gladys Bolhouse; Old Salem, Inc., Jan Hiester; Philadelphia City Institute, Free Library of Philadelphia, Paul E. McAdam, Marianne Promos, and Hope D. Ritz; Temple University, Samuel Paley Library, Thomas M. Whitehead; United States Military Academy, West Point, New York, Major Bill Smullen; United States Naval Academy, Annapolis, Maryland, Del Malkie; Veterans Administration, James M. Griffin, Nicholas G. Hamaty, and John W. Mahan; Department of Conservation and Cultural Affairs, Virgin Islands, June A. V. Lindqvist; and the Chamber of Commerce in both Montgomery, Alabama, and Saint Augustine, Florida.

The offices of many cemeteries sent me information in answer to my queries. Many did not. Among those who were most helpful with specific material, I remember with appreciation the following: Albany Rural Cemetery, Robert G. Killough; Arlington National Cemetery, R. J. Costanzo; Bellefontaine Cemetery, Donald W. Meyer; Blandford Cemetery, James H. Bailey; Christ Church Burial Ground, Sandra R. Thornton; Cimitero degli Inglesi, Rudolf Schenk; Crown Hill, Horace Moorman and Stewart D. Tomkins; Ferncliff Cemetery, V. E. Angerole; Forest Lawn Cemetery, Buffalo, New York, Fred R. Whaley, Jr.; Forest Lawn Memorial—Parks and Mortuaries, Paul Berthelot and Dick Fisher; Gate of Heaven Cemetery, Louis Anguish; Gettysburg National Cemetery, Thomas J. Harrison; Glasgow Necropolis, James Stevens Curl; God's Acre, Mary Creech; Green Mount Cemetery, John D. Mayhew; Highgate Cemetery, Valerie Winter and Michael Wright; Hollywood Cemetery, John W. Brown, Jr.; The Iona Community, Mary MacKechnie; Jewish Cemetery, Newport, Rhode Island, Rabbi Theodore Lewis; Jews' Burying Ground, Nevis, Robert D. Abrahams, Esq., and Peter Renerts; Laurel Hill Cemetery, Mary Jane and Drayton M. Smith; Moravian Cemetery, Staten Island, New York, Bradley Gramprey; Mount Auburn Cemetery, Alan D. Chesney; National Memorial Cemetery of the Pacific, Ernest C. Schanze; Old Jewish Cemetery, Prague, Erik Klíma; Protestant Cemetery, R. Hichens-Bergström, ambassador of Sweden to Italy, and Karin Melin-Fravolini of Kungliga Biblioteket, Stockholm; Rock Creek Cemetery, Stanton L. Wormley; Spring Grove Cemetery, Leo J. Mistak; Swan Lake Cemetery, James P. Black; Trinity Churchyard, Helen Rose Cline and Reverend William B. Gray; and Woodlawn Cemetery, Kennerly Woody.

To all the following for providing information or photographs, I am also grateful: Seymour Adelman, Louise Allen, Ronald and Sheila Arculus, Hettie Bachman, Elizabeth and D. C. Brooks, Stephen D. Budrow, Ann S. and Robert J. Cahn, Eleanor R. Callahan, Steven Lee Carson, Frances Cavanah, Ida B. DePencier, Harold S. Diehl, Caroline Dosker, Elizabeth Cabell Dugdale, Anne and Hilda Einselen, Niki Ekstrom, Parmenia Migel Ekstrom, Duncan Cairnes Ely, Hugh D. Ford, Seaborn P. Foster, Madeline and Joseph Fox, Doris Y. and James R. Frakes, Pauline R. Frazier, Muriel Fuller, Alice R. Gautsch, Susan J. Gibbons, Henry F. Gill, Esq., Kathryn H. Greenwood, Martin Greif, Gene Gurney, Eric W. Halbig, Keith F. Harris, Armason Harrison, Mildred Hopkins, Carol-Joyce Howell, Ellen S. Jacobowitz, Dorothy Hayes Johnson, Julie Kernan, Milton Kenin, Caroline Klein, Joseph P. Lash, Mary Louise Lindsay, Beverley Lord, John Maass, John McGrath, Mary S. and James E. Marion, Kenneth D. Matthews, Jr., Marjorie Maurer, Lidie Miller, Miriam B. Milligan, Rabbi Ezekiel N. Musleah, W. Glen Myers, Ralph Paterline, Kin Platt, Samuel D. Porpora, Henry Hope Reed, Jr., James K. Robertson, Frankie McKee Robins, Anthony Roma, Theodore Roosevelt III, Ruth Sarner, Foster Schmitt, Clarkson Schoettle, Doris P. and John H. Shalley, Jr., Anne and Thomas J. Shanahan, Della M. and Martha L. Simonetti, Grahme T. Smallwood, Dorothy Valentine Smith, Eugene E. Smith, Margaret Smith, Harry Soviak, Joseph R. Spector, Esq., Rabbi Malcolm H. Stern, Edward Stranix, Daniel B. Strickler, Esq., Miriam H. Tees, Betty Anne and Gordon B. Tribble, W. Douglas Varn, Marion von Rosenstiel, Vida B. Wentz, Georganne Woessner, Harvard C. Wood, Jr., Harvard C. Wood III, Karl Wurzer, and Joseph J. and Helen Hughes Zimmer.

Introduction

AS 1976 was itself dying, Julian Moynahan, writing in *The New York Times Book Review,* made a statement that represents much of the present attitude toward death: "In modern literature dying seems the last frontier . . . it is the only one left veiled and mysterious enough to solicit the over-informed modern imagination."

It is that last frontier that has intrigued me since childhood. Death has always held a certain mystery, a great fascination; never the fear that it has for most people. This, I suspect, has accounted in part for my love of cemeteries.

No American of Irish ancestry could possibly not be aware of death, burial, and its trappings. In my childhood journeys to Albany, New York, my mother's home, a visit to Saint Agnes Cemetery was a certainty. Soon after we arrived, my grandmother would suggest we ride up the river road to see the plot. Such an undertaking has little relevance to today's generation; most do not know where their grandparents are buried. For me it had great importance. (The Victorians used the word "plat" as we do "plot," and both are used interchangeably in this book.)

We drove along the Hudson toward Watervliet and once inside the gates of Saint Agnes, we soon found the plot. Then followed the timeworn ritual. We simply stood about admiring and discussing it: of providing Perpetual Care someday when we had more money, the exact locations of my great-grandparents' graves and those of my grandfather, various aunts, uncles, and cousins. It was always mentioned that great-grandmother's body had been lowered at one point—since she was one of the first buried there—to make room for someone else. All these bits of information were turned over like so many jewels, ruminated on, and carefully stored away by one young member of the group. Aunt Kathryn, not having a garden of her own, once cut the roses and peonies to take home, declaring the dead could not see and appreciate them as she did.

Thus, my imagination was piqued. Since my great-grandparents on both sides of my mother's family were immigrants, and no photographs of them survived, this plot was for me the site of my heritage in America. This most detractors of cemeteries fail to grasp: The cemetery is often the one tangible link with a family's past.

It has been said: "Show me your cemeteries and I'll show you a nation's society." The observant visitor can readily grasp much of the history of an area by examining a cemetery. J. M. C. Toynbee in *Death and Burial in the Roman World* tells us: "The appearance of all city cemeteries was, naturally, largely determined by the tombs of the wealthy and reasonably well-to-do who could afford to buy a piece of land on which a personal or family grave-monument or house-tomb could be erected."

One can often observe social position by the elaborateness of the monument. True, some of the great—Benjamin Franklin, Sir Winston Churchill, Franklin and Eleanor Roosevelt, and Charles de Gaulle, to name a few—have simple stones over their graves, but the monuments of the affluent and prominent in many cemeteries reflect their wealth and position in society. In the cemeteries and burial practices one sees much of the life of a particular epoch. This is especially true in our age of mediocrity when architecture and decorative ornamentation have been so watered down that even our cemeteries lack personality. Like most things constructed today, our modern cemeteries seem to show all the impermanence man now seems to feel about life. These new memorial parks with their tidy lawns and bronze plaques flush with the grass have the same uniformity that today's fashion in dress has. We all represent the least common denominator. How different from our ancestors!

It is this time past that I have endeavored to recall. Because there have been studies made of the burial practices of primitive peoples and of the classical world, the present book was never intended to be a history of cemeteries from ancient time to the present. I have selected certain cemeteries for their intrinsic interest, their place in a community's history, or because they are repositories of the famous. Some are seventeenth and eighteenth century in origin, but most are of the nineteenth century, when the movement for rural, or garden, cemeteries gained momentum. In certain cases there are ancient ones, such as the Reilig Odhrain on the island of Iona and the Old Jewish Cemetery in Prague. Both, I felt, were germane to the book.

These burial grounds are legacies of the past. Through them we see monument and architectural design, the role of the cemetery in city planning. John Maass, who has made a study of the Victorian world and consequently of cemeteries, reminds us that the subject straddles several disciplines: history, social customs, symbology, religious rites, social anthropology, and economics. They are, in essence, parks, horticultural and arboreal oases in the city, bird sanctuaries.

Maass tells us that "Victorian cemeteries survive as fine and unspoiled examples of nineteenth-century architecture and town planning. The Victorian necropolis had its public buildings (gateways, chapels, offices) on squares and boulevards, its mansions (mausoleums) on large lots with a view along fashionable drives, its middle-class homes (tombs) on winding urban and suburban streets (walks); some cemeteries also boasted apartment buildings (catacombs, columbariums) and transient accommodations (mausoleums for rent). The Victorian cemetery was also the people's museum which displayed sculpture in communities which had few other specimens of the art."

In the past cemeteries were sought as places of promenade, or of solitary contemplation. Families were wont to spend a Sunday at the cemetery. Once having viewed their own family plot, they would stroll about, often stopping to admire a particular monument, and to picnic there. Pilgrimages were made to the graves of the famous. It was not worship of the dead, but homage to them.

The neglect of cemeteries brought about deterioration, then obliteration. The rise of our twentieth-century cities and towns, and the consequent desire for every inch of land within them, suddenly made the older cemeteries anachronisms. Preservationists are seeking now to save those that remain. If this book has a raison d'être apart from the author's lifelong love of cemeteries, it is that it may revive interest in the subject and provoke preservation and restoration efforts. Several have been placed on the National Register of Historic Places in the United States and there is a similar movement afoot in the United Kingdom.

Ironically, a cemetery lot may be the only piece of property a person ever owns. This was mentioned poignantly in *A Tree Grows in Brooklyn* when the mother holds the deed to the cemetery lot in her hand and realizes she is a property owner at last. Since many of us may eventually be such owners, and later dwellers in a cemetery, it is hoped that the stories told here will enable the reader to consider burial grounds as pleasant, peaceful places—cities of silence within the more noisy world about us. Now, let us open the gates, stroll along the paths, and discover the wonders within.

John Francis Marion
Philadelphia

I. Europe
and the
West Indies

PERCY BYSSHE SHELLEY

COR CORDIUM

NATUS IV AUG. MDCCXCII.

OBIIT VIII JUL. MDCCCXXII

Nothing of him that doth fade,
But doth suffer a sea-change
Into something rich and strange

Père-Lachaise, an early view showing a funeral procession. *Print and Picture Department, Free Library of Philadelphia*

1. Père-Lachaise

PARIS, FRANCE

PÈRE-LACHAISE is more than a necropolis. It is, in fact, a small city of thousands—all dead—within the larger city of Paris. It is never empty of life; there is movement here constantly. It is Paris's conscience and Parisians are continually aware of its existence. Père-Lachaise is as much a part of the City of Light as the Arc de Triomphe, the Eiffel Tower, and Notre-Dame.

The name derives from the confessor to Louis XIV, whose estate it was in the eighteenth century. That monarch had sent the Jesuit a crew of gardeners who landscaped the property in the planned, romantic manner of the French country seats during the reign of the Sun King. Mont-Louis, as it was then called, had a succession of owners, one of whom, a certain Baron Desfontaines, was in possession in 1804 when, by decree of Napoleon (then first consul), Père-Lachaise, outside Paris, became the new burial place for the city.

Nicolas Frochot, prefect of the Seine, was the first consul's architect for the scheme. By what means he con-

vinced the baron to sell the villa, outbuildings, mews, belvedere, and gardens for a trifling sum, we do not know. How he persuaded him to leave the property of seventeen acres within eight days is even more puzzling. On June 12, 1804, Napoleon issued a decree stressing the ban against burial within, or just outside, churches, synagogues, and temples. Père-Lachaise officially opened the week Napoleon was named emperor of the French on December 2, 1804.

The condition that brought about the Napoleonic decree and the establishment of Père-Lachaise was one common to all old cities of Europe, but especially to Paris. For centuries the dead had been buried on top of one another. Finally the earth was filled and the tombs aboveground were equally crowded. It was not uncommon to observe bones and skeletons protruding from graves. In truth, it was a *danse macabre*. In 1763 there was a parliamentary investigation but like so many French procedures, although it produced reports, statis-

3

tics, and proposals, nothing further was done and the findings were abandoned. The powerful clergy benefited by the fact that corpses populated church property that was beyond local control. They controlled the selling of graves and burial fees.

By 1780 nature took a hand in the situation. An apartment block abutted the ancient Cimetière des Innocents. In that year its cellar walls gave way from the pressure of thousands of corpses buried nearby. More than two thousand tumbled through the breach. The stench permeated the quarter. Paris was scandalized—and almost asphyxiated. This led to the closing of the Innocents—and other cemeteries—and the opening in 1786 of an ossuary south of the city called The Catacombs.

The bones of the dead were transferred to The Catacombs with great regularity from 1786 until 1788 and, excepting two small burial places in Montmartre and Vaugirard, and the cemetery of Sainte-Catherine, there was little outward sign that burials had taken place for centuries in Paris. This situation continued with certain recommendations by lesser city officials—until the proposal was made for Père-Lachaise.

Frochot began his plans as early as 1801 (the prefectural authorities had suggested in 1794 that four distinct cemeteries be planned outside the city) and three years later saw his vision take form. In 1814 alone, a total of 509 monuments were erected (more than had been previously constructed), and Baron Desfontaines, who purchased a spot for himself on his former estate eighteen years after selling Mont-Louis, paid 272 times the original rate for which this small piece of ground (three square yards) was sold to Frochot.

In the beginning events moved slowly. The first burial was that of a police commissioner's errand boy, hardly the sort to attract the better classes. What was needed were names and Frochot was not to be thwarted in his pursuit of them. Two dear to the heart of every Frenchman—Molière, born Jean Baptiste Poquelin (1622–1673), perhaps France's greatest comic dramatist; and Jean de La Fontaine (1621–1695), poet and author of *Fables Choisies*—came to mind and were immediately sought. The bones of these immortals lay, in actuality, in Alexander Lenoir's Museum of French Monuments, where they had been on deposit since the National Assembly had them exhumed a dozen years before—Molière's from Saint-Joseph's graveyard, La Fontaine from the Cimetière des Innocents. They were moved to Père-Lachaise in 1817.

Earlier the remains of Louise de Lorraine, queen to Henri III, the last male member of the House of Valois, were discovered by workers demolishing a Capuchin convent near the Place Vendôme. Molière and La Fontaine are still at Père-Lachaise. Louise remained only a decade, but long enough to give the cemetery a royal cachet before Louis XVIII, after the Bourbon Restoration, had her moved again to the Church of Saint-Denis.

Those legendary lovers Héloïse and Abélard came to rest finally at Père-Lachaise after having been separated and reunited six times since the twelfth century. Pierre Abélard (1079–1142), the French scholastic, fell in love with and secretly married his pupil Héloïse, niece of Fulbert, a canon of Notre-Dame. When her uncle had him emasculated by hired ruffians, Abélard retired to a monastery to become a monk; Héloïse eventually an abbess to a company of nuns. Their figures on the tomb have hands clasped. He is tonsured, his feet resting on a small stone dog; she wears a nun's headdress. Their monument is covered with a Gothic canopy constructed of fragments from the Paraclet Convent.

Because of certain municipal manipulations, although the land within Père-Lachaise rose in value as the cemetery's acceptance increased, that adjacent to it depreciated. In 1850 the area of Père-Lachaise was doubled—and again at a ridiculously low price. Louis Napoleon Bonaparte, nephew of the founder of the Imperial dynasty, was now emperor of France. In 1853, according to his directive, the poor would be buried as others and not stacked seven deep as before. During the Crimean War he granted the Turks, allies of France, one square block of Père-Lachaise—enough ground to erect a mosque and bury their dead.

It remained for Rachel—the greatest actress of her time, and occasional mistress of Napoleon III (she was also the paramour of his cousin "Plon-Plon," Prince Napoleon)—to have one of the memorable funerals of the Third Empire. Rachel (1821–1858), the great tragedienne who illuminated the works of Corneille, Racine, and Sardou, died at Le Cannet, a tiny village overlooking the Mediterranean, not far from Cannes. Her body was returned to Paris for burial.

At high noon from the Place Royale the procession set out for Père-Lachaise. Six horses drew the hearse, the coffin was covered with a white pall sprinkled with silver stars. On it lay the Crown of the Immortelles. Sixteen carriages of mourners followed. Madame Anita de Barrera, who published the *Memoirs of Rachel* in 1858, describes the occasion:

> The funeral obsequies were performed according to the Jewish rites, in the Israelite division of the cemetery of Père la Chaise. The hearse was preceded by the Grand Rabbi of the Jewish Consistory of Paris, and followed by the father, brother, and youngest boy as the chief mourners. The ribbons were held by MM. Alex. Dumas (the elder), Auguste Maquet, Chairman of the Society of Dramatic Authors, M. Geoffroy, *sociétaire* of the Théâtre Français, and Baron Taylor.
>
> Not withstanding the inclemency of the weather, the crowd was immense. Perhaps no dramatic artist was ever followed to the grave by so numerous a *cortège* of distinguished writers. Among them were MM. Scribe, Alphonse de Vigny, Saint Beuve, Emile Augier, Legouvé, Viennet, and other members of the Academy; M. Camille Doucet, from the Ministère d'État; M. Emile de Girardin; MM. Halevy, Alexandre Dumas, Auguste Barbier, Fiorentino, Mario Nehaud, Ar-

sène Houssaye, Louis de Ratisbonne, Latour de Saint Ybars, Michael Levy, and the managers of the Parisian theatres. The majority of the *artistes* of the Grand Opera, Théâtre Français, Opera Comique, &c., &c., were also there.

Funeral orations were spoken by MM. Jules Janin, Auguste Maquet, and Bataille.

March Cost, Rachel's greatest biographer, gives a touching picture of the final moments at Père-Lachaise:

Virginie Déjazet was the name on every lip.

None had seen her till the critical moment. None had expected it. Least of all, Dumas. But her timing had been perfect.

One moment she had not been there. The next she was revealed as the only person present, for as the coffin descended, her two hands were seen to part above it and a shower of violets fell.

As Déjazet left Père-Lachaise, Miss Cost tells us:

"Nor had this been all. At the gates she had paused as she saw the mob waiting. And her face had cleared like an April day. With a gesture that embraced everyone, she had exclaimed to the crowd's delight: 'Wonderful ... wonderful! What would not I give to have half this number at my own funeral!' "

The Bonapartes are present too, although the greatest of them, Napoleon I, is in Invalides and others are buried elsewhere in Europe. His sister, Caroline Bonaparte (1782–1839), and her husband, Joachim Murat (1767–1815), lie in Père-Lachaise, and several "connections," such as Marie Walewska (1789–1817), the Polish countess who was Napoleon's mistress (portrayed by Greta Garbo in the film *Conquest*), are here. Not far from her burial place is their natural son, Alexandre Walewski (1810–1868), by whom Rachel bore a son.

Victor Noir, not a Bonaparte but who achieved a certain fame in death because of his brush with one on his final day of life, has his spot in Père-Lachaise too. In 1870 a Parisian journalist who contributed to *La Marseillaise* accused Prince Pierre Bonaparte, nephew of Napoleon and son of Lucien, of having insulted him in an article the prince had written. He sent his seconds to Pierre, challenging him to a duel. The prince refused the challenge; an altercation ensued; and one of the seconds, Victor Noir, a young journalist, was shot by Bonaparte. Noir, whose real name was Yvan Salmon, became a Republican martyr. More than twenty thousand climbed the stairs to his fifth-floor room where his body lay; over a hundred thousand crowded the streets leading to Père-Lachaise on the day of his funeral. Indignation ran high in Paris. The public outcry was against not only Pierre, but the family, who were compared to the Borgias. Noir is forgotten today, but the scandal surrounding his murder led to the downfall of Napoleon III.

By 1860, with the annexation of the suburbs, Père-Lachaise was taken into the city of Paris, no longer an orphan beyond its walls. Napoleon III's reign was not without its dramatic moments. With his flight during the Franco-Prussian War, the Bonapartes toppled from the throne the second, and last, time. In 1871 the Communards who were driven from the city proper took refuge and set up their batteries in the most unlikely of spots—Père-Lachaise. Eleven artillery pieces were dragged there, eight set up near the cenotaph of the Duc de Morny (1811–1865).

Three artillery pieces were placed near the pyramid over the grave of the financier Nicolas Beaujon. Feeling in Paris ran high at the thought of this desecration; the press depicted the Communards in orgies of debauchery among the graves and mausoleums. On May 27 a company of marines managed to breach the wall. Guerrilla warfare ensued as the Republicans and the Communards played a cat-and-mouse game. The Communards' final stand was against the eastern wall and resulted in a terrible slaughter—seven hundred men and women fell and their bodies were thrown into a common grave with five hundred others from Mazas Prison and seventy from the streets of the city. This carnage was not enough for the Republicans, and 147 fédérés (or Communards) were lined against the wall and executed the following day. These "expiations" (as Adolphe Thiers called them) weighed heavily on the French conscience. In 1883 that portion of the wall—the Mur des Fédérés—that served as a place of execution was dedicated to the memory of the Communards.

All was not egalitarian, nor had it been in this city of *Liberté! Égalité! Fraternité!* From the beginning most graves were held for five years by lease and when these expired the holders' bones were ignominiously thrown into a common grave. Eternal ground went to the wealthy for high prices. In 1804, for instance, cemetery property was granted in perpetuity to them. For a hundred francs the first square meter of land could be purchased and, at competitive rates beyond that, one could buy as many as sixteen square meters, "ownership of which will be assured, whatever may befall, for time immemorial." Jews, such as Rachel and the Rothschilds, were in a walled ghetto. All this changed after the establishment of the Third Republic. In 1874 the Municipal Council ruled that the temporary leases and the resultant common grave would cease (but it was eight years before the ruling was official), and in 1882 the ghetto wall was razed. By 1887 the Turkish mosque had disappeared and a crematorium had taken its place, but it was another two years before anyone was farsighted enough to use it.

One of the most remarkable monuments is that to Oscar Wilde (1854–1900), the Irish-born playwright whose adventures in the purple world of London's decadence led to his downfall, trial, imprisonment, and eventual exile. For years it was considered scandalous, almost a phallic symbol in the city of the dead. Commissioned of Jacob Epstein by "a lady," it is a large, square plinth with a male angel on one side. His face and headdress are Egyptian in character.

The facts of Wilde's life—except those of his fall from grace—are recorded on the other side of the monument. We now know, as a result of the publication of Violet Wyndham's *The Sphinx and Her Circle,* a memoir of the novelist Ada Leverson, whom Wilde called "The Sphinx," that "a lady" was Helen Kennard Carew. At a dinner at the Ritz Hotel in London on December 17, 1908, Robert Ross (who handled the Wilde estate) told the assembled guests, including the prime minister, according to Mrs. Wyndham, "that he had received a gift of £2,000, on the condition that the giver should be anonymous, to place a suitable monument to Oscar Wilde at Père-Lachaise and that this work should be carried out by the brilliant young sculptor, Mr. Jacob Epstein."

Père-Lachaise lies at the juncture of the Avenue de la République, the Avenue Gambetta, and the Boulevard de Ménilmontant. The French in their desire for order laid it out in eight sections and within these are ninety-seven divisions. All are encircled, bisected, and separated by a series of avenues, *chemins* (roads), and *allées.* The avenues have rather commonplace names—Avenue Circulaire, Avenue de la Chapelle, Avenue Principale, but some of the streets are more memorable: Chemin Talma, Chemin de Lesseps, and Chemin du Mont-Louis. Along these walkways is the most amazing collection of mausoleums, temples, mosques, obelisks, pyramids, broken columns, ziggurats, chapels, menhirs, tiny Gothic cathedrals, miniature basilicas, urns, and altars.

Sarah Bernhardt (1844–1923) did not suffer the fate of her fellow actress Rachel, who was buried in the walled enclosure reserved for Jews. During her lifetime the walls came down. (Sarah, who was born illegitimately to a Jewish mother, was baptized a Roman Catholic.) However, the Divine Sarah, according to Alexander Woollcott, had other plans for her final resting place and they did not include Père-Lachaise. She intended to be buried "in a tomb cut deep into the seawashed rock of her own Belle Isle, that little, white edged island which lies just off the ugly port of Saint-Nazaire." She later lost the island in one of her many financial crises.

Bernhardt had early in life a strange predilection—she persuaded her mother to purchase for her a satin-lined redwood coffin. She occasionally slept in it, as when she was caring for her tubercular sister, Régina, and the physician in charge forbade her to sleep in the same bed with the invalid. There is no record that she was buried in *that* coffin, but we do know what her last words were. On being told there were reporters outside her home, waiting for news of her condition, Bernhardt replied: "All my life reporters have tormented me enough. I can tease them now a little by making them cool their heels." Cornelia Otis Skinner reminds us that the French government for unexplained reasons failed "to give their

great actress a national funeral, but the people of Paris gave her one as many ... walked behind the hearse ... as had at the time of Victor Hugo's obsequies. During the slow journey from the church of Saint-François-de-Sales the cortege stopped for a minute of silent tribute outside the Théâtre Sarah Bernhardt, then continued on its way."

The world of the theatre is well represented at Père-Lachaise. Mlle. George (1787–1867), a favorite of Napoleon I, who was born Marguerite-Joséphine Weymer; François Joseph Talma (1763–1826), the greatest tragedian of his time; and those darlings of the music halls—Yvette Guilbert (?1867–1944) and Edith Piaf (1915–1963). Lying beside her last husband, Théo Sarapo, Piaf is as popular in death as in life. Her grave is continually covered with vases of fresh flowers left there by the faithful. The other grave that seems to have the most floral offerings is that of Alain Kardec, called the "pope of spiritism." Those interested in the occult line up before his black bust to commune with the spirit world and come laden with flowers.

It would be an impossibility to list all the notables in Père-Lachaise, but among the artists are Amedeo Modigliani (1884–1920), Eugène Delacroix (1798–1863), Jean Auguste Dominique Ingres (1780–1867), Camille Corot (1796–1875), Honoré Daumier (1808–1879), Jean-Baptiste Isabey (1767–1855), Gustave Doré (1833–1883), and Camille Pissarro (1830–1903). Musicians include Francis Poulenc (1899–1963), Reynaldo Hahn (1875–1947), Gustave Charpentier (1860–1956), Frédéric Chopin (1810–1849), Luigi Cherubini (1760–1842), Vincenzo Bellini (1801–1835), Gabriel Fauré (1845–1924), and François (Esprit) Auber (1782–1871). Among the writers are Marcel Proust (1871–1922), Guillaume Apollinaire (1880–1918), Honoré de Balzac (1799–1850), Alphonse Daudet (1840–1897), Benjamin Constant (1767–1830), Alfred de Musset (1810–1857)—at his request a willow stands by his grave—Jules Romains (1885–1972), Colette (1873–1954), and Gertrude Stein (1874–1946).

Three of Napoleon's marshals—François Christophe Kellermann (1735–1820), André Masséna (1758–1817), and Michel Ney (1769–1815); a well-known lady of uncertain virtue, la Comtesse Verasis de Castiglione (1840–1900), who was very close to Napoleon III; Samuel Hahnemann (1755–1843), who was responsible for the development of homeopathy; and that monstrous old lecher and astute maneuverer of destinies and dynasties, Charles Maurice de Talleyrand-Périgord (1754–1838), deposed bishop of Autun and prince de Benevento, are all neighbors at Père-Lachaise.

Reminders of the tragedy, suffering, and the murder of European Jews during the Hitler years are seen in the memorials to those who died at Buchenwald, Mauthausen, and Sachsenhausen. The Mauthausen monument forms a series of steps—a symbolic stairway from prison to freedom—to which the tragic form of an emaciated inmate clings, clutching a step. The attitude of the figure tells of its despair; the hanging head and lifeless arms relate that he did not achieve his goal. The story on the monument's face tells all: 180,000 imprisoned, 154,000 exterminated. Small pots of flowers are placed with regularity before these memorials.

Père-Lachaise has achieved a place in history—and in literature. Perhaps no description is more evocative of this repository of all that is near and dear to the French than the figure of Eugène de Rastignac in Balzac's *Père Goriot,* standing in Père-Lachaise, his arm raised, fist clenched, shouting at Paris: "Now it's between the two of us!"

The monument to General Foy at Père-Lachaise. Engraving, circa 1830, by Fenner Sears & Company. *Print and Picture Department, Free Library of Philadelphia*

The monument to actor François Joseph Talma. Engraving published by Robert Jennings and William Chaplin, Cheapside, August 1, 1830. *Print and Picture Department, Free Library of Philadelphia*

Rachel's tomb. *Photograph by Eric W. Halbig*

Above, left: The tomb of Héloïse and Abélard at Père-Lachaise. *Photograph by Eric W. Halbig*

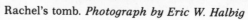

The grave of Edith Piaf and her husband, Théo Sarapo. *Photograph by Eric W. Halbig*

Jacob Epstein's monument to Oscar Wilde. *Photograph by Eric W. Halbig*

Above, left: The monument to the victims of Mauthausen. *Photograph by Eric W. Halbig*

< Frédéric Chopin's grave. *Photograph by Eric W. Halbig*

9

The Reilig Odhrain. *British Crown Copyright. Reproduced by permission of the Department of the Environment*

The cemetery before the roof was replaced on the chapel. *The Iona Community*

2. Reilig Odhrain

IONA, SCOTLAND

IONA is a sacred isle. One of those treasured ones of the Inner Hebrides, it has been called the Canterbury of the Celtic Church. Seemingly, it floats between sea and sky, an island out of time.

Its ancient name is Icolmkill (I Chaluim-Chille in Gaelic)—meaning Columba's isle of the church—and it lies just 1½ miles off the Ross of Mull, its larger neighbor. In ancient times—eons ago—it must have been attached to Mull, but that was in some remote prehistoric age. The tiny island is 6½ miles from Staffa, the island of Fingal's Cave. All about it are islets, rocks, juttings, and in the distance mountains on the larger islands. Iona is 3½ miles long, 1½ miles wide and is dominated by Ben Buirg (sometimes called Ben I), the hill fort of Iona, 332 feet

high. On the island's eastern side it looks to Mull, on the west to Ireland and the vast stretches of the North Atlantic. It was a Western outpost and, naturally, in the sequence of history, a port of call.

Early in the century William Sharp, the Scottish writer who wrote under the pseudonym of Fiona Macleod, described Iona eloquently:

In spiritual geography, Iona is the mecca of the Gael.

It is but a small isle, fashioned of a little sand, a few grasses salt with the spray of an ever-restless wave, a few rocks that wade in heather and upon whose brows the sea-wind weaves the yellow lichen. But since the remotest days sacrosanct men have bowed here in worship. In this little island a lamp was lit whose flame lighted pagan Europe from the Saxon in his fens to the swarthy folk who came by Greek waters to trade the Orient. Here Learning and Faith had their tranquil home, when the shadow of the sword lay upon all lands, from Syracuse by the Tyrrhene Sea to the rainy isles of Orcc.

Viking warriors, marauders, roving bands of brigands, and plunderers came to Iona through the centuries, and killed the monks and stole the church treasure. Some of these died and were buried here; if not in the burial ground, they often lay where they fell.

Most important of all who put ashore on the strand was Saint Columba (521–597), born in Gartan, Donegal, student, teacher, monk, abbot, theologian, and man of great organizational ability. A great-grandson of King Conall of Ireland, he might, in the natural course of events, have been king had he not chosen the church. However, his fiery temper involved him in a bloody battle with King Diarmit. Although he was victorious, he was excommunicated. When the sentence was lifted, as an act of penance he set out to live in exile and carry Christianity to Alba (Scotland).

Columba and his band of twelve beached their coracles of wicker and hide on the south side of the island at what is now Port na Churaich on Pentecost, on May 12, 563. This might be called the emergence of Iona into the mainstream of civilization. It was certainly the dawn of Christianity in Scotland, although earlier there had been missionaries. Before Columba's arrival Iona had been called Innis nan Druinidh (Island of Druids) and there had been a settlement on the island from the most ancient times. Columba and his disciples brought learning to Iona—he was one of the great scribes of his time—and his teaching and conversions extended throughout Scotland.

Before Columba the Reilig Odhrain—the burial place of kings—was here. Its history goes back to antiquity, lost in the mists of time in some long-forgotten Celtic twilight. Alec Ritchie, who lived on Iona and wrote about it, said: "The Reilig Odhrain, aptly called the Westminster Abbey of Scotland, is claimed by some writers to have been used as a royal burying ground even before the advent of Saint Columba. One fact is certain, that for many centuries King and Chief, Noble and Commoner have been buried in the churchyard."

The burial ground surrounds Saint Oran's Chapel (eleventh century), within sight of the restored Iona Cathedral (Abbey Church of Saint Mary). The lonely skies mirrored in the water in the distance emphasize the isolation of Iona, and the churchyard its remoteness in time. Although their graves cannot all be individually found, forty-eight Scottish kings lie here and tradition has it that eight Norwegian, four Irish, and two ancient French kings do as well. In actuality, there are more kings in the Reilig Odhrain than in Westminster Abbey. It was traditionally the burial place of the Dalriadic (Argyllshire) kings from the earliest times to Gabhran Mac Domongart, who died in 560. Two rulers who are familiar even outside Scotland are buried here—Duncan and Macbeth, kings of Scotland. Macbeth's body was carried over the water in 1057 to the keening of his followers and the cry of the curlew.

In *Macbeth,* Shakespeare has Ross ask Macduff where Duncan's body is. Macduff replies:

Carried to Colmkill,
The sacred storehouse of his predecessors
And guardian of their bones.

The spot was also remembered by Sir Walter Scott, a keen student of Scottish history, in *Lord of the Isles* when his hero—who had assisted the Bruce in the Battle of Bannockburn—is buried in the chapel, until 1957 roofless to the sky after years of being ruined. It is thought that Queen Margaret, who died in 1093, restored it, which makes it one of the oldest historical ruins in Scotland. In 1868 when the Iona Club collected the monuments there to protect them, the Ridge of Kings and the Ridge of Chiefs were formed. The monuments are of great interest with motifs on the stones of the lotus leaf, vine spirals, swords, Norse galleys with sails furled, and the stag being chased by dogs. During World War II a German airman shot down was buried here beside a British pilot. Strange companions for the Celtic rulers!

For an island as peaceful as Iona now is, its history has been fiery, tumultuous at times. The Danes massacred the monks in 806 and again in 825. By 1098 it was annexed by Norway and remained Norwegian until 1266. The monks were expelled in 1561, the nuns in 1574, and about 1688, the year of the Glorious Revolution, Iona passed to the Duke of Argyll. In 1899 the eighth duke gave the ruins to the trustees of the Church of Scotland, who administer the cathedral, the chapel of Saint Oran, and the Reilig Odhrain.

The Celtic cross of Saint Martin (also known as the Iona Cross), a sentinel before the cathedral, can be seen from the Reilig Odhrain, a talisman to the Celtic Christians through the ages. The stump of Saint Matthew's cross, and fragments of that of Saint John remain too. About ten feet from the doorway of Saint Oran's Chapel, between it and the road, lies the stone called Clach Brath. Pilgrims to the burial ground believed the world would end when the stone was worn through. These wayfarers turned pebbles in the cavity of the stone in the direction the sun traveled, hoping to hasten the day of reckoning.

Iona's past and present are intertwined in history, myth, and folklore.None is more evocative than the legend, writes Otta F. Swire, that "before the end of the world a great flood will sweep over and drown all the islands 'even Islay,' but Iona will rise on the waters and float there like a crown and the dead who are buried in her will arise dry and so be recognised at the Last Day."

The mass of gravestones in the Old Jewish Cemetery. *State Jewish Museum, Prague*

3. Old Jewish Cemetery

PRAGUE, CZECHOSLOVAKIA

IN that section of Czechoslovakia's capital city preserved as a memorial to the ancient Jewish population of Bohemia and Moravia stands a series of monuments that comprise the State Jewish Museum in Prague. The Staronova (Old-New) Synagogue, built in 1270, is the oldest in continuous existence in Europe and one of Prague's early Gothic architectural treasures. The Jewish Town Hall, first erected in the 1680s and rebuilt in 1763; the High Synagogue, repaired at the end of the seventeenth century; and the old Jewish Cemetery are some of the components of the State Jewish Museum, and serve as an indication of the highly individual character of the old Jewish community.

A tumble of tombstones, with their ancient Hebrew inscriptions, jumbled higgledy-piggledy on top of one an-other, give the walled burial ground a distinctly Eastern European, Slavic cast. The beginnings of the cemetery date back to the first half of the fifteenth century, which is borne out by the oldest tombstone preserved, that of Abigdor Karo. This scholar-poet's death is recorded as occurring on 25.4.1439 (April 25, 1439). Through the centuries—more than three hundred years—burials took place to such an extent that the cemetery had to be enlarged several times. In spite of this, it was still too small for the rapidly growing Jewish population of the city.

The expedience of covering the old graves with fresh soil and burying on top of them was resorted to. The layers of burials built up so that the cemetery soon began to resemble the Parisian one, the Cimetière des Innocents, where, as we have seen, the pressure of the graves caused the collapse of the wall of an adjacent apartment building in the late eighteenth century. Eventually—in 1787—burials in the Jewish Cemetery ceased. However, these graves, one layer on top of another, give a faithful picture for the visitor of life and death within the old ghetto of Prague.

Tombstone inscriptions are always a source of historical information, but those of the Jewish Cemetery are even more valuable than most. They usually include such genealogical information as the name, profession, dates of death and of the funeral, and, even more valuable, the name of the deceased's father and—in the case of a married woman—that of her husband.

In an age when tombstone rubbing has become increasingly popular, especially in Great Britain and the United States, the Prague cemetery is a rich source of examples of the stonemason's art. Some reliefs are traditional ones (hands raised in benediction, a jug, a vine); others are symbols of the deceased's name (bear, lion, stag), his age, and profession (medical instruments, tailor's scissors). Occasionally, a representation of the person buried is used.

Some of the early burials were of leading members of the Prague Jewish community, such as the Renaissance astronomer David Gans (1541–1613); Joseph Solomon Delmedigo (1591–1655), astronomer and philosopher; and Judah Löw ben Bezaleel, better known as Rabbi Löw, who died in 1609. He is credited with having created the golem (from the Hebrew word meaning embryo), who in medieval Jewish legend was an automaton of clay, given life through the invocation of religious symbols in order to help the Jews persecuted by Emperor Rudolf II.

Visitors follow Jewish custom and place pebbles on the grave, each signifying a separate visit. Through the years the pebbles have covered Rabbi Löw's grave. Others drop notes into the marble mausoleum of the rabbi, hoping this mysterious ancient scholar's spirit will make their wishes come true.

Mordecai Maisl (1528–1601), who is buried here, was one of the wealthiest and most influential members of the Prague Jewish community. A wonderfully evocative painting—from a cycle of pictures of the Funerary Brotherhood—by an unknown eighteenth-century painter shows eight pallbearers carrying a corpse on a board, the body in a winding sheet. They are followed by mourners, one of whom carries a silver vessel. Several of the leaning tombstones can be seen at one corner of the canvas, indicating the entry to the Jewish Cemetery.

Also interred here is David Oppenheimer, an eighteenth-century ancestor of the late American nuclear physicist J. Robert Oppenheimer.

The Old Jewish Cemetery by its very existence alone provides a link with seven centuries of Judaism in Prague. Jewish life and thought were powerful factors in the intellectual, artistic, and architectural development of the city.

The tombstone of Judah Löw ben Bezaleel (Rabbi Löw), who died in 1609. *State Jewish Museum, Prague*

The tombstone of David Gans, outstanding Prague scientist, astronomer, and historian, who died in 1613.
State Jewish Museum, Prague

A painting from the cycle of pictures of the Funerary
Brotherhood by an unknown artist of the eighteenth
century. *State Jewish Museum, Prague*

Greyfriars Churchyard with Edinburgh Castle in the background. *Photograph courtesy of The Scotsman*

4. Greyfriars Churchyard

EDINBURGH, SCOTLAND

It was Queen Mary who threw open the gardens of the Grey Friars: a new and semi-rural cemetery in those days [1562], although it has grown an antiquity in its turn and been superseded by a half a dozen others. The Friars must have had a pleasant time on summer evenings; for their gardens were situated to a wish, with the tall castle and the tallest of the castle crags in front. Even now, it is one of our famous Edinburgh points of view; and strangers are led thither to see, by yet another instance, how strangely the city lies upon her hills. The enclosure is of an irregular shape; the double church of Old and New Greyfriars stands on the level at the top; a few thorns are dotted here and there, and the ground falls by terrace and steep slope towards the north. The open shows many slabs and table tombstones; and all round the margin the place is girt by an array of aristocratic mausoleums appallingly adorned.

IT was Robert Louis Stevenson—one of the greatest Scottish writers and one of the most sensitive—who thus recorded Greyfriars in 1878 when *Edinburgh: Picturesque Notes* was first published. A century has not much altered the cemetery, although the town, now a city, has seen changes.

The kirk—or church—itself is considered one of the most important buildings in Scotland's history. To go back to most ancient times, its name "derives from the Franciscan Observantines (so called for their strict adherence to the ascetic standards of their founder, St. Francis of Assisi), who had their friary by the north end of the present kirkyard." We know that the friary was damaged here in 1544 by the English during an invasion of this northern kingdom, so that the first buildings on the spot were here before that date. During the Reformation the Greyfriars community was dispersed and in 1562 their yards were acquired as a public burial place. Rising here too was to be the first reformed kirk built in Scotland.

The ancient kirkyard of Saint Giles was overcrowded and no longer was it able to serve the city's four parishes adequately. This was the situation that brought about the edict from Mary Queen of Scots. Edinburgh was growing, the population increasing, and in 1601 the Greyfriars' yards were thought best for the new kirk. The "heiche," or upper yard, was chosen for it. Progress was slow and not until 1611 did the Town Council declare that "the kirk foundit in the buriell yaird suld be bigget with pilleris."

15

Work proceeded through the years, and in 1619 it is recorded that the funeral service for William Couper (born 1568), bishop of Galloway and dean of the Chapel Royal, was the first held in the kirk. Its great importance historically and the kirkyard's too was the signing here in 1638 of the National Covenant to oppose the innovations of William Laud, archbishop of Canterbury. This document was Scotland's protest against the efforts of its kings of the House of Stuart, who now reigned over England as well as Scotland, to foist episcopacy upon Scotland against its will and remonstrance. It signaled that a nation was covenanted to defend the Reformed religion (Presbyterianism) and to forbear the practice of all innovations and corruptions in the worship or government of her church. The "Killing Times," one of Scotland's great sorrows, followed, when the Covenanters were an outlawed people—one who bore witness and died for their beliefs.

This churchyard—the scene of so much history—was at first only the northernmost part of the present area, its entrance on the site of the modern gateway on Candlemaker Row. Old customs die hard and it appears few burials took place in the "heiche" before 1590, although its first extensive use was during the plague of 1568. An early burial—and that of the first member of the peerage to be interred here—was James Douglas, earl of Morton, regent of Scotland (1572–1578), who was executed in 1581 for his role in the murder of Lord Darnley, husband of Mary Queen of Scots. (He had earlier been involved in that of her favorite, David Rizzio.) The next year saw the burial of George Buchanan (1506–1582), the historian and humanist. Records show the planting and pruning of trees was done in 1609–1610, in 1624 an entrance to the upper yard was formed on the site of the present east gate, and in 1679 the prisoners from Bothwell Brig were confined, after the defeat of the Convenanters who had taken up arms against King Charles II.

Both Morton's and Buchanan's graves are unmarked—a circumstance not uncommon in old churchyards, but a monument to Buchanan was later erected by the historian Dr. David Laing, and a short column marks what is thought to be the site of the regent's grave. Other unmarked graves are those of the painters George Jamesone (1588–1644), Sir John Medina (1659–1710), and Allan Ramsay (1686–1758), the Scottish poet who was a major figure in the revival of vernacular poetry (*The Gentle Shepherd,* 1725). With them are Robert Rollock, first principal of Edinburgh University, and two who succeeded him—John Adamson and Gilbert Rule, as well as Robert Traill, the Greyfriars' minister banished because of his allegiance to the Convenanters.

The monuments, reflecting so much of the fabric of Scotland's history, are unique and of as great interest to visitors from abroad as to the native Scot. Most meaningful of all, at the foot of the east walk, is the Covenanters' Monument, erected in 1771 in place of the 1706 stone (now at Huntly House, Canongate). James Brown, in his

The Epitaphs & Monumental Inscriptions in Greyfriars Churchyard (1867), writes: "No monument within the grounds attracts so much notice as The Martyr's Monument.... It may easily be supposed that it was not erected during the persecution, but some years after the execution of the last of this noble company, James Renwick, 1688."

The inscription itself, beginning with the words "Halt, passenger, take heed what you do see—" contains four particularly significant lines:

**Their lives were sacrifi'd unto the lust
Of prelatists objur'd: though here their dust
Lies mixt with murderers and other crew,
Whom justice justly did to death pursue.**

They indicate the Covenanters, long after their unnatural deaths, and burial in Greyfriars, shared the same soil with many of their mortal enemies. During these "Killing Times" many Scots sailed for the New World to take root in a land where they were free to worship as they pleased.

Stevenson speaks of the haunted mausoleum of Sir George Mackenzie of Rosehaugh (1636–1691), lord advocate during the troubles. Called "Bloody Mackenzie," he was the author of "some pleasing sentiments on toleration." He "continues to sleep peacefully among the many whom he so intolerantly helped to slay." "It was here," Stevenson continues, "on the flat tombstones, that the Covenant was signed by an enthusiastic people. In the long arm of the churchyard that extends to Lauriston, the prisoners from Bothwell Bridge—fed on bread and water and guarded, life for life, by vigilant marksmen—lay five months looking for the scaffold or the plantations. And while the good work was going forward in the Grassmarket, idlers in Greyfriars might have heard the throb of the military drums that drowned the voices of the martyrs."

A grisly and dramatic coda to the scene was played out forty-five years later. Patrick Walker, who witnessed the later drama, wrote a full report of it, saying James Renwick told him of the hanging of five Covenanters at the Gallowlee between Leith and Edinburgh. The men's heads, and the right hand of Patrick Foreman, "were brought and put upon five pikes on the *Pleasaunce-Port.*" The bodies, first buried at the foot of the gallows, were carried by Renwick and his friends to the West Churchyard—"not Greyfriars this time"—and buried there. Later the heads and hand were recovered, "and Day being come, they went quickly up the *Pleasaunce;* and when they came to *Lauristoun* Yards, upon the Southside of the City, they durst not venture, being so light, to go and bury their Heads with their Bodies." Alexander Tweedie, a gardener, buried them in the Lauristoun Yard, "where they lay 45 years except 3 Days." Tweedie marked the spot by planting a white rosebush over the box containing the heads and hands, but took the precaution of telling his son, Daniel, about the secret burial. In 1726, when the box was exhumed, "many came out of Curiosity." They "concluded to bury them upon the Nineteenth Day of *October* 1726, and every One of us to acquaint Friends with the Day and Hour, being *Wednesday,* the Day of the Week on which most of them were executed, and at 4 of the Clock at Night, being the Hour they went to their resting Graves." They were interred "closs to the Martyrs Tomb, with the greatest Multitude of People Old and Young, Men and Women, Ministers and others, that ever I [Patrick Walker] saw together."

N. Brysson Morrison, the Scottish novelist, historian, and biographer, said:

> It is native to Scotland that their plot of mother earth should shelter alike the famed and the unknown. In Greyfriars amongst the nobility and lord provosts, poets, professors and painters, lie the forgotten and the humble. One such was John Gray, known as Auld Jock. He used to come into Edinburgh on market day from his small farm when he always went with his Skye terrier Bobby to Traill's Eating House for his dinner. Gray died suddenly in 1858, there were few mourners at his funeral but his dog was one of them.
>
> Bobby did not return to the farm that had been his home. Instead he spent the rest of his 14 years keeping vigil at his master's grave. Each day Bobby was a regular customer at Mr. Traill's, his dinner-gong the gun fired from the castle daily at one o'clock. When they tried to keep Bobby in during bad weather, he howled until they let him out.
>
> The little dog's devotion to his dead master aroused the liveliest interest and visitors used to go to the kirkyard just to see Greyfriars Bobby. One of these was the Baroness Burdett-Coutts (1814–1906), the philanthropist, who after Bobby's death in 1872 had a drinking-fountain erected to him outside what had been Traill's Eating House.

Years later he became the hero of Eleanor Atkinson's book *Greyfriars Bobby.*

No cemetery is richer in monuments or epitaphs. Stevenson says: "We Scots stand, to my fancy, highest among nations in the manner of grimly illustrating death." He speaks of every mason being a pedestrian Holbein with a deep consciousness of death, who "loved to put its terrors pithily before the churchyard loiterer; he was brimful of rough hints upon mortality, and any dead farmer was seized upon to be a text. The classical examples of this art are in Greyfriars. In their time, these were doubtless costly monuments, and reckoned of a very elegant proportion by contemporaries; and now, when the elegance is not so apparent, the significance remains." He speaks of Latin mottoes, "some crawling endwise up the shaft of a pillar, some issuing on a scroll from angels' trumpets." One memorable epitaph is on a

tombstone one man raised to his spouse, who departed this life on November 11, 1818, aged fifty-six years. The husband, Peter Leslie, mourns:

She was!
But words are wanting to say what.
Think what a wife should be,
And she was that.

There is another, touching on the infant mortality of earlier times. The Laird of Enterkin's wife died on February 5, 1676, aged forty, and is extolled:

Twice five times suffered she the childhood pains
Yet of her children only five remains.

Others who are in Greyfriars and left their mark on Scotland's history are the father of Sir Walter Scott; a number of the Boswells of Auchinleck (the family of James Boswell, companion to Dr. Samuel Johnson); Henry Mackenzie (1745–1831), the novelist best remembered for *The Man of Feeling* (1771); Captain John Porteous of the town guard, whose lynching in 1736 at the hands of an Edinburgh mob is described in Sir Walter Scott's *Heart of Midlothian;* the Gaelic bard Duncan Ban MacIntyre (1724–1812); William Adam (1689–1748), an architect himself and the father of the more famous ones, Robert and James; Henry Siddons, son of the actress; and James Hutton (1726–1797), thought by many to be the father of geology.

Ancient and peaceful, Greyfriars' calm is only disturbed by the sunshine that dapples its tombstones or an occasional cat that sits on one of its monuments. Greyfriars dreams on—symbolizing the strength of the Scots and their history.

An old photograph of Greyfriars Churchyard, showing the variety of tombstones. *Photograph courtesy of the Central Library, Edinburgh*

The portico of the Anglican chapel and the tomb of Princess Sophia, daughter of King George III. *Photograph by James Stevens Curl*

5. Kensal Green Cemetery

LONDON, ENGLAND

KENSAL Green Cemetery today is a forlorn orphan of the Victorian age; faded, shabby, the grass in need of cutting, the entire effect is that of a widow whose weeds worn too long have turned from black to green.

Almost a century and a half ago when Kensal Green was born, it reflected a change in attitude toward death and burial. In 1830 when the first meetings of the General Cemetery Company were in progress, George IV, the first of King George III's sons to reign, was on the throne. The situation of the London churchyards was intolerable. Noxious fumes arose from overcrowded burial places, which were dangerous to the health of the community. Charles Dickens campaigned against the practice of burial in churchyards within the city. Other Londoners began to express themselves in the press as John Claudius Loudon, a well-known horticulturist who is buried at Kensal Green, did on May 4, 1830, in a letter to the *Morning Advertiser.* He urged a series of cemeteries, "all, as far as practicable, equi-distant from each

other, and from what may be considered the center of the metropolis." A royal commission was formed and eventually the cemetery system of Inner and Outer London was foreseeable.

The founders of Kensal Green—technically All Souls' Cemetery—had in the late 1820s looked at various sites, and in 1830 both the Eyre estate and Primrose Hill were under consideration. As early as 1827 Augustus Charles Pugin exhibited a design at the Royal Academy for an entrance gateway to a cemetery. Then in 1830 Benjamin Wyatt was invited to serve as architect. He declined but recommended Charles Fowler, and Pugin and Fowler joined the committee.

The General Cemetery Company was formed with nontransferable shares until three-fifths of the purchase price was repaid. The following year the company secured an act of Parliament to facilitate its activities, and the first trustees were Andrew Spottiswoode, M.P., Viscount Milton, G. F. Carden, and Sir John Dean Paul. Fifty acres, in the boroughs of Kensington and Hammersmith, were purchased in 1831 for £9,400. The cemetery, just off the Harrow Road, lay northwest of London, a little beyond Paddington in an area then completely rural.

The ground plan design was based on that submitted by an architect named Liddell, who had been in the Crown Office under the great Regency architect John Nash. The plan was picturesque in every way. A circular drive, from which meandered winding roads and paths, was the focal point of the plan, and "an extraordinary fantasy in Gothic for the chapel, a delightful water-gate through which funerals could proceed from the canal, and a robust entrance gateway on the Harrow Road."

Eight hundred trees were planted, and within this growing wonder the public could erect whatever monuments it chose to. Soon obelisks, broken pillars, angels, and figures of grief and mourning began to dot the landscape and could be seen through the trees. In fact, the public's fancy knew no bounds. The principal entrance gateway and lodges—a broad Doric treatment over a triumphal arch—were designed by Henry Edward Kendall (1776–1875), a pupil of Nash and a friend of Pugin. All Souls' was consecrated in 1833 and the first interment was that of Margaret Gregory. The directors were so happy to have her that, at their own expense, they erected a tablet to her memory. From the beginning London took Kensal Green to its heart.

The grand design began to take shape. The Anglican chapel—designed by John William Griffith and William Chadwick—was Greek Revival, rather than the Gothic first contemplated. It was Doric where the Nonconformist chapel was Ionic. Of Portland stone and Roman cement, each had a brick vaulted catacomb beneath, which has been described as "Piranesian in intensity, with stone coffin racks and cast-iron protective grilles of similar detail to typical domestic balconies of the period."

The large cemetery, of course, took away from the parish churches certain revenues connected with death and burial. It was determined, according to James Stevens Curl, a historian of London cemeteries, that the "clergy of the parish from which a body was taken were to be paid a fee of 5s for every body so removed, if interred in a vault, catacomb or brick grave; and 1s 6d each if interred in the open ground; the rector of St. Marylebone to receive an additional 2s 6d for each body, his salary being 'principally composed of burial fees.'"

Such planning was bound to lure the great to Kensal Green: Anne Scott (1803–1833) and Charlotte Sophia Lockhart (1799–1837), daughters of Sir Walter Scott, came here, as well as Charlotte's husband, John Gibson Lockhart (1794–1854), biographer of both Scott and Robert Burns. Mary Scott Hogarth (1819–1837), Dickens's sister-in-law, whom he loved and from whose death he never fully recovered, is also here. (Most of the Dickens family are in Highgate and the novelist is buried in Westminster Abbey.)

The Byron circle—and it was an extensive one—comprises his publisher, John Murray (1778–1843), who in 1812 purchased the house at 50 Albermarle Street where the firm's offices still are situated; poet Leigh Hunt (1784–1859), the feckless friend of the sixth lord; and John Cam Hobhouse (1786–1869), later Baron Broughton de Gyfford, who in 1815 was best man at Byron's wedding to the Honorable Anne Isabella Milbanke, and was also executor of his will.

The literary world is represented further by three novelists: William Makepeace Thackeray (1811–1863)—Dickens attended his funeral; Anthony Trollope (1815–1882); and William Wilkie Collins (1824–1889). Trollope, once a post-office clerk, claimed it was he who suggested the introduction of the postal pillar box.

And there is an exceptional woman here too—James Barry, probably born in the early 1790s. Dr. Barry, dressed in men's clothes, outwitted everyone, including army and naval officers, as to her sex. It was only at the death of the Inspector General of Hospitals (and after forty-six years of active army service) that Dr. Barry was discovered to be a woman by the charwoman who prepared her for burial in the summer of 1865.

Queen Victoria purchased sites for royal mausoleums in 1849, but by the time the Prince Consort died in 1861 she had changed her mind and he was buried at Frogmore. However, other members of the royal family did select Kensal Green as a resting place. At the funeral of his brother, King William IV, in 1837, the aged Augustus Frederick, duke of Sussex (1773–1843), sixth son of King George III, became so enraged at the delay, confusion, and the question of etiquette at Windsor that he is reported to have said: "This is intolerable. Now, recollect what I say to you. If I should die before I return to Kensington [Palace], see I am not buried at Windsor, as I would not be buried there after this fashion for all the world."

The irascible uncle of Queen Victoria did live to return to Kensington Palace, but when his time came he was interred at Kensal Green. Opposite him in what has been called a "quattrocento sarcophagus" is his sister Princess Sophia (1777–1848). Her tomb, before the Anglican chapel, dominates the chapel's façade. Sophia, one of the tragically unhappy daughters of George III, had been involved in a love affair with General Thomas Garth, one of her father's equerries, and it has long been suspected that a child was born to them. Her monument bears the inscription: "Come unto me all ye that labour and are heavy laden and I will give you rest."

A royal love affair with a happier ending was that of George, duke of Cambridge (1819–1904), first grandson of George III to be born and the last to die. A field marshal and commander of the British army, he was also personal aide-de-camp (1882–1895) to his first cousin Queen Victoria. Because his beloved morganatic wife, Sarah Louisa Fairbrother (1816–1890), known as Mrs. Fitzgeorge, was buried here, he joined her in the course of time. When Louisa's funeral cortege reached Kensal Green the crowd was so large that barriers had to be erected, and the entrance gates closed. On his death the duke's sister, Princess Augusta, wrote to her niece, Princess Mary of Wales [the future Queen Mary, consort of George V]: "He will not be laid to rest in the family vault at Windsor, and is to be taken to a strange resting place, so far away from us all."

Burials of the well known were such that Kensal Green provides a good cross section of British life in the nineteenth century. There were Michael William Balfe (1808–1870), composer of *The Bohemian Girl;* Sir Julius Benedict (1804–1885), another composer remembered chiefly for *The Lily of Killarney;* the acrobat Charles Blondin (1824–1897), who crossed Niagara Falls on a tightrope; Sir Marc Isambard Brunel (1769–1849) and his son, Isambard Kingdom Brunel (1806–1859), the great engineers of the last century—the father was responsible for the Thames tunnel (1825–1843) and the son for ocean-going iron ships, notably the *Great Eastern.* Here too is Samuel Lover (1797–1868), Irish composer of "The Low-backed Car" and grandfather of Victor Herbert; and Madame Vestris (1797–1856), actress and singer.

The actor who created the greatest furor at Kensal Green was Andrew Ducrow (1793–1842), known as the king of mimics and also the lessee of the Royal Amphitheatre in London. When his wife died in 1835, Ducrow ordered a tomb for her and paid £100 for the site and £40 for the vault. When the funeral day arrived, the ground around the tomb was a sea of clay and mud, and the tomb had three feet of water in it. The irate actor threatened to take his wife's body home again, but was persuaded to leave it in the chapel. To ensure its safety, he took the keys with him. The present tomb cost £3,000 to build and was—before the cemetery began to deteriorate—one of the most noteworthy points of interest.

Although its image is tarnished, and few notables are buried here any longer, Kensal Green is an absorbing place for both the architectural historian and the scholar interested in nineteenth-century life. James Stevens Curl, who has made an exhaustive study of the period and its burial practices, says: "The whole range of Victorian taste is displayed in this cemetery, from chaste classical tombstones to wild Gothic fantasies, like Gibson's high Victorian Gothic octagon. Ducrow's Egyptian style mausoleum of 1837 looks as though it could have been by Geary, who published books of designs which are incredibly coarse." It is just this wild phantasmagoria that has made Kensal Green a marvelous relic of Victoria's age.

The Dissenters' Chapel (no longer standing). *Photograph by James Stevens Curl*

The main avenue at Kensal Green, showing the Kiralfy monument. *Photograph by James Stevens Curl*

Catacombs arcade near the wall on the Harrow Road. *Photograph by James Stevens Curl*

The Rossetti family monument. *Photograph © by Michael Wright*

6. Highgate Cemetery

LONDON, ENGLAND

"HIGHGATE Cemetery must have first claim to being the most unashamedly romantic of all cemeteries in Britain," writes James Stevens Curl in *The Victorian Celebration of Death.* It is just this romantic quality that has made Highgate the object of pilgrimage by those who treasure old cemeteries and who seek out the graves of the famous.

Gothic in quality, Highgate guards both sides of Swain's Lane in that section of the Parish of Saint Pancras known as Highgate Village. When it was consecrated on May 20, 1839, by the Bishop of London, the cemetery was an answer to the overcrowding of the old churchyards of the city that had become health hazards.

The older section once formed part of the grounds surrounding the mansion of Sir William Ashurst. The cemetery was founded by Stephen Geary (1797–1854), who is buried here. A colorful figure, he is remembered as the designer of the first gin palace in London circa 1830. The first burial was that of Mrs. Elizabeth Jackson of Little

Windmill Street, Golden Square. It was not long before Londoners of substance began to adopt the cemetery as one of their favorite burial grounds. Among the early arrivals were the parents of Charles Dickens, John (died 1851) and Elizabeth Barrow (died 1863). Although the novelist is not here (he is in the Poets' Corner at Westminster Abbey), his wife Catherine Hogarth (1815–1879) and their ninth child, Dora Annie (1850–51), are. So are John Singleton Copley (1738–1815), the portrait painter born in Boston, and his son, John (1772–1863), later Baron Lyndhurst. In 1820 the younger Copley conducted the prosecution of Queen Caroline, consort of George IV, in the House of Lords.

The London Cemetery Company, which established Highgate, overlooked no innovation in planning the cemetery with "Paths, Walks, Avenues, Roads, Trees, Shrubs, and Plantations as may be thought necessary." As was the custom of many of the large commercial cemeteries in England in the nineteenth century, most of

Highgate was for members of the established church, but a portion was set aside for Dissenters.

Catacombs were peculiar to Highgate. They are somewhat reminiscent of the wall tombs in the cemeteries of New Orleans (each has an iron door, opening to a compartment with shelves for the coffins), but there the similarity stops. Those in Highgate flank the Egyptian Avenue and ascend the slope to the Circle of Lebanon, which, in turn, has another bank of catacombs facing it. These Egyptian tombs leading to the circle are ingeniously designed: The walls of the tombs facing the avenue graduate lower and lower as they approach the crest of the hill, giving the illusion that the avenue is of greater length than it really is.

The Egyptian Revival is evident here as it is in the gate to Mount Auburn Cemetery in Cambridge, Massachusetts, and that to the Grove Street Cemetery, New Haven, Connecticut. Above all, dominating this part of Highgate, is the enormous mausoleum of Julius Beer, built in 1877–1878 of Portland stone and designed by John Oldrid Scott. Some of the famous who are scattered throughout the cemetery lie about the circumference of the Circle of Lebanon. Here are Carl Rosa (1843–1889), founder of an opera company bearing his name; Radclyffe Hall (1886–1943), whose novel *The Well of Loneliness,* describing the attachment of a young girl for an older woman, was a *cause célèbre* when it was published; and Mrs. Henry Wood (1814–1887), whose *East Lynne* (1861) was one of the best-selling novels of the last century.

Tom Sayers (1826–1865) was a member of that breed of bareknuckle fighters who thought nothing of going sixty rounds. He was beaten only once in his life, and his fight with John C. Heenan went two hours and six minutes and was declared a draw. Tom was the darling of London, especially of the working classes. At his death some ten thousand people attended the funeral procession. It was a day of mourning—and festivity. Tom's admirers drank ale or gin, the blinds in the public houses along the route were lowered, and crape was seen everywhere. His faithful dog, with a collar of crape, rode in state in a phaeton behind the hearse, the lone official mourner. Appropriately, a replica in stone of Tom's best friend rests on his monument.

Nothing creates an air of the Gothic or romantic as does an exhumation. Highgate has had three of importance. Karl Marx (1818–1883), father of modern socialism, whose grave is in the new cemetery on the other side of Swain's Lane, and his family were moved to a spot nearer the path, presumably to enable the faithful to find this place with greater ease. Since the monolithic bust of Marx dominates the scene in this part of Highgate and is easily accessible, it seems to have been a target for vandals who topple it with frequency. The bust was erected in 1956. Beneath it is the legend: "The philosophers have only interpreted the world in various ways. The point however is to change it." His daughter, Eleanor (1855–1898), a suicide, lies in the same plot.

The other exhumations were not for the transferral of bodies. In 1896 England was awakened to the charge by Mrs. Anna Druce that her father-in-law, Thomas Charles Druce (1793–1864), was not, in fact, Druce at all but William John Cavendish Bentinck-Scott (1800–1879), the fifth duke of Portland, an eccentric who was also a recluse. In 1907 the grave was opened (after Mrs. Druce had been placed in a mental institution), and the following year it was officially announced that the body was not that of His Grace but of Thomas Druce.

The grave opening that most captured the imagination was that of Elizabeth Eleanor Siddal, wife of Dante Gabriel Rossetti (1828–1882), the poet and Pre-Raphaelite painter. When she died of an overdose of laudanum in February 1862, the distraught poet, unseen by other mourners, placed in her coffin a manuscript book of his poems—the only complete copy he had. It was buried with her in Highgate.

Seven years later his own ambition, and the persuasion of his friends, led to the recovery of the buried manuscript. One early October evening in 1869 there was enacted in Highgate Cemetery a scene worthy of Edgar Allan Poe. Rossetti's friend C. A. Howell, Dr. Llewellyn Williams of Kennington, and Henry Virtue Tebbs exhumed Elizabeth's body. They built a large fire by the open grave as the only protection they could devise against infection. Howell reported that Mrs. Rossetti's red hair had continued to grow after her death, filling her coffin. The manuscript was recovered, Dr. Williams drenched it with disinfectants, and dried it leaf by leaf. Strangely enough, although Rossetti referred to the exhumation in his sonnet "Life in Love," and although he loved Elizabeth and felt great remorse at her death, he left instructions that he was not to be buried beside her. His words were: "Let me not on any account be buried at Highgate, but my remains burnt as I say." He was buried at Birchington-on-Sea, near Margate, but his parents, his brother, William, and his sister, Christina Georgina (1830–1894), the poet, are here.

The new cemetery, opened seventeen years after the old one, does not have as many famous names, but two who lie near one another in death as they did in life are George Eliot (1819–1880), the novelist, and George Henry Lewes (1817–1878), the man of letters with whom she formed a lasting liaison.

There are others of interest here: Michael Faraday (1791–1867), the chemist whose electricity experiments made him one of the scientific giants of his age; Frederick Tennyson (1807–1898), elder brother of the poet; William Betty (1791–1874), the child actor who played Romeo at the age of twelve; and Herbert Spencer (1820–1903), philosopher and author. A memorial to John Galsworthy (1867–1933) is near the Circle of Lebanon, although his ashes were scattered on Sussex Downs, and Samuel Taylor Coleridge (1772–1834), the poet, while not in Highgate itself, lies in a crypt in Saint Michael's Church, adjoining the cemetery.

Highgate reminds one of Miss Havisham, the eccentric in Dickens's *Great Expectations.* It is a relic of another age, a bit down at the heels and out of fashion. There is decay, the undergrowth has taken over to such an extent that the tombs and gravestones are toppled and broken. Foxes can often be heard at night. It seems forgotten to all but the antiquarian. Often those who do enter are vandals or individuals such as the president of the British Occult Society, who was brought to trial in 1974. Reports were that stakes had been driven through the hearts of bodies, and it was thought that ceremonies of a necromantic nature occurred.

Reflecting the past in a bizarre manner, Highgate Cemetery still commands the magnificent prospect of London. In the words of Richard Church, the poet: "Few, if any, mourners enter, and nothing molests the solitude of this strange retreat, as remote as an Aztec village deserted in the jungle."

The grave of Sir Rowland Hill, founder of the postal system. *Photograph © by Michael Wright*

Below, left: The tomb of George Wombwell. The recumbent lion was popular in cemetery art in the nineteenth century. *Photograph © by Michael Wright*

The monument to Thomas Sayers, the pugilist, showing his faithful dog. *Photograph © by Michael Wright*

The Glasgow Necropolis. *Photograph by James Stevens Curl*

7. Glasgow Necropolis

GLASGOW, SCOTLAND

THE ancient city of Glasgow, thought by most as only industrial, has been a seat of culture for centuries and it has always maintained with Edinburgh what March Cost, the Scottish novelist, spoke of as a "certain civic rivalry between these two magnificent but entrenched positions."

The industrialism that brought employment to thousands in the shipyards and factories also brought wealth and prosperity to the merchants and industrialists. Glasgow, which has had a university since 1451, has been termed purse-proud rather than nobility-proud like Edinburgh. It was these purses that provided support for the necropolis.

In 1832 Kensal Green was a reality in London, but it was to Paris and Père-Lachaise that the Glaswegians looked for inspiration. James Ewing, dean of Guild (later provost and a member of Parliament), presented the original proposal for the necropolis. In this he was abetted by Laurence Hill, the collector, and John Strang, the chamberlain. Strang was motivated, he later said, by a desire to awaken the Scots to the neglected condition of their churchyards. A contemporary characterized him as a "brilliant super-orthodox luminary burning in a dense cloud of Scotch prejudice and Glasgow smoke."

What these men did for the gray and often fog-shrouded port was to select the most theatrical eminence available. They chose a hill two hundred feet above the Clyde that was separated from the cathedral precincts by the Molendinar Ravine through which, at an earlier period, the Molendinar Burn had coursed.

The ground itself had once formed part of the estate of Wester Craigs, which was purchased in 1650 by the Merchants' House (established in 1605) from Stewart of Mynto for £1,291.13s.4d. In the years between, it had been feud—or rented—to different individuals and companies, but the Merchants' House reserved the right to quarry rock or stone there "at pleasure."

A promontory known as Fir Park was laid out as a

The Glasgow Necropolis, showing the circular Ionic temple over the grave of John Dick, professor of theology and minister of Greyfriars Church in Glasgow. The tallest monument is the John Knox monument. *Photograph by James Stevens Curl*

plantation but by 1804 many of the firs had died or were in decaying condition, so it was uprooted and developed with other species. A stone wall was built, a resident keeper appointed, and in 1825 the monument to John Knox, later one of the chief attractions of the necropolis, was erected by public subscription. Thus, the stage was set, the land available and desirable, and certain Glaswegians anxious to put it to even more spectacular use.

The necropolis was formally opened in March 1833, although Joseph Levi was buried in the Jewish sepulchre the previous year. He was followed by Elizabeth Miles Mylne on February 9, 1833. Purse-proud it might be and, as a consequence, a certain snobbishness developed on the part of the citizenry to be interred in this, the first major cemetery in Scotland.

Several years later John Strang wrote: "Its surface is broken and varied, its form is picturesque and romantic, and its position appropriate and commanding. It is already beautified with venerable trees and young shrubbery, it is possessed of several winding walks, and affords from almost every point the most splendid views of the city and neighborhood. The singular diversity, too, of its soil and substrata, proclaims it to be of all other spots the most eligible for a cemetery; calculated, as that should be, for every species of sepulture, and suitable as it is for every sort of sepulchral ornament."

A lithograph of the last century allows us to hark back to the early time. A bridge across the ravine—"The Bridge of Sighs"—formed a Roman arch spanning sixty feet and led to the façade erected by John Park in 1835 (gates were added in 1838), which it was said "forms a conspicuous architectural ornament at the entrance to the Necropolis." What set the tone then, and captures it now, is the inscription over the gate:

> The adjoining bridge/ was erected by/ The Merchants' House of Glasgow/ to afford a proper entrance to their new cemetery combining/ convenient access to the grounds with suitable decoration to the/ venerable cathedral and surrounding scenery to unite the tombs of many generations/ who have gone before with the resting places destined for generations yet/ unborn where the ashes of all shall repose until the resurrection of the just when that which/ is born a natural body shall be raised a spiritual body when this corruptible must put/ on incorruption when this mortal must put/on immortality when death is swallowed up in victory./ A.D. MDCCCXXXIII./ "Blessed is the man who trusteth in God and whose hope the Lord is."

Because the Scots, like Peter, built on rock, there were certain complications. Some tombs, or "lairs," had to be literally blasted, and hinged slabs placed over them as covers. Another peculiarity to Glasgow and the necropolis were the craft stones that indicated a man's trade or profession.

Rock and hinged doors did not protect the dead from grave robbing and body snatching. The passing in 1832 by Parliament of the Anatomy Act at least provided cadavers to anatomy schools and lessened the practice somewhat, but the Scots to protect their prosperous dead placed iron safes, cages, and other heavy structures on the graves until the bodies had sufficiently deteriorated to make them unsuitable for anatomy schools.

James Stevens Curl comments on Scottish cemeteries: "The visually receptive traveller visiting Scotland for the first time will see much to interest him and delight the eye. He will not fail to notice the important part that cemeteries and burial grounds play in the landscape of both town and country. Cemeteries in Scotland are dominant features. They are not discreetly played down or hidden from view: rather they assert themselves, and mirror the scale of towns and villages, hamlets and countryside which they serve."

The necropolis asserts itself in a manner of which no visitor or Glaswegian could be unaware, for this burial place owes a visual debt to ancient Attica. Curl states: "The influence of Greece is strong, and the Necropolis is so astonishing that a constant effort has to be made to realize one is actually in Glasgow when viewing it. Yet Greek Revival is a style found frequently in Scotland, a country that, like Prussia, favoured the mathematical precision of that crisp and rational atmosphere."

The Mansion House continued to oversee the necropolis until 1966, when the Corporation of Glasgow acquired the cemetery and the Parks Department of the city began a program of tree planting to enhance the hills and monuments.

The monuments defy description. Their variety is infinite, ranging from temples, Egyptian vaults, obelisks, draped urns, and miniature cathedral spires, "from purest Greek to dissenting Gothic, and from chaste slab to Moresque mausoleum." Their variety gives an uneven rhythm to the landscape, a visual diversity, and an architectural complexity that is at once exciting and awing. Glasgow set its heart on not being outdone—and it succeeded.

The triumph is, of course, the John Knox Monument, a towering Doric column with a twelve-foot statue of the reformer in a Geneva gown, clutching the Bible in his right hand. Another clergyman, this one more controversial, is also a resident of the necropolis. Edward Irving (1792–1834) created his own furor with his emphasis on the supernatural and the second coming of Christ. In 1833 these and other teachings led to his expulsion from the Church of Scotland. He was the founder of the Catholic Apostolic Church, whose members are often referred to as Irvingites. William Motherwell (1797–1835), antiquary and man of letters, known best for *Poems, Narrative and Lyrical* (1832), rests in a Gothic tomb; his fellow writer Michael Scott (1789–1835), author of *Tom Cringle's Log* and *The Cruise of the Midge* (both published in 1836), and James Sheridan Knowles (1784–1862), the dramatist who is best remembered for *Virginius* (1820), lie here as well. James Ewing, one of the founders of the necropolis, is buried in a massive sarcophagus of polished Peterhead granite, and John Dick, professor of theology and minister of Greyfriars Church in Glasgow, is immortalized by a "little temple of the Ionic order crowned with a circular canopy resting on six fluted columns."

John Claudius Loudon, who visited the Glasgow Necropolis in 1841, gave an accurate description of it. Loudon noted that the "impression made by the first view of this hill, studded with trees and tombs and scars of solid rock, when looking from the town, with the cathedral in the foreground, is grand and melancholy; and the effect if heightened as we pass along an elevated road towards a bridge which crosses the valley at the point where the Necropolis commences and is, as it were, joined to the ancient churchyard, so as to unite the tombs of many generations with those of generations yet unborn."

The graves of John Keats and Joseph Severn with the pyramid in the background. *Photograph by Massimo Ascani. Courtesy Ab Allhems Förlag, Malmö, Sweden*

8. Protestant Cemetery

ROME, ITALY

ONE of the more sorrowful aspects of death is the burial of the deceased on foreign soil, among alien corn so to speak. Rome, which for years has attracted the expatriate and the traveler, the occasional sojourner and the diplomatic messenger, the artist, writer, and wanderer, provides a last resting place for many.

The Protestant Cemetery, or as it is sometimes called, the English Cemetery, is nonsanctified ground according to the laws of the Roman Catholic Church, but it contains the remains of two who were the most sanctified of poets —John Keats and Percy Bysshe Shelley—and pilgrims have found their way to these graves for over a century and a half now.

The cemetery, which contains the graves of German, English, Russian, Greek, Scandinavian, American na-

tionals, and others, has been located here for over two hundred years. Italian Protestants, atheists, and agnostics are not permitted to be buried here unless married to a foreigner or related to one. This is hallowed ground for historians and was originally part of the *Ager,* the fields of the Roman people.

Situated close by the Porta San Paolo, it is marked in particular by the pyramid of Caius Cestius, the praetor and tribune of the people, who was a member of the Septemviri Epulones, a group that prepared sacred feasts for the gods. In 12 B.C. when he died, in the last years of the Republic, his will directed that a tomb be erected in the Egyptian fashion within 330 days of his death. In medieval times it was known as the tomb of Romulus. Near the pyramid and the Protestant Cemetery stands a section of the Aurelian wall (which once stretched eleven miles), built in A.D. 271 to keep out the barbarians. In the distance is the basilica of Saint Paul, erected over the spot where the Apostle was buried, following his martyr's death in A.D. 67. The first church was erected by the Emperor Constantine; a larger one was later built at the end of the fourth century. The present edifice dates from 1823 when the former one burned. Saint Paul walked past the pyramid on his way to his beheading, a fact visitors often forget. This setting then, historic by both Roman and papal standards, is the backdrop for the pine- and cypress-filled burial ground.

On the city side of the gate to the left, the Via Caio Cestio leads to the cemetery itself. Elizabeth Bowen called it "Rome's permanent foreign colony," and said "the aislelike walks are trodden by pilgrims, no longer by mourners." The first burial, in 1738, as far as can be ascertained, was that of a young Oxford student whose surname was Langton. Records of this early time no longer exist. However, we do know that Baron George Werpup of the Kingdom of Hanover died as a result of a fall from his carriage. The baron, who was only twenty-five in 1765 and had not yet made his mark in the world, is remembered today because of his early burial here. Rome at that time was a port of call on the Grand Tour for others, such as Sir James McDonald, Bart., who was only twenty-four when he followed the young baron here in 1766.

Children are buried here too. William, the year-old son of the Shelleys; two children of Wilhelm von Humboldt, philologist and naturalist, lie here as well. A grandson of Wordsworth is here also. Goethe's son August—named for his father's patron, Grand Duke Charles Augustus of Saxe-Weimar, and the only one of the poet's five children to reach young manhood—was his father's secretary when he died of smallpox three weeks after arriving in Rome. Bertel Thorvaldsen, the Danish sculptor, did the bas-relief monument for young Goethe's tomb.

Of course, it is Keats and Shelley who give the cemetery focus today. Keats languished and died—on February 23, 1821—in his rooms near the Piazza di Spagna. The date was recorded as the twenty-fourth because he died after nightfall and in papal Rome the day ended with the Angelus. Events occurring after the Angelus had rung were recorded with the following day's date. His burial here first brought distinction to the ancient ground, then increasing fame, and now immortality. Miss Bowen recalls that many buried here "once dreaded the rigours of Roman sunshine: here is ensured for them the protective shade that in life they sought."

Joseph Severn (1793–1879), the painter who was with the poet at his death, buried his infant son, Arthur (he later gave another son the same name), at Keats's side in 1837. The baby died tragically when he slipped through the rail on his cot while sleeping and broke his neck. And in 1879, at the age of eighty-five, Severn himself was laid to rest beside the poet. Arthur Severn's stone records that

the "poet Wordsworth was present at his baptism in Rome." Joseph's states he was eminent for his representation of Italian life and nature in his paintings.

Keats's grave is marked with the following inscription that is familiar to many a wayfarer in Rome:

This Grave
contains all that was Mortal
of a
Young English Poet
Who
on his Death Bed
in the Bitterness of his Heart
at the Malicious Power of his Enemies
Desired
these Words to be engraven on his Tomb Stone

"Here lies One Whose Name was writ in Water."

Actually, Keats wanted only the final line on the stone. Severn felt otherwise, but later regretted it. Shelley, moved by sorrow at Keats's death, wrote the elegaic "Adonais" to commemorate his passing. In the preface to the poem, Shelley wrote: "The cemetery is an open space among the ruins, covered in winter with violets and daisies. It might make one in love with death to think that one should be buried in so sweet a place."

It remained for Edward John Trelawny (1792–1881), rogue, adventurer, consummate liar, buccaneer, and literary hanger-on, to carry an association even further than Joseph Severn had. It was he who burned Shelley's body on the beach at Viareggio after it had earlier been buried in quick lime, following the drowning off Leghorn. Trelawny and Severn decided to exhume the remains of the infant William, so they could be reburied next to his famous father, but it was discovered—according to legend—that a skeleton more than five feet in length lay beneath the infant's stone. Sheila Birkenhead in *Illustrious Friends,* her memoir of the Severn, Keats, and Ruskin families, says that they did not search further for, as Joseph wrote to a friend, they were "in the presence of many *respectful* but wondering Italians."

Shelley's burial was in the newer section because the papal government had forbidden further interments in the ground where Keats lay. Lady Birkenhead mentions that so many heretics' tombs had been defaced by the Catholic populace that the English colony appealed for permission to surround the graves with a wall. The papacy refused because it felt a wall would mar the view. However, a new burial ground was granted nearby, which had a wall around it. The pope stationed soldiers there to protect it. Today the two burial grounds, the older with Keats, the newer with Shelley, are one, and a still newer common wall encloses both.

Trelawny lived to an advanced old age, as Joseph Severn had and, fifty-nine years after Shelley's death, died at the age of eighty-eight. He had made a life's work of his association with Byron and Shelley and thus established a place for himself in the literature devoted to both poets' lives. This wild, enigmatic pirate was laid to rest next to Shelley. It has been his good fortune to have been placed here, a spot most agree he usurped and did not deserve. Shelley, deemed Ariel by his friends, lies beneath a stone bearing the lines from that charming character's song in *The Tempest*:

Nothing of him that doth fade
But doth suffer a sea-change
Into something rich and strange.

Leigh Hunt actually wrote the Latin inscription giving the vital facts of the poet's birth and death. Trelawny added the lines from Shakespeare. Early in this century, in 1902, the young Virginia Stephen, later Virginia Woolf, asked her sister, Vanessa, when in Italy to lay red roses on Shelley's grave.

And here are also the obscure, only remembered because of more famous relatives. Jane Gallatin Powers, who lies here, was the sister of Grace Gallatin Seton, author of numerous travel books, and the first wife of the naturalist Ernest Thompson Seton and mother of the novelist Anya Seton (*Dragonwyck, The Winthrop Woman*). Margaret and Joshua Jones came here even earlier. They contracted tuberculosis and were sent to Rome to recover their health. Instead they died and were buried, as all Americans of good family were expected to be, in the Protestant Cemetery. They were the brother and sister of George Frederic Jones, father of the novelist Edith Wharton.

Others include John Addington Symonds (1840–1893), the Victorian art critic whom we now know to have had an active sexual as well as artistic life. He was buried in the shadow of the pyramid in 1893. William Wetmore Story, a native of Salem, Massachusetts, and son of Justice Joseph Story of the Supreme Court, found fame in Italy as a sculptor. He did the head of Charlotte Cushman, the actress, and other literary lights of the Roman colony. The kneeling angel over the grave of his wife was his last work. Wilhelm Waiblinger, a minor German poet, was interred here in 1830. Ronald Firbank, the effete British writer, was first buried in the Protestant Cemetery after his death in 1926, but—because it was said he became a convert to Catholicism at Cambridge—he was later interred in the Monumental Cemetery on the Via Tiburtina. George Santayana stayed an even shorter time: His body was in the mortuary chapel one night in 1952 before being transferred to the Tomb of Spaniards in the Campo Verano.

Santayana's nocturnal stay brings to mind that daytime funerals were not permitted in the early days, because the processions were often attacked by

Percy Bysshe Shelley's grave. *Photograph by Massimo Ascani. Courtesy Ab Allhems Förlag, Malmö, Sweden*

anti-Protestant citizens. So burials were after nightfall, stealthily held by torchlight. Until fairly recently—in 1870—crosses were not permitted on the graves either.

Today, dreaming of the past, the Protestant Cemetery stands as a symbol of the traveler to Rome: a historic memento in a strangely personal way. At one end is Monte Testaccio, wholly formed from shards of wine and oil vessels from ancient Roman transports and from warehouses on the Tiber. The cats, those familiar citizens of the Eternal City, prowl silently among the graves; violets and daisies grow at will among silent stones; occasionally, the tinkle of a bell at the gate summons the shuffling caretaker. Otherwise, Adonais and Ariel and their famous and little-known companions sleep here among the crooked paths, running vines, and the quiet birdsong—for the ages.

The sculpture *Angel of Death* by William Wetmore Story is over the graves of the artist and his wife. *Photograph by Massimo Ascani. Courtesy Ab Allhems Förlag, Malmö, Sweden*

9. Cimitero degli Inglesi

FLORENCE, ITALY

H. V. MORTON, that inveterate traveler, describes the way to this fascinating cemetery: "As you travel toward the Porta S. Gallo, along that stretch of the boulevard known as the Viale Antonio Gramsci, you come to a remarkable object in the centre of the road. It is a rise of ground upon which grows a number of venerable trees; and as you approach nearer, and see the road dividing respectfully on each side, you realize that this must be the old Cimitero degli Inglesi [English Cemetery], in the Piazza Donatello."

This is a little bit of England in Italy. It is no longer used and is a twentieth-century phenomenon, a traffic island. The British have always had a love affair with Florence from ancient times, but since the eighteenth century—the age of the Grand Tour—and the nineteenth, when the expatriates seemed to gravitate toward

Florence, a part of the city has always been a British colony.

The most famous of those to be buried here is Elizabeth Barrett Browning (1806–1861), who left Wimpole Street for life with Robert in Florence. Elizabeth was only fifty-five at the time of her death. Near her grave is that of Isa Blagden, a devoted friend of the Brownings.

Some names on the tombstones have a familar ring for students of English literature. There is Arthur Hugh Clough (1819–1861). He died of a fever in this Renaissance city on the Arno, and two generations later Winston Churchill quoted lines by him during the dark days of World War II. The marriage lines of the British are fascinating; the relationships that crisscross and dovetail are often startling. Clough, true to this, married a cousin of Florence Nightingale. At his death Matthew

Elizabeth Barrett Browning's tomb. *Courtesy Rudolf Schenk*

The grave of Walter Savage Landor. *Courtesy Rudolf Schenk*

Arnold wrote a monody, "Thyris," in memory of Clough.

The octogenarian Walter Savage Landor (1775–1864) is in the English Cemetery as well. H. V. Morton spoke of him as an aged, confused King Lear. Landor himself wrote a four-line poem, "Finis," which could be his epitaph:

I strove with none, for none was worth my strife.
Nature I loved and, next, to Nature, Art:
I warm'd both hands before the fire of life;
It sinks, and I am ready to depart.

Frances Trollope (1780–1863), mother of the novelist Anthony and a denigrator of the United States (*Domestic Manners of the Americans*) finished out her life in Florence too. Mrs. Trollope lived to the advanced age of eighty-three, irascible and acerbic to the end. Before her death she developed a morbid fear of being buried alive and she told her son Thomas Adolphus that Italian law allowed too short a time for a body to remain unburied after death. She extracted a promise from him that he would, following her death, have a vein opened in her arm. True to his promise he followed her instructions, but he had great difficulty in persuading a physician to carry out her request. The lovely Italianization of her given name—Francesca—is inscribed on this ubiquitous traveler's stone.

Another Trollope, Theodosia Garrow (1825–1865), who married Thomas Adolphus, is buried here too. Fanny Trollope loved Theodosia and pushed Thomas Adolphus, who was fainthearted about proposing, into marriage. Another lady with literary connections who found her way to the English Cemetery was Fanny, the wife of W. Holman Hunt, who died in Florence on December 20, 1866, in the first year of her marriage. Hunt, a British painter, was a member of the Pre-Raphaelite brotherhood.

The *cappelle,* or chapels, cover the hillside.

10. Cimitero di Staglieno

GENOA, ITALY

GENOA, although it has been described as the most vital of Italian cities, has taken second place to the more romantic ones of the peninsula: Florence, Pisa, Rome, Venice, and Verona. Yet Genoa, with its harbor and backdrop of hills, is as dramatic as its sister towns and cities. An ancient wall, wide enough for thirty men to march abreast, stretches almost ten miles across the Apennines. This rampart, with its castlelike keeps, is a reminder of Genoa's great days as a city-state. From the vantage point of the hills the visitor can see the Ligurian riviera stretching to Savona on the west and Portofino to the east.

Here, high above the port on the northeast slope (the right bank of the Bisagno), lies the magnificent Cimitero di Staglieno, the largest in Italy. Begun in 1844, and designed for the Commune of Genoa by the architect C. B. Resasco, the grandiose burial ground covers 418,000 square meters. An open square dominates the whole and from it stretch colonnades in each direction, which, in turn, draw the entire cemetery toward its axis—the square. Paved with marble, the square has been crossed with still other colonnades since it opened. This ancient concept was used earlier in the campo santo at Pisa (built between 1278 and 1283) and later in Salzburg, Austria.

From the center of the colonnades, or galleries, Santo Varni's heroic statue *The Faith,* a figure holding the cross, stands before the circular church or, as it is sometimes called, the pantheon. It covers a room below where the coffins of the recently deceased are kept. Groves of cypress are enclosed by myrtle hedges.

The church, built by the architect Barabino, is surrounded by sixteen columns of black marble from Varenna. Here in the niches are statues of Adam and Eve, and the prophets Ezekiel and Daniel. Eve, by Giambattista Villa, is chastely holding a large tropical leaf before her. Long, curly locks reach to her hips. The serpent, seduction on his mind, is slithering from the vege-

33

tation at her feet. Adam, by Lorenzo Orengo, is quaintly described in an old guidebook:

> The sculptor sculpted Adam, with long hair and long nails, quite naked, less a large leaf fixed around the body, and who lacerated by the remorse leans on a stick, bending under his heavy weight. Splendid and admirable the moulding of the legs, of the arms and of the bust, who reveal the precision and the anatomical knowledge.

Beneath Adam at the base of the monument are the words *Sol per mia colpa qui la morte impera,* which the same chronicler translates as "It is only by fault that death commands here."

The realistic sculptures that defy belief fill the colonnades. Some are heroic in concept, others amusing, still others sentimental. One very touching monument was erected by Caterina Campodonico, a peddler, before her death. On its base, in the Genoese dialect, is Caterina's testament:

By selling my wares at the sanctuaries of Acquasanta, Garbo, and St. Cipriano, defying wind, sun and rain in order to provide an honest loaf for my old age I have also put by enough to have myself placed, later on, with this monument, which I, Caterina Campodonico (called the Peasant) have erected while still alive.
1881. Oh, you who pass close to this my tomb, if you will, pray for my peace.

Her statue, also by Lorenzo Orengo, shows a small woman attired in her Sunday best. A shawl with fringe covers her shoulders, she holds a giant-sized rosary in both hands. The curls and waves of her hair, the fringe on the shawl, the lace on her apron, are lifelike enough to entice the beholder to reach out and touch them.

Grief and despair are often the themes nearest and dearest the hearts of sculptors. Pietro Badaracco's monument pictures his widow, her head bowed, holding a small wreath in one hand while the other is raised to knock at the door of the tomb. The sculptor Cevasco superbly chiseled the lace on her shawl. The Mangini monument (1887) depicts Father Time in a state of exhaustion at the foot of Life's Stairway. Below him is the legend: "All meet here from every country."

In front of Carlo Erba's tomb (1883), a serene woman, representing Everlasting Sleep, sits, holding poppies in her hand. Father Time is again in evidence in the 1876 sculpture in memory of Captain Erasmo Piaggio, R.N. (This memorial lends its name to the arcade—the Arcade of Time.) Francesco Oneto's tomb is guarded by an angel, arms crossed on her bosom, a trumpet, almost as long as she is tall, clutched in one hand. Cristoforo Tomati's tomb (1881), on the other hand, depicts his orphaned daughter kneeling before the sarcophagus on

which Tomati's full-length figure lies. Christ stretches his arms protectively over the deceased and the bereaved.

Still another—that of F. G. Casella—shows a mother holding a child to kiss the medallion of his father on the face of the tomb, while an older child kneels in prayer, the broad collar and decorative buttons on his coat realistically sculpted. These and hundreds more stretch as far as the eye can see down the corridors of the colonnades. Each is unique, some more extravagant than others. Each depicts the deceased or the survivors graphically as in life.

Italian opera in the works of Puccini, Mascagni, and Leoncavallo is spoken of as *verismo.* The sculpture here is *verismo* in stone rather than music.

The cappelle, a group of tiny chapels that dot the hillside, is often considered the most artistic spot in the campo santo. The Raggio Chapel, the most spectacular of these, Gothic in style and conceived by the architect

Monument to Pietro Badaracco, showing his widow knocking at the tomb.

Rovelli, was inspired by the cathedral in Milan.

Giuseppe Mazzini (1805–1872), the Italian patriot and revolutionary who was a pivotal figure in the Risorgimento and who spent most of his life in exile (much of it in London), is the most famous of those buried here. George Trevelyan records that on Garibaldi's 1864 visit to London he declared publicly that Mazzini "alone watched when all around slept, he alone kept and fed the sacred flame." Thomas Carlyle spoke of him as the "most pious man I know." Mazzini, now returned forever from his long exile, sleeps in native ground. His tomb, an austere yet massive one, is situated in an irregular grove. It is unusual here because no realistic sculpture of the man stands before it. Instead two Doric columns of granite without bases sustain an architrave without a frieze. His name—cut in large letters—is his memorial. The entrance is in the wall opposite the atrium. Here in the campo santo, all about him, are other members of the Risorgimento.

Caterina Campodonico, a peddler, had her monument erected before her death.

F. G. Casella's monument depicts his widow and children at the tomb.

The tomb of patriot Giuseppe Mazzini.

The central gallery.

11. Cimitero di San Michele

VENICE, ITALY

EVERYTHING in Venice is somewhat different than in other cities. The architecture is peculiar to Venice; its decay is too. This tiny island city, laced with canals, facing a lagoon and the Adriatic, is more water than land.

Venice's cemetery is an island—that of San Michele. The church of the same name was begun by Mauro Coducci in 1469 and is familiar to all with its semicircular pediment and its hexagonal Cappella Emiliana added in 1530. The island sits in isolated splendor, off the Fondamenta Nuove, in the lagoon.

William Dean Howells remembered his visit to this white Carrara marble islet, jutting from the sea like the top of some submerged city: "As we go by the Cemetery of St. Michele, Piero the gondolier and Giovanni improve us with a little solemn pleasantry. 'It is a small place,' says Piero, 'but there is room for all Venice in it.' 'It is true,' assents Giovanni, 'and here we poor folks become land-owners at last.' "

The island has been called "handsome, well-manicured," and it is lovely in its strangeness, its isolation, and its sense of peace. The tombs in the garden about the church are ornate, some are enormous, and the paths are shaded with cypresses. Death in Venice, since the publication of Thomas Mann's novella of that name, has had a romantic aura about it. Virginia Woolf wrote: "Venice is a place to die in beautifully." Thousands of Venetians have died here through the ages, but except

for the rich and the famous, their bones are taken from their graves after a time and put into a common one. Land is scarce enough for the living, but for the dead it is at more of a premium. The procedure is even more drastic than in New Orleans, where many of the graves do remain intact for eternity.

In 1797 when Napoleon annexed Venice he issued a decree that terminated burial in the city's small and overcrowded campos santos. The new cemetery emerged from the union of two islands—San Michele and San Cristoforo—which were joined by landfill. The name of San Michele was retained, for here the first Renaissance church in Venice had been built on the site of a Camaldolese monastery.

The new cemetery inspired a burial society much like those that developed at the same time in New Orleans. In 1824 Giacomo Massaggia and Bernardo Pasini founded the Primo Suffragio dei Morti (First Help of the Dead), which was much valued by the Venetians who joined, for subscribers paid less for land than the city asked, or nothing at all if they could not afford it.

Three years later it was called the Archiconfraternia di S. Cristoforo e Compagnia della Misericordia (Archconfraternity of Saint Christopher and Guild of Mercy), which was recognized by the Patriarch of Venice. This organization provided mausoleums, and in-ground burial could be arranged for twelve-, twenty-, fifty- or one-hundred-year periods. Here are mausoleums much like those in New Orleans where members' bodies are placed in crypts.

Venice has always attracted an international group of

The monument over Diaghilev's grave. *Photograph copyright © 1976 by Niki Ekstrom* expatriates, visitors, and émigrés. Some have remained here to die. (Browning did, but his body was returned to England for burial in Westminster Abbey.) The famous here are not Venetians, but visitors from other lands. One of the earliest was Léopold Robert, described as one "who specialized in the painting of brigands and committed suicide in 1835 on the tenth anniversary of his brother's death." An epitaph by Lamartine distinguishes his monument.

Frederick Rolfe, Baron Corvo, the eccentric Englishman who came into the prominence again when his novel *Hadrian the Seventh* was dramatized in our time, lies in one corner of the cemetery. An enigmatic figure who wove fantastic tales from his background and history, he bore a title, "which he claimed to have acquired through the gift of some estates by a former Duchess of Cesarini-Sforza." His spirt hovers over San Michele in death as his phantom figure did in life in the streets and on the canals of Venice.

Sergei Diaghilev (1872–1929), the Russian impresario who brought the Ballet Russe out of Imperial Russia before World War I and who was the Svengali-like figure behind Nijinsky, lies in the Orthodox section. His funeral was spectacular and memorable, particularly marked by the emotional scene caused by the dancer Serge Lifar. Overwrought by the ceremonies, Lifar leapt into the open grave—a scene never forgotten by those present and now part of ballet history.

Another Russian, composer Igor Stravinsky (1882–1971), who died in New York, was brought back to San Michele for burial. Later a marble and lapis lazuli slab by Manzus was placed over his grave. In 1975, when his widow arrived in Venice, red paint had been, unexplainedly, poured over the new slab. Next to Diaghilev and Stravinsky lie Monsieur and Madame (born Countess Wolkoff) Alexandre Mitropen. Her Palazzo Wolkoff, adjacent to the Palazzo Dario on the Grand Canal, is one of Venice's loveliest. It is worth noting too that the Russians are about the only group at San Michele who cannot ever be moved from their graves and placed in wall niches.

Ezra Pound (1885–1972), after being an expatriate American for most of his life, chose Venice as his final home. Following his burial in San Michele, a sculptural likeness of Pound (based on a drawing by Henri Gaudier-Brzeska) was turned in sculpture by Isamu Noguchi, who also designed the circular base that holds it.

Perhaps it is the children's graves that are remembered longest. Each has a little statue and some, in the Continental style, have photographs under glass. The pathos of the children's section is very moving, an aspect of Venice seldom mentioned by her chroniclers.

The graves of Eamon de Valera and his family. *Photograph by Ruth and S. Alexander Smith*

12. Glasnevin Cemetery

DUBLIN, IRELAND

IN that part of Dublin north of the River Liffey and between the Royal Canal and the River Tokla, facing the Finglas Road, is Glasnevin Cemetery (opened in 1832), the burial place of Irish heroes.

The most conspicuous memorial, one that dominates the cemetery and the area around it, is that to Daniel O'Connell (1775–1847), the "Liberator," a replica of an Irish round tower. Rising some 160 feet above the crypt containing his remains, it commemorates O'Connell, who founded in 1823 the powerful Catholic Association whose pressure led to the Catholic Emancipation Act of 1829. It was he who urged the repeal of the union with Great Britain and who strove to solve the Irish land question. To the left of his grave is a Gothic memorial chapel, also in his memory, designed by a Doctor Petrie.

Beyond the chapel is the grave of Charles Stewart Parnell (1846–1891), the Irish nationalist whose career was ruined when he was named correspondent in a divorce action by the husband of his mistress Kitty O'Shea. Par-

nell's grave is marked with a huge boulder, the area is fenced in, and the trees around it form an unplanned grove. Nearby Parnell's grave is a statue to Barry Sullivan (1824–1891), the Irish actor. John Philpot Curran (1750–1817), Irish statesman, orator, and trial lawyer who defended Wolfe Tone, Lord Edward Fitzgerald, and other anti-British rebels, is also interred here (his remains were moved here in 1834) in a tomb of impressive simplicity.

The funeral that brought Glasnevin to the attention of the literary world was a fictional one—Paddy Dignam's in James Joyce's *Ulysses.* Occurring on Bloomsday, June 16, 1904, probably the most celebrated day in all literature, Paddy's funeral evoked comments from the mourners and moved Joyce, through Bloom, to ruminate: "Extraordinary the interest they take in a corpse."

The funeral procession, much like the actual ones, passed from the Finglas Road. Simon Dedalus murmured that they were at the O'Connell Circle, which moved Mr. Power to declare O'Connell was at rest among his own people, "but his heart is buried in Rome."

There is nothing the Irish love more than a funeral unless it is the wake preceding it. Joyce understood this and in writing of the life of Leopold Bloom on this memorable day in Dublin, he would of necessity include a funeral to give a true picture of Dublin life. Bloom's comment—"The Irishman's house is his coffin"—crystallizes this. Bloom walked in Glasnevin, reflecting on decomposing bodies and the "shadows of the tombs when churchyards yawn and Daniel O'Connell must be a descendant, I suppose."

The Fenian Plot, usually called the Republican Plot, or the Young Irelanders' Plot—dedicated to those members of the Irish secret revolutionary society (organized about 1858) who advocated independence from England by force—has a memorial group in Sicilian marble in memory of those buried here, notably Terence Bellew MacManus (1823–1860), Colonel John Francis O'Mahony (1816–1877), Charles Patrick McCarthy, Daniel Reddin, Patrick W. Nally, and James Stritch. The plot contains the graves of others who were prominent in the struggle for Irish independence, and the 1916 plot (in Saint Paul's section) contains the graves of those who fell in the Easter Rebellion. (All these plots are under the care of the National Graves Association.)

The monument is "to commemorate the lives, principles and sacrifices" of these men, "members of the Irish Republican Brotherhood, whose remains lie below. All outlaws and felons according to English Law, but true soldiers of Irish Liberty; Representatives of successive movements for Irish Independence. Their lives thus prove that every generation produces patriots who were willing to face the gibbet, the cell, and exile to procure the liberty of their nation and afford perpetual proof that in the Irish Heart Faith in Irish Nationality is indestructible."

Both Michael Collins (1890–1922), leader of the Sinn Fein, and Arthur Griffith (1872–1922) are here, as well as Kevin O'Higgins (1893–1927). Collins organized the guerrilla warfare that caused the British to sue for peace, and Griffith and O'Higgins were responsible for the establishment of the Irish Free State in 1921. Griffith was its first president (1922); Collins was assassinated that same year.

One of Ireland's great heroines, Constance, Countess Markievicz (1868–1927), was sentenced to death for her part in the 1916 Easter Rebellion. The "Rebel Countess" served in the Sinn Fein parliament (1918–1922) and in the Dail Eireann (1922, 1923, 1927). Daughter of a distinguished and ancient family (Gore-Booth) of the Anglo-Irish Ascendancy, she became a twentieth-century heroine to her people and to those of the rest of the world who supported a free Ireland. Five days before her death on July 15, Kevin O'Higgins—whose vision of a modern Eire she opposed—was assassinated on his way to mass.

While half of Dublin mourned O'Higgins, the other half grieved for Constance. Her body lay in the Rotunda —the City Hall and the Mansion House were refused by her political opponents—and her funeral was the occasion for a great outpouring of affection. The esteem in which she was held was demonstrated by eight trucks bearing floral offerings. Even an old countrywoman arrived with an offering of three fresh eggs, keeping a promise she made when it was thought the countess might live.

Thousands of Irish turned out, lining the streets of Dublin, to watch the Sinn Fein, Fianna Fail, the Irish Citizen Army, and other organizations march in the funeral procession to Glasnevin. There her Irish Citizen Army uniform was placed in her grave. Eamon de Valera delivered the oration, calling her the "friend of the toiler, the lover of the poor."

De Valera (1882–1975), the man whose name is most associated today with Irish independence, came to Glasnevin finally on September 2, 1975. De Valera's wife, Sinead (1878–1975), his son Brian (1915–1936), and daughter, Vivion (1910–1951), are here also. As his funeral moved through Dublin—past the great buildings, through the slums, along the Liffey—it passed the General Post Office, the scene of the unsuccessful attempt to free Ireland from British rule. Cries of "Up Dev" were heard above the band playing "Wrap the Green Flag Round Me." His grandson, the Reverend Shan O'Cuiv, sang the requiem mass in Gaelic, his two surviving sons read the lesson in the same tongue, and the eulogy was delivered in Gaelic as well.

The great Irish nationalist was buried in the shadow of O'Connell's tower and near the graves of Parnell, Collins, and Griffith. The ordinary folk of Dublin—those De Valera devoted his life to—climbed up on Celtic crosses or on the gray headstones to silently witness the coming home of the old campaigner. A few tottering survivors of the Easter rebellion stood at his graveside, their medals picking up the sunlight. An honor guard of army cadets from the same unit De Valera sent to Washington for John F. Kennedy's funeral held their rifles upside down at the graveside. Just before the Last Post was sounded, the air was shattered by sound as a tall tombstone collapsed. It fell under the weight of five spectators perched on its angel wings. De Valera's coffin, covered with the tricolor of the Irish republic, was slowly lowered into the ground devoted to Irish patriots.

Two others who were involved in the cause of Irish independence are also here. The bones of Sir Roger Casement (1864–1916), the controversial Irish patriot, were returned to Glasnevin after lying in English soil for many years following his hanging by the British. And Maud Gonne (1866–1953), the legendary English beauty who was "obsessed with a burning desire to free Ireland," was buried among her fellow patriots. Yeats, who first met Maud in 1889, proposed to her on several occasions, declaring that from the time they met life was "changed, changed utterly." Although they did not marry, she found her own immortality in Yeats's *The Countess Cathleen* and in being called Ireland's "last great romantic heroine."

The grave of Roger Casement. *Photograph by Ruth and S. Alexander Smith*

A view of Glasnevin Cemetery, showing the O'Connell tower. *Photograph by Ruth and S. Alexander Smith*

The boulder marking the grave of Charles Stewart Parnell. *Photograph by Ruth and S. Alexander Smith*

A view of the Republican Plot. *Photograph by Ruth and S. Alexander Smith*

13. Central Cemetery

VIENNA, AUSTRIA

WIEN! City of dreams, where life has always been—according to Franz Lehár and Oscar Straus—one round of gaiety: wine, women, and song. Even Johann Strauss gave one of his most popular waltzes that title. Where there is life and music, there must also be death. In Vienna there are several small and old cemeteries such as those in the districts of Heitzing and Meidling, but the Zentralfriedhof, or Central Cemetery, has for the city become *the* burial ground. Located in Simmering, the 11th district, and surrounded by woods, it was planned in 1873, the year the Vienna Universal Exhibition attracted thousands of visitors to the capital from elsewhere in Europe and America.

To provide what is now one of Europe's largest and most elaborate cemeteries, the city purchased an area that had formerly been low-yield farmland. The city's other burial grounds—as in Paris and London—were overfilled. Population was increasing, and thousands flocked to Vienna from all parts of the Austro-Hungarian empire, many never again to return to their birthplaces.

The city fathers were concerned at the time the cemetery was in its first stages of development, thinking it was too close to a brewery. Nothing is closer to a Viennese than his beer, and it was felt that the bodies might poison underground fountains used in beer production. Another worry was that the Zentralfriedhof tended to flood the moment it rained.

<

The monuments to Beethoven and Mozart. *Photograph by Adrianne Onderdonk Dudden*

Two German architects were imported from Frankfurt am Main and it was they who suggested the idea of subdividing the cemetery into square blocks, enabling visitors to have easy access to the graves by creating a number of straight, tree-lined avenues stretching from one end of the cemetery to the other.

The first burial took place on All Saints' Day on November 1, 1874. Since that time about 1.5 million people have been buried here (almost the number of the present population of Vienna), among them all the post-World War II presidents of Austria.

It is the musicians, of course, who give the Central Cemetery its wide tourist appeal. The bodies of Ludwig van Beethoven (1770–1827) and Franz Schubert (1797–1828) had been buried next to one another in what is now Franz Schubert Park. The bodies were exhumed and reburied here, but the original headstones remain along the walls in the old park. Johann Strauss (1825–1899) and Johannes Brahms (1833–1897) both died after the Central Cemetery opened and were buried here. Strauss's monument is marvelous in its romantic yet rococo style. Below a circular medallion of his head stands a languorous female figure, her right hand lightly touching the strings of a small harp. Between the muse and the musician are cherubim and seraphim, dancing and playing their instruments. Johann's wife Adélé (1856–1930), to whom he was not always faithful, lies beside him. Johann Strauss the Elder (1804–1849), founder of this remarkable dynasty, and his sons Josef (1827–1870) and Eduard (1835–1916) are not far away. Josef is entombed beneath a black monument. Leaning against it in sorrow is a classical figure in white marble, a small lyre in one hand.

As Brahms lay dying, he accepted a glass of wine from Frau Celestina Truxa, his faithful housekeeper. This was also the last act of both Beethoven and Goethe. In his native city of Hamburg, flags flew at half-mast both in the city and on the ships in the harbor. The streets of Vienna were thronged with mourners.

At his grave the words from two of his greatest works were part of the funeral service. The Protestant clergyman gave as the benediction the words of the last movement of the German Requiem: "Blessed are the dead which die in the Lord, from henceforth; 'Yea,' said the Spirit, 'that they may rest from their labors: and their works to follow them.' " As the coffin was slowly lowered, a choir sang the last farewell, Brahms's chorale *Fahr Wohl* (Blessed Journey).

Franz von Suppé (1819–1895), known today for his *Poet and Peasant* Overture, has cherublike angels hovering over his bust. Between the Beethoven and Schubert graves is a memorial to Wolfgang Amadeus Mozart (1756–1791). It was placed there by the grateful city of Vienna, which had neglected to mark his grave in the Saint Marxer Friedhof nearby—one of the great ironies of musical history. Had the grave of the greatest of all Viennese composers been known, undoubtedly his remains would have been moved here with Beethoven's and Schubert's.

A modern Viennese waltz king, Robert Stolz (1882–1975) was buried not far from Johann Strauss, whom he knew and who advised him as a young musician. Stolz composed fifty operettas, the scores for a hundred films (he won two Academy Awards), and 2,500 songs. The one for which he is best known is "Two Hearts in Three-Quarter Time." Karl Millöcker (1842–1899), who composed *The Dubarry,* which starred Grace Moore on Broadway, is among the lesser composers here. Hugo Wolf (1860–1903), one of the greatest composers of German *lieder* (more than three hundred, including the settings for poems by Goethe), is here too.

Flowers as much as music are the heart of Vienna. At the gates flower stalls bank the entrances with pansies, daisies, daffodils, verbena, and roses. For a small tip the visitor can collect a shovel and watering can to garden at the family graves. These are usually marked by a large stone, setting forth the family name and the members buried within the plot.

While flowers are expected, and the landscaping of the cemetery is enough to make it an arboretum or even a small pleasure park, it is probably the only cemetery in the world where hunting was not only allowed but encouraged. Hunters were issued special licenses to hunt small game—rabbits, hares, partridges, pheasants, and occasionally a deer—that were damaging graves, trampling flowers, and even toppling tombstones, especially in the long winter months when food was difficult to forage. The Vienna City Council finally took action, and in the late 1960s, in an unprecedented move, issued hunt-ing licenses. One—at a fee of $300—was granted to Ludwig Siehs, a sixty-one-year-old retired grocer. It permitted him, and a small group of friends, to hunt small game among the grave sites from nightfall—when the cemetery gates are closed—to sunup, just before they are reopened, during the regular hunting season, which extends from November 1 to mid-April.

This decision was not made lightly, and not without consultation. Catholic, Protestant, and Jewish clergymen were approached and none objected, so the City Council proceeded. The alternative to this would have been to raise the annual charges for caretaking in order to provide for additional exterminators. Herr Siehs and his friends formed a private—and very exclusive—cemetery hunting club, probably the only one in the world.

No picture of the Zentralfriedhof is more moving than that on All Saints' Day, when the observer looks upon the cemetery after night has fallen. Then the lights of Vienna are lit. Small candles on thousands of graves flicker in the darkness, a myriad of fireflies as the Viennese remember the departed. It is then a City of Dreams.

The monument over the grave of Johann Strauss. *Photograph by Adrianne Onderdonk Dudden*

The grave of Franz von Suppé. *Photograph by Adrianne Onderdonk Dudden*

< The monument over Josef Strauss and his three wives. *Photograph by Adrianne Onderdonk Dudden*

Family monuments in the Central Cemetery. *Photograph by Adrianne Onderdonk Dudden*

The monument to Johann N. Prin, a mayor of Vienna. *Photograph by Adrianne Onderdonk Dudden*

Above, right: Franz Schubert's grave. *Photograph by Adrianne Onderdonk Dudden*

The grave of Marie Wilt (1834–1891), chamber music singer. *Photograph by Adrianne Onderdonk Dudden*

The monument to Hugo Wolf, composer of *lieder. Photograph by Robert J. Cahn*

Above, left: The monument to Brahms. *Photograph by Robert J. Cahn*

Beethoven's grave. *Photograph by Adrianne Onderdonk Dudden*

The grave of Nikita Khrushchev. *Photograph by W. Douglas Varn*

14. Novo-Devichy Cemetery

MOSCOW, RUSSIA

IN Soviet Russia the highest honor accorded the dead is burial in Red Square. There in splendor Vladimir Ilich Lenin (1870–1924), father of the Russian Revolution, lies embalmed in the massive mausoleum that is the most photographed structure in Russia. Joseph Stalin (1879–1953) shared that honor with Lenin until Premier Nikita S. Khrushchev ordered his body removed. It was then placed in the secondary place of honor, the burial ground beside the Kremlin wall where cosmonaut Yuri Gagarin

and John Reed (1887–1920), the American revolutionary and author of *Ten Days that Shook the World,* are.

Often called the Soviet Forest Lawn. Novo-Devichy, or New Virgin, is but a short distance from Red Square. Here lie some of Russia's great: playwright Anton Chekhov (1860–1904), whose *The Three Sisters* depicted the longings for the pleasures of Moscow; Nikolai Gogol (1809–1852), author of *Dead Souls*; and the great composer Dmitri Shostakovich (1906–1975), whose funeral brought forth great displays of emotion and grief.

Contemporary Soviet art at Novo-Devichy is a mé-lange of the bad and the not so good. One of the most tasteless memorials is that to a Moscow heart surgeon who died in 1967, "a huge granite hand clutching a plastic ruby-colored jewel." An airplane propeller encased in glass is to the memory of those who died in the crash of a transport plane in the White Sea.

More than 2,500 graves cover Novo-Devichy. The monuments over Klavdia, wife of Premier Aleksei Kosygin, and Sergei Eisenstein (1898–1948), the film director (*Potemkin, Alexander Nevsky,* and *Ivan the Terrible*), are simple and dignified. The most popular grave is that of Nadezhda Alliluyeva Stalin, first wife of the dictator. Near her is their grandson, Vassily Vassilivich Stalin, who died at the age of twenty-three in 1972, reportedly of an overdose of drugs. Nadezhda's grave is a simple white shaft with a sculptured head of her at the top.

Nothing seems to appeal to the Soviet temperament more than officialdom—political figures, military leaders, astronauts, and cosmonauts. In 1974 the first authorized memorial to Premier Nikita S. Khrushchev was raised. An eight-foot marble monument with a bronze head of the statesman by Ernest Neizvestny, it cost the family about $13,000, with a small contribution made by the government. It is ironic that Neizvestny was chosen. He is the nonconformist artist who openly quarreled with Khrushchev over modern art. In fact, their shouting match made international headlines; eventually he won the premier over to his side.

An equal number of black and white marble blocks in the monument represent the two sides of Khrushchev's personality and also the "fact that he stood at the point where, thanks largely to him, one epoch in our history ended and another began." Observers felt this referred to Khrushchev's efforts to end the repressions of Stalinism.

Others buried here are Premier Nikolai A. Bulganin (1895–1975); Andrei Tupolev, father of Soviet jet aircraft; the cosmonaut Pavel I. Belyayev; and the folk heroine of World War II—Zoya Kosmedemyanskaya. This sixteen-year-old partisan was tortured to death by the Nazis and her grave is a place of pilgrimage for schoolchildren.

Novo-Devichy is an anachronism in Russia, and perhaps that is why more than two thousand citizens and foreigners visit it each weekday. (The numbers increase on weekends and holidays.) In Russia—an atheistic society—cremation is encouraged as ritualistic religious burials are not. The newer section of the cemetery is noticeably free of crosses and angels. In the older section is a touching sight—and one dear to the West. A special corner contains the graves of the actors of the Moscow Art Theatre.

Everything is regulated at Novo-Devichy by the Moscow Soviet, or City, Council. A grave costs as little as $13.50 and an urn in the cemetery wall a mere $1.35. In 1974 families and friends of those interred planted ten thousand trees and shrubs to help beautify Moscow's great cemetery.

The grave of Georgií Nikolaevich Babakin. *Photograph by W. Douglas Varn*

A physician's grave. *Photograph by W. Douglas Varn*

An example of Moscow cemetery art.
Photograph by W. Douglas Varn

The restored Jews' Burial Ground. *Photograph by Peter Renerts*

15. Jews' Burial Ground

CHARLESTOWN, NEVIS

ON the tiny island of Nevis, one of the Leeward necklace stretching between the Atlantic Ocean and the Caribbean Sea, the ancient and restored Jews' Burial Ground, situated in the shadow of Mount Nevis, provides a continuity with the island's historic past. Nevis, first settled by the English in 1628, was a port of call in 1607 for the Jamestown, Virginia, settlers en route to the New World.

Jewish traders are thought to have visited Nevis as early as the 1650s, but the first record of Jewish settlement is on the rolls of 1678. (In 1671 England separated those Leeward Islands under her control from the government of Barbados; by 1678 Nevis had the largest population in the Leewards.) These first Jews were evidently the purchasers of the ground for the cemetery, and it must have been about this time, for the oldest grave is that of Ester Maraché, who died on February 20, 1679. It was not until 1688, however, that the Jewish population was large enough to build a synagogue.

On every Caribbean island both nature and imperialism took their toll. Nevis was no exception. There was a major epidemic of malignant fever in 1689–1690. The death toll from a 1706 raid by the French—who controlled Martinique, Guadeloupe, and Marie-Galante—reduced the island's population (and the Jewish one as well) by one-third. The population in 1724 was nearly three hundred whites, about a quarter of whom were Jews, but it declined afterward, especially after the emancipation of the slaves in 1838.

The cemetery gradually fell into disuse. The last known burial—that of Jacob Vas Mendes—dates from 1768. In 1772 a violent hurricane caused extensive damage and is thought to have driven out the remaining Jews, or they may have perished in it.

The Nevis cemetery—abandoned, overgrown, the

51

stones disintegrating—was saved through the efforts of Robert D. and Florence Abrahams of Philadelphia, and Rabbi Malcolm H. Stern of New York. Samuel Hunkins, a leading builder on the island, designed and built the wall. Norman Kalcheim, law partner of Mr. Abrahams, designed the gates, which were forged on the nearby island of Saint Kitts, and Mrs. Hester Marsden-Smedley of London, a descendant of the Pinney family, early island plantation owners, lent encouragement. The Ministry of Agriculture provided prison labor for clearing the rubble, replanting the cemetery, and restoring the tombstones. The rehabilitation of the old burial ground became very much a community project.

In February 1971, the Jews' Burial Ground was rededicated. Nineteen recognizable gravestones—not all legible—survive, the earliest dated 1684, the latest 1768. The restored wall surrounds the 200- by 75-foot plot; the handsome wrought-iron gates, opposite the Jews' Walk (which leads to the ruins of what is thought to be the old synagogue and school), enhance this hallowed ground. The names are of Spanish-Portuguese origin, the wording Portuguese or Hebrew.

Of the extant stones, that of Bathsheba Abundiente (wife of Rohiel), who died on August 8, 1684, is the most elaborate. She is buried beside her son, and the visitor is cautioned: "For she did what was right in the eyes of the Lord. May her soul be bound up in the bond of eternal life." As befits a woman with an exotic biblical name, her stone is decorated with lotus blossoms whose stems are intertwined, crossed palm branches surmounting a wreath, and a winged hourglass resting on a sloping mound with wheatlike plants on either side.

The role of the Jews' Burial Ground in the island's history, and its significance now—historically and religiously—is best expressed in the poem Robert D. Abrahams wrote for the rededication ceremony on February 25, 1971:

Poem of Reconsecration

Long, long ago they walked this lovely isle,
And lived and died within Mount Nevis shade;
Far was their coming, here found rest awhile,
Enjoying what their fruitful labors made.

We know not why they came, nor where they went,
But these remained, reposing in this spot—
Their wanderings at end, their voyaging spent:
A while they were remembered, then forgot.

Standing close today beside their graves,
We say the ancient prayer they would have known;
"All men are brothers"—this the truth that saves,
And may the Lord of all here, bless each stone.

The marker for the Jews' Burial Ground. *Photograph by Peter Renerts*

The surviving stones in the Jews' Burial Ground. *Photograph by Peter Renerts*

One of the stones that has its inscription intact. *Photograph by Peter Renerts*

One of the stones that is in excellent condition. It is over the grave of Bathsheba, widow of Rowland Gideon. *Photograph by Peter Renerts*

The most unusual of the stones in the Jews' Burial Ground. *Photograph by Peter Renerts*

II. The United States

The Mary Baker Eddy memorial. © *1918, Renewed 1946. The Christian Science Publishing Society*

16. Mount Auburn Cemetery

CAMBRIDGE, MASSACHUSETTS

INSPIRED by Père-Lachaise in Paris, Mount Auburn became the first natural landscape cemetery in the United States—a garden cemetery in a rural setting. Founded during the administration of Andrew Jackson, it was fortunate in having Jacob Bigelow—botanist, physician, poet, and author of *American Medical Botany* —as the genius behind its conception. Dr. Bigelow was for years the foremost botanist in New England and he saw at once the botanical possibilities of Mount Auburn.

The land itself—originally known as Stone's Wood, but popularly called Sweet Auburn—was the country estate of George W. Brimmer. In June 1831, Bigelow and other prominent Bostonians announced they were offering lots at $60 each to one hundred subscribers; the $6,000 thus raised was used to purchase the original seventy-two-acre estate. Not only were these citizens very much involved in the creation of Mount Auburn, but the Massachusetts Horticultural Society was as well. "It was determined to devote it to the purpose of a rural cemetery, and experimental garden." Mount Auburn became

the model for similar cemeteries near large cities across the nation.

The situation could not have been more felicitous. The view from Mount Auburn itself was spectacular, the highest point rising to a height of 125 feet above the Charles River. Boston's spires could be seen in the distance; below, the Charles snaked its way in its meandering course. The land was of great diversity: grassy knolls and hillocks, bosky dells, copses, small woods, pools, and ponds gave it a natural setting, the "first example in modern times of so large a tract of ground being selected for its natural beauties, and submitted to the processes of landscape gardening, to prepare it for the reception of the dead."

Bigelow was authorized to give names to the various features of Mount Auburn—the hills, ponds, and tracery of paths. He responded, botanist that he was, by naming many after plants. Today we find them still—Aralia Path, Bellwort Path, Laurel Avenue, Viburnum Avenue, and even Primrose Path! He did not stop with plants and flowers, but named some for birds—Meadowlark Path, Eagle Avenue, Hummingbird Path, and Swan Avenue.

Boston and its environs took Mount Auburn to their heart. Wealthy Bostonians became subscribers, and, with money contributed specifically for a chapel, Bigelow designed one—named for him and still standing—and an Egyptian-style gate. An 1846 guide to the cemetery described a "fence of wooden pales, with a lofty entrance-gate in the centre, constructed of wood, the form of which was in imitation essentially of some of the gateways of Thebes and Denderah. In 1843 this gate was taken down, and reconstructed of Quincy granite, after the same design, at an expense of somewhat less than $10,000." At that time there was great interest in the Egyptian Revival, which, however, never attained the popularity of the Greek Revival.

In September 1831, the cemetery was consecrated, with Judge Joseph Story of Marblehead delivering the oration. The following summer the first burial—that of a child—took place. The same 1846 guide noted some of the early lot holders: Edward Everett; Horatio Greenough, whose residence was listed as Florence, Italy; Samuel F. Morse (the B. was omitted); Pierce Butler of Philadelphia (husband of Fanny Kemble, the British actress); Harrison Gray Otis; and H. W. Longfellow of Cambridge. The list also contained such distinguished New England names as Crowinshield, Bradford, Bowditch, Sawyer, Snow, Dana, Sturgis, and Hosmer, and there was more than a sprinkling of those charmingly original ones that New Englanders of the last century bore: Mace Tisdale, Temperence C. Colburn (of Lowell), Supply C. Thwing (of Roxbury), and Zebedee Cook, Jr., of New York.

Mount Auburn is a pantheon and has been termed the "Westminster Abbey of America," because of the noted Americans buried here. Among the poets are James Russell Lowell (1819–1891); the autocrat of the breakfast table, Dr. Oliver Wendell Holmes (1809–1894); Henry Wadsworth Longfellow (1807–1882); and Amy Lowell (1874–1925), the Boston Brahmin whose cigar smoking was almost as famous as her poetry. Here too are John Bartlett (1820–1905), whose *Familiar Quotations* is a standard reference work today, the publishers George H. Mifflin (1845–1921), Charles Little (1799–1869), and James Brown (1800–1855), whose names still grace Boston publishing houses. Edwin Booth (1833–1893), the only member of the famous theatrical family not buried in Green Mount Cemetery in Baltimore, lies beside his first wife, Mary Devlin; not far away lies Charlotte Cushman (1816–1876), the foremost American actress of her time. All but two of the deceased presidents of Harvard since 1810 lie here near many professors and students of that university.

Others who lie in Mount Auburn are Isabella Stewart Gardner (1840–1924) and Mary Baker Eddy (1821–1910). Isabella, "Mrs. Jack," mistress of Fenway Court, who, aided by Bernard Berenson, amassed a superb art collection, left it and her home as a museum. Mrs. Eddy, the founder of the Christian Science Church, is buried on the shores of Halcyon Lake. Her monument is a charming Greek temple, a derivation of the Choragic Monument of Lysicrates in Athens.

Perhaps the greatest funeral in Boston's history, and certainly in Mount Auburn's, was that of Charles Sumner (1811–1874). Sumner, an ardent abolitionist, was attacked on the floor of the senate in 1856—after he delivered a notable antislavery speech—by Congressman Preston Brooks of South Carolina, and caned so severely that his health was affected long afterward.

It was said that the procession of mourners accompanying the body from King's Chapel to Mount Auburn was over a mile long, many on foot, including hundreds of black citizens who came to pay homage to a man who had fought so ardently for their cause. More than a hundred carriages joined the procession and five thousand people—an unforgettable sight—ringed the hills surrounding Mount Auburn; thousands more were unable to get near the cemetery. It was the largest funeral in the history of New England until then.

Only one president is associated with Mount Auburn, but not in death. Franklin Pierce (1804–1869), of New Hampshire, the fourteenth president of the United States, attained that office in 1852. At the Democratic nominating convention in Baltimore, Lewis Cass, Stephen Douglas, and James Buchanan were deadlocked and Pierce was named the compromise presidential candidate. He was resting under a tree at Mount Auburn when a messenger sent to find him relayed the news of his nomination.

The list of the famous here is unending: Henry Cabot Lodge (1850–1924), who opposed the Treaty of Versailles and the League of Nations; Francis Parkman (1823–1893), author of *The California and Oregon Trail;* Edward Everett (1794–1865), the famed orator who spoke at Gettysburg at the same ceremony at which Lincoln delivered his famous address; Louis Agassiz (1807–1873), zoologist and geologist; Gamaliel Bradford (1863–1932), American biographer; Charles Bulfinch (1763–1844), the great architect responsible for the Massachusetts State House and other notable Boston buildings; Nathaniel Bowditch (1773–1838), navigator and author of *The New American Practical Navigator;* Winslow Homer (1836–1910), painter; William Ellery Channing (1818–1901), poet; Charles Eliot Norton (1827–1908), editor of the *North American Review* and a founder of *The Nation;* Dorothea L. Dix (1802–1887), pioneer reformer in the movement for more humane treatment of the insane; Julia Ward Howe (1819–1910), whose words for "The Battle Hymn of the Republic" made it almost a second national anthem, and her husband, Samuel Gridley Howe (1801–1876), reformer and philanthropist.

Here, in truth, is the flowering of New England—the men and women who helped make that section of the United States unique.

Pilgrim Path, Mount Auburn. Engraved by James Smillie. *Print and Picture Department, Free Library of Philadelphia*

A lamb over a grave always indicated that a child was buried there. *Photograph by Clive E. Driver*

One of the older roads in Mount Auburn. *Courtesy Mount Auburn Cemetery*

A view of Mount Auburn showing the magnificent trees and shrubbery. *Courtesy Mount Auburn Cemetery*

The Jacob Bigelow Chapel. *Courtesy Mount Auburn Cemetery*

Above, left: The grave of Henry Wadsworth Longfellow. *Courtesy Mount Auburn Cemetery*

A newer section of Mount Auburn. *Courtesy Mount Auburn Cemetery*

The early days of Laurel Hill. *Print and Picture Department, Free Library of Philadelphia*

17. Laurel Hill Cemetery

PHILADELPHIA, PENNSYLVANIA

"DESCENDING a steep declivity, immediately beside the north boundary fence, persons of taste cannot but be gratified with the rural character of the picturesque scene; fine old trees of beech, oak &c., cast a solemn shade, while the river meanders in peaceful quiet below." Thus, the anonymous author of *Guide to Laurel Hill Cemetery Near Philadelphia With a List of Lotholders* described in 1854 the nation's second oldest rural cemetery.

He was endeavoring, of course, to interest prospective buyers of lots and remind them that "morning is decidedly the most agreeable time of day to visit Laurel Hill, particularly to the bereaved mourner. It is then comparatively unfrequented."

In those days Laurel Hill was a stroller's paradise and it was more often frequented than not. Philadelphians took their children there in pleasant weather to wander along the paths that wound round the hills overlooking the Schuylkill River. They never tired of looking at the

monuments to the famous, the prosperous, or the well-born.

Cambridge, Massachusetts, anticipating Philadelphia by several years, created Mount Auburn Cemetery in 1831, the first cemetery of any size detached from a church or a parish in the United States, and the first to be nonsectarian, although some Roman Catholics and Jews continued to use their own burying grounds. Philadelphia followed with Laurel Hill, although Green-Wood in Brooklyn has often been credited with being the second oldest commercial cemetery in the United States. Organized by John Jay Smith (with Nathan Dunn, Frederick Brown, and Benjamin W. Richards), after a meeting of the commissioners in November 1835, the ground was purchased the following February and an act of incorporation, 1836–1837, was granted by the Pennsylvania legislature. (Green-Wood's act of incorporation was filed on April 11, 1838).

Laurel Hill was formed from several estates along the

scenic river, just above the falls of the Schuylkill, the first of which was Laurel, the country seat of Joseph Sims, Esq., who "fully appreciating its many and remarkable beauties, had left the river front to the care of nature." It was covered with a fine growth of trees—a small forest—and only here and there intersected by paths. Rocks were "piled in picturesque confusion on some portions." Later the estates of Harleigh and Fairy Hill were purchased to complete the cemetery as it stands today.

There was a drama—in fact, high drama—connected with the establishment of Laurel Hill. A prominent person—or, better still, several—had to be found to help attract purchasers from better families. In 1838 Charles Thomson (1729–1824), was selected. Secretary of the Continental Congress, he was an Irish immigrant whose father died when the ship bearing him and his motherless children was in sight of the Delaware capes. A self-made man, he contributed richly to the development of his adopted city. In fact, John Adams called him the "Sam Adams of Philadelphia." He lived almost to the age of ninety-five, dying only twelve years before the first burial here, and was buried beside his second wife at Harriton, her family's home in Bryn Mawr. In 1838 his bones were removed to Laurel Hill and the repercussions are still felt in certain Philadelphia circles. John Thomson, Charles's nephew and heir, claimed when Thomson was buried at Harriton that it was thought the title to the burial ground could never be contested, but in time it had reverted to the new owners of the estate. John wanted a suitable stone erected over his illustrious forbear and the graves better cared for.

Taking matters into his own hands, John consulted several lawyers and then wrote to a "respectable undertaker," giving him his instructions. This man and his assistants, in the midst of the disinterment, were surprised by several farmers and questioned as to their right in removing the bodies from Harriton.

Levi Norris wrote to the *National Gazette,* excoriating those who had perpetrated this dire deed, but he had not bargained for John, who replied righteously in the *American Daily Advertiser,* defending his position. The entire contretemps has not yet died down, for the present owners of the burial ground declare Thomson is there and not at Laurel Hill.

Thomson's was not the first burial. That honor belongs to Mrs. Mercy Carlisle. A few weeks before her death she visited Laurel Hill and selected the spot she wanted—under a group of large pine trees. She was laid to rest here on October 19, 1836.

Laurel Hill was conceived as a rural cemetery, "where family affection could be gratified in the assurance that the remains of father and child, husband and wife could repose side by side undisturbed by the changing interests of man; where the smitten heart might pour out its grief over the grave of the cherished one, secure from the idle gaze of heartless passers-by, and where the mourner could rear a flower, consecrated to memory and hope."

Not only the monument to Thomson rose above the rolling hills of Laurel Hill, but memorials of all shapes and sizes. The managers felt a word of caution might be appropriate:

There is another suggestion which the Managers feel it their duty to make the lot-holders; they trust it will be received as an evidence that they are anxious to unite in carrying out the original intention of creating Laurel Hill *a tout ensemble,* which shall evince that, with superior facilities, there is growing up an improved taste in monumental sculpture. It has been a frequent remark of visiters—our own citizens, as well as Strangers—that a monotony already begins to be apparent in the style and form of the improvements; obelisk succeeds obelisk, &c., with only slight variation, and if this is continued, we shall see, in time, too dull a uniformity to strike the mind with agreeable sentiments. This may be obviated by a little *inquiry before ordering a monument,* and not by always taking the advice of a stone-mason, often himself willing to suggest the greatest bulk for the least money, and thus allowing marble to usurp the place of good taste.

Today the monuments are relics not of good or bad taste, but of an age given to extravagance and fancy in cemetery art. Angels with outstretched arms, childlike angels, classical figures, urns, even a recumbent lion, help make Laurel Hill a monument to Victorian taste. The rustling of the pines on a windy day gives the place a mournful air; in summer it is friendlier, with the foliage softening the marble necropolis. Like so many old cemeteries, Laurel Hill has been a haven for birds, for it is an extension of Fairmount Park, which borders it.

Thomas Godfrey (1704–1749) lies here. He invented the mariner's quadrant and although he died before Laurel Hill was opened, his body and those of his parents were brought here from a Germantown farm. Thomas McKean (1734–1817), signer of the Declaration of Independence, and David Rittenhouse (1732–1796), astronomer, clockmaker, inventor of a collimating telescope, and first director of the United States Mint, lie here too.

Beside Admiral John Adolphus Bernard Dahlgren (1809–1870), the "father of modern naval ordnance," lies his son, Colonel Ulric Dahlgren, who was killed on March 2, 1864 in the Civil War. Admiral Dahlgren was commander of the South Atlantic Blockading Squadron in the same war. Young Dahlgren's arrival at Laurel Hill was preceded by a saga worthy of the finest Civil War novelist. On February 28, 1864, an army of more than five thousand Union soldiers, including Dahlgren, under the command of General Judson Kilpatrick, bore down on Richmond. Dahlgren, who was fitted with a wooden leg and used a crutch, rode like the wind when mounted. He, with several thousand soldiers, was to make a thrust at Richmond from one direction while Kilpatrick attacked the Confederate capital from the other. The plans went awry and Ulric Dahlgren was killed in a retreat in the rain under cover of darkness.

The Confederates buried the body close to a road, after having cut off a finger to obtain a ring and removing the wooden leg, which could be used again. After his burial, word spread throughout Richmond that, had the attack been successful, Dahlgren was under orders to burn and sack the city, and kill Jefferson Davis and his cabinet. Although this was never proven, Confederate passions reached fever pitch. Union prisoners were described as assassins, and compared to the Huns, the Goths, and the Saracens in cruelty. It was suggested by one publication that Dahlgren's corpse be disinterred and exhibited publicly as a "monument of infamy."

The body, unknown to the aroused populace, had been placed in a coffin (it would not have been difficult to identify with one leg and one finger missing) by order of Jefferson Davis and was reburied secretly among thousands of other Union graves. A Negro sympathetic to the North watched the reinterment and reported it to Elizabeth Van Lew, a Richmond lady whose dispatches to the Union forces kept them appraised of the situation behind Confederate lines. He marked the grave and told Elizabeth its location. The intrepid Miss Van Lew, whose grave in Shockhoe Cemetery in Richmond was appropriately marked by northern admirers, had Colonel Dahlgren's body removed and spirited away (but not before it was identified).

Furtively, it was carried to the farm of W. C. Rowley. There, in a seed house, the body was placed in a metal coffin and reburied on another farm—that of Robert Orrick—outside of Richmond. To accomplish this, Rowley placed the coffin in a wagon, and covered it with a dozen peach trees carefully and tightly packed. By sheer good fortune and the carelessness of the sentry at the pickets, Rowley succeeded in passing through the lines. Miss Van Lew then sent a report in cipher to General Ben Butler.

There is still another short chapter to this story. Admiral Dahlgren requested the return of his son's body and President Davis acceded to the request, but when the body was not found where it should have been, Richmond was alive to the mystery of the situation. After the war's end, Elizabeth Van Lew revealed Colonel Dahlgren's third grave and he was then transferred to his fourth, and present, one in Laurel Hill.

Joshua B. Lippincott (1840–1896), of the distinguished publishing family, and numerous members of the Fitler family, ancestors of Margaretta Fitler, wife of former Vice-President Nelson Rockefeller, are buried here too. They lie among little temples, broken columns, stone crosses, marble coffins, and life-sized statues of the deceased that dot the cemetery, such as the seated figure of Thomas S. Reed, M.D. (1822–1889), in bronze. He faces away from the cemetery toward the more spectacular view over the Schuylkill. Captain Henry J. Biddle (1817–1862), who is buried near Dr. Reed, was assistant adjutant general in the Pennsylvania Reserves. He was mortally wounded in the Battle of New Market Cross Roads, and his monument is decorated with a sword belt and crossed banners.

The most widely publicized monument in Laurel Hill is just inside the Ridge Avenue gates of the north section. *Old Mortality with Sir Walter Scott and a Pony,* by James Thon (1779–1850), cannot be mistaken—at least the author of *Ivanhoe, Old Mortality,* and *Rob Roy* is easily recognizable. In the Scott novel Old Mortality was a stonecutter, who incised names and dates on tombstones. Thon immortalized him and Scott in this group, which was exhibited in Edinburgh, London, and elsewhere before being permanently installed in Laurel Hill. Old Mortality is seen bringing into fresh relief the decayed and dubious inscription on the grave of a Covenanter.

Laurel Hill is a microcosm of Philadelphia history. Here we find General Jonathan Williams (1750–1815), grand-nephew of Benjamin Franklin, who headed the Engineers Corps of the army during the Revolution and who published *Elements of Fortification* and Thaddeus Kosciusko's *Manoeuvres for Horse Artillery;* and Andrew Bradford (1686–1742), publisher of the first newspaper in Pennsylvania and a son of William Bradford, who is buried in Trinity Churchyard, New York City. Benjamin Franklin applied for a job to William, who owned the only printing press in that city, and was told to try at Andrew's shop. So Benjamin Franklin came to Philadelphia and helped change the face of the city and the history of the nation.

William John Duane (1780–1865), who was responsible for drawing up the will (thirty-seven pages in length) of Stephen Girard and was later secretary of the treasury in Andrew Jackson's cabinet; William Pepper (1843–1898), founder and editor of the *Philadelphia Medical Times* and medical director of the Centennial Exposition of 1876; and George W. Childs (1829–1894) are also here. Childs, owner and developer of the *Public Ledger,* built the Shakespeare memorial fountain in Stratford on Avon and gave a window in Westminster Abbey in memory of the poets Cowper and Herbert.

Thomas Buchanan Read (1822–1872), a poet, who wrote "Sheridan's Ride," is here. So is General Jospeh Reed (1741–1785), George Washington's aide and secretary, president of Pennsylvania, and a signer of the Articles of Confederation; and William Short (1756–1849), who received from George Washington the first appointment to public office ever conferred under the Constitution of the United States. General Hugh Mercer (1721–1777), assistant surgeon at the Battle of Culloden in 1746, emigrated from Scotland, was the companion of Washington in the Indian Wars (1755–1756), and died at the Battle of Princeton.

The list is unending: Thomas Sully (1783–1872), artist; Colonel Charles Ellet (1810–1862), who planned and built the first wire suspension bridge in the United States and died at the Battle of Memphis; Commodore Isaac Hull (1773–1843), hero of the War of 1812; Commodore

Richard Dole (1756–1825), first lieutenant under John Paul Jones in the engagement between the *Serapis* and the *Bonhomme Richard;* General George Gordon Meade (1815–1872), who distinguished himself at Antietam, Fredericksburg, and Chancellorsville, and is credited with the victory at Gettysburg; Sarah Josepha Hale (1788–1879), for forty years editor of *Godey's Lady's Book* and responsible for the establishment of Thanksgiving Day; and Louis Antoine Godey (1804–1878), publisher of that magazine, in part make up the hall of fame that dominates the east bank of the Schuylkill River.

Laurel Hill is deserted today. Burials are fewer; people now select graves in the memorial parks in the suburbs or in the newer West Laurel Hill on the other side of the river. However, it stands as a reminder of nineteenth-century life and death in Philadelphia, and an application has been made to place it on the National Register of Historic Places. Motorists, cyclists, and walkers along the East River Drive below can look up and see the brooding, peaceful, tree-covered cemetery, virtually hanging precipitously over the drive.

Nathaniel Parker Willis, the nineteenth-century writer, described it best:

[We] made an excursion to Laurel Hill, certainly the most beautiful cemetery in the world, after the Necropolis of Scutari. It seems as if it were intended to associate the visits of the departed more with our pleasures than our duties. . . . The views down upon the river and through the sombre glades and alleys of the burial ground, are unsurpassed for sweetness and repose. . . . I look upon this and Mount Auburn, at Cambridge, as delightful indications of a purer growth in our national character than politics and money-making.

The sarcophagus of Commodore Isaac Hull was designed by architect William Strickland and features an American eagle clasping the colors in one talon. *Photograph by Clarkson Schoettle*

Above, left: Examples of Laurel Hill's magnificent sculpture. *Photograph by Marjorie R. Maurer*

Two highly individualistic monuments stand side by side. General Francis E. Patterson's grave is marked by the bare-bosomed mourning figure. A recumbent lion marks that of General Robert Patterson. *Photograph by Clarkson Schoettle*

The Warner family's classic yet macabre tomb was designed by Alexander Stirling Calder and shows the soul escaping from the half-open sarcophagus. *Photograph by Clarkson Schoettle*

Above, right: Sarah Harrison's tomb, designed by John Notman, architect of Laurel Hill, is a small Gothic enclosure that shelters a sleeping lamb. *Photograph by Drayton M. Smith*

The mother and her twins were the work of Henry Dmochowski Saunder (1858) to the memory of his wife and sons, who are buried together. *Photograph by Clarkson Schoettle*

Lawn-Girt Hill in Green-Wood. Etched by James Smillie. *Print and Picture Department, Free Library of Philadelphia*

18. Green-Wood Cemetery

BROOKLYN, NEW YORK

GREEN-WOOD evolved, like Mount Auburn in Cambridge, Massachusetts, and Laurel Hill in Philadelphia, as the result of conditions similar to those in European cities: the overcrowding of churchyards in the late eighteenth and early nineteenth centuries, and the resulting unsanitary conditions. The solution was the establishment of cemeteries on the periphery of cities and in a natural landscape. Green-Wood was, in fact, the third such commercial, rural cemetery in the United States. Only Mount Auburn and Laurel Hill are older.

In 1835, a year after the incorporation of the City of Brooklyn, Henry E. Pierrepont was appointed chairman of a commission to lay out the streets of the new city. A man of foresight and vision, Pierrepont made provision in the new city for eleven parks and he also reserved land for what was to become Green-Wood, taking his initial inspiration from Père-Lachaise in Paris, which was the model for so many nineteenth-century cemeteries. Earlier, in 1832, he had visited Mount Auburn, a year

after its establishment, and had come away impressed with its situation on the hills behind Cambridge and with its spectacular view of Boston. Mount Auburn, rather than Père Lachaise, eventually became his model for Green-Wood.

Often called the "Garden City of the Dead," because of its superb landscapes, rolling hills, ponds, lakes, drives, and meanders, Green-Wood eventually became the inspiration for later cemetery planners. Pierrepont was aided in his project by Major David B. Douglass, who had been trained as an army engineer. Douglass thought it would be advantageous to have an astronomy laboratory, a plan that was abandoned. The site finally selected was dominated by low hills overlooking the Gowanus Canal, an area that was then open farmland, which provided unparalleled views of Brooklyn and New York.

An act of incorporation was filed on April 11, 1838, and the name selected was one "indicating that it should always remain a scene of rural quiet, and beauty, and leafiness, and verdure." Land holdings originally in the possession of the Bennet, Bergen, Schermerhorn, and Wyckoff families—early settlers in the region—were purchased from descendants of these families. The largest purchase was from the Schermerhorn family, who were paid $650 an acre, a considerable amount for that time. In the following decade additional land purchases were made until the cemetery reached its present size of 474 acres—twice the size of Père-Lachaise and four times that of Mount Auburn. For more than sixty years it was the largest landscaped cemetery in the world.

Green-Wood was planned to the smallest detail with Major Douglass supervising the layout of walks and drives, recontouring the land when necessary, and deepening and regularizing the six small lakes. He also supervised the initial plantings. Eventually, twenty-two miles of roadway and more than thirty miles of meandering paths resulted. In 1841 Major Douglass left to become president of Kenyon College and Pierrepont continued for more than twenty years to keep a watchful eye on his creation.

Douglass and Pierrepont appointed as Green-Wood's architect Richard Upjohn, the architect of Trinity Church in New York, who, with his son, designed and constructed most of its original rustic and Tuscan buildings for Green-Wood during its first thirty years. He was the architect for Henry Pierrepont's house in Brooklyn Heights and also the founder of the American Institute of Architects, a rather remarkable achievement when we consider that he was trained as a cabinetmaker and draftsman and only became an architect by accident. The story is told that when teaching drawing in New Bedford, Massachusetts, he saw an architect's drawing for the Custom House in Boston, and said: "If that is architecture, I am an architect."

There were other architects concerned with Green-Wood too. The cemetery commission intended building a chapel in the center of the grounds, which would in inclement weather shelter the marble sculptures as well as visitors, and also provide a focal point architecturally. Carrère and Hastings were commissioned to design the building and when their design was not accepted, they redid it and today we see it as the New York Public Library at Fifth Avenue and 42nd Street.

The landscape effect Upjohn, Pierrepont, and Douglass were endeavoring to realize was an English one, based on descriptions by the English romantic poets. Occasionally, the ideal and the practical was realized. More often it was not. Of the original rustic wooden buildings in Green-Wood, the only survivor is a shelter house, which was a refuge for mourners in wet weather and also served as a temporary chapel for small funerals, since it was fitted with stoves and a bell.

In their efforts to re-create multiple aspects of the romantic landscape, the planners found it necessary to introduce special features. An example is the Indian mound with a monument above it that records that an Indian princess, Do-Hum-Mee, the daughter of Nan-Nouce-Rush-ee-toe and wife of Cow-Hick-Kee, lies buried here. Actually, she was an unfortunate member of the Sac tribe who died of pneumonia in New York while a member of a family deputation seeking to persuade the United States government to live up to one of its treaties with the Indians.

Like Laurel Hill and Père Lachaise, it was felt that Green-Wood needed someone of note. Such a burial served as a lure for would-be purchasers of plots, even if the poet buried here—McDonald Clarke—was a half-mad one. He was buried on "Poets' Mound" in 1842, and over his grave on a classical obelisk is a cameolike relief portrait of Clarke, reminiscent of the classical portraits of Roman poets.

There are others of note here. Samuel Finley Breese Morse (1791–1872), the portrait painter who invented the wireless telegraph; De Witt Clinton (1769–1828), governor of New York and sponsor of the Erie Canal; Elias Howe (1819–1867), inventor of the sewing machine, who changed the face of American domestic life; Lola Montez (?1818–1861), dancer, adventuress, and mistress, among others, of mad King Ludwig of Bavaria; William S. Hart (1872–1946), the original motion picture cowboy; Nathaniel Currier (1813–1888) and J. Merritt Ives (1824–1895), noted lithographers of hearth and home; Leonard Jerome (1818–1891) and his wife, Clara Hall (1825–1895), grandparents of Sir Winston Churchill; and those eternal rivals, James Gordon Bennett (1795–1872) of the New York *Herald* and Horace Greeley (1811–1872) of the *Tribune* ("Go West, young man, go West!") are all buried here.

More curious than these are the graves of Henry Ward Beecher (1813–1887) and his wife, Eunice White Bullard. Beecher, brother of Harriet Beecher Stowe and one of the most influential clergymen of his time, was rector of the wealthy Plymouth Church in Brooklyn Heights. One of his parishioners, Mrs. Elizabeth Tilton, confessed to her husband, Theodore—editor of both the *Independent* and the *Union* newspapers—that she had been having a love affair with her minister and had committed adultery.

The scandal shook Brooklyn Heights, all of New York, and the entire country because of Beecher's fame. The trial in 1875 ended with a hung jury, which the judge dismissed. The public at large was divided for years to come as to whether he was guilty or not. Beecher and his wife lie side by side in Green-Wood and on the stone above them, between their names, are the words: "He thinketh no evil." (No one ever accused Beecher of thinking evil; it was what he did that got him into trouble.) Elizabeth Tilton is also buried in Green-Wood.

There were other aspects than the burials of the famous or infamous to attract the curious. After the Brooklyn Bridge opened in 1883, there were trolley tours to Brooklyn to see the cemetery, a prime tourist attraction. By 1862 there were over one thousand stereopticon views of the cemetery in its New York office. In 1852, through the interest of a felicitously named bird lover, Thomas S. Woodcock, birds were imported from Manchester, England—forty-eight skylarks, twenty-four woodlarks, forty-eight goldfinches, twenty-four English robins, twelve thrushes, and twelve blackbirds. None are known to have survived long, but, because of its landscaping, Green-Wood, like so many cemeteries, is a bird sanctuary in the heart of a city.

In the first twenty years of Green-Wood's development, nearly every then-available variety of weeping tree was planted. The most spectacular remaining examples are the row of weeping mulberries just inside the main gate, and several magnificent weeping beeches, now in their prime. Conscious of the trend it was setting, in 1875 the cemetery issued a list of deciduous trees for cemeteries.

There are monuments in Green-Wood that predate the establishment of the cemetery. When the Dutch Reformed Church in Brooklyn Heights moved, the stones from the churchyard were reerected in Green-Wood. The founders hoped other churches would follow suit and continue their former churchyard practices in this beautifully landscaped setting. Very few did.

Trinity Church had originally agreed to buy twenty acres but unexpectedly withdrew. Eventually Trinity established its own cemetery, larger than twenty acres, at 155th Street between Amsterdam Avenue and Riverside Drive in Manhattan. There was a certain rivalry between Manhattan and Brooklyn, and there was a distaste on the part of New Yorkers for being buried in Brooklyn. This also might have been due to the cemetery's distance from Manhattan, and to the presence of six sizable bodies of water within its borders, which gave the mistaken impression that the ground was swampy.

The Upjohns designed receiving vaults that were capable of storing 1,400 bodies ventilated and hermetically sealed. Between 1859 and 1863 as Brooklyn expanded, it became apparent that Green-Wood's purely rustic character could not be maintained, so its post and rail fence was gradually replaced by one of iron manufactured in England, which can be seen today. The monumental gateway, erected in 1861, was probably the work of the younger Upjohn. Erected five hundred feet within the cemetery, rather than at the street, it has been described as English pointed Gothic, and the trustees boasted that "it belongs not to Pagan but to Christian architecture." This was another expression of the rivalry between Green-Wood and Mount Auburn, where the gates were examples of the Egyptian Revival.

Green-Wood remains a monument to the Victorian attitude toward death and the consequent hope of resurrection. And Green-Wood has become more cosmopolitan, for, although Peter Cooper (1791–1883), who in 1830 built the *Tom Thumb,* the first steam locomotive to be used successfully on an American railroad; Duncan Phyfe (1768–1854), the cabinetmaker who lent his name to a style; and Henry George (1839–1897), founder of the Single-Tax movement and grandfather of dancer Agnes de Mille, are buried here, so too are the Mafia members Frank Anastasia and Joey Gallo. Strange bedfellows indeed!

Far left: The classicism of the past. *Photograph by Clive E. Driver*

The Angel of the Resurrection. *Photograph by Clive E. Driver*

The monument to John Matthews, the "Soda Water King." He owned 500 soda fountains in New York when he died. *Photograph by Clive E. Driver*

Above, right: The variety of sepulchral art in Green-Wood is unending. *Photograph by Clive E. Driver*

>

John William Mackay's mausoleum reportedly cost $300,000. *Photograph by Clive E. Driver*

The Garretson mausoleum is a rare example of the Turkish Revival. *Photograph by Clive E. Driver*

>

The Builder's Creed on the façade of the Great Mausoleum at Forest Lawn in Glendale. *Courtesy Forest Lawn Memorial—Parks and Mortuaries*

19. Forest Lawn Memorial Park

GLENDALE, CALIFORNIA

WHEN the funeral of Jeanette MacDonald (1903–1965), the motion picture soprano, was held at Forest Lawn, the 250 friends and relatives inside the Church of the Recessional, and the 400 admirers of the film star outside, heard her recorded voice singing "Ave Maria" and "Ah, Sweet Mystery of Life." It was a funeral in the Hollywood tradition. Stars were there: Greer Garson, Mary Pickford, Buddy Rogers, and Irene Dunne, and many who appeared opposite her on the screen—Allan Jones *(The Firefly),* José Iturbi *(Three Daring Daughters),* Jack Oakie *(Let's Go Native),* and Buddy Ebsen *(The Girl of the Golden West).*

Pallbearers included Barry Goldwater, once a presidential candidate; Leon Ames, the actor; Meredith Willson, composer of *The Music Man;* and General Lauris Norstad, former Supreme Commander of the North Atlantic Treaty Organization. Honorary pallbearers included two former presidents of the United States, Harry S. Truman and Dwight D. Eisenhower (a massive cross

of white roses bore a card reading "Ike and Mamie"); and a former vice-president who would later be president—Richard M. Nixon; as well as Senator George Murphy of California; Earl Warren, chief justice of the United States; Tom Clark, associate justice; and Lauritz Melchior, the famed *heldentenor.* Other leading men of Miss MacDonald—Joe E. Brown *(The Lottery Bride),* Lew Ayres *(Broadway Serenade),* Maurice Chevalier *(The Merry Widow),* Spencer Tracy *(San Francisco),* James Stewart *(Rose Marie),* and Nelson Eddy *(Naughty Marietta)*—were honorary bearers, as well as Alfred Hitchcock, Ronald Reagan, Joseph Pasternak, and John Mack Brown (who had also been an usher at her wedding to Gene Raymond in 1937).

The service opened with the organ playing some of the star's favorite songs, "Indian Love Call," "I'll See You Again," and "Smilin' Through"—all of which she sang in her films. Following these, an orchestral recording of "Beyond the Blue Horizon," which Miss MacDonald introduced in the 1932 film *Monte Carlo,* was heard over the loudspeaker. Small birds in cages chirped through the music. Then came the sound of Jeanette Mac-Donald's own voice in Schubert and Victor Herbert songs.

Lloyd Nolan, who starred with her in her last film, *The Sun Comes Up,* delivered the eulogy, remembering Miss MacDonald's courage (she died after a long history of heart ailment) and her devotion to music. "When she sang," the actor reminded his listeners, "she sang to you. And through her songs she sent her message of love." Among the crowd outside the church was one woman who revealed she had driven from Texas, another had flown from Manila, a third from Montreal. The funeral had all the trappings of Hollywood, even to the faithful and adoring fans. Black-suited attendants gave the mourners a printed pictorial map and guide to Forest Lawn, directing them to "world famous art treasures" within the cemetery, and urging them to consider Forest Lawn's "outstanding advantages—before need."

Forest Lawn, which is undoubtedly the best-known cemetery in the United States, with the exception of Arlington, is a memorial park; in fact, it was the first. It presents a different aspect of a burial ground: a cemetery as memorial park. Few, however, know the background and history of this remarkable undertaking.

Though it is older than most Americans realize—there has been a cemetery on the spot since 1906—it was not until 1916, when Dr. Hubert Eaton (1881–1966) took over the management of the then Forest Lawn Cemetery at Tropico, on the outskirts of Los Angeles, that a new concept emerged. Dr. Eaton, who was called The Builder, had a glimpse of what the cemetery might become when on New Year's Day 1917, he stood on a hill overlooking this part of Southern California and from his vantage point had a glimpse of the future. This dream became a reality, and today the entire complex of Forest Lawn—now four separate memorial parks—is a tribute to Dr. Eaton's foresight and energy. The memorial parks have been planned to the smallest detail; nothing has been left to chance.

Dr. Eaton conceived the cemetery as a "sacred, protected, permanent resting place for the departed but also a place of service to the living." In effect, the memorial park is a complete museum, containing representative architecture and art of the past. In 1941 Dr. Eaton said: "Forest Lawn shall be not only a safe repository for our beloved dead, but a place for the sacred enjoyment of the living as well."

What was only fifty acres in 1917 had grown to three hundred by 1941, and an aggregate of twelve hundred acres in four separate parks today. In 1941 there were twenty thousand trees and shrubs, more than sixty-five thousand owners, and in excess of four thousand burials a year. These were in columbaria, where space is provided for the remains to be placed in niches; inurnment —urns for the ashes; mausoleums for families and, sometimes, larger ones for many families; cenotaphs to commemorate those buried elsewhere; and burial in the earth. Today one out of ten California burials—eight thousand annually—is at Forest Lawn.

Such a place of rest, to be a thing of beauty, must have art objects, and art was provided to a degree seldom contemplated before in any cemetery. Dr. Eaton spared no expense. The mortuary was housed in a building of Tudor architecture, modeled after a sixteenth-century English manor house, Compton Wynyates. The first of the replicas of historic churches was the Little Church of the Flowers, inspired by the fourteenth-century church at Stoke Poges, Slough, England, where more than two hundred years ago Thomas Gray composed his "Elegy Written in a Country Churchyard." The Wee Kirk o' the Heather, a faithful reconstruction of the tiny church in Glencairn, Scotland, where Annie Laurie worshiped 250 years ago, was also added. Mementos linked with the Scottish heroine are inside and the stained glass windows in the nave were inspired by Annie's love for William Hamilton. Nearby in a quiet grove is a sylvan retreat, suitable for prayer and contemplation, graced by a reproduction of Albert Bertel Thorvaldsen's *Christus.* The Church of the Recessional, on the other hand, is named for Rudyard Kipling's poem, and is modeled after its twelfth-century Norman counterpart, Saint Margaret's in Rottingdean, not far from the south coast resort of Brighton. Weddings often take place in these chapels. One of the more than fifty thousand people married here was Ginger Rogers.

One of the basic concepts in the planning of Forest Lawn was the assembling of sculpture to enhance the landscape. The majority of more than five hundred bronze and marble figures are original; others are reproductions of world-famous masterpieces. *Duck Baby* and *Frog Baby,* evocations of infancy, are the work of Edith Barrett Parsons. (Children are laid to rest in Lullabyland, which has a fairy-tale castle monument, and Babyland.) There are also *The Dying Chief* by Gutzon Borglum; *Mark Twain* by Gladys Lewis Bush; and *Klods Hans* (Clumsy Hans), a character from Hans Christian Andersen, a memorial to Jean Hersholt, actor and humanitarian.

The Builder sought inspiration beyond the British Isles for other buildings. The Great Mausoleum was inspired by the campo santo in Genoa, and rises in eleven massive terraces. On the Memorial Terrace are the Hall of Memory; the Cathedral Corridor, housing reproductions of Michelangelo's Moses (in fact, there are more reproductions of Michelangelo's work here than in any other place in the world); and the Memorial Court of Honor, containing Rosa Caselli-Moretti's stained glass version of *The Last Supper.*

The Memorial Court of Honor houses crypts that are not offered for sale. Interred in this "New World Westminster Abbey" are Gutzon Borglum (1871–1941), the sculptor who is best known for the Mount Rushmore memorial; Carrie Jacobs-Bond (1862–1946), composer of "I Love You Truly," "Just A-wearyin' for You," and "A Perfect Day"; Robert Andrews Millikan (1868–1953), physicist and educator who received the Nobel Prize in 1923 for his research on the isolation and measurement of the electron, and the proton theory of light; and Jan Styka (1858–1925), whose painting *The Crucifixion*—the largest (45 by 195 feet) in the world—is housed in the Hall of the Crucifixion-Resurrection, which also displays *The Resurrection* by Robert Clark.

In the newer Forest Lawn-Hollywood Hills, America's past is evoked by the panoramic *The Birth of Liberty* mosaic, which re-creates twenty-five scenes of American history with ten million pieces of multihued Venetian glass. Scenes include a depiction of Patrick Henry uttering his immortal words, Paul Revere on his equally famous ride, Washington at Valley Forge and also crossing the Delaware, the Battle of Bunker Hill, the signing of the Declaration of Independence, and Betsy Ross sewing the first flag. The Court of Liberty, where the 165-foot outdoor mosaic is displayed, also holds a replica of the Liberty Bell. Another feature is the Lincoln Terrace, with Venetian glass mosaic scenes from the Emancipator's life, flanking a reproduction of Augustus Saint-Gaudens's portrait statue of the sixteenth president.

The Gardens of Memory within Forest Lawn-Glendale are secluded, walled for privacy, beautifully landscaped, and embellished with memorial statuary. The bronze doors guarding the entrance to this garden are closed to the general public, unlocked only by the Golden Key of Memory given to those whose interment property is within. A bronze plaque near the entrance is inscribed with the words of the poem "Death Is Only an Old Door." Within is the family memorial of Mary Pickford, with *Motherhood* by Silvio Silva contemplating the scene. A memory of the Pincio Gardens in Rome is the reproduction of Pharaoh's daughter finding the infant Moses in the bulrushes, another of the spectacular sculptures in Forest Lawn-Glendale.

The memorial park in Glendale also contains the Court of David, a reproduction of Michelangelo's statue, towering 20½ feet in the air. (Dr. Eaton wanted David without the fig leaf, but was overruled.) Bronze bas-reliefs in the wall of the court depict biblical scenes from David's life. Here also are the Mystery of Life Garden and the Forest Lawn Museum, containing the Hubert Eaton gem collection and the James R. Eaton collection of ancient coins, as well as medieval arms and armor, paintings on ivory from India, and the first reproduction in America of the fifteenth-century Ghiberti doors on the Baptistry at Florence.

The Court of Freedom extends for 750 feet along the crest of a hill, with the feminine figure of *The Republic* by Daniel Chester French at one end and George Washington by John Quincy Adams Ward at the other. The central feature is the mosaic *The Signing of the Declaration of Independence.* The Court of Freedom adjoins the Garden of Everlasting Peace.

The architecture of Forest Lawn-Hollywood Hills is Colonial American as opposed to the English influence at Forest Lawn-Glendale. The mortuary here is a replica of Mount Vernon. There is also the Church of the Hills, a copy of the old First Parish Meeting House in Portland, Maine, where Henry Wadsworth Longfellow worshiped in his youth. Just off the church foyer is the Longfellow Historical Room, an exact reproduction of the poet's study in Craigie House, Cambridge, Massachusetts, containing a chair and cabinet that were once his, in addition to reproductions of the poet's other furnishings. Here too is the Bride's Garden. (Marriages are performed in each of the memorial parks.) There is also a replica of Boston's Old North Church, an integral part of the Court of Liberty, where many services and special meetings take place.

Newer still are Forest Lawn-Cypress, in Orange County, in the Lakewood and Long Beach area, with the architecture Virginia Colonial; and Forest Lawn-Covina Hills, adjacent to San Gabriel and Pomona valleys. Here the architecture is Georgian Colonial and the church is modeled after Saint George's Church, Fredericksburg, Virginia, where Washington, James Monroe, and John Paul Jones worshiped. In June 1975, the *Life of Christ* mosaic, portraying twenty-six of the most familiar events of Christ's life, was dedicated. The mosaic fronts the Mausoleum of Christian Heritage, and the rotunda of the mausoleum contains replicas in Venetian glass of many of Michelangelo's paintings in the Sistine Chapel.

These four memorial parks have carried out Dr. Eaton's idea that a cemetery should be "restful, beautiful, remove man's fear of oblivion and bolster his faith in immortality, that a cemetery should be a bright and lovely garden where happiness is recalled and sorrow forgotten."

Among the great and near-great of Hollywood who are buried here are Humphrey Bogart (1900–1957), Lon Chaney (1883–1930), Errol Flynn (1909–59), Ernie Kovacs (1919–1962), Charles Laughton (1899–1962), Stan Laurel (1890–1965), Tom Mix (1880–1940), Spencer Tracy (1900–1967), Clark Gable (1901–1960) and Carole Lombard (1909–1942) (side by side in marble vaults in the Great Mausoleum), Jean Harlow (1911–1937), and Irving Thalberg (1899–1939).

W. C. Fields, the comedian whose witticisms have become part of American folklore, when questioned in 1925 by a writer for the magazine *Vanity Fair* concerning his choice of an epitaph, replied with the now-classic answer (often garbled and misquoted): "Here Lies W. C. Fields. I Would Rather be in Philadelphia." Unfortunately, instead of those now-immortal words, only his name and dates (1880–1946) appear on the simple bronze marker at Forest Lawn.

Entrance gates to Forest Lawn in Glendale, which are larger than those at Buckingham Palace after which they were modeled. *Courtesy Forest Lawn Memorial—Parks and Mortuaries*

The entrance to Forest Lawn—Covina Hills, showing a fountain and the Court of the Masters in the foreground. *Courtesy Forest Lawn Memorial—Parks and Mortuaries*

The scenic esplanade at Forest Lawn in Glendale, with a vista of Los Angeles and Glendale below. *Courtesy Forest Lawn—Memorial Parks and Mortuaries*

The Court of David, Forest Lawn in Glendale. *Courtesy Forest Lawn Memorial—Parks and Mortuaries*

Below, left: The Great Mausoleum in Forest Lawn, Glendale, modeled after the campo santo in Genoa. *Courtesy Forest Lawn Memorial—Parks and Mortuaries*

The Little Church of the Flowers at Forest Lawn in Glendale. It was dedicated in 1918. *Courtesy Forest Lawn Memorial—Parks and Mortuaries*

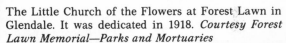

20. Congressional Cemetery

WASHINGTON, D.C.

THE capital was in deep mourning on April 4, 1841; the newly inaugurated William Henry Harrison (1773–1841) had died on that day, only a month after taking the oath of office. The sixty-eight-year-old veteran of the Indian wars, elected as ninth president on the slogan "Tippecanoe and Tyler Too," lay in state in the East Room of the White House. On April 8 the new president, John Tyler, former President John Quincy Adams, and Daniel Webster were among those of official Washington who attended the services.

Then the deceased president's body was borne to the Congressional Cemetery at 18th and E streets, S.E., and placed in a newly built public vault. President Harrison, like Andrew Jackson and John Quincy Adams after him (and Dolley Madison in 1849), did not remain long. In June, when summer arrived, and the frozen roads were again passable, his body was taken from the vault by his family to North Bend, Ohio, and placed in a tomb, "facing out over the fields which he had loved, past which the Ohio flows quietly on its long journey to the Mississippi."

Established in 1807, the original 4½ acres were purchased from the federal government for $200 as a private burial ground by a group of citizens. Five years later and seven years after Christ Church, the oldest religious body on Capitol Hill, was built (1805), Henry Ingle deeded the cemetery to the church as "The Washington Parish Burial Ground."

The first congressman to be buried here—Senator

<
A superb example of Victorian extravagance in cemetery art. *Photograph by J. A. Horne. Reproduced from the collection of the Library of Congress*

Uriah Tracy of Connecticut—was interred on July 19, 1807, after his body had been transferred from Rock Creek Cemetery. This led, in 1817, to the selection by the vestry of one hundred burial sites, which were to be used for interring members of Congress who died in Washington. From that time the name Congressional Cemetery was used, and it has endured to the present. (On May 30, 1849, the vestry of Christ Church changed the name to Washington Cemetery, which is its correct name today.)

Custom ruled and it soon became traditional to bury here senators and representatives and (temporarily in three instances) presidents of the United States. One hundred graves appeared to be too few, so in 1823 an additional three hundred were donated for congressional use. The interest of Congress itself from 1824 to 1834 is apparent when we consider that both Houses made appropriations for the erection of a keeper's house, a neo-baroque receiving vault, a chapel, and a wall around the burial ground, and for planting trees and placing boundary stones. From 1849 on, the Congressional Cemetery was gradually enlarged by the purchase of additional ground until it reached its present size of some thirty acres. Throughout the nineteenth century— until the 1870s—Congress continued to make irregular appropriations for its improvement.

Two large groupings of cenotaphs—each monument a square sandstone block on a sandstone slab, surmounted by a short segment of column topped with a squat cone —are the work of Benjamin Henry Latrobe, the architect who left his own special imprint on the city of Washington. These serve as reminders of many members of Congress who died between 1807 and 1877. Several hundred were erected, but only fourteen senators and forty-three representatives were interred here. These monuments were discredited when Senator George Frisbie Hoar of Massachusetts remarked that being buried beneath one would add new terror to death.

Others besides members of Congress are buried here, including the early architect Dr. William Thornton (1759–1828) and a Choctaw Indian chief with the improbable name, Push-Ma-Ta-Ha. Dr. Thornton, a Scottish physician, supervised the construction of the Capitol until he was replaced by Latrobe and designed Washington's Octagon House, as well as Woodlawn in Fairfax County, Virginia. The chief, designated on his tombstone monument as the "White Man's friend," fought under Andrew Jackson in the Pensacola campaign, dying of diphtheria in Washington in 1825. The United States army accorded him a full military funeral. His last words, on his monument, were: "Let the big guns boom over me."

Several vice-presidents, by their presence in the Congressional Cemetery, lend distinction to it. George Clinton (1739–1812), the fourth holder of that office, lies here as does his successor, Elbridge Gerry. Clinton has the distinction of having been vice-president (1805–1809) in the second administration of Thomas Jefferson and in the first (1809–1812) of James Madison. At his death from pneumonia, he was a senile and cantankerous old man no longer fitted to assume the mantle of the presidency. His children, who viewed him differently, erected a monument in his honor, "bearing an inscription more faithful to his past service to the state of New York than to his more recent efforts as Vice-President." It reads: "While He lived, His Virtue, Wisdom and Valor were the Pride, the Ornament and Security Of his Country, and when He Died, He Left an Illustrious Example of a Well Spent Life, Worthy of all Imitation."

Elbridge Gerry (1744–1814), a notable figure, in fact a formidable one, in his lifetime, is all but forgotten today except in his native Massachusetts. He was a signer of the Declaration of Independence and a delegate to the Constitutional Convention (although he refused to sign that document "in the belief that it would lead to civil war"). Gerry was vice-president (1813–1814) under James Madison and lent his name to the word "gerrymander."

Gerry, who had earlier made a fortune as a Boston merchant, which had since been depleted, was buried at public expense. His neoclassical monument, a truncated pyramid of marble twelve feet high, is topped by an urn and flame. It records that his death on the way to the Capitol as president of the Senate fulfilled "his own memorable injunction: 'It is the duty of every citizen, though he may have but one day to live, to devote that day to the good of his country.'" Sol Barzman, the historian who has made an in-depth study of the vice-presidency in *Madness and Geniuses,* reminds us that President Madison was the "only president to lose two successive vice-presidents through natural causes." As we have seen, they are both buried in the Congressional Cemetery.

There is always a certain pathos associated with the death of a child. The Victorians and Edwardians often memorialized them with tiny lambs on their graves, or a broken pillar, denoting a life cut short. The monument to Marion Ooletia Kahlert, who died in 1901 at the age of ten, has a special poignancy. Marion was the city's first traffic fatality, the victim of a motor vehicle (which were slower then, but still capable of killing). Her mother commissioned the monument in Rome. It shows Marion in the fashion of the day, a lace collar capelike on her shoulders, high button shoes, and with the sausage curls so popular in the first year of the new century. She stands erect, correct, modest, her right hand resting lightly on the pillar, her childhood captured in stone for all time.

Alexander Macomb (1782–1841) has no bust or figure of himself on his neoclassical monument. (Monuments are generally neoclassical or Victorian in the Congressional Cemetery.) The son of an Irish immigrant who was in the fur trade with John Jacob Astor, Macomb was Detroit-born and entered the army as an officer at the age of sixteen.

He brought honor to himself at the Battle of Niagara in the War of 1812, and also in the Battle of Fort George. He also drove the British forces back into Canada. A grateful Congress voted him a gold medal. In 1828 he became commanding general of the army. His monument is unique: a massive base supports four pairs of lion paws, which, in turn, hold a marble obelisk. Surmounting this is a draped American flag and a Roman officer's helmet. The faces of the monument contain the symbols of life, death, and burial: laurel leaves and a Roman sword; a butterfly and a snake (symbols of the Resurrection); an hourglass, a scythe, and a pair of wings (indicating the transitoriness of life on earth); and the willow branch (sorrow). Typical of the elaborate pre–Civil War monuments, it incorporates many of the symbols used at that time.

One of Washington's greatest funerals of the Civil War years, attended by President Lincoln and Secretary of War Edwin Stanton, was held for twenty-one women killed in an explosion at the Washington Arsenal on June 18, 1864. They were buried in a mass grave two days later and over it rises a monument paid for by donations from the citizens of Washington. A marble shaft rises twenty feet in the air. At its apex is a figure of a sorrowing woman, Grecian or classical in concept, her head slightly bowed, her hands clasped as her robes fall in graceful folds about her feet. At the front of the monument on the base is a panel portraying the arsenal fire. Washington was aroused by the tragedy—the greatest civil disaster in the city during the war—and 150 carriages bore the mourners from the arsenal to the cemetery.

Because it was once our national cemetery, and, although it fell into general disuse with the official opening of Arlington National Cemetery after the congressional settlement with Robert E. Lee's son, Congressional Cemetery has had its share of famous graves: Mathew B. Brady (1823?–1896), the Civil War photographer; Scarlet Crow, Sioux chief and United States scout; the son of Cochise; Colonel Tobias Lear (1762–1816), friend and personal secretary to George Washington; John Philip Sousa (1854–1932), bandmaster and composer, and his family; and the nineteenth-century architects George Hadfield (c. 1764–1826) and Robert Mills (1781–1855). One of the most recent burials was that of J. Edgar Hoover (1895–1972), former head of the Federal Bureau of Investigation.

The monuments have been called the "most historic collection of funeral sculpture in the city" by James M. Goode, an architectural historian who has painstakingly recorded the statues, monuments, and sculpture of Washington. Application was made in 1969 to place the cemetery on the National Register of Historic Places, and in 1973 a bill was introduced into Congress "for the transfer of the cemetery from private control to the care of the National Park Service, which would be able to restore and maintain this historic site as a national landmark."

In 1976, for the first time in twenty-six years, Congress authorized funds for the maintenance of portions of the cemetery. The architect of the Capitol was authorized to spend $250,000 in the following two years "to prevent further deterioration" of sections of the cemetery, which are of "historic significance." Another $50,000 was approved for the architect to prepare a permanent maintenance program. The architect's office intends to plant trees, institute a program of tree surgery, and repair an old chapel on the grounds.

At the same time the Association for the Preservation of Historic Congressional Cemetery (which is working with the Capitol Hill Restoration Society and the Smithsonian Institution on plans for an unused section of the cemetery) held a Halloween party on the afternoon of October 31, 1976, which it is hoped will be held annually. The money raised aided the Association in its preservation work and enabled the community to feel a part of the project.

The monument to Alexander Macomb. *Photograph by J. A. Horne. Reproduced from the collection of the Library of Congress*

The grave of Marion Ooletia Kahlert, Washington's first traffic fatality. *Photograph by J. A. Horne. Reproduced from the collection of the Library of Congress*

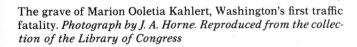

The Adams memorial is within the enclosure formed by the grove of trees in the background. *Historic American Buildings Survey. Jack E. Boucher, photographer*

21. Rock Creek Cemetery

WASHINGTON, D.C.

MARK TWAIN, who could be counted on to comment on almost every aspect of life in America, in contemplating the Adams Memorial in Rock Creek Cemetery, said the Saint-Gaudens statue seemed to embody all human grief. From then on the figure has been known popularly as *Grief.* It was probably the most widely known grave in the United States until the Tomb of the Unknown Soldier was dedicated at Arlington National Cemetery.

Rock Creek Cemetery, located on Rock Creek Church Road and Webster Street, N.W., not far from the District of Columbia-Maryland line, was originally the churchyard of Saint Paul's Episcopal Church (established 1712), often called Rock Creek Church. In 1719 the Reverend John Frasier, rector of the Piscataway Parish (Saint John's, Broad Creek) who since 1712 had regularly

conducted services in the neighborhood of what is now Rock Creek Church, called a meeting of the local inhabitants to select a site for the building of a "chapel-of-ease." At that meeting Colonel John Bradford, a tobacco planter and vestryman of Broad Creek, gave "one hundred acres of Land whereon is Timber for building said Chappell and necessary houses for a Gleab for the use of the present and future Minister for which Intent the Said hundred Acres of Land is given forever."

A glebe is land belonging to a parish church intended to produce revenue. Originally its strong stand of timber provided lumber for the construction of the chapel, houses for the minister, stables, and other buildings, as well as for firewood. As the land was cleared, the gardens of the glebe provided food for the tables of the rectors and their families. At various times cleared land was leased to farmers, at other times timber was sold from it to professional builders for construction purposes. From the earliest years a portion of the glebe near the church was used as a burial ground for parishioners. By the early nineteenth century grave lots were sold to nonparishioners.

It remained a simple burial ground—a small, private enclosure—until 1871 when the vestry, in response to an obvious need in the growing city of Washington and mindful of the natural beauty of the legacy, established a public cemetery on the glebe. Eighty-six acres of gently rolling land (one of the highest points in the district) were added and a more formal cemetery laid out. Some of the trees have been estimated to be 450 years old, and these, with the landscaping of flowers and more than a hundred varieties of imported evergreens, make Rock Creek a place of peace and beauty.

Most visitors come to see the Saint-Gaudens statue, then linger to examine other graves. The preponderance of the sculpture here is of the fifty-year period from 1875 to 1925, but there are earlier tombs of great interest. Most notable because of its neoclassical style and because of John Lenthall (1762–1808), whose memory it honors, is the templelike tomb over his grave. Erected in 1809, it incorporates a low-relief portrait medallion of Lenthall, another figure representing grief or mourning, and an angel with an hourglass and scythe. The latter denotes the shortness of Lenthall's life—forty-six years—but it does not in any way hint at his dramatic ending.

A son of Sir William Lenthall, speaker of the House of Commons, he emigrated to America in 1792 and married Jane King, whose father and brothers had assisted Pierre L'Enfant in his survey of the area that was to be the city of Washington. This proximity to architecture must have brought him into contact with Benjamin Henry Latrobe, the architect. In 1803 we find Lenthall a special assistant to Latrobe in the construction of the Capitol building. Five years later he was killed when one of the arches of the Supreme Court Chamber in the Capitol collapsed. His epitaph makes no mention of this doleful happening, but does proclaim: "He was an industrious and upright citizen, a lover of Justice, and zealous in the discharge of his duty. When living, he was esteemed by those who know the value of talent and integrity in his profession."

A grave such as Lenthall's, although not without its attraction, never lured the curious, the art student, and scholar as did the monument that Henry Adams (1838–1918) commissioned for the grave of his wife, Marian (1843–1885). Mrs. Adams, with a long history of illness and periods of depression, committed suicide soon after the death of her father. Adams, son of Charles Francis Adams, ambassador to Great Britain, grandson of President John Quincy Adams, and great-grandson of President John Adams, was a distinguished biographer (Thomas Jefferson, Albert Gallatin, and John Randolph),

but his fame today rests on his two classics, *Mont-Saint-Michel and Chartres* (1904) and *The Education of Henry Adams* (1906).

Before leaving for a voyage to the South Seas with architect and artist John La Farge, Adams conceived of having Augustus Saint-Gaudens (1848–1907) create a monument for his wife's grave. The result was called by the artist *The Mystery of the Hereafter,* or *The Peace of God That Passeth Understanding.*

John Hay, assistant private secretary to President Lincoln and Henry Adams's neighbor on Lafayette Square, wrote to the travelers: "The work is indescribably noble and imposing. It is to my mind St. Gaudens' masterpiece. It is full of poetry and suggestion, infinite wisdom, a past without beginning, and a future without end, a repose after limitless experience, a peace to which nothing matters—all embodied in this austere and beautiful face."

The figure, neither male nor female, shrouded in a cloak that cowl-like shields the head, has a sense of mystery which, in turn, draws and baffles the observer. Stanford White created the setting and base for the work, and a grove of holly trees encircled by evergreens gives it the privacy Adams sought. The rector of Saint Paul's was scandalized and thought the statue agnostic in concept, declaring he hoped to get the "unchristian monument out of his churchyard." Letters pro and con appeared in *The Nation* and other publications, and the intrepid tourists began to arrive, so much so that Adams, who often came here to be alone, could find no peace. Here, by this masterpiece he endowed, Henry Adams was interred next to his wife in an unmarked grave, according to his wish.

Another association with *Grief,* and equally poignant, remained unknown until revealed in 1971 by Joseph Lash in *Eleanor and Franklin.* After Eleanor Roosevelt's discovery of Franklin D. Roosevelt's infidelity with her social secretary, Lucy Page Mercer, the future First Lady found solace here, sitting before the Saint-Gaudens statue. Lash writes that after Eleanor Roosevelt's death, among her bedside papers was found a sonnet about the haunting figure written by Sir Cecil Spring-Rice, onetime British ambassador to the United States:

> *O steadfast, deep, inexorable eyes*
> *Set look inscrutable, nor smile nor frown!*
> *O tranquil eyes that look so calmly down*
> *Upon a world of passion and of lies! . . .*

Christian Heurich (1842–1945) engaged in an active business life to the end of his 102 years. A native of Germany, he emigrated in 1866 and six years later founded the Christian Heurich brewery. The handsome family mausoleum, erected in 1895, was the work of Louis Amateis, architect and sculptor, and is in the Beaux Arts tradition with its four caryatids and stained glass window executed by Tiffany. Originally erected on the family farm, it was moved to Rock Creek Cemetery at Mrs. Heurich's request before her death in 1956.

Sculptors of the period from 1875 to 1925 are well represented at Rock Creek with Gutzon Borglum's memorial to Charles Mather Ffoulke, *Rabboni;* it portrays Mary Magdalene finding Christ in the tomb at Easter; the Frederick Keep monument by James Earle Fraser (two seminude figures before a marble backdrop); and William Ordway Partridge's *The Seven Ages of Man* for the grave of Samuel H. Kauffman (1829–1906), owner of the Washington *Evening Star* from 1867 until his death. A seated figure in repose contemplates the bronze panels of the seven ages in the stone wall beside her. And Laura Gardin Fraser created the Art Deco monument, erected in 1938, to the memory of Robert Stockwell Reynold Hitt (1876–1938), whose father of the same name represented Illinois in Congress for twenty-four years. The younger Hitt served as minister to Panama and Guatemala. Inscribed on the face of the memorial are the words: "Out with the ebb tide/ On some farther Quest."

Among the great and near-great at Rock Creek are: Abraham Baldwin (1754–1807), signer of the Constitution of the United States; David Burnes, one of the original proprietors from whom land was acquired for the city; Nicholas King, surveyor for Thomas Jefferson; William J. Stone, engraver of the Declaration of Independence; Rosalie Poe, sister of the poet; Montgomery Blair, postmaster general in Lincoln's cabinet; Dr. Robert King Stone, the president's family physician; Harlan Fiske Stone (1872–1946), justice of the Supreme Court; and Under Secretary of State Sumner Welles. (1892–1961).

Saint Paul's Church, guardian of the cemetery, is the oldest and the only colonial church within the District of Columbia, and has been an independent parish since 1726. Although it has been damaged by fire and has had structural changes since the present building was constructed in 1775, the pre-Revolutionary walls remain intact.

A scene in Rock Creek Cemetery after the funeral of General John Alexander Logan. *Reproduced from the collection of the Library of Congress*

The Adams memorial. *Historic American Buildings Survey. Jack E. Boucher, photographer*

The National Cemetery of the Pacific, showing the punch bowl in the volcano.
Courtesy of the Veterans Administration

22. National Memorial Cemetery of the Pacific

HONOLULU, HAWAII

THE name Puowaina was known to the ancient Hawaiians as "Consecrated Hill," or "Hill of Sacrifice." Nothing could be more appropriate for the National Memorial Cemetery of the Pacific. The presence of the old gods of the Pacific whose spirits hover over the islands of the Hawaiian chain is felt within the bowl of the crater of this centuries-old volcano.

Known popularly as the "Punchbowl Crater" because of its shape, it became the National Cemetery of the Pacific in 1948. In 1941 the Seventy-seventh Congress authorized an appropriation for the establishment of a national cemetery at Honolulu. By 1943 the Governor of Hawaii (it was still a territory of the United States at the time), with the approval of the legislature, offered Puowaina to the government for a cemetery. Because the original congressional appropriation was too small "to

enable further action for the establishment of a cemetery ... the matter was deferred until after the conclusion of World War II."

Peace brought thoughts of properly honoring the men and women of all services who died in far-flung outposts across the wide Pacific. Many lay in temporary graves marked by wooden crosses; others were unidentified and would always remain so. A grateful and sorrowing nation, seeking to bind the wounds of war, brought the bodies to the cemetery from such islands as Wake, Ie Shima, Guam, Guadalcanal, Iwo Jima, Japan, Saipan, and from Burma and China on the mainland.

In 1948 the Eightieth Congress passed the necessary legislation and President Truman approved it. Funds of more than one million dollars were allocated and the simple yet imposing cemetery we see today began to take form. The remains of an unknown serviceman killed in the attack on Pearl Harbor, on December 7, 1941, were interred here on January 4, 1949—the first burial. He is one of thousands of unknown men and women of all races, ranks, and creeds from many United States wars who now sleep beneath Hawaiian skies.

The cemetery was dedicated on September 2, 1949, the fourth anniversary of V-J Day. The remains of thirteen thousand World War II servicemen who died in battle or in prison camps constituted the initial burials. Many of these were Hawaii's own sons come home. Four years later, on October 23, 1953, committal services were held for the group burial of 44 marines, 3 navy men, and 131 civilians who perished in the defense of Wake Island. A specially designed marker, larger than the individual ones but also flush with the ground, lists the names of the 178 men. Of the individual markers throughout, some bear the Latin cross, others the Star of David, and many the Buddhist emblem of the wheel.

The most famous of those buried here is Ernest Taylor Pyle (1900–45), the war correspondent known to thousands as "Ernie." This reporter captured the hearts of those at home by his firsthand accounts of life on the beaches, in the foxholes, on the destroyers, and in the forefront of battle. His death by Japanese machine gun fire on April 18, 1945—just a few days after that of President Franklin D. Roosevelt—saddened an already shocked nation.

Here, on May 15, 1958, Master Sergeant Ned Lyle, Twenty-fifth Infantry Division, stood in the hushed cemetery, facing four flag-draped caskets on a grassy oval opposite the cemetery entrance. The biers contained the remains of four servicemen killed in the Korean War. His decision was an important one, for the casket he chose, of an unknown **Korean War** comrade, would be given a place of honor beside the Unknown Soldier of World War II in Arlington National Cemetery. Bearing a large circular wreath of blue and white carnations, arranged at the center to represent the Korean Service Medal, he slowly walked to the end casket to his left and by laying the wreath there bestowed on his unknown fellow American his nation's greatest honor.

Dominating the circular bowl of the extinct volcano, at the head of the east end of the cemetery and backed by the rising slopes of the crater, is the Honolulu Memorial, dedicated by the American Battle Monuments Commission in 1966. A series of eight courts, four on each side, flank the steps leading to the monument itself. On the walls of these Courts of the Missing are inscribed the names of 26,280 American heroes (18,093 from World War II, 8,187 from the Korean War) from every state, the District of Columbia, Puerto Rico, the Panama Canal Zone, Guam, the Philippines, Mexico, Canada, and Samoa. Each was recorded as missing, lost, or buried at sea in the central, northern, southern, or western Pacific regions. (Those from the Southwest Pacific are recorded at the Manila American Military Cemetery. Nor does the memorial list the names of those whose individual graves are marked.)

The visitor is attracted at the first court by an inscription in the Trani marble, which is reminiscent of that of the tomb of the Unknown Soldier in Arlington National Cemetery:

In these gardens are recorded the names of Americans who gave their lives in the service of their country and whose earthly resting place is known only to God.

The courts lead almost like stations of the Cross to the core of the monument. In the center of each court grows a frangipani tree surrounded by Ficus ramentacea close to the ground. Flowering monkeypod trees surrounded by Allamanda shrubs line the sides of the stairway, and on the outer edges of the courts is a hedge of orange jasmine, as well as rainbow shower and Chinese banyan. At the crest of the slope are planted beds of cup of gold and star jasmine. This tribute of marble and the glories of the Hawaiian landscape are even more moving among the ashes of the volcano and memories of the dead.

The Court of Honor at the top consists of a central tower with a North and South Map Gallery to the sides. The effect of the galleries is that of arms embracing the whole. A thirty-foot female figure, designed by Bruce Moore, holding a laurel branch, stands on the symbolized prow of a navy carrier looking out to sea. Beneath her, incised in the marble, are President Lincoln's words to a bereaved mother: "The solemn pride that must be yours to have laid so costly a sacrifice upon the altar of freedom."

The frieze of the map galleries reads like the roll call of the Pacific War: Pearl Harbor, Wake, Coral Sea, Midway, Attu, Solomons, Gilberts, Marshalls, Marianas, Leyte, Iwo Jima, Okinawa, Tokyo, Korea. The maps themselves are a record of the battles in which these 26,280 men died.

Most times gentle winds touch the flags on the memorials, furling them softly. At other times the ancient Hawaiian gods invoke winds of hurricane force that lash the Punchbowl Crater. During the years when Hawaii was a monarchy (until 1898), the site was closely associated with the defense of the kingdom. Heavy cannon were placed strategically to protect Honolulu harbor. Later the Hawaii National Guard used it as a training ground, and from 1940 until the end of World War II it was an observation and fire control point in the harbor defense system. Once associated with war and defense, the ground is now appropriately one of the sacred places associated with those fallen in battle.

Here America remembers.

A Court of the Missing. *U.S. Army Photograph. Courtesy of the Veterans Administration*

23. Calvary Cemetery

EVANSTON, ILLINOIS

CHICAGO, the second city of the United States, was called "Hog butcher for the World" by poet Carl Sandburg. It was and is much more. There were settlements here on the shore of Lake Michigan from the time French explorers Jacques Marquette and Louis Joliet arrived in 1673, and in the eighteenth century a trading post was established. However, despite its earlier origins, Chicago was a nineteenth-century city and today few traces of the first seventy years remain other than the cemeteries. The twentieth century has made Chicago its own and this is in part due to the great fire of 1871. A new city emerged—a greater city of steel and stone, the seat of the grain and livestock markets, a railroad terminus between East and West, an inland port.

Twelve years before the 1871 holocaust that changed Chicago's face, its Catholic population felt the need for a new burial place for its dead. The *Chicago Daily Democrat* of November 3, 1859, announced the opening, reporting: "Calvary Cemetery is situated about two miles north of Rose Hill, and within about a mile of Evanston on the Milwaukee Road. It comprises about one hundred and twenty acres, beautifully situated on the Lake shore."

In 1843 the first Catholic burial ground (bounded by what are today North Avenue, Dearborn Parkway, Burton Place, and State Street) was opened by the Reverend William Quarter, bishop of Chicago, from 1844 to 1848. When this became inadequate for the needs of the population the Reverend James O. Vandervelde (bishop from 1849 to 1853) purchased forty acres of land from John Davlin in 1851 and eight years later Bishop Duggan acquired another forty from John O'Leary. (The cemetery now totals ninety-two acres.)

These were modest beginnings, but from them Calvary Cemetery, the largest Catholic burial ground in the Chicago area, developed. Bishop James Duggan had the ground plotted for cemetery use in 1859 and had the receiving vault—the oldest structure standing in the cemetery—built. Later that year on All Souls' Day the bishop consecrated the ground.

The first mass celebrated in the cemetery—also the first offered in Evanston—took place on August 15, 1865, in a grove of trees just opposite the main entrance, with a kitchen table for an altar. The occasion was not without incident, for the Reverend Patrick M. Flannagan, the celebrant, was late in arriving. Father Flannagan took the scenic drive along the north shore in his buggy, which became mired in the heavy sand. Traveling con-

ditions were far from ideal at that time and only one train—a funeral train—ran on Sunday, a journey of an hour.

Since then Calvary Cemetery has become the burial place of Governor Edward S. Dunne of Illinois; three mayors of Chicago—John P. Hopkins, William E. Dever, and Edward J. Kelly; and four bishops (including the founder, James Duggan). In all, over three hundred priests and eight hundred nuns are interred here. And the Cuneo family, to be distinctive in an age of conformity, placed Oriental rugs in their family mausoleum.

By 1894 the author of *Chicago The Garden City: Its Magnificent Parks, Boulevards and Cemeteries* could tout many of its virtues: "Among the chief beauties of Calvary are the great number of forest trees, which together show a harmonizing of the mixture in summer," and "the skill and taste of the sculptor and architect have been exerted in a remarkable manner in the construction of elaborate monuments and mausoleums."

In an age when the word ecumenical was seldom heard and the burial of non-Catholics in Catholic cemeteries was in most cities virtually unknown, the *Chicago Daily Democrat* (November 28, 1859) reported Bishop Duggan's extraordinarily advanced views:

> We find in the last number of the *Western Banner,* the Catholic paper of this city, the rules and regulations established by the Right Reverend Bishop Duggan, for the government of the New Catholic Cemetery lately opened and dedicated by that Prelate on the Green Bay Road, North of this city.... We are pleased to observe that by one of these rules it is allowable for non-Catholics to be interred within the limits of the Cemetery, in the lots owned by the families of which they may be members, although no religious ceremony will be allowed to take place on such occasions within the precincts of the Cemetery.

The writer went on to say that this policy was, he believed, first instituted by the "first presiding Priest of Chicago, Father St. Palais, now Bishop of Vincennes [Indiana], but the first Bishop appointed here, the Right Reverend Bishop Quarters, reversed this arrangement, and strictly forbade the interment of non-Catholics in holy ground, which order, we believe, has existed until now again reversed by the direction of the present Bishop."

At the centenary of Calvary Cemetery the statistics since the interment of Daniel Maloney—the first burial —on November 16, 1859, were impressive. On July 20,

1899, Mary Byrne became the 100,000th person buried there; Helen McLaughlin became the 200,000th on July 13, 1955; and at the start of the second century the total burials were 202,209.

Although florid in the manner of the late nineteenth century, the author of *Chicago The Garden City* evokes a climate that still permeates Calvary: "There are few who would not choose such a peaceful place as Calvary Cemetery where the great companionship of death gives a sense of fellowship. There is no jarring noise of life; no hustle recalling the pain and travail of existence; not even the murmur of the lake close by; or the low breathing of the distant city, its roar being softened here to a whisper."

24. Graceland Cemetery

CHICAGO, ILLINOIS

THIS remarkable monument to the past has been called "overwhelmingly Victorian grandiose, right down to the swans on Lake Willowmere." It is to the Midwest what Laurel Hill and Green-Wood are to the East, or Hollywood Cemetery in Richmond is to the South. Jory Graham, writing about Graceland in *Chicago: An Extraordinary Guide,* declares: "It's unlikely you'll come across one in this country in which so much has been built by private citizens on a scale usually reserved for kings and emperors."

Some of these private citizens were rulers of industry and wielded more power in their time than their enthroned counterparts did in Europe and Asia. Some of the Chicago mighty interred in Graceland include George M. Pullman (1831–1897), builder of railroad equipment: Cyrus Hall McCormick (1809–1884), inventor of the first successful harvesting machine, and his wife, Nettie Fowler, leader in Chicago society; Marshall Field (1834–1906), the merchant prince; Joseph T. Ryerson, steel magnate; and Potter Palmer (1826–1902) and his wife, Bertha.

Founded by Thomas A. Bryan, the cemetery was dedicated on August 30, 1860, and received its charter the following February. Almost immediately it gained social acceptance. "Checagou," the Indian name for the city, had earlier become Chicago, and Alexander Beaubien, the first male child born to permanent residents of the city, found his final resting place at Graceland. So, too, did John Kinzie (1763–1828), the first white settler, but not before he had been moved a great many times. At his death they buried Kinzie north of the Chicago River in one of the earliest cemeteries. By 1835 he was disinterred and moved to the old North Side Cemetery (now Lincoln Park) and, finally, to his last resting place at Graceland. Some thirty to forty other members of his family surround him.

Lorado Taft (1860–1936), the sculptor who during his lifetime exerted a great influence on young artists of the West, was responsible for several monuments at Graceland. His statue of a knight marks the grave of Victor Lawson, founder of the *Chicago Daily News,* and his *Death,* a shrouded bronze figure with the skull covered by the shroud, stands sentinel over the Graves family plot (just opposite the Kinzies). It has been described as terrifying in the rain.

Louis Henry Sullivan (1856–1924), who was so influential in the evolution of modern American architecture and was responsible for the Chicago School, designed a number of mausoleums (among them the Wainwright tomb in Bellefontaine Cemetery, Saint Louis, Missouri). He is buried at Graceland, his stone erected by friends and associates after his death. It bears only his name and dates. Graceland proudly displays two examples of Sullivan's celebration of death. The mausoleum for Martin Ryerson is not far from Sullivan's own grave. Egyptian in concept, it has been described by Sullivan's biographer Willard Connely as a "truncated pyramid with its four main lines curving out at the base, and a smaller pyramid superimposed, the whole in blue-black granite, polished to reflect the greenery close by."

At the other end of the cemetery, on the shores of Lake Willowmere, stands Sullivan's masterpiece of cemetery art, the Getty tomb erected for Elizabeth Getty, a cubical gray limestone mausoleum with folding doors in pierced bronze. Sullivan's disciple Frank Lloyd Wright called it "entirely Sullivan's own, a piece of sculpture, a statue, a great poem." Erected in 1890, and designated a Chicago architectural landmark in 1960, it draws students of architecture from all parts of the world.

On the island in Lake Willowmere is the grave of Daniel Hudson Burnham (1846–1912), architect and city planner whose plan (with his partner John Wellborn Root, whose grave is marked with a Celtic cross) for the Columbian Exposition of 1893 had enormous influence on the contemporary design of cities. The cremated remains of the father of the Chicago, Cleveland, San Fran-

The Getty tomb designed by Louis Henry Sullivan. *Reproduced from the collection of the Library of Congress*

tampering by vandals) by having his coffin "wrapped in tar paper and bolted with steel bolts, then embedded in a room-size chamber filled with concrete and topped with bolted steel rails." A Corinthian column rises over this and there is not even the smallest hole for the soul to be released!

Chicago has always been a city devoted to sport. Several likely candidates for immortality are buried at Graceland. Bob Fitzsimmons (1862–1917), who held the heavyweight championship from 1897 after defeating Gentleman Jim Corbett until he lost it two years later to James J. Jeffries, and Jack Johnson (1878–1946), who defeated Jeffries in 1910 and held the title until 1915, lie here. (Johnson was the subject of *The Great White Hope.*) Here too is William A. Hulburt, the man who founded what became baseball's National League. Appropriately enough, his grave is marked by a large granite baseball complete with stitches cut in stone. Unusual monuments are the rule at Graceland and that of Marshall Field, an allegorical bronze monument, is reflected in a sunken pool. In addition to the merchant's name, the words "Equity-Integrity" appear on it.

Augustus Dickens, brother of the author of *David Copperfield,* lies far from home among many who helped make Chicago famous: Philip D. Armour, founder of a meat-packing empire; John Jones, the first Chicago black to gain prominence and be elected to a county office; Joseph Medill, founder of the *Chicago Tribune;* Edith Rockefeller McCormick, philanthropist and daugher of John D. Rockefeller; and Philip Henrici, who is remembered because it was he who opened Chicago's first old-world coffeehouse.

cisco, and Washington, D.C., "plans" lies under a boulder surviving from the glacial period. (Graceland had one of the earliest crematories, built in 1893.)

Allan Pinkerton (1819–1884), founder of the detective agency bearing his name, guardian of President Lincoln, and a Union spy during the Civil War, is buried beneath a monument whose inscription includes the words: "A friend to honesty and a foe to crime." George Pullman, for whom railroad passenger cars were called Pullmans, forever ensured the safety of his remains (and to prevent

25. Oak Woods Cemetery

CHICAGO, ILLINOIS

AS American cities go, Chicago, compared to the older ones along the eastern seaboard, is one of the youngest. The city was incorporated in 1833 and when one zealous citizen declared there would be a population of five thousand five years from that date, he was called a dreamer.

Although a new cemetery was not the first matter of importance, it soon became so for the growing community on the shores of Lake Michigan. We learn from the *Chicago. City Manual* for 1909 that:

Chicago's first cemetery was laid out in 1835. In earlier times each interment was made on or near the residence of the friends of the deceased. Later, the settlements about where the river branches had a common acre on the west side of the North Branch, where the dead were buried. The dead from the fort [Dearborn] were buried generally on the

north side of the main river, east of Kinzie's old house, near the lake shore. There John Kinzie was buried in 1828. The soldiers who died of cholera in 1832 were interred near the northwest corner along the borders of the two branches, wherever settlements had been made and deaths had occurred. In later days the forgotten graves were often opened in excavating, which led to much speculation as to whom the disinterred remains belonged. As late as March 12, 1849, the *Daily Democrat* records the fact that during the spring freshet, "two coffins were seen floating down the river, supposed to have been from some small burying-ground on the North Branch in the Wabansia addition."

One of Chicago's forgotten early citizens was Henry Gherkin, a Prussian immigrant who arrived in 1836. He was the city's first recorded gravedigger. Earlier, on August 15, 1835, the town surveyor was ordered to lay out two tracts suitable for cemetery purposes: sixteen acres on the south side and ten acres north of the river. These two lots, the first established cemeteries in Chicago, were fenced in during September, and burials were forbidden elsewhere within the city.

This situation did not remain long. Two years later the city's charter was amended in the interests of public health to permit the establishment of a city burial ground. The amendment also gave Chicago the right to regulate burials. By 1840, with the city sprawling in all directions, the City Council decreed that the early cemeteries should be abandoned and a new large one established. This new location was on the site of what is now Lincoln Park.

In 1855 nine men of foresight banded together and, as the incorporators, founded Oak Woods Cemetery. The rural cemetery movement, which had begun in the eastern states in the 1830s and gained momentum in the next decade, inspired them. They too wanted a beautifully planned park with winding roads and judiciously placed lakes. Adolph Strauch, one of the foremost landscape architects and designers, was engaged, and the 183 acres began to take the form we now see.

A decade later, in the waning years of the Civil War, when Chicago named its new park on the site of the City Cemetery after the president, hundreds of bodies were moved to Oak Woods from what is now Lincoln Park. This procedure was a familiar one across the country as older city cemeteries were closed and rural ones developed. The war also brought a tragic note to the city, and to Oak Woods.

Camp Douglas, located at 34th Street and Cottage Grove Avenue, had housed some ten thousand captured Confederate soldiers. When a few escaped, Chicago felt there would be an organized mass break. To ensure security, the 109th Pennsylvania Infantry was ordered to Camp Douglas. Fate intervened, cholera and smallpox broke out, and the death toll was estimated at six thousand.

In 1867 the federal government acquired two acres in Oak Woods for the reburial of the Confederate dead, who had up to this time been buried at Camp Douglas. They were interred (with twelve federal guards who also died at the camp) in what is known today as the Confederate Mound, overlooking Magnolia Terrace and the Lake of Reverence. The spot was marked appropriately in later years with a Confederate monument, erected largely through the efforts of southern sympathizers, but also with contributions received from all over the country. At the monument's dedication on May 30, 1895, President Grover Cleveland and his cabinet attended the ceremonies, along with more than a hundred thousand people.

There was to be another ceremony of note at the spot in 1953, the one hundredth anniversary of the granting of Oak Woods's perpetual charter. Governor Robert Kennon of Louisiana presented the cemetery with a memorial magnolia tree to be planted at the Confederate Mound. Jimmy Pope, five-year-old descendant of President John Tyler (who died in Richmond, Virginia, during the Civil War), planted the tree in honor of the Confederate dead in soil sent by Governor Hugh White of Mississippi from the battlefields of Vicksburg.

The names of those buried at Oak Woods reflect a wide spectrum of Chicago life: two governors—Charles S. Deneen and John M. Hamilton; William Hale Thompson and Monroe Heath, former mayors of the city; Lyman Trumbull, senator from Illinois at the time of the impeachment proceedings against President Andrew Johnson; Judge Kenesaw Mountain Landis (1866–1944), the legendary first commissioner of baseball; Jessie Bartlett Davis, the singer who made "Oh, Promise Me" from *Robin Hood* her own; Enrico Fermi (1901–1954), physicist, Nobel Prize winner, and "Father of the Atom Bomb"; and Walter Gresham (1832–1895), secretary of state during Grover Cleveland's second administration. (The president and his cabinet attended Gresham's funeral.)

Well into its second century now, Oak Woods Cemetery has kept pace with the times by erecting the Tower of Memories on the shore of the Lake of Memories. Constructed of Portuguese marble, the mausoleum includes a six-story columbarium, the tallest in the world. No expense was spared in using the rarest of carved tropical woods and beautifully etched marble. The stained glass window in the Chapel of Hope, spectacular in its conception, is a modern evocation in glass of Katharine Lee Bates's poem "America the Beautiful."

With the monuments of the past are some unusual conceptions of the present. One of the most touching of the former is that constructed of twisted bits of iron and glass, all that remained of the cemetery's office in downtown Chicago after the great fire of 1871. Another is to the heroic firemen who lost their lives in the 1893 fire on the grounds of the World Columbian Exposition. Oak Woods donated a lot for their interment; the Chicago Fire Department erected a memorial bearing their names. Among those memorials of the present is the Eternal Light Monument, an unusually beautiful and impressive granite structure created and erected by the Oak Woods Cemetery Association as a memorial to the six million martyrs who died in World War II.

The old Jewish section of the cemetery is European in character as well it should be, for many of the early burials were those of immigrants. Many of these tombstones have small framed pictures of the deceased.

Oak Woods was interracial before knowing it. In the last century the attitude of restricting burial to whites was a common one. However, unknown to everyone, a black woman was buried here in 1862 and it was not until recent years, according to Jory Graham in her *Chicago: An Extraordinary Guide,* that a graduate student investigating the early history of blacks in the Windy City found the grave of the woman. This discovery settled historically the controversy of when "mixed burial" began in Chicago.

The gates to Crown Hill. *Historic American Buildings Survey. Jack E. Boucher, photographer*

26. Crown Hill

INDIANAPOLIS, INDIANA

> *I cannot say and I will not say*
> *That he is dead. He is just away!*
> *With a cheery smile and a wave of the hand,*
> *He has wandered into an unknown land,*
> *And left us dreaming how very fair*
> *It needs must be, since he lingers there.*

THESE words from "Away" by James Whitcomb Riley were in memory of W. H. H. Terrell (1827–1884), financial secretary during the Civil War to Governor Oliver Perry Morton of Indiana. Reflecting the Victorian attitude and sentiment toward death, the poem appeared in the *Indianapolis Journal* on May 31, 1884. Both Riley and Terrell rest at Crown Hill, one remembered, the other forgotten.

Crown Hill occupies the same position in the hearts of the people of Indianapolis, for that matter of all Indiana, that Père-Lachaise does for the citizens of Paris.

Indianapolis was founded in 1819 and has a rich his-

torical past. In 1821 the city established Greenlawn Cemetery, a modest burial ground, of twenty-five acres but certainly not one for a capital city (a role it undertook in 1825) on the march so to speak. It was near the railroads, shops, and factories, and lacked the amenities Indianapolis felt should be extended to its dead.

By 1863, when the Civil War was at its height, Indianapolis was a hive of activity—a northern city, but in a sense in a border state. The census for 1860—18,611—indicates its growth. A decade earlier it had ten thousand fewer people. Troops were sent to or returned there from the front lines. "Unsettled conditions, anxiety over the war and uncertainties as to the future" affected the community, and Greenlawn was becoming crowded, especially with the hundreds of soldiers buried there who had died in Indianapolis hospitals.

Although thriving and growing, Indianapolis retained a leisurely approach to the affairs of life and death. Several public-spirited citizens met casually, discussed the civic problem of a new cemetery, but the status quo did not change. It was Hugh McCulloch, later secretary of the treasury, who told one of these men—James M. Ray, a banker—about the cemetery planned and laid out at Fort Wayne.

The spot itself—then known as Strawberry Hill—was included in the farm of Martin Williams, and was selected by John Chislett (his son and grandson later became superintendents of Crown Hill), a landscape gardener and cemetery superintendent from Pittsburgh. The hill was the highest point near Indianapolis and was two hundred feet higher than the level of the White River. This was added to the other land purchases, totaling 252 acres. It was decided that the cemetery would never exceed six hundred acres. One other point should not be forgotten: The articles of association specified "that the entire funds arising from the sale of burial lots, and the proceeds of investment of said funds shall be . . . dedicated to the purchase and improvement of the grounds of the cemetery, and keeping them durably and permanently enclosed and in perpetual repair . . . that no part of such funds shall, as dividend, profit, or in any manner whatever, inure to the corporators."

It was not a native of Indianapolis who in 1864 first entered Crown Hill, but Lucy Ann Seaton, "who with her husband were spoken of as 'strangers to the town.' " Lucy Ann died of tuberculosis. She was thirty-three, the wife of Captain John L. Seaton, and had been born in Halifax, Virginia, in 1831. The *Indianapolis Journal* urged all to attend the services at Crown Hill, a customary gesture of the day when funerals were a matter of civic pride and participation. Captain Seaton's farewell cry is recorded on Lucy's stone: "Dear Lucy, God grant that I may meet you in heaven." There was, however, a feeling of dismay in the community that the widower could leave Lucy Ann here alone, far from her own.

One result of Lucy Ann's burial—although she is forgotten today except as a historical footnote—was that removals from Greenlawn Cemetery began several years later, for one interment led to others and soon Crown Hill gained acceptance.

The Civil War marked Indianapolis for all time. In 1861 it was a country town, but there was an absolute passion among the citizens of Indiana to enlist. The state sent 208,767 soldiers to the battles in the Confederacy: Men flocked to Indianapolis to enlist from farms, villages, and towns throughout Indiana. Some from rural areas, in haste to answer the call to arms when Fort Sumter fell, arrived in overalls and bare feet.

The federal ground is in actuality a national cemetery within a city burial ground. Those unfortunate soldiers who died in Indianapolis hospitals during the war are interred here: The War Department purchased 1½ acres in Crown Hill for those who wore the red badge of courage. The bodies of others who died in battle or in camp were also sent home. (They, too, were removed from Greenlawn on Kentucky Avenue—708 were reburied in 1866, including 36 unknowns.)

Crown Hill is the final resting place of Benjamin Harrison (1833–1901), twenty-third president. President Harrison was a great-grandson of a signer of the Declaration of Independence, and grandson of William Henry Harrison, the ninth president. His first wife, Caroline Scott Harrison (1832–1892), lies here too. She was the first president general of the National Society of the Daughters of the American Revolution. Harrison, after the death of his wife, married her niece, Mary Scott Lord Dimmick (1858–1948), who survived the president forty-seven years before she joined him and her aunt in Crown Hill.

Presidents are of prime interest to cemetery visitors, but vice-presidents—unless they achieve notoriety—are generally forgotten men. Three are at Crown Hill as well as three who were nominated for the office but were not elected. The first of these was Thomas Andrews Hendricks (1819–1885), who held the office under Grover Cleveland but died eight months after inauguration. He was joined here thirty-three years later by Charles Warren Fairbanks (1852–1918), who held the office from 1905 to 1909 under Theodore Roosevelt. He is best remembered today because Fairbanks, Alaska, was named in his honor. Fairbanks had presidential aspirations, but McKinley's assassination thwarted them. Fairbanks and Charles Evans Hughes ran on the Republican ticket in 1916, which "was a classic cliffhanger." Their opponents were Woodrow Wilson and Thomas Riley Marshall, and it was the only time that two vice-presidential candidates came from the same state.

The third member of the triumvirate, Governor Thomas Riley Marshall (1854–1925), is remembered for an American maxim: "What this country needs is a good five-cent cigar!" This imperishable remark was made to a clerk while Mr. Marshall presided over a Senate debate—an especially tiring one—in which Senator Bristow of Kansas labored through a speech called "What This Country Needs." The three Indianans buried here who received the nomination (but were not elected) are George W. Julian, who was the Free Soil Candidate in 1852; William H. English, nominated in 1880 with General Winfield Scott Hancock by the "War Democrats"; and John B. Kern, Democratic nominee in 1908 with William Jennings Bryan.

These six men and President Harrison *are* buried at Crown Hill. Of this there is no doubt. What then of Caleb B. Smith (1808–1864), secretary of the interior in President Lincoln's cabinet? Smith is not at Crown Hill, although it was intended he be here, and he should in all likelihood be. However, the mausoleum bearing his name and the year of his death does not, as far as it is known, contain Smith's body—and never did!

Crown Hill was not open for burials until six months after Smith's death, so the body was temporarily placed in a vault at old Greenlawn. The records are sketchy. Legend has it that his widow, apparently without formal permission, had a mausoleum built for her husband, which was partly set in a hillside. In this she placed Mr. Smith's remains—but not for long! Crown Hill's management ordered her to abandon the tomb as unsanitary, and Caleb Smith's long and mysterious journey to oblivion began once more. From this time Smith's body disappeared. All manner of theories were offered: that it was at Connersville, his family home, or in a Cincinnati cemetery. His widow later built another stone mausoleum (this time a sanitary one!) where she, their daughter, and another relative were laid to rest, but not Caleb Smith. Indiana's first cabinet member is remembered by name, but there are doubts that he was ever formally buried.

The Hoosier poet James Whitcomb Riley (1849–1916) created "Little Orphant Annie" and "The Old Swimmin' Hole," and published such sentimental collections as *Afterwhiles* and *An Old Sweetheart of Mine.* In 1912, four years before his death, the schools throughout the country observed his birthday. When he died in his house on Loekerbie Street he was accorded a funeral in keeping with his national stature. Today his grave, on the highest point of Crown Hill, is distinguished by the elegantly simple Greek temple above it, a reminder to all those for miles around of him who celebrated Indiana's bucolic life and rustic virtues, and made them and Indiana's Poet Laureate universally loved. One of his poems—it could be about a procession to Crown Hill at the time—records:

A thing that's 'bout as trying as a healthy man can meet
Is some poor feller's funeral a-joggin' 'long the street:
The slow hearse and the horses—slow enough to say the least,
Fer to even tax the patience of the gentleman deceased!
The slow crunch of the gravel and the slow grind of the wheels—
The slow, slow go of every woe that everybody feels,
So I ruther like the contrast when I hear the whiplash crack
A quickstep for the horses
When the
Hearse
Comes
Back.

Equally appealing—for he too celebrated the idyllic life of America's coming of age, the period from the turn of the century until the end of World War I—was Newton Booth Tarkington (1869–1946). *Penrod* and *Penrod and Sam* extolled the joys of boyhood. *Seventeen* did the same for adolescence. The gentleman from Indiana was a beloved figure in American letters when he died just after World War II and joined Riley and Kin Hubbard here. Frank McKinney Hubbard (1868–1930) introduced in 1904 another rustic Hoosier character in Abe Martin, and brought caricature and satire to new heights in this syndicated cartoon. (Although somewhat forgotten today, in his own lifetime his fellow humorist Will Rogers thought highly of his work.) Meredith Nicholson (1866–1947), author of *The House of a Thousand Candles* (1905), was United States minister to Paraguay (1933–1934), Venezuela (1935–1938), and Nicaragua (1938–1941).

Here also is Catharine Merrill (1824–1900), an educator who volunteered as a nurse in the Union army during the Civil War and was the second woman in the United States to hold a full college professorship; Frederick S. Duesenberg (1876–1932), German-born automobile manufacturer who gave his name to one of the most expensive cars (and whose Duesenberg racing cars won the famed Indianapolis 500 in 1924, 1925, and 1927); Colonel Roscoe Turner (1895–1970), aviation pioneer and three-time winner of the Thompson Trophy; Sarah T. Bolton (1814–1893), Hoosier poet who gained national prominence with her poem "Paddle Your Own Canoe"; Colonel Eli Lilly (1838–1898), founder of the pharmaceutical concern; W. D. McCoy, the black educator appointed by President Harrison as minister and consul general to Liberia in 1892 (he died there of tropical fever the following year); and the never-to-be-forgotten John Dillinger (1903–1934).

Dillinger, the bank robber who terrorized the Midwest, was betrayed by the "Woman in Red" and shot by agents of the Federal Bureau of Investigation. His funeral was the only occasion when Crown Hill had to close its gates and restrict attendance, honoring the Dillinger family's desire for privacy. In the years since, his grave markers have been chipped beyond recognition by souvenir hunters and in 1976 the marker over his grave was dug up and taken away by a ghoulish collector. Through the years Crown Hill has paid for the replacements.

Perhaps no happening in Crown Hill's existence than the funeral of an obscure citizen better illustrates that Indianapolis through its years of growth has never lost the touch that James Whitcomb Riley and Booth Tarkington recorded for others beyond its boundaries. For twenty-five years Herbert A. Wirth (1898–1971), a modern-day tinker, successor to the drummers of the past, a peddler carrying on a lost tradition, went from door to door through Indianapolis's north side, selling his wares. Lugging two shopping bags filled with washcloths, potholders, scouring pads, and shoelaces, he had become a fixture in the community. Folks were used to seeing Herbie and, in many ways, took him for granted. Herbie had paid for his funeral expenses in advance. At his death he might have been interred quietly, but with dignity. At this point the *Indianapolis Star* published a feature about Herbie Wirth, saying that he never feared death so much as being sent off alone. His only wish was that someone would come to mourn his passing.

Never let it be said that Indianapolis lacks heart. The city responded and over one thousand citizens turned out on a cold, blustery day for his funeral, one of the largest in Crown Hill's history.

The monument to Thomas Andrews Hendricks, vice-president of the United States. *Photograph by Fred Abel*

Above, left: The grave of Vice-President Charles Warren Fairbanks. *Photograph by Fred Abel*

‹ The grave of Lucy Ann Seaton, first to be buried in Crown Hill. *Photograph by Fred Abel*

The Booth Tarkington mausoleum. *Photograph by Fred Abel*

The James Whitcomb Riley memorial. *Courtesy Caldwell-Van Riper, Inc.*

The grave of "Public Enemy Number One." *Photograph by Fred Abel*

The chapel at Crown Hill. *Historic American Buildings Survey. Jack E. Boucher, photographer*

The grave of President Benjamin Harrison. *Courtesy Caldwell-Van Riper, Inc.*

Trees are the exception in Saint Louis I. *Photograph by the author*

27. Saint Louis Cemetery I

NEW ORLEANS, LOUISIANA

"THEY told me to take a streetcar named Desire, and then transfer to one called Cemeteries and ride six blocks and get off at—Elysian Fields."

Spoken by the tragic Blanche Dubois in Tennessee Williams's play *A Streetcar Named Desire,* these words raise more faint echoes of the romantic aura that surrounds New Orleans cemeteries than a factual account might. They indicate the importance of the cemeteries in New Orleans, more so than in any other city with the possible exception of Genoa. The city has removed itself from the heat by means of air conditioning, from fever by drainage, from floods by the levees, from disease by the advances of medicine, but the cemeteries are, and have been, an accepted part of the life of New Orleans.

Founded by the French in 1718, an early plan of New Orleans in 1725 shows a cemetery outside city limits. Since the city was Roman Catholic, the cemetery fell under the jurisdiction of the church of Saint Louis.

Although burials did take place in the cemetery, most —following European custom—were within the church. However, in 1784 when Spain ruled Louisiana (Spanish rule began in 1762), the Cabildo, the Spanish governing body in the colony, ordered that church burial be no longer permitted except for distinguished citizens. That early cemetery—the Saint Peter Street Cemetery— served for almost seventy years. It took a major crisis— an epidemic of fever—to bring about a new one. In 1788 the Mississippi River overflowed, a fire followed with almost a thousand homes destroyed, and sickness and death filled the city.

New Orleans, which is low-lying near the delta of the Mississippi, was in a precarious state. The authorities knew that the position of the cemetery in relation to the city could bring about a greater pestilence. In an effort to avoid this, they ordered that a new cemetery site be selected. Thus, Saint Louis Cemetery I was established in

1789, making it the oldest extant cemetery in New Orleans today.

Located at Basin and Saint Louis streets, and enclosed with a whitewashed wall, it appears at first glance to be well kept. Once inside, this illusion is dispelled. The decay of almost two centuries hangs over the quiet cemetery. It is decay without eeriness. The sounds of the city without the walls bring the twentieth century close, but the crumbling old tombs, many open to the eye, are a testimony of neglect.

The paths follow no apparent pattern. Instead, they run a haphazard course, one into the other. The absence of extensive planting is obvious at once. There is occasionally a lone cypress, a small patch of grass; mostly, it is a closely packed hodgepodge of tombs, one on top of the other. The lack of planning and order is especially striking here. The growth that is most evident are those tufts of grass, or small trees, that have rooted on the roofs of the high tombs.

The tombs themselves are unique in many ways. Because there was no natural stone quarried near New Orleans and it had to be brought great distances, the tombs themselves were made of brick, a soft red variety fired locally. A plaster, which was then whitewashed, was laid over the brick and acted as a preservative. On occasion, marble was used as facing, but with the passage of years exposure to the elements has warped and broken it. Only a few of the tombs are newly whitewashed and plastered today. Families have died out, or no longer care to preserve their vaults. Neither the parishes nor the archdiocese can afford to allocate money, the decay creeps in, and once it has a foothold it seems difficult to stop—the way a jungle takes over ancient cities. Here the remnants remain, but they are forlorn and bedraggled by time and neglect.

The earliest inscription we know of was fortunately recorded in 1903 before time and the weather erased it: "Here lies a poor unfortunate who was victim of his own imprudence. Drop a tear on his tomb and say, if you please, the psalm 'out of the depths I have cried unto Thee, O Lord,' for his soul. He was only 27 years. 1798."

The names on the tombs are generally of French origin (although some are Spanish), some so exotic as to evoke echoes of New Orleans's romantic past. The stones have often fallen from the walls and lie scattered about. In French we read: "Mlle. Josephine Duclos décédée le 15 Septembre 1867 à l'age de 4 ans et 4 mois." The given names—Zoë, Victorine, Élie, Edouard, Eugénie, Bastien, Arsène, Hippolyte, Archille, Amélie, Odile, Suzette, and Léontine—set the French tone as do the surnames—Cenas, Thibaut, Charbonnet, Redon, Moncharveaux, and Peyrefitte.

Here lies Prince Albert Monteculli, son of Charlotte, Countess Laderche and Princess von Oettingen Wallenstein. Prince Albert died in 1822 and cannot be found even in old copies of the *Almanach de Gotha*.

Among the illustrious of New Orleans buried here are Jean Étienne Boré (1741–1820), first mayor of the city; Paul Morphy (1837–1884), the greatest chess player of his time; and Marie Laveau, the voodoo queen. Marie's tomb is bizarre and of interest to citizens of New Orleans and tourists alike. It is marked with X's in colored paint or crayon—for good luck.

Benjamin Henry Latrobe (1764–1820), the distinguished architect, designed a charming tomb for Eliza Lewis, first wife of Governor William C. C. Claiborne; their daughter, Cornelia Tennessee Claiborne (who died at the age of three); and Mrs. Claiborne's brother, Micajah Green Lewis, private secretary to the governor, "who fell in a duel February 14, 1805 in the 25th year of his age." The monument, set in a recessed well, was created in Philadelphia and sculpted by Franzoni. It is reminiscent of ancient commemorative altars and is unlike the other monuments in character. In fact, it is similar to those found in European or in old northern cemeteries rather than in southern ones.

Stanislaus Fournier, born in Saint Aubin, France, in 1814 and who died in New Orleans in 1883, was the city's only commercial clockmaker during his lifetime. Present-day horologists convening in New Orleans find their way to Saint Louis I to stand at his grave. (It has been marked anew by the Creole Chapter of the National Association of Watch and Clock Collectors, Inc.)

William P. Canby (1796–1814) was a midshipman in the navy, "who fell in that unequal contest between the United States Gun Boat Squadron and the British Flotilla on Lake Borgne, near New Orleans." Next to his monument is one to those who fell in the Battle of New Orleans on January 8, 1815.

The ovenlike tombs, famous the world over as characteristic of New Orleans, are nowhere more in evidence than in Saint Louis I. Their condition is generally deplorable. Vandalism and neglect have taken their toll; a historic-minded group called "Save Our Cemeteries" is making an effort to enlist citizen help in restoring them.

The principle of the oven vaults was that the remains were placed on a shelf in the wall, which was then sealed, to eventually disintegrate. As the coffin fell to bits, only the bones remained and these were then swept through a small grating to join other family bones in a receptacle *(caveau)* below. In some cases, the remains were pushed to the back of the enclosure, the casket (or what was left of it) burned, and the space left to receive another body. There are as well two-vault tombs, one above the other. The bones are also placed in the pit below after a suitable time and the space cleared for future use. Vaults are often rented for a year or two, then the bones consigned to the *caveau,* and the vault free to be rented once more.

Oven vaults had to be used because of New Orleans's water level. Ground burial became impossible because as soon as a grave was dug—often before the casket was placed in it—it would fill with water. Grisly stories are told of gravediggers standing on coffins to weigh them down, or worse still of a shovel being thrust into the coffin. Once broken, it would fill with water and sink!

Especially peculiar to Saint Louis, and other New Orleans cemeteries, are the tombs of the various benevolent societies: the Portuguese Benevolent Association, the Cervantes Mutual Benevolent Society, the New Orleans Battalion of Artillery, and the New Orleans Italian Mutual Benevolent Society. The latter tomb was designed by Pietro Gualdi and erected in 1857 at a cost of $40,000. There are vaults in the tomb for society members, and three handsome statues—one on top holding a cross, and *Italia* and *Charity* in niches—make the tomb especially spectacular even in its present state of decay.

In and about this dilapidation one finds small, new, rectangular stones in memory of servicemen who died in World War II, the Korean War, and the Vietnam conflict. They are not attached to a base, are movable, and resemble a sidewalk curb. Engraved with the name and rank of the deceased, they are simply placed before the family's tomb, reminders of those buried elsewhere.

The floral arrangements, purposeful or accidental—a lone yellow wax rose twined about an iron cross at the head of a grave or a flowering vine growing from an opened oven vault; the forlorn, brooding look of the benevolent societies' tombs; the rusted iron fence; the metal door of a tomb hanging by one hinge; a single cypress or palm tree; or the sound of nearby church bells tolling the hours—all contribute to the romantic picture of a deserted ancient burial ground. The streetcar may be marked Desire or Cemeteries, but Saint Louis I is far from being an Elysian field.

Tombs are literally built on top of one another. *Photograph by the author*

The Claiborne monument designed by Benjamin Henry Latrobe. *Photograph by the author*

Decay is everywhere in Saint Louis I. *Photograph by the author*

The tomb of the New Orleans Italian Mutual Benevolent Society in Saint Louis I. *Photograph by the author*

28. Saint Louis Cemetery II

NEW ORLEANS, LOUISIANA

IN New Orleans the juxtaposition of life and death is nowhere more apparent than in the contrast between Saint Louis Cemetery II, consecrated in 1824, and the overhead freeway (Claiborne Avenue Overpass). The silence in the cemetery is broken by the hum of traffic, the rumble of trucks, the screech of tires. The twentieth century is virtually on top of Saint Louis II.

Preserving the city's cemeteries has been an uphill fight and Saint Louis II does seem to have fared better than Saint Louis I, although it is a shabby sister beside the grander, more opulent Metairie Cemetery.

The cemetery, located between Claiborne Avenue and North Robertson Street, is in three sections with Iberville Street, Bienville Avenue, and Conti Street bordering it. Saint Louis II has a uniformity that Saint Louis I lacks; it is rectangular, well laid out, with a main aisle and parallel side aisles. There isn't the haphazardness here one encounters in the older Saint Louis I. Perhaps this can be attributed to Antoine Philippe LeRiche, the Paris-

born architect and engineer who was inspector of cemeteries at the time of Saint Louis II's planning. Also, in the first quarter of the nineteenth century, cemetery planning in any city followed a more orderly scheme.

Saint Louis II evolved as did so many European and American burial grounds. Disease—not as a cause of death—was one of the prime movers for its inception. By 1820 the City Council was alarmed enough by the epidemics, plagues, outbreaks of fever, and the expected spread of disease from city cemeteries to seek a solution. One fact was certain—the new cemetery must be 2,400 feet from city limits. The result we see today is a cemetery with a curiously Mediterranean look, even to the extent of a lone cypress providing a touch of occasional green to the whitewashed tombs. The absence of color, except in the *allées,* and the occasional flower or plant before a tomb, is heightened by the intensity of the sun upon this singularly exposed piece of open ground.

The French names are evident in Saint Louis II as in

A view of Saint Louis II, circa 1855. *Print and Picture Department, Free Library of Philadelphia*

Saint Louis I. Here we find Julie-Mathilde, Amilcar, and Amédée, as well as Chopin, Breaux, de la Ronde, Lavillebeauvre, La Peyre, Bouligny, Lhote, Chaudet, and St. Pe. But some of Spanish origin creep in: Rojas, Estrada, Fuentes, Fernandez, and Canto. The tombs are more imaginative, more spectacular, and more generally individualistic than in Saint Louis I. One finds more ironwork fencing, an occasional ornate miniature chapel, a mausoleum suggesting one found in ancient Rome, and a plethora of tombs of benevolent societies.

No one interred here is more romantic than Dominique You, a pirate captain under Jean Lafitte and still legendary in New Orleans, where legends die slowly. Dominique, an expert cannoneer, later became a reformed pirate, fought in the Battle of New Orleans, and led a life of service to the community. "When he died in 1830 military honors were paid to his memory, banks and business houses were closed, and flags on ships and public buildings were placed at half-mast." Here too is

Alexander Milne (1744–1838), a Scot who emigrated to New Orleans and at his death at the age of ninety-four left his fortune to provide homes for destitute children. The monument over Milne, who came to New Orleans prior to 1770, is a handsome one with superb lettering that should endure as long as Saint Louis II does. The base and the elongated shaft above it are inscribed with extracts from his will and Section I through Section V of an act of the state legislature setting up the Milne Asylum for Destitute Orphan Boys. Newton Richards (1805–1874), one of New Orleans's better-known tomb designers, was responsible for this little gem.

At one time Margaret Gaffney Haugherty (1813–1882) was interred in the tomb of the Sisters of Charity of Saint Vincent de Paul. When the tomb was demolished in 1920, Margaret's remains (and those of the other nuns) were moved to Saint Louis Cemetery III. Margaret, as she was known to the people of the city, fed and clothed the poor and the homeless. A statue of her stands in a small park bounded by Camp, Prytania, and Clio Streets, but no stone marks her present grave.

Dominating the smaller individual or family tombs are the vaults built by the mutual benefit societies for their members. That of the Cazadores de Orleans, a group attached to the Louisiana Legion, was built in 1836 at a cost of $15,000. Inscribed on it is the reminder that "every man belonging to the company of the Cazadores de Orleans shall find here a retreat where his mortal remains may rest in peace. R.I.P." A further legend is in French:

**La compagnie des
Cazadores D'Orléans
formée in 1829
et attachée de la légion de la Louisiane
a erigé a ses membres
ce monument, où leurs dépouilles Mortelles
Gisent dans un repos eternal
1836
AMEN**

Saint Louis II shares one ceremonial in common with all New Orleans cemeteries. On November 1—the Feast of All Saints—all New Orleans descends on the city's burial places to honor the dead. For weeks beforehand, intense activity takes place: The tombs are whitewashed, names of the recently dead are cut into their monuments, and the plantings around the graves are cut and trimmed. *Immortelles,* the bead and wire wreaths often embellished with a porcelain or wax rose, which are indigenous to New Orleans, are in evidence throughout the cemeteries. (Before the mid-nineteenth century they were often imported from France. After that time they were created in the workrooms of the Vieux Carré.) Tiny vases are hung from the walls of the oven tombs, sometimes holding a single flower such as the artificial blue rose once found on the Saliba tomb (bearing the single word "Heine") in Saint Louis I. Small wooden shelves jut out from the walls of some tombs and often a pathetic small canopy above affords little protection. In these cases, a common glass jar holds a floral offering.

All this is a prelude to the great day itself. From dawn to sunset the people of New Orleans descend on the cemeteries carrying chrysanthemums, and by nightfall these old burial grounds are a mass of flowers. The dead have not been forgotten.

The cemetery has a Mediterranean character. *Photograph by the author*

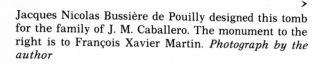

Jacques Nicolas Bussière de Pouilly designed this tomb for the family of J. M. Caballero. The monument to the right is to François Xavier Martin. *Photograph by the author*

The Barelli tomb. *Photograph by the author*

The Oliver Blineau and Antoine Carrière mausoleum, built in 1845. *Photograph by the author*

The ironwork is often of singular design. *Photograph by the author*

Decoration on the vault of the Jefferson Fire Company Number 22, which has been standing since 1852. *Photograph by the author*

The open, empty, and desolate vault of the Edward W. Sewell family. *Photograph by the author*

29. Lafayette Cemetery I

NEW ORLEANS, LOUISIANA

ONE of the striking differences between New Orleans cemeteries and those farther north is the sparsity of trees, or complete absence of them, in the cemeteries of the delta city. The exception to this is, of course, Metairie Cemetery, which has more trees than all the other New Orleans cemeteries combined. However, in recent years some fine magnolias have been planted in Lafayette I to replace those that have died or been destroyed during storms.

The square of land on which Lafayette I stands was acquired for $6,000 from Cornelius Hurst and laid out by Benjamin Buisson, the city surveyor. Earlier the land had been part of the Livaudais plantation, which in 1832 had been subdivided into city squares. Lafayette Cemetery I was the municipal cemetery for the city of Lafayette. (It became part of New Orleans twenty years later in 1852.) As a cemetery, it has the advantage of being perfectly square with two main crosswalks, or aisles, meeting at right angles. This gives the cemetery

a sense of order not always found in the old ones of the city, but still some overcrowding is evident.

Lafayette I has the advantage of being situated in the Garden District, which has the greatest diversity of architectural style, ornament, and charm. While Saint Louis I and II are now part of the urbanization of New Orleans and tall commercial buildings can be seen from the cemeteries themselves, and Metairie Cemetery is in the heart of an area subjected to suburban sprawl, freeways, and shopping centers, Lafayette I is surrounded by evidences of the past. The superb dwellings in the district are, with the cemetery, all of a piece. The visitor easily could be back in 1832, when it was subdivided, or in 1852 when the city of Lafayette was annexed to New Orleans but did not lose its individuality in the process.

In 1858 the cemetery was enclosed by a wall and the handsome gates were erected to the memory of Theodore Von La Hache, musician-composer. The names on the stones here indicate a preponderance of Irish and German families, although some French and Spanish are here as well. The tombs show great diversity in style and their inscriptions leave the reader with a sense of sadness. The Schifferstein tomb tells its own story. Lafayette I was used for burials during the great yellow fever epidemics and perhaps this child was a victim of one of these plagues:

Family tomb of
A. B. Schifferstein
In Memory of

Phaon

only child of
A. B. & Catharine Schifferstein
who departed this life

April 17, 1851
Aged 5 years 1 month & 1 day

That once loved form now cold and dead
Each mournful thought employs
We weep our earthy comforts fled
And withered all our joys.

The Civil War brought its own tragedy. The empty, forlorn tomb of Edward W. Sewell, who died in 1864 at the age of sixty, is witness to this. A native of Cork, Ireland, he had been a resident of New Orleans for thirty-three years when he died on May 12. On the twenty-eighth his only son, Corporal William Washington Sewell, was killed in the Battle of New Hope Church, Georgia. The inscription on the tomb, which has been destroyed, said his death left "his widowed mother childless." She, née Teresa J. Murray and a native of Sheepwalk Avoca, Ireland, lived until 1882. Today the Sewell tomb is one of the decaying ones in Lafayette I, open to the cold eye of the living. The covering protecting the coffin shelves has fallen off, and the remains have been swept away. Vines cover what is left; the grass is uncut. The tomb stands as a mute reminder of the transitoriness of earthly existence.

One of the memorable tombs here is that of the Jefferson Fire Company No. 22. A fine but rusting ironwork fence surrounds the many-vaulted tomb, and on the façade, near the roof, is an example of the variety of decoration found here. The stonecutter has fashioned a fire engine of the period—the horse-drawn, hand-pump variety. It is effects like this that make a walk through Lafayette I an adventure for those interested in architectural decoration. And it is monuments such as these that enabled interested citizens to have the cemetery placed on the National Register of Historic Places.

There is a hint of antebellum days here and those postbellum years too, before the turn of the century. It is almost a whiff of a faded, romantic past in a setting probably best expressed by the French inscriptions on two of the stones. That of Joseph Uzee (1807–1850) reads: "Il fut bon époux, bon ami et chéri de ses enfants." Justine Babin (1833–1851) is remembered thus: "Et rose elle a vecu ce que vivent les roses. L'espace d'un matin."

A neglected corner of Lafayette Cemetery I. *Photograph by the author*

A mausoleum at Lafayette I. The iron fence is in a better state of preservation than most. *Photograph by the author*

The tomb of the Garibaldi Society Italian Benevolent Association. *Photograph by the author*

30. Metairie Cemetery

NEW ORLEANS, LOUISIANA

METAIRIE Cemetery is 150 acres in a suburban district that was undeveloped when it was planned in the nineteenth century. Today traffic on Pontchartrain Boulevard, a large expressway, and Metairie Road, passes as if on a racetrack.

In the romantic days of New Orleans's antebellum past, when river gamblers and fancy ladies found their way to the city—in the days of *Show Boat* and *Saratoga Trunk*—what is now Metairie Cemetery was then the Metairie Race Course. In 1838 the racetrack was laid out on the somewhat high ground of Bayou Tschoupitoulas (Bayou Metairie), and until the Civil War it was one of the leading racing centers of the South.

Following the war, which brought great changes to all sections of the South, the racecourse was closed when beset by constant financial difficulties. As with any historic spot south of the Mason-Dixon line, a number of legends surrounding this metamorphosis from racetrack to cemetery have become part of New Orleans folklore.

One that may be apocryphal concerns Charles T. Howard, who was blackballed from the exclusive Metairie Jockey Club, which owned the racetrack. It was said he swore he would see a cemetery on the property before he died. When he died in 1885 his elaborate mausoleum was surmounted by a marble figure with a finger to his lips!

Word had been carried back to New Orleans of the rural, garden-type cemeteries of New England and the Middle Atlantic states: Mount Auburn, Laurel Hill, Green-Wood, and Woodlawn. Many of the early New Orleans cemeteries were almost filled. All except one (Greenwood) were surrounded by wall vaults. Most were small, too small for a growing city, one of the largest in the South. From the 1830s on, more elaborate small tombs or mausoleums had replaced the earlier boxlike ones aboveground, but in cemeteries such as Saint Louis I and Saint Louis II they were hemmed in and not shown to advantage as in a garden cemetery.

The time was propitious and the Metairie Cemetery

Association was chartered in 1872. Benjamin F. Harrod, the architect engaged to develop it, followed the plan of the 1 1/16-mile racetrack for the main avenue (now Metairie Avenue). An ambitious landscaping of trees, shrubs, and bushes followed, and two lakes, crossed by charming stone bridges, were developed—Lake Prospect and Horseshoe Lake. (The latter was an enlarged part of Bayou Metairie but has since been filled in.) The entire effect was that of a large-scale city park, developed with winding roads and paths. It was in this setting that the first burial, that of Dr. James Ritchie, took place in 1873. His tomb bears the inscription: "More Bent to Raise the Wretched than to Rise."

Metairie Cemetery immediately became the most desirable of New Orleans burial places, and it still is. Associations such as the Benevolent Association of the Army of Tennessee, the Garibaldi Society Italian Benevolent Association, the Cristoforo Columbus Society built tombs for their members, and although Metairie has few world-famous figures, it once held the remains of Jefferson Davis, president of the Confederate States of America, who died in New Orleans in 1889. All the states in the Confederacy, in a move to call Jefferson Davis their own, offered burial places. The president of the Metairie Cemetery Association decided the issue when he sent Mrs. Davis a note reading: "While the entire South claims him as her own, New Orleans asks that Jefferson Davis be laid to rest within the city where he fell asleep."

He was given a state funeral (the ceremonies lasted five days; his body lay in state in City Hall), for he was perhaps the most revered figure in the South since the death of Robert E. Lee. The silver plate on his coffin was inscribed: "Jefferson Davis at Rest." At his funeral thousands (at least fifty thousand) passed the bier, a death mask was taken of his face. Every available room in New Orleans was occupied as people continued to arrive by train, riverboat, and horse-drawn carriage. *Immortelles* of every conceivable design and flowers arrived in tribute. Among them were two bouquets of violets from South Carolina, packed in damp sponges in an old shoebox. The card enclosed told its own story: "From an old soldier and his son." Catholic priests, a rabbi, and ministers of the Presbyterian, Baptist, Methodist, and Episcopal faiths officiated. It took an hour and twenty minutes for the funeral procession to pass any given spot. Thousands of Confederate veterans marched as did thirty from the Mexican War in a funeral that lasted from noon until sundown.

Jefferson Davis's body was placed in the tomb of the Army of Northern Virginia until 1893, when it was removed to Richmond, Virginia, the capital of the Confederacy, for reburial in Hollywood Cemetery. Then his crypt in Metairie Cemetery was sealed and never used again. Thus, New Orleans lost the most famous burial it had or ever was to have.

The tomb of the Association of Northern Virginia, often called the Stonewall Jackson Monument because of the granite statue of the general thirty-eight feet in the air that surmounts the column, dominates a circular site. In the fifty-seven vaults are the remains of twenty-five hundred Confederate veterans who fell from the Battle of Manassas until the surrender at Appomattox. At the dedication of the monument, more than five thousand attended, hearing General Fitzhugh Lee, a nephew of Robert E. Lee, give the address.

Leading the roll of Civil War leaders buried here is General Pierre G. T. Beauregard (1818–1893), whose body lies in the tomb of the Army of Tennessee. (His son-in-law, Charles Larendon, is in another part of the cemetery in a Moorish tomb.) The Army of Tennessee (Louisiana Division) dedicated the tomb site in 1883 with General Charles E. Hooker and Jefferson Davis participating. In the cornerstone, in a copper casket, are articles and mementos of the Confederacy. Topping the vaulted Gothic chapel (covered by a tumulus, or grassy mound) is an equestrian statue by Alexander Doyle of General Albert Sidney Johnson. By the entrance to the tomb (which contains forty-eight vaults) stands a statue of a Confederate soldier calling the roll. The face, according to Leonard V. Huber, historian of New Orleans's cemeteries, was modeled by Doyle from a photograph of the New Orleans Confederate soldier William Brunet, sergeant of the Louisiana Guard Battery, who died in 1864 at the Battle of New Hope Church, Georgia. It was a gift of Charles T. Howard, the man who swore he would see the racetrack a cemetery. Other Civil War figures here are General Richard Taylor (son of President Zachary Taylor), General John Bell Hood, and John A. Stevenson, builder of *Manassas,* a Civil War ironclad used in the defense of New Orleans in 1862.

The graves of the diverse and highly individual personages buried here are fascinating. None was more colorful than Josie Arlington, proprietor of one of the city's most extravagant bordellos, or, as they were called then, "sporting houses." Josie, born plain Mary Deubler, led a life highlighted by such incidents as her brother's death at the hands of Lobrano, her lover. Lobrano had first led Josie down the path from respectability; then he let her support him with her earnings as a madam. Later, after having set Lobrano adrift on his own, Josie ran an even more refined establishment, the Château Lobrano d'Arlington (she was faithful to his name), but she would not permit chaste young girls to work for her, declaring no girl would be ruined under her roof!

Josie's success enabled her to build a $15,000 pink marble tomb in Metairie Cemetery, with a bronze figure of a young woman, seemingly about to knock at its doors. The statue led to theories that it typified Josie, knocking at her father's door in vain, when he locked her out following her fall from grace with Lobrano; or that it represented Josie's dictum against virgins in her Château.

Her mausoleum was more talked about after her death in 1914 than Josie had been before. A signal pole erected outside the cemetery shone its light on Josie's tomb. The light was red. The furor among the curious who came to view this phenomenon caused the city to move the signal. Josie is no longer in her tomb (although locally it is still referred to as the Josie Arlington tomb). Her thrifty relatives sold it to J. A. Morales and moved her bones to a less costly resting place.

Josie's tomb was equaled in notoriety only by the one Daniel Moriarty raised in memory of his late wife. Mrs. Moriarty loomed great in Daniel's life and her loss was equally as great, so when her remains were removed here in 1905 (she died in 1887), he had erected what is the largest monument in the cemetery. The granite for it was so heavy that a spur from the railroad line had to be specially constructed into the cemetery. This was not enough. Later, in 1914, when a walk of Mount Airy granite was laid around the plot, the stones each weighed eleven tons (Moriarty built for the ages) and the drays hauling them cut deep ruts into the gravel-paved Canal Street.

Moriarty wanted four graces at each corner of the base of the monument's shaft and this led to a local sobriquet being applied to them: Faith, Hope, Charity—and Mrs. Moriarty!

The Lucien Brunswig (died 1892) tomb, an excellent example of late Egyptian Revival. *Photograph by the author*

The tomb of Charles A. Larendon (died 1888). *Photograph by the author*

The mausoleum of Stanley W. Ray, Jr. *Photograph by the author*

A Pietà in gold on black marble decorates the monument to the Clark family. *Photograph by the author*

The approach to the chapel at Green Mount Cemetery. *Photograph by J. H. Schaefer & Son*

31. Green Mount Cemetery

BALTIMORE, MARYLAND

FEW cities in the United States occupy the unique position Baltimore does: a border city between North and South which is, technically, southern. Sectional barriers have fallen, especially during and since World War II, but the characteristics and personality of the city remain. Baltimore retains a charming blend of the old, romantic South with the hurry and bustle of the North.

In 1839 when Green Mount Cemetery opened, Baltimore (founded in 1729) was little over a century old, but its population (102,313 in 1840) made it the nation's second city. The year before the proprietors of Green Mount Cemetery were "created a body politic and corporate,"

but not until July 13, 1839 was the spot—once the estate of Robert Oliver—formally dedicated.

As with so many other cemeteries, Green Mount was a rural estate possessed of a pastoral beauty to delight the eye of either John Constable or Old Chrome. The tract itself was composed of portions of three original grants made by the various lords Baltimore (there were six in the Proprietary period) in the latter part of the seventeenth and the early years of the eighteenth century; their names—Salisbury Plain, Haile's Folly, and Hanson's Wood Lot—as picturesque as their setting. Oliver, a leading Baltimore merchant of his day, began to acquire land in 1793 and continued to add to his holdings until shortly after his death in 1834.

At the dedication of Green Mount Cemetery, the Baltimore Musical Association marked the occasion by singing a chorale from Felix Mendelssohn's then-new oratorio *Saint Paul.* The Reverend Dr. William Edward Wyatt, rector of Saint Paul's Church, gave the invocation described as a "prayer ... replete with references to dirges and abysses and charnel-houses." Benjamin Henry Latrobe's son, John Hazelhurst Boneval Latrobe, a railroad lawyer who supported African colonization of Liberia, composed a poem for the occasion "sung to the tune of the 100th Psalm."

John Pendleton Kennedy, a congressman, later secretary of the navy (1852–1853) and novelist (*Horse-Shoe Robinson, Swallow Barn,* and other popular favorites now forgotten), was moved by the ornate style and florid oratory so esteemed in 1839. He declared: "I know not where the eye may find more pleasing landscapes than those which surround us." He spoke of "sylvan embellishments ... this venerable grove of ancient forest ... the thicket begemmed with wild flowers ... embowered alleys ... the cool dell where the fountain ripples over its pebbly bed ... a landscape rife with all the charms that hill and dale, forest-clad heights and cultivated fields may contribute to enchant the eye."

Such rhetoric enchanted those Baltimoreans present for the dedication ceremonies, and some were convinced of the value of Green Mount even if it was far out in the country. This, then, was the beginning of a civic enterprise—nonprofit and nonsectarian. Gerald W. Johnson tells us: "Although a small group constituted the corporation and had charge of its affairs, the town from the very beginning regarded Green Mount in somewhat the same light in which it regarded the city churches—legally, the possession of certain trustees, but in every other sense the property of the city."

It was a child who first led Baltimore to Green Mount. Olivia Cushing Whitridge, daughter of a Baltimore physician, died in December 1839 at the age of two years, two months, and twenty days, and was the first to be buried here. Severn Teackle Wallis (who has achieved an immortality of sorts because unwittingly his name came down to the Duchess of Windsor), moved to verse, wrote of Olivia and Green Mount:

Green home of future thousands! how blest in sight of heaven
Are these, the tender firstlings, that death to thee has given!
Though prayer and solemn anthem have echoed from thy hill,
This first, fresh grave of childhood hath made thee holier still!

A remarkable bit of civic foresight concerning the finances of the cemetery was the proprietors' effort to bar profiteering. A sum of $65,000 might be realized by the proprietors from the sale of lots and this would be used to pay the notes given as part of the purchase price to the heirs of Robert Oliver. Then a surplus fund of $40,000 could be set aside, but all other sums were to be used two-fifths exclusively for cemetery purposes, one-fifth to the common schools of Baltimore city, one-fifth to promote "the cause of Sunday schools," and the remaining fifth to establish a seamen's home and apprentices' library. This unusual philanthropy was a deterrent against private profit and a boon to the city itself.

Originally, it was intended to make the cemetery a "sort of mutual-benefit association, in which lot-holders would elect the management by ballot." This arrangement was not to come to pass until the last of the outstanding notes, representing the purchase price, had been paid. To offset such a situation, successive proprietors have purchased the unpaid notes from their predecessors and refused to present them for payment! There is an amusing footnote to this original agreement. In 1938 (after the repeal of the 18th amendment to the Constitution) the 1840 arrangement for one-fifth to go to schools was used to promote the cause of temperance.

Poe, who died in Baltimore but is buried in the Westminster Presbyterian Churchyard, could in one of his tales easily have established the climate of Green Mount. It soon became a sculptural garden, with obelisks, broken pillars, raised sarcophagi, ornate monuments of every sort marching in disordered array over its lawns and hills. The acceptance of gloom and terror, the macabre and the grisly, was part of the nineteenth-century attitude toward death. It was the age when death had a romantic aura associated with it and its sting was lessened by the trappings of burial and mourning.

Those who left their mark on the physical property were Robert Carey Long, architect of the cemetery, and Benjamin Henry Latrobe, Jr. (1806–1878), who laid it out. The winding drives, circles, prospects, and horticultural amenities are evident today. The plot areas bear such designations as hickory, linden, cypress, fern, oak, willow, cedar, maple, walnut, holly, yew, beech, poplar, spruce, chestnut, rose, tulip, lilac, lily, rosemary, and heartsease.

In the American theatre no name radiates more luster than that of Booth—or more of a sense of infamy. Edwin Booth, legendary even in our time, made Shakespearean heroes part of the American tradition. His brother John Wilkes Booth brought disgrace to a family that lived to distinguish its name again. The first of the family to come to America was Junius Brutus Booth (1796–1852), a strolling player whose road led him across America to California gold fields. When he died on a Mississippi River boat near Louisville on his journey home, his widow hastened to Cincinnati to claim his body and bring it to Maryland for burial. (He was first buried in

Baltimore Cemetery.) At the head of his coffin, during the wake held on Exeter Street in Baltimore, stood a bust of Shakespeare. After Edwin returned home from California, with some of the first money he earned in the East, he had a monument erected over his father's grave. A medallion head of the noble thespian was carved in profile on the obelisk and beneath it the epitaph:

> Behold the spot where genius lies,
> O drop a tear when talent dies!
> Of tragedy the mighty chief,
> His power to please surpassed belief.
> Hic jacet matchless Booth.

It is not the grave of Junius Brutus that the curious come to see, but that of his fifth son, named for the great English political leader who championed the cause of the American colonists. It was John Wilkes Booth's hand that held the pistol that fateful April evening in 1865 when President Lincoln was shot in Ford's Theater. The nation, Booth's family, and the theatrical profession were plunged into grief, the latter two into shame.

For four years the body of Booth (1838–1865) lay at the Naval Arsenal in Washington. In 1869 Edwin Booth wrote to President Andrew Johnson, asking that the body of his disgraced brother be returned to the family. In this his third attempt Edwin succeeded, and John's remains were exhumed and transported to Baltimore. He could not bring himself to identify the body, but his mother, brother Joseph, and sister Rosalie did in a back room at the undertaking establishment of John Weaver. A lock of the assassin's hair was snipped and given to the bereft Mrs. Booth.

While these necessary formalities were attended to, and while the body (in the Weaver family vault) awaited reburial, those of his father, grandfather Richard Booth, and two sisters and brother, along with the elaborate monument, were moved to another lot in Green Mount. Eleanor Ruggles, Edwin Booth's biographer, tells of the exhumation of the children Mary Ann, Frederick, and Elizabeth: "The remains of the children that had lain for over thirty years in the willow-shaded burying ground at the farm under a shattered tombstone (shattered with an ax, the legend ran, by Mr. Booth in his frenzy over little Mary Ann's death) were brought to Green Mount so that all the Booths might rest together—all except Henry Byron [another son of Junius Brutus], dead in his thirteenth year in England." (Edwin is buried at Mount Auburn, Cambridge, Massachusetts, beside his first wife, Mary Devlin.)

One of the last acts of the Lincoln drama was being enacted. On June 26 the Booth family—Mrs. Booth and her children, Edwin, Junius Brutus, Jr., Rosalie, and Joseph—"drove openly" to Green Mount. A few loyal friends joined them. Fellow actors carried the casket to the grave; placed beside it was a smaller box that contained all that was left of the three younger children, all dead before John Wilkes was born. The Episcopal clergyman from New York had not been told beforehand the name of the deceased. He read the burial service, but because he had done so over Lincoln's murderer, his congregation voted to dismiss him. John Wilkes Booth lies in an unmarked grave in the Booth plot, although his name is on the stone with those of other family members.

The story does not end with Booth's final interment. Legend grew, myths abounded about the disposition of his body. One report said it was buried near the old Washington jail, "and a battery of artillery drawn over his grave to obliterate all traces of it," according to General David D. Dana. The author of *Ben-Hur,* General Lew Wallace, claimed Booth was buried under the brick pavement in a room in the old Washington penitentiary, while Captain E. W. Hilliard reported that he was sunk in the Potomac River. And still another military officer, Colonel William P. Wood, vowed he had been buried secretly on an island twenty-seven miles from Washington. After a century, however, his grave has become the most visited in Green Mount and John Wilkes Booth seems no longer to be reviled as he once was.

If the grave of Booth, who by a rash act changed the course of American history, is the most visited, certainly of equal interest to Baltimoreans is that of Elizabeth Patterson (1785–1879), the Baltimore belle who on Christmas Eve 1803, married Jérôme Bonaparte, Napoleon's youngest brother. The emperor had the marriage annulled, but Betsey and her son Jérôme ("Bo"), were part of the European and Baltimore scene for the better part of the century. She outlived her son and is buried in a lot all to herself. The words from Shakespeare on her tomb delineate her life and career: "After life's fitful fever, she sleeps well." Not far from Madame Bonaparte, as she was called, lies Sidney Lanier (1842–1881), poet, musician, and author of "The Marshes of Glynn" and "The Song of the Chattahoochee." He was a Confederate soldier during the Civil War, and his health was broken during his confinement in a federal prison. His grave is fittingly marked with a rough boulder from his native Georgia, on which is inscribed a line from one of his poems: "I am lit with the sun."

One by one, those who contributed richly to the fabric of Baltimore's history came to rest at Green Mount: Johns Hopkins (1795–1873), founder of the university and medical center that bear his name; Enoch Pratt (1808–1896), whose name was given to the Baltimore library system following a large donation for that purpose; William T. and Henry Walters, founders of the Walters Art Gallery; General Joseph E. Johnston and fifteen other Civil War generals; eight Maryland governors and six mayors of Baltimore; Allen Dulles, former director of the Central

Intelligence Agency; three senators; Louis McLane (1786–1857), secretary of state in Andrew Jackson's cabinet; and Harriet Lane Johnston (1830–1903), niece of President James Buchanan, who served as hostess in the White House for the bachelor from Pennsylvania. Harriet is remembered in Baltimore for her ongoing bequest to the city—a hospital for sick children that is today the children's clinic of the Johns Hopkins Hospital. The Oliver family lot near the gatehouse entrance is a link with the original owners of Green Mount, and the grave of Ross Winans brings to mind that this Baltimore & Ohio executive was the first to build a railroad from Moscow to Leningrad (then Saint Petersburg).

The Duchess of Windsor, whose romance and marriage caused dynastic rumblings, will not be interred here, but in the royal burial ground at Frogmore (Windsor), beside the former King Edward VIII. In her memoirs, *The Heart Has Its Reasons,* she speaks of her uncle, S. Davies Warfield: "Uncle Sol was sleeping his last sleep in the Warfield family vault at Green Mount Cemetery."

On a hill, a Gothic chapel erected in 1856, is romantic, almost airborne, with its tiny spires and graceful buttresses. Gerald W. Johnson spoke of its interior "with its vaulted roof and slender, clustered columns . . . in spirit much farther back—back to the cathedrals of the Middle Ages, to Chartres and Rheims. Such a chapel a French king, or a great feudal lord, might have erected for the private devotions of himself and his family." Concealed from sight beneath it is a modern crematory. [Thus, the chapel serves as a reminder of another age, but now has a new use since cremation has become more widely accepted.]

As a bicentennial contribution, the proprietors selected seventy-three grave sites from the more than sixty thousand within the cemetery's walls (erected soon after its opening), numbered, and marked them with floral arrangements. Visitors entering the timeworn Gothic gateway saw the sleeping figure over the grave of the sculptor William H. Rinehart (1825–1874). He also did the sleeping children on the Sisson family lot, *Love Reconciled with Death* over the Walterses' graves, the design for the bronze doors of the Capitol in Washington, D.C., and the Celtic cross marking the graves of banker Robert Garrett (president of the Baltimore & Ohio Railroad) and his wife, Mary, a founder of Bryn Mawr College. They observe the sailing ship on the stone over "Commodore" Thornton Rollins (1840–1935), owner of a fleet of Chesapeake Bay clippers, and the angel holding his trumpet, guarding the grave of Mary McEvers Taylor Tucker.

They come away feeling as a woman did who told John D. Mayhew, secretary-treasurer and manager: "I know I'm going to heaven because I'm going to be buried at Green Mount." As Baltimoreans they are in full agreement with the proprietors that Green Mount is an "island of beauty within the city for memorable Marylanders."

The chapel at Green Mount Cemetery.

The mausoleum at Green Mount. *Photograph by J. H. Schaefer & Son*

The interior of the chapel. *Photograph by J. H. Schaefer & Son*

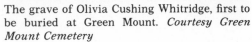

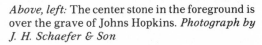

The grave of Olivia Cushing Whitridge, first to be buried at Green Mount. *Courtesy Green Mount Cemetery*

Above, left: The center stone in the foreground is over the grave of Johns Hopkins. *Photograph by J. H. Schaefer & Son*

The grave of W. H. Rinehart, sculptor. The bronze figure was executed by him several years before his death. *Photograph by J. H. Schaefer & Son*

32. Granary Burying Ground

BOSTON, MASSACHUSETTS

NO visitor to Boston, interested in burial grounds or not, should miss the Granary on Tremont Street, north of Beacon Hill. In the heart of the business district, hemmed in by buildings on three sides, it is but a stone's throw from King's Chapel Burying Ground in one direction and the State House in the other.

The cemetery was established in 1660, the same year as Copp's Hill Burying Ground, making it one of the oldest extant in the United States. A barn once stood on the spot—hence the name. The early records state: "The weevils have taken the wheet, and mice annoy the corn much, being very numerous."

Three Massachusetts men who signed the Declaration of Independence are here: John Hancock (1737–1793), president of the Continental Congress (1775–1777), whose signature on that document is the most prominent; Samuel Adams (1722–1803), the firebrand who was largely responsible for inflaming his fellow citizens; and Robert Treat Paine (1731–1814). This could be called the patriot's burial ground for James Otis (1725–1783), who led the radical wing of colonial opposition to British policies and also proposed the Stamp Act Congress; Peter Faneuil (1700–1743), who gave Faneuil Hall, "the cradle of liberty," to Boston; and Paul Revere (1735–1818), the silversmith and engraver whose legendary ride (April 18, 1775) alerted the Massachusetts countryside of the advance of British troops, are here as well.

For many years the small burial ground has attracted the curious because the grave of Mother Goose, she of the nursery rhymes, is not far from Revere's. She was, in fact, Mary Goose, wife of Isaac, and she died on October 9, 1690. The parents of Benjamin Franklin are here, their grave marked by a large obelisk, the victims of the Boston Massacre (1770), and a number of French Protestants who fled the Edict of Nantes in 1685.

The grave of Mother Goose. *Photograph by Clive E. Driver*

In a Boston that has destroyed much of its past—houses and public buildings—and replaced them with a concrete city, this pocket handkerchief burial ground in the heart of the city is a memorable link with the early days of the nation.

33. Sleepy Hollow Cemetery

CONCORD, MASSACHUSETTS

THIS is a place of pilgrimage and to it come men and women from all walks of life, some students, and especially those devoted to American literature and the New England mystique.

Situated on Court Lane, just north of the town square, and reached from Bedford Street, "for many years the hollow lay in natural beauty, its amphitheater a farmer's field, its steep surrounding ridges wooded," according to Allen French, a historian of old Concord.

The newer section, the hollow, dates as a cemetery from 1855, although earlier there was a burial ground nearby. The dedication featured an address by Ralph

The Alcott family plot. *Photograph by Clive E. Driver*

Waldo Emerson, a poem read by William Ellery Channing, and this ode by Frank B. Sanborn was sung:

> *These waving woods, these valleys low,*
> *Between these tufted knolls,*
> *Year after year shall dearer grow,*
> *To many loving souls.*

Actually, the name Sleepy Hollow was given to the section before it was used as a burial ground. It may have been taken from Washington Irving's *The Legend of Sleepy Hollow*—because of its romantic setting—and if it was, the literary associations of many of the dead certainly bear out its name. These associations began early. Emerson sat here in October 1837, "to hear the harmless roarings of the sunny south wind." Five years later Hawthorne came upon Margaret Fuller "meditating or reading." Margaret, that strong-willed transcendentalist who was part of the experiment at Brook Farm, was not to be buried here. In 1850, as the Marchesa Ossoli, she drowned off Fire Island, New York, with her child and

her Italian nobleman-husband when their ship foundered.

The Melvin Memorial, erected to three brothers who died in the Civil War by a fourth who did not, is of particular interest because it is the work of American sculptor Daniel Chester French (1850–1931), who also executed the Lincoln Memorial. French is buried in Sleepy Hollow as well.

It is "Authors' Ridge" that draws the visitor, however. Here sleep the great of Concord, those who created the "flowering of New England"—Nathaniel Hawthorne, Emerson, Henry David Thoreau, and the Alcotts.

Hawthorne and his beloved Sophia Peabody, one of the three remarkable sisters of Salem, used to walk out here from Wayside, the house he bought from Bronson Alcott. A man who believed he would never die was said to have once lived at Wayside. Hawthorne had no such belief, but he did have intimations of immortality. He and Sophia earlier spoke of building a castle on the spot that Sophia selected for his grave. (She is not buried beside him, but in London, where she died.) Along the top of the ridge where Hawthorne rambled, Van Wyck Brooks says of his path there: "He fancied that the grass and little shrubs shrank away as he passed them because there was something in his broodings that was alien to nature."

Hawthorne's grave is near the crest, hidden in a small, secluded spot. At his burial Emerson, who would one day lie nearby, followed the bier. The old guard were all there: Longfellow, Oliver Wendell Holmes, Louis Agassiz. Mr. and Mrs. James T. Fields brought a sheaf of lilies of the valley to lay on the coffin beside the manuscript of Hawthorne's unfinished novel, *The Doliver Romance.* His stone bears a single word—Hawthorne.

Just opposite Hawthorne is the Thoreau family plot. Henry David (1817–1862), his brother, John, and sisters, Helen and Sophia, have only their first names on the small stones, an indication that the entire family approached life and death with the simplicity Thoreau expounded. On the one hundredth anniversary of Thoreau's death—May 6, 1962—led by amateur flutist Harry Gatos (Thoreau often played the flute in solitude), some two hundred townspeople walked to his grave from the house where Thoreau died. They carried bouquets of wild flowers, which were placed there.

Next to the Thoreaus is that prodigious family, the Alcotts. Louisa (1832–1888) has a stone marked L.M.A. and all her family's are likewise incised with only their initials, but Louisa May, the most famous, has her name in full. The author of *Little Men* and *An Old Fashioned Girl* is remembered especially at Memorial Day, and her grave is decorated because of her service as a nurse in the Civil War. Her family are all about her: her parents Amos Bronson Alcott (1799–1888), educational reformer and philosopher, and Abigail May; and the *Little Women* —"Beth" (Elizabeth Sewall Alcott) and "Meg" (Anna Bronson Alcott; her husband, John Pratt, lies beside her); there is a stone for "Amy" (Abba May Nieriker, who was buried in France. She was also the first teacher of sculptor Daniel Chester French.)

Farther along the ridge one comes to the Emerson graves. The poet's own lines are on his rose quartz monument:

**The passive master lent his hand,
To the vast Soul which o'er him planned.**

Those Emerson (1803–1882) loved lie near him for all time—his mother, his second wife, his daughter, his son, Waldo, who died in 1841 at the age of five. Emerson described him:

**The hyacinthine boy for whom
Morn well might break and April bloom.**

The stone over his aunt, Mary Moody Emerson, also contains Emerson's tribute: "She gave wise counsels. It was the privilege of certain boys to have this immeasurably high standard indicated to their childhood, a blessing which nothing else in education could supply."

The Hawthornes, Thoreaus, Emersons, and Alcotts are the more famous, but here is also the grave of "Margaret Sidney," who was Harriet Mulford Stone (Mrs. Daniel Lothrop), author of the *Five Little Pepper* series, popular with generations of children.

In September 1971, on his second and last visit to the United States, R. F. Delderfield, the British novelist (*God Is an Englishman, Theirs Was the Kingdom*) and his wife, May, were taken to Sleepy Hollow on a visit. Not knowing he had less than a year to live, Delderfield surveyed Authors' Ridge with great emotion for he loved the works of those buried here. Turning to his guide, he said: "I hope you will save a place here for me." (He died the following June and his ashes were scattered along one of his favorite walks on the cliffs of Devon.)

Although Sleepy Hollow is a shrine to those of the Concord school, there are other graves of interest here. That of Ephraim Wales Bull, breeder of the Concord grape, bears the inscription: "He sowed, others reaped." Bull, unfortunately, died in poverty.

Elizabeth Hoar was engaged to Charles Emerson, who died before they could marry. Emerson always thought of her as a sister. Her father, Samuel ("Squire") Hoar, is remembered for his protest in Charleston, South Carolina, in 1844 against regulations affecting free Negro seamen. One son, George Frisbie Hoar, was a Massachusetts senator and another, Ebenezer Rockwood Hoar, was attorney general in President Grant's administration. Squire Hoar was adamant in preventing Sunday travel past his home on Main Street. Concord, like any New England town, had its share of eccentrics and strong-willed citizens, and many of them are buried here.

Not far from Sleepy Hollow, on the same side of town, is Concord Bridge, the spot where the "shot heard round the world" rang out. Emerson, who wrote the words schoolchildren have memorized for generations, lies within sound of a musket shot, in company with Daniel Chester French, sculptor of *The Minuteman,* and those men and women who made Concord the intellectual focus of America in the nineteenth century.

Joseph Brown's grave. *Photograph by Clive E. Driver*

34. Old Burial Hill

MARBLEHEAD, MASSACHUSETTS

NO town in New England appeals more than Marblehead, made famous a century ago by John Greenleaf Whittier's poem "Skipper Ireson's Ride." In our own time Anya Seton dramatized its colonial history in her novel *The Hearth and the Eagle.*

Dominating the harbor in its individualistic way is Old Burial Hill on Orne Street, near Redd's Pond. Here are the graves of the earliest known burials in Marblehead. The town was settled in 1629 by men and women from the islands of Guernsey and Jersey and from Cornwall, England, and the first meetinghouse was built on top of Old Burial Hill in 1638. The oldest gravestones are found in the hollows on each side of the meetinghouse site.

The burial ground is recorded as early as 1736 in the minutes of the town meeting, although the oldest known gravestone is that which records the life of Mary Lattimore, who died on May 8, 1681, at the age of forty-nine. Her much older husband, Christopher, was "aged about 70 years" when he died nine years later on October 5, 1690. The earliest gravestones were probably carved and brought from England for it was not until 1723 that any old records mention the presence of a gravestone maker in Massachusetts. It is the exception in the United States to find seventeenth-century gravestones, but if they are to be found, New England, and particularly Marblehead, is the logical place to discover them. Seventeenth- and eighteenth-century stones have exceptional epitaphs and some beautiful carving, which is highly appropriate for gravestone rubbing.

Marblehead's most famous grave is that of the "Hon. John Glover, Esquire, Brigadier General in the Late Continental Army," who was sixty-four years of age when he died on January 30, 1797. It was General John Glover and his Marblehead mariners who ferried Washington across the ice-strewn Delaware to launch the attack against the Hessians at Trenton on December 25, 1776. His wife, Hannah, lies near him as does Mrs. Tabithy Jillings, the "relict of Mr. Thomas Jillings, but formerly the wife of Captain Jonathan Glover [brother of General John], from whom the present families of this name are descended."

Here too lies Captain James Mugford, Jr. (1749–1776), the first of Marblehead's revolutionary soldiers to die. In the summer of 1913, the Mugford monument was moved to its present location by a vote of the townsmen. Its inscriptions tell their own tale: "A tribute of Marblehead to the memory of the brave Capt. Mugford and his heroic crew, who in the schr. *Franklin* of 60 tons and four 4 pounders, May 17, 1776, under the guns of the British fleet, captured and carried into Boston, the transport *Hope,* 300 tons, 10 guns, loaded with munitions of war including 1,500 barrels of powder." Then the crew of the

Franklin, "as far as known," is listed. The monument was erected in the centennial year—on May 17, 1876—a century after the capture. It praised Captain Mugford as one who died "while successfully defending his vessel against 13 boats and 200 men from the British fleet." There are an estimated six hundred veterans of the rebellion interred on Old Burial Hill, most of the graves unmarked.

Ministers' Row on the brow of the hill contains the graves of Samuel Cheever, John Barnard, William Whitwell, and Ebenezer Hubbard, all ministers of the town. Mr. Whitwell's stone records the facts of his life and work first in Latin, then in English. He is described as "pastor of the first Church of Christ in Marblehead" and "he was a scribe well instructed unto the kingdom of Heaven." We learn he was "fervent, pertinent & solemn" and that "he loved all mankind; and was most strongly attached to his country." This paragon died on November 8, 1781, "in the 19th year of his ministry, & 45th of his Age."

On the other hand, the Reverend Mr. Barnard was a "faithful pastor of the first Church in Marblehead . . . a learned Divine, a judicious & profitable preacher," who died January 24, 1770, in his eighty-ninth year. In Ebenezer Hubbard, the "Parish has lost a faithful Minister, Christianity an able Advocate & his Country one of her best Citizens." Mr. Whitwell's stone and that of Anna Barnard ("the worthy and exemplary consort of the late Venerable & Reverend John") are embellished with handsome portrait carvings.

Beneath a headstone decorated with an eagle (almost the coat of arms of Marblehead!), his wings outspread and a banner in his beak, reading "Victory—Peace," lies: "Joseph Brown 1750–1834. Marblehead's 'Black Joe.' A Revolutionary Soldier. A Respected Citizen." And not far away is that of a slave, Agnis, described as a "Negro Woman Servant to Samuel Russell." When Agnis died on "July Ye 12, 1718," aged "about 43 years," Mr. Russell thought highly enough of her to erect this stone, which has endured for over 250 years.

Often quoted is that which proclaims the most vital of statistics:

**Here Lyes Ye Body
of Mrs. Miriam Grose
Who Decd in the
81st year of her
age & Left 180 children
Grand Children &
Great Grand Children**

That of Mrs. Susanna Jayne (died 1776) is unbelievable in its complexity of design. It is a bizarre example of the stonecutter's imagination: an hourglass, bats, angels, a snake eating its tail, and a skeleton with a scythe and laurel wreath, the specter holding in his hands the sun and the moon. Mrs. Jayne gained her independence from life in the same year the colonies did from the Mother Country.

Many of the old stones testify to the passing of Marblehead names that are no longer heard in town: Dupuy, Hawkins, Hulen, Fosdick, Bexford, Darrell, Nance, Calley, Furness, Hubert, Beenean, Nurse, Tawley, Story, Neck, Egglestone, Powsland, Sarel, Darling, Dolhonde, and Rayment. Others such as that of Mrs. Mary Crowningshiel (died 1807) bear equal testimony to the survival of surnames—hers has become Crowninshield in our time.

Old Burial Hill, almost the counterpart of Edgar Lee Masters's *Spoon River Anthology,* is the resting place of Captain Joseph Lindsey, master of the United States schooner *Ticonderoga,* who distinguished himself at the battle of Plattsburg on Lake Champlain in 1814. Edward Fettyplace, Esq., who died in 1805 in his eighty-fourth year, had a "warm and generous heart"; Samuel Brimblecom (died 1807)—"an honest man is the Noblest work of God." His daughter-in-law, Lucey (buried beside seven small children), died "aged 39 years 1 month & 30 days," on June 12, 1757. Perhaps childbirth, as was so often the case then, caused Lucey to achieve the heavenly ramparts at an early age.

The largest monument, appropriately enough, is that of white granite, which dominates the top of the hill. It commemorates the tragic time in 1846 when the men who went down to the sea in ships left Marblehead in eleven vessels, never to return. Sixty-five men and boys perished in a storm off the Grand Banks. Nothing speaks more mutely for this ancient sailing town than this record of its adventurous and brave seamen.

35. Bellefontaine Cemetery

SAINT LOUIS, MISSOURI

1849. NO year was more crucial in the development of the American West. Purists might suggest 1803, the date of the Louisiana Purchase, or that of the Lewis and Clark Expedition (1803–1806). However, the discovery of gold at Sutter's Mill caused the greatest migration westward, one which brought about the fusion of the East, the Plains states, and the West.

At this time Saint Louis was a thriving city, having been founded by Auguste Chouteau and Pierre Laclède Liguest in 1765, and was the center of river traffic to and from New Orleans. It was a period when expansion of the city was vitally necessary if it was to grow and prosper. In 1849 the older cemeteries along Jefferson Avenue —the City Cemetery, the Catholic, Presbyterian, and Methodist ones—were directly in the path of progress.

William McPherson, a prominent banker and member of the Second Baptist Church, and John F. Darby, a lawyer who had been mayor several times, headed the drive for a new cemetery. Others joined them and the committee was able to purchase 138 acres of land that included the Hempstead farm and the adjoining La Beaume farm. It was originally called the Rural Cemetery, but that name was soon abandoned in favor of Bellefontaine because the land was located on the old military road leading to the former Fort Bellefontaine.

Epidemics were natural to the low-lying river communities and in June 1849, one originating in New Orleans soon spread upriver with devastating effect. By mid-August more than 10 percent of the population of Saint Louis died, and it was said that more than thirty funerals a day were held at the Catholic cathedral and at other city churches. The nonsectarian cemetery was put to use even before official planning could begin.

It was accepted practice in the nineteenth century to lure architects and planners of established cemeteries from other cities. James E. Yeatman, a member of the Bellefontaine Association, persuaded thirty-year-old Almerin Hotchkiss to leave his post at Green-Wood Cemetery in Brooklyn, New York, and go West. He held the position of superintendent for forty-six years and at his death his son, Frank, succeeded him for the next twenty, surely a family record in the United States. Hotchkiss was responsible for the broad roadways, gently curving drives (to preserve the trees then existing on the hills), rich plantings, and the abundance of trees, which soon made Bellefontaine the most desirable cemetery in the area.

Although Bellefontaine was incorporated in 1849, the earliest tombstones are those from the family burying ground on the Hempstead farm, which dated from 1817. Stephen Hempstead, a veteran of the Revolution who ventured West from Connecticut, lies here. In this old burial plot is also interred Manuel Lisa (1772–1820), one of the giants of the early fur trade. (He helped form the Missouri Fur Company.) Lisa was first buried in the Catholic Cemetery, and his body and monument were moved to this spot in 1830.

A walk through Bellefontaine is one through early Western history. General William Clark (1770–1838), one of the two explorers who lent their names to the Lewis and Clark Expedition and who later served as governor (1813–1821) of the Missouri Territory, is buried here. He was originally buried in a small Gothic tomb in the O'-Fallon family burial ground (now part of O'Fallon Park), but was transferred here soon after the Civil War along with the bodies of his three deceased children and his second wife, Harriet Radford. Later his eldest son, General Meriwether Lewis Clark, and his wife joined them. When his youngest son, Jefferson Kearney Clark, died in 1900 (he and his wife are here too), he left $25,000 to erect a suitable monument to his father's memory. In 1904, during the World's Fair (held to celebrate the centenary of the Louisiana Purchase), the granite obelisk was unveiled, with ceremonies attended by surviving members of the Clark family and dignitaries. The bronze bust of Clark before the obelisk is the work of William Ordway Partridge of New York.

Clark's nephew, Colonel John O'Fallon, a veteran of the War of 1812, who sold the cemetery association part of his farm in the 1850s (which increased its size to 333 acres), is buried in what is the largest plot—on Magnolia Hill—and which was part of the original O'Fallon farm holdings. The central monument, holding a classic figure aloft, dominates the plot. All about it are buried the numerous descendants of John and Caroline O'Fallon.

Saint Louis is noted for its bridge and its beer. James Buchanan Eads (1820–1887), the engineer responsible for the steel arch bridge (1875) across the Mississippi (now designated a historic monument), also constructed ironclad gunboats used in the Civil War that were especially valuable to Ulysses S. Grant during the siege of Vicksburg. He is buried here as is Adolphus Busch, the brewer who died in 1913. Eads lies beneath a simple monument. Not so Busch. The beer baron's mausoleum is a striking Gothic one, built in 1915 of unpolished Missouri red granite, with bronze gates and a bronze flèche at the peak of the roof.

Thomas Hart Benton (1782–1858), senator from Missouri (1821–1851) and a member of the House of Representatives (1853–1855), who had the vision to encourage Western expansion and aid the settlers, lies in Bellefontaine, as does Taylor Blow, the man who gave Dred Scott his freedom after prolonged litigation.

In every cemetery there are interred those who did not play leading roles in history, but whose lives can be described as being footnotes to history. Such was that of Kate Brewington, wife of William Bennett, one of the cemetery's founders. At her death in 1855—which was sudden at the age of thirty-seven—Kate Brewington Bennett was considered the most beautiful woman in the city. To achieve the pallor that was then so fashionable, and to preserve it, Kate resorted to taking small doses of arsenic. What she did not realize was that arsenic is a cumulative poison. To memorialize his vain and foolish wife, William Bennett erected an elaborate canopy monument for her. The sarcophagus is protected by the stone canopy, which is crenellated and decorative. An iron fence, popular in the nineteenth century, enclosed the grave and the smaller family stones, but has since been removed.

Not so dramatic as Kate's story is that of Susan Blow (1843–1916). She founded the first kindergarten in the United States at Des Pères School in Saint Louis in 1873 and is buried next to her father, Henry T. Blow, minister to Brazil during the first administration of President Grant. Also special to Saint Louis, and the Mississippi, was Captain Isaiah Sellers. This steamboat captain, a familiar river figure between the ports of Saint Louis and New Orleans, was the first to use the pseudonym Mark Twain. As is fitting, the stone over Captain Sellers's grave shows a bas-relief of the riverman standing at the wheel of his boat. Samuel Gaty, the first manufacturer in the West of steamboat machinery, was a native of Pittsburgh. Gaty's lot is dominated by a most unusual monument. A shaft of white marble has at its base high relief carvings representing the four seasons. About it are a series of small stones, erected in the 1850s, every other one suggesting one of the ages of man.

The monuments scattered over the rolling hills reflect the memorial art that dominated the last three-quarters of the nineteenth century and the early years of the twentieth; it displays an embarrassment of riches in its diversity and its devotion to detail and ornamentation. Several of the monuments are fine examples of this extravagance. That of Brigadier General Richard B. Mason, who died in 1850, is of brown freestone, designed in Philadelphia by John Struther, who established himself as a master of cemetery art when he created the sarcophagus for George and Martha Washington at Mount Vernon. General Mason, the first military and civil governor of California, reposes beneath an ornate monument. Struther used examples of the accouterments of Mason's career—cannon, twined rope, topped by a romantically draped cloak. What makes this plot distinctive—apart from the monument—is the fact that General Mason's widow, who died in 1881, and her second husband, Major General Don Carlos Buell, who lived until 1898, are here as well. Saint Louisans like to remember that the widow had the distinction of mourning one general on this lot and being mourned by another on the same spot.

The tomb of the greatest architectural interest today is that of Charlotte Dickson Wainwright, who died in 1891. Her husband, Ellis, who survived her until 1924, commissioned Louis Sullivan to design a mausoleum for her. Willard Connely wrote: "The architect responded like a poet moved to elegy." Small, of gray limestone, Oriental in style and conception, it is distinctive because of its small dome embellished with a series of star patterns and angels. It, said Connely, "bore some further witness to his [Sullivan's] distinction. . . . Both inside and out, the architect once again proved his kingship in the art of contrast: just enough decoration, but of the richest quality, against surfaces left otherwise emphatically smooth." Since Sullivan's buildings in our large American cities have gradually disappeared, examples such as the Wainwright tomb (declared a national landmark), which have a better opportunity of survival, are valuable reminders of our architectural heritage.

The avenues—Red Bud, Myrtle, Woodbine, Cypress, Wildwood, and Wild Rose—all have botanical or arboreal names, as do the hills—Magnolia, Mulberry, Locust, and Pine. Cascade Lake and Cypress Lake are romantic, Gothic touches to the cemetery. No cemetery of consequence in the nineteenth century lacked a small lake or two.

At Bellefontaine is the grave of Sara Teasdale (1884–1933), a poet whose work assures her own niche in the annals of American literature. The grave served as the final scene of a love story that has particularly sad overtones. Sara was born at 3668 Lindell Boulevard, and was to bring honor to her native city in her own lifetime. She divorced Ernst Filsinger in 1929 and took her own life four years later. At the funeral service in Bellefontaine were her nephews, her sister-in-law, Mrs. Willard Teasdale, and the two sisters of her former husband. (He was out of the country at the time.)

The stone placed over her ashes reads "Sara Teasdale Filsinger," as she directed in her will. The story has a bittersweet finale. Filsinger, who never ceased to love Sara, was buried not far away. Before the families were connected, both the Teasdales and the Filsingers purchased family lots near each other in Bellefontaine. When Ernst died in Shanghai in 1937 his ashes were returned here and placed in that part of the Filsinger lot nearest Sara's grave.

Trinity Churchyard is used as a park by the neighborhood. *Photograph by Frank H. Bauer*

36. Trinity Churchyard

NEW YORK, NEW YORK

IN New York, where few evidences of the past remain, and those that do are fast disappearing, no preservationist society has kept Trinity Church and the surrounding churchyard inviolate. Trinity Church itself has been able to maintain its building and churchyard with income from endowments and from the commercial property that descended from its grant from Queen Anne in 1705. It remains an enclave in the heart of the great financial district, a monument to the time when New York life was more gracious, less hurried.

Standing at the head of Wall Street, the church—architecturally reminiscent of English ones—and the churchyard give emphasis and balance to a section of Gotham that is dominated by concrete and steel. Here the past and present meet in lower Manhattan. History breathes through these narrow, winding streets.

There has been a cemetery on the spot for almost three hundred years. First used as a burying ground by the city, the north section of the present churchyard was granted to the parish in the Royal Charter of 1697 during the reign of William III. It was formally granted to the parish in 1703 by Mayor Philip French, and two years later the parish acquired the south section, which had been the Queen's Garden and was included in property grants to the church by Queen Anne. There are many stones dating from the reign of Anne and, in fact, in all there are 1,186 stones and 90 private family vaults. In 1897 a survey was made and it was found that 1,018 inscriptions were legible at that time. Trinity Church has always cared for its graves and these stones were recorded and many recut.

As befits such a churchyard, the famous lie here beside

the stout burghers and good wives of the eighteenth century, the solid middle-class and upper-class merchants, businessmen, and financiers of the nineteenth and twentieth centuries. Most famous of all is Alexander Hamilton (1757–1804), statesman, patriot, Founding Father. Fittingly enough, the first secretary of the treasury lies near the offices of the present great financial empires. Killed by Aaron Burr, vice-president under Jefferson, as a result of a duel in Weehawken, New Jersey, Hamilton lies beneath a monument typical of the Federal period. It is topped by an obelisk, with urns at each corner of the tomb, and a flowery inscription bids us remember that the Corporation of Trinity Church raised the monument: "In testimony of their Respect/ For/ The Patriot of incorruptible Integrity,/ The Soldier of approved Valour/ The Statesman of consummate Wisdom;/ Whose Talents and Virtues will be admired/ By/ Grateful Posterity/ Long after this Marble shall have mouldered into Dust." Beside Hamilton lies his wife, Elizabeth (1757–1854), daughter of General Philip Schuyler of Albany, who survived him by fifty years, dying in Washington, D.C.

Here too lie Robert Fulton (1765–1815) and Albert Gallatin (1761–1849). Fulton, painter and inventor, whose *Clermont* was the first steamboat to make a successful voyage when it sailed from New York to Albany in 1807, and Gallatin, a Swiss immigrant who achieved prominence in politics and business, are two who contributed vitally to the growth of the new nation. Gallatin served as secretary of the treasury during both administrations of Jefferson, and also in the first of James Madison. He distinguished himself by drawing up the Treaty of Ghent (1814), which concluded the War of 1812. Later he served as United States minister at Paris (1816–1823) and ambassador to the Court of Saint James. He was a founder of New York University. The Gallatins were influential in New York business and society for generations.

Important to most Americans, although known to the few, is William Bradford (1663–1752). The stone itself records his birth as being in 1660. Bradford was "Printer to the Government" for more than fifty years. He emigrated to Philadelphia in 1682, the year of William Penn's first landing. Bradford was a pioneer in maintaining freedom of the press. As early as 1689, when he filled an order to print the charter of the Commonwealth of Pennsylvania, Governor John Blackwell reprimanded him, saying authorization should have come from him. Bradford stood his ground in the face of the governor's criticism. In 1692, when he went on trial for printing material of the Keithian Friends, he spoke in his own defense and successfully established a point of libel, which protects each publisher today. In 1693 he moved to New York and held the office of Public Printer for over a half century. Among his accomplishments were the first printing in America of the Book of Common Prayer and the founding of New York's first newspaper, the *New York Gazette,* in 1725. One of his apprentices was John Peter Zenger, whose own trial in 1735 further established the freedom of the press in America.

There are graves of those not so well known. That of Richard Churcher is the oldest in the churchyard. He died on August 5, 1681, sixteen years before Trinity Church was founded. John Watts (1749–1836), the last Royal Recorder of the City of New York (1774–1777) is here too. So is Captain James Lawrence (1781–1813), who is remembered for his dying command "Don't give up the ship" during the engagement between the *Chesapeake* and the British frigate *Shannon.* The inscription reads that "the Enemy contended with his Countrymen who should most honor his remains." This refers to the fact that Lawrence, wounded in an engagement off Boston Light, died a few days later at sea. The British gave him full honors when they buried him at Halifax, Nova Scotia. His remains were later transferred to Salem, Massachusetts, and finally to Trinity Churchyard. The monument to Lawrence and his widow, Julia (1788–1865), also honors his aide, Lieutenant Augustus C. Ludlow (1792–1813). The black, coffinlike monument is enclosed with looped chains, connected to upended cannon, an appropriate touch to the grave of naval heroes.

The saunterer in the churchyard finds evidences of infant mortality, sad reminders of personal loss two or three centuries ago. Walrond LeConte lived only a week beyond his first birthday in 1692. Richard J. Leaycraft died on August 21, 1787, only four days old; his brother, John J., lived to be three years and four months, expiring on August 23, 1793; another Richard J. (babies were often named for deceased brothers and sisters) lived eighteen months, dying on August 23, 1791.

The stone over the grave of James Leeson, who died in 1794, aged thirty-eight, contains a cryptogram, which is indeed cryptic when deciphered: "Remember Death." The graves of the Right Reverend Benjamin Moore and his wife, Charity Clarke Moore, are here. Dr. Moore was president of Columbia University (which as King's College was granted land by Trinity Church for the first college building) from 1801 to 1811, but he and Charity are best remembered as the parents of Clement Clarke Moore, author of the classic *A Visit from St. Nicholas* (" 'Twas the night before Christmas, when all through the house"). The poet is buried uptown in Trinity Church Cemetery. Catharine Nicholson Few, wife of Colonel William Few, first United States Senator from Georgia and a signer of the Constitution, is also buried at Trinity.

The names of families associated with old New York —Astor, Livingston, Onderdonk, and Schermerhorn— are recorded on these stones. Titled Britons who happened to die in New York are here—Catharine, Lady Cornbury (1673–1706), was the daughter of Henry, Lord Obrian and Lady Catharine, and was the sister and heir to Charles, duke of Richmond and Lennox. Lord Cornbury was royal governor of New York, assuming his post in 1702. Every burying ground or churchyard of historic importance in the United States *should* have a grave of one signer of the Declaration of Independence. Trinity is no exception and contains all that was mortal of Francis Lewis (1713–1803). A native of Wales, he was a vestryman (1784–1786) and the only signer buried on Manhattan Island. Here too is John Jones, who emigrated from Cornwall in the early eighteenth century. He was the first American ancestor of Edith (Newbold Jones) Wharton, the novelist who characterized New York society of the late nineteenth and early twentieth centuries.

There are actors here—Adam Allyn (died 1768), comedian; revolutionary soldiers—Charles McKnight, M.D., senior surgeon in the Continental Army during the rebellion; natives of Barbados, Londonderry, Nova Scotia, Sutherland and Aberdeen in Scotland, many from France, and a Dane, Lars Nannestad, who had been the Danish king's weigh and postmaster on the island of Saint Thomas, but evidently fled to New York in 1807, when England and Denmark were at war, so as not to be forced to give evidence to the enemy.

There are the graves of wayfarers—Robert Aire (died 1779), purser of H.M.S. *Deal Castle;* landowners— Adrieen Hoghland (died 1772), who owned the Bloomingdale farm of 235 acres on Riverside Drive, which he purchased before the Revolution for £237; and an Irishman with the improbable name of Hercules Mulligan, who lived to be eighty-five years of age. Nor can we forget Commodore Silas Talbot (died 1813), first commander of the United States frigate *Constitution* ("Old Ironsides"), or Charlotte Temple, whose stone is supposed to mark her grave, but there is some controversy as to whether Charlotte is buried here. She was the alleged heroine of *The History of Charlotte Temple Founded on Fact* (1801), by Mrs. Susanna Rowson. (Charlotte's unhappy love affair was the background for this book, which was extremely popular when first published.)

Three monuments command our attention. The churchyard cross to the memory of Caroline Webster Astor, widow of William (a grandson of the first John, the fur trader), was erected by her daughter, Caroline Astor Wilson. At night the floodlit cross is a symbolic beacon in the darkened churchyard midst the silent streets.

A charming Firemen's Monument faces Broadway, called the "Broad Way" by the earliest settlers. Erected in 1865, it commemorates the men of the Empire Steam Engine Company, Number 42, who were killed in the Civil War "or in the discharge of their duty as firemen."

Most imposing of all is the Soldiers' Monument (sometimes called the Martyrs' Monument) at the northeast corner of the churchyard. Reminiscent of the Sir Walter Scott Monument on Princes Street in Edinburgh, although smaller, it was suggested in 1852 to honor the memory of "heroic men who sacrificed their lives in achieving the independence of the United States, many of whom died while in captivity in the old Sugar House

(on Liberty Street) and are interred in Trinity Churchyard." Many of these victims of British captivity during the Revolution are buried in the northern part toward Pine Street.

Today Trinity Churchyard is a park, much like those of London, where office workers sit on benches and read or eat their lunches in the open air. It closes only two days a year, in January, in order to protect the church's right of way. It is a green spot in the heart of the megalopolis and, consequently, a refuge for birds as well as people. It is no longer used as a cemetery.

Aerial view of Trinity Churchyard. *Trinity Parish Office of Communication. Photo by Eric Hass*

Here surrounded by the graves of the famous, the average, and the lowly, with the church dominating it, the visitor with a penchant for the past can cast his eye on the tomb of Alexander Hamilton and then turn toward Wall Street and see Federal Hall (built 1842) on the corner of Nassau and Wall streets. On the site of Federal Hall stood City Hall (1703–1788). From its balcony George Washington took the oath of office for his first term as president, with Alexander Hamilton looking on. And just below and slightly to the north is the South Street Seaport, where vessels plying between Europe and the new republic discharged their cargoes. It is a historic bit of early America, dominated by the churchyard on the hill, where sleep the men, women, and children who made New York the lively city it was even long ago.

The Robert Fulton monument. *Wurts Brothers Photographers*

Above, right: Alexander Hamilton's grave. *Photograph © 1968 by V. Sladon. Courtesy Trinity Parish Office of Communication*

The Soldiers Monument, erected by the vestry in 1852. *Photograph by Frank H. Bauer*

Trinity Church in 1790. *Trinity Parish Office of Communication*

<

Churchyard cross, a memorial to Caroline Webster Astor.
Photograph by Frank H. Bauer

The monument marking the grave of Alexander Hamilton, erected by the Corporation of Trinity Church in 1804. *Photograph by Frank H. Bauer*

The monument to John Watts.

View of Woodlawn Memorial Chapel. *The Woodlawn Cemetery*

37. The Woodlawn Cemetery

BRONX, NEW YORK

MOUNT Auburn in Cambridge, Laurel Hill in Philadelphia, and Green-Wood in Brooklyn had already set the pace for the large rural cemetery movement in the United States when Woodlawn was organized in 1863, soon after the Battle of Gettysburg and President Lincoln's proclamation of the first Thanksgiving Day.

New York had grown from the thriving city it was early in the century, and was then the nation's largest and on its way to becoming a metropolis. Immigration from Europe increased and gained impetus, but had not reached the proportions it would achieve in the next fifty years. However, the sprawling city that was to evolve was apparent (although most did not feel it would grow northward the way it did), and the churchyards were reaching the point where they could no longer absorb additional burials. The need for larger cemeteries—separated from the churches themselves and on the outskirts of the city—was apparent.

Green-Wood in Brooklyn was a showplace, the desirable spot for New Yorkers in search of a final resting place. However, Green-Wood was across the East River, and the necessity of putting funeral chaises aboard the ferries was a problem in itself. There was an additional situation in Manhattan too. Street traffic had become unmanageable—something we fail to realize today. They may not have had automobiles, but there were numerous horse-drawn vehicles, whose drivers shouted at one another, and an absence of sufficient police to handle the situation. Traffic in Manhattan was chaotic. How could a funeral procession make its way to the East River in dignity, carriages placed aboard the ferry, or ferries, and then proceed in state to Green-Wood? Not only were the logistics impossible, but the time element was too.

The selection of Woodlawn's site must be credited to the Reverend Absolom Peters. He assembled eight prominent New Yorkers at a time when the Broncks (the original Dutch spelling) seemed like a far-distant rural country to Manhattan dwellers to the south. They purchased 313 acres of what was the Bussing family farm, which had been in that family for generations. It was not only desirable land, but it was historic as well. On the southeast border of the property—the Gunhill Redoubt—General Heath, at George Washington's behest, constructed a redoubt (which is on the southeast corner of the present cemetery). When Washington, in moving from Long Island to Westchester in 1776, evacuated his army across the East River to Manhattan, he then moved it north to Westchester County and White Plains.

The Fordham Ridge was a peaceful place of quiet farms after the Revolution. It was deep country; no one ever expected—even in his wildest imagination—that greater New York would expand and grow the way it was to do in the century ahead.

The first burial—even if of an unknown person—takes on an added aura in the years afterward. To Mrs. Phoebe E. Underhill, who was interred here in January 1865, goes that honor. Soon after this, the cemetery managers acquired additional land from Samuel Valentine.

As the century progressed and the cemetery became more beautiful, the desire for burial plots among the rich and famous became intense. One of the most distinguished men of American letters—Herman Melville (1819–1891), author of *Moby Dick*—lies in Woodlawn, although most Americans would unwittingly place him in a New England burial ground. Melville lies beneath a tall oak; his wife, Elizabeth Shaw (1822–1896), is beside him, her stone in the shape of a cross. The novelist's stone, on the other hand, has an unrolled scroll and quill pen carved on it. Their children are near them—Malcolm, who shot himself at eighteen; Elizabeth, who was unmarried; and Stanwix, who died at thirty-five. Their granddaughter, Eleanor Melville Metcalf (daughter of Frances Melville), is here too. (His mother, brother, and maternal grandparents are upriver in the Albany Rural Cemetery.) Melville's grave remains a place of pilgrimage for scholars from all parts of the world. The Melville grave was the scene of a nocturnal meeting of dramatic proportions in the twentieth century. Here Dr. John F. ("Jafsie") Condon, the intermediary in the Lindbergh kidnapping case, met with the man later suspected to be Bruno R. Hauptmann in an effort to recover the kidnapped infant.

The world of the theatre and music is represented by Victor Herbert (1859–1924), the Dublin-born composer of *Naughty Marietta* and *Mademoiselle Modiste;* Oscar Hammerstein (1847–1919), the impresario; and Fritz Kreisler (1875–1962), the Viennese violinist whose artistry endeared him to several generations of concertgoers. George M. Cohan (1878–1942), the song and dance man, and Sam H. Harris (1872–1941), the producer, are buried in mausoleums that stand side by side. That of Cohan has the names Cohan and Niblo worked into the ironwork on the doors. The Niblo is for Josephine Cohan

Niblo, the Yankee Doodle Dandy's sister. The Four Cohans ("My father thanks you, my mother thanks you, my sister thanks you, and I thank you") are all here together in death as they were in life.

A tiny white mausoleum, almost like a miniature Greek temple—simple, graceful, and elegant—contains the body of Marilyn Miller (1898–1936), the blonde sprite who as *Sally, Sunny,* and *Rosalie* danced her way into the hearts of all America in the twenties and thirties. Her name in sans serif letters is across the pediment. Below it and across the door cap is that of Frank Carter, the Ziegfeld star's first husband.

The glorious Laurette Taylor (1884–1946), who captured America and England at the beginning of her career in *Peg o' My Heart,* and had an equally great success at the end of her life in *The Glass Menagerie,* is here with her parents, James and Elizabeth Cooney, her brother, Edward, and her second husband, J. Hartley Manners, the playwright who created "Peg" for her.

Woodlawn provides a greenbelt in this section of New York. (Van Cortlandt Park nearby can be considered an extension.) From the ridge where the redoubt is marked by a boulder, the ground rises and falls in gentle slopes. Woodlawn becomes a park, a bird sanctuary (over one hundred species have been identified), and an arboretum. Walking or driving about its twenty miles of winding roads means leaving the city behind, achieving a sense of peace among the graves of the city's dead. A small lake attracts mallard ducks and Canada geese. Even an occasional seagull can be seen standing on a rock, silently surveying the scene. The rock formations in this part of the Bronx are evidences of the Fordham Gneiss, a rocky ridge that extends southward through Connecticut and Westchester County.

The diversity of cemetery art and sculpture is itself astounding. There are the ornate mausoleums of the past of which the finest example is that of John H. Harbeck, a financier. It towers above the graves and other mausoleums and is distinguished by ornate carving, exceptional stained glass windows, and decorative lighting fixtures over the two sarcophagi within. The tomb is wired for electricity but was never connected to utility wires, although the original plan was to do so. In addition to the fixtures, there is an electrical music box which would play masses if wired.

In contrast to the larger mausoleums and monuments are two simple and distinguished pieces of sculpture. Backed by a small peristyle, the grave of Vernon Castle, the ballroom dancer, is graced by the unclothed figure of a young woman who has completed her final dance and has sunk gracefully to the floor in repose. It is called *The End of the Day* and was created by Sally Farnham (who also did the statue of Simón Bolívar at Central Park South). Irene Castle explained that Miss Farnham took the pose from a tired member of Isadora Duncan's troupe who had dropped into the position at the end of a long rehearsal. The figure was never conceived as a memorial to a fallen soldier. The dancer's widow had erected the pillars of the peristyle but waited ten years to find a suitable piece of sculpture, a "statue that would please my eye while expressing my grief." In Neysa McMein's studio (a gathering place for artists and writers), Irene Castle saw the Farnham sculpture and knew at once that she had ended her quest with "this glorious figure."

The legend below, placed there by his wife, Irene (née Foote), his dancing partner, reads:

My Beloved Husband
Vernon Castle Blyth
Born May 2, 1887
Was Killed February 15, 1918
In the Service of His Country
Croix De Guerre

It was the end of the day for Vernon Castle, the end of an era for Americans who danced the "Castle Walk," and for the women who styled themselves after Irene (1893–1969). Her ashes were placed here after her death, and she also had her last husband, George Enzinger (1892–1959), buried here. In a more contemporary vein is the statue above the graves of Alexander Archipenko (1887–1964), the sculptor, and his wife, Angelica (1893–1957). It is a mother figure, a green madonna, with hands folded and expression serene.

In direct contrast—there is no sculpture here—is the grave of Fiorello La Guardia (1882–1947), New York City's most famous mayor (although some might accord that honor to James J. Walker). The stone, a lovely warm yellowish brown, simply states:

La Guardia
Statesman
Humanitarian

Above the name, carved out of the stone, is one small blossom for the "Little Flower."

Similarly, the enclave where Samuel Untermyer (1858–1940), an attorney, and his wife, Minnie Carl (1859–1924), and other members of the family lie entombed, is reached by ascending a slight hill. An urnlike fountain dominates the crest. Then to the right, a long walk over the slabs of the tombs brings the visitor to the bronze monument of the Untermyers. Almost a small outdoor reliquary, it seems to be a Greek-like monument, its figures protected by bronze doors (always open) on three sides.

A sylvan retreat nearby could be expected to be found in the heart of a forest. This is the burial ground of Robert Louis Levy and Beatrice Levy. The approach leads to flagstone steps, then to a bench beneath one of the ceme-

tery's largest trees. Here in a stone wall—contemporary in concept—are places for the ashes of other family members. It is, in its own distinct fashion, Thoreau-like, Walden-like, and most unlike the usual cemetery memorial sites.

In an age when spiraling costs of cemetery maintenance are continually mounting, and investments do not provide adequate income, certain new measures have been adopted. When a family no longer cares for a single grave, the upright stones are often laid flat and ivy and other plantings removed so that grass can be more easily cut.

The Memorial Mausoleum, where single crypts or those for two or four members of a family can be purchased, is a relatively new addition to Woodlawn's facilities. The various rooms of the mausoleum have names that are carried out in the theme of the faceted glass windows created by the Willet Studios of Philadelphia: magnolia, laurel, lilac, azalea, dogwood. Those crypts on the outside of the mausoleum are designated garden crypts. Nearby is the Woolworth Memorial Chapel, simple and airy, decorated in the most subtle combination of green, cream and gold leaf. There have been over a quarter of a million burials at Woodlawn and the Memorial Mausoleum is a precaution against the cemetery's becoming a "closed cemetery."

Among the 3,500 trees (about fifty are replaced every year) are the graves and tombs of such distinguished families as Vanderbilt, Whitney, Webb, Belmont, Goelet, Gould, Havemeyer, Lamont, Macy, and Woolworth. Oliver Hazard Perry Belmont, the financier, lies in a mausoleum created by Richard Howland Hunt, which is an exact copy of the Chapel of Saint Hubert at the Château d'Amboise in the Loire Valley (decorated with gargoyles, buttresses, and finials). Jules S. Bache, another Wall Street giant, rests in one modeled after the Temple of Isis at Phylae, while that of Clyde Fitch, the first American playwright to achieve international acclaim (*The Trial*), is a Tuscan temple housing his swag-draped sarcophagus. One which is completely opposite in treatment and concept is that of the Harkness family. A teakwood gate in a semicircular stone wall leads to a small enclosed garden. A boxwood hedge follows the line of the wall. The miniature ivy-covered chapel could be found in rural England. At Christmastime a holly wreath with red ribbon hangs from the gate.

Nearby is a stone that is Victorian in concept and execution. The statue is that of the young woman buried here. Only the trained eye will see the mouse—a human touch—the sculptor provided near the hem of her skirt. Legend has it that her heart was weak and a mouse frightened her to death.

There are suffragettes in Woodlawn—Carrie Chapman Catt (1859–1947) and Elizabeth Cady Stanton (1815–1902); actresses—Lotta Crabtree (1847–1924); statesmen—Chief Justice Charles Evans Hughes (1862–1948); nobility—Princess Anastasia of Greece (1883–1923); opera singers—Herbert Witherspoon (1873–1935); jazz musicians—Joseph (King) Oliver (1885–1938), William C. Handy (1873–1958), and Edward Kennedy ("Duke") Ellington (1899–1974); "Nellie Bly" (Elizabeth Cochrane Seaman) (1867–1922), the journalist who went round the world in eighty days; and the daughters of Francis Scott Key and Robert Fulton—Alice Key Pendleton (1824–1886) and Cornelia Livingston Fulton (1812–1893), remembered only because of their famous fathers.

Woodlawn is nonsectarian and there has never been any racial discrimination here in burial. In addition to Ellington, Oliver, and Handy, the polar explorer Matthew A. Henson (1866–1955) lies here.

In a city of concrete and brick—the borough of the Bronx—there is little relief: the rows of apartment houses, the ugliness of urban sprawl, the absence of the reminders of the past that do stand farther south on Manhattan Island. Woodlawn Cemetery, and Van Cortlandt Park, provides a sense of green relief to the city dweller's tired eyes. Here for well over a century New York has guarded its dead wisely.

One of the community mausoleums that flank the Woolworth chapel across cloisterlike enclosures. *The Woodlawn Cemetery*

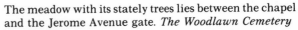

The lake at Woodlawn. *The Woodlawn Cemetery*

The meadow with its stately trees lies between the chapel and the Jerome Avenue gate. *The Woodlawn Cemetery*

The brook that runs from the lake down to the Bronx
River. *The Woodlawn Cemetery*

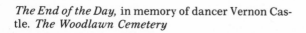

The End of the Day, in memory of dancer Vernon Castle. *The Woodlawn Cemetery*

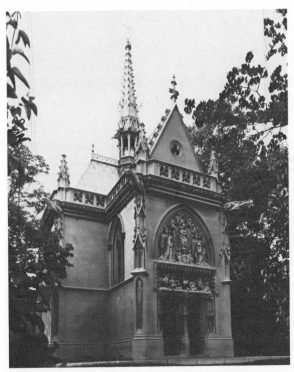

The Oliver Hazard Perry Belmont mausoleum. *The Woodlawn Cemetery*

Bronze doorway of the Moritz B. Philipp memorial. A. Franco was the sculptor. *The Woodlawn Cemetery*

Two examples of the 1,300 or more private mausoleums on Woodlawn's grounds. *The Woodlawn Cemetery*

38. Albany Rural Cemetery

MENANDS, NEW YORK

ALBANY, the capital city of New York since 1797, takes its name from the title of James, duke of York and Albany, later King James II. The date of its name-taking was 1664, when the English unceremoniously relieved the Dutch of New Netherland. However, Albany as a community traces its beginnings to 1614 when the Dutch established the trading post of Fort Nassau (the name was later changed to Fort Orange) on the west bank of the Hudson River. Albany is said to be the "oldest city in the United States in continuous existence."

It was only natural then that Albany would be one of the first American cities to establish a rural cemetery—in this case but a scant nine years after the opening of Mount Auburn in Cambridge, Massachusetts. Today cemeteries are planned and opened without much—if any—civic participation. This was not so in the nineteenth century. A group of citizens of the city gathered at the YMCA on New Year's Eve 1840, "to take into consideration the propriety and importance of purchasing a plat of ground for a new public cemetery, on a plan similar to the cemetery at Mount Auburn." Mount Auburn had captured the fancy and imagination of other towns and cities throughout the country and each wanted to emulate the beautiful rural burial ground on the banks of the Charles.

The meeting in Albany was spirited and marked by the florid rhetoric of the time. "Resolved, That among the indications of an enlightened age, we hail with peculiar pleasure the attempts so successfully made and making to accomplish through the repose of the dead, high moral purposes beneficial to the living, and that we cordially unite in the earnest hope that the citizens of Albany may feel deeply and effectively all the advantages derived from this solemn and interesting source of pure and true instruction."

Thirteen committeemen formed the Albany Cemetery Association, which was incorporated on April 2, 1841. Two tracts of 120 acres were purchased for $12,500. (Other purchases since have brought the total acreage to 467.) Three years later—April 20, 1844—the governor attended the dedication and Daniel D. Barnard, member of Congress, was the principal speaker. It was a civic occasion in which all segments of society participated. The Albany Republican Artillery and the Van Rensselaer Guards, conducted by General Rufus H. King, marshal, led the procession of dignitaries and citizenry from downtown Albany to the cemetery site. Such fraternal groups as the Hibernian Benevolent Burial Society, "The

Temperance Societies," and the Albany Burgesses Corps were joined by "Revolutionary Officers and Soldiers in Carriages." Four bands played, including the Lothian, the "unsurpassed band from the City of New York, numbering some twenty-one pieces."

Once here in the country—for the spot was truly rural then—a chorus of more than three hundred voices sang hymns, two of which were written especially for the occasion by Miss Sarah McDonald and Miss A. D. Woodbridge of the Female Academy. The men were not to be outdone and Arthur Billings Sweet read a poem—all sixty-four lines of it—beginning with the words:

When life's last breath has faintly ebb'd away
And naught is left but cold unconscious clay.

The Honorable Mr. Barnard was not to be overshadowed either. True to his kind and the custom of the day, his lengthy oration was as solemn, stately, and as flowery as Mr. Sweet's poem had been. The congressman reminded his listeners: "Here the dead will possess quiet graves, which friends may watch over and beautify at leisure. Here Nature will put on all her loveliness to tempt the mourner forth to frequent communion with her, with the spirits of the departed, and with God, the Author of all."

The first business at hand was the selection of an architect, and Major David B. Douglass, who had been responsible for the beautiful landscaping of Green-Wood in Brooklyn, journeyed upriver to begin the formal planning of The Evergreens, as the cemetery was named originally. In the meantime, the first choice of lots went to those making the highest bids. Bidders were arranged in classes according to the amount of their bids (which ranged from one to eighty dollars). "Days on which they would have priority of selection in each class were determined by member." Edward C. Delavan is remembered as the citizen to have the first lot recorded by deed (registered July 4, 1845). The first interment was that of David Strain. He died in May 1845, at the age of twenty-one. A marble memorial (the first monument erected) marks his resting place.

The years brought the great and the well known to the Albany Rural Cemetery (popularly known today as, simply, the Rural Cemetery). Forgotten now except by the student of presidential history is John Van Buren (1810–

1866), son of President Martin Van Buren, eighth president of the United States. John died at sea on October 13, 1866, en route from Liverpool to New York. An Italian marble cross marks his grave. The Van Burens were from Kinderhook, a village downriver, but had long been associated with Albany life. Another lot is in the name of the president himself. Near John's grave is a triangular plat bought by the president for Roger Skinner, his law partner, who died in 1825. The custom of reburial was a more usual one then than now and when a new, more desirable cemetery opened, bodies were transferred from older burial grounds. (For a city of its age, it is paradoxical that there are no ancient burial grounds or churchyards remaining in Albany.)

Among the notables in the Albany Rural Cemetery are a number of relatives of Herman Melville, the author of *Moby Dick*. (Melville himself is buried in Woodlawn Cemetery, Bronx, New York.) His brother, Allen, secretary to the American legation in London, died in that city in 1832 and is interred here as is their mother, Maria Gansevoort. Their maternal grandparents, Brigadier General Peter Gansevoort (1749–1812) and his wife, Catherina Van Schaick, are here as well. General Gansevoort, a Revolutionary War hero, distinguished himself at the siege of Fort Stanwix in the Upper Mohawk Valley.

Chester Alan Arthur (1830–1886), twenty-first president of the United States, lies here beside his parents (his mother was Malvina Stone) in a lot purchased by his father, the Reverend William Arthur. On June 15, 1889, the handsome dark granite monument (which resembles Napoleon's in Invalides), designating the president's grave, was dedicated. Designed by Ephraim Keyser, the sarcophagus was paid for with $10,000 contributed by friends of the late president. A bronze Angel of Sorrow stands sentinel at one side of the tomb, placing a palm leaf on it. Each year on Memorial Day three services are held in the cemetery—one at the grave of President Arthur, one at the Civil War Memorial, and one at the Soldiers and Sailors Plot, where members of the Disabled War Veterans conduct the ceremonies.

President Arthur is the most famous of the politicians buried here. Lesser ones are Daniel Manning (1831–1887), secretary of the treasury in the first administration of Grover Cleveland; William Learned Marcy (1786–1857), secretary of war (1845–1849) under President James Knox Polk during the Mexican War and later, in the administration of President Franklin Pierce, secretary of state from 1853 to 1857. (The term "spoils system" supposedly originated from a speech of his defending the practice.) Thurlow Weed (1797–1882), who is all but forgotten, lies here too. The editor of the Albany *Evening Journal*, Weed was a force in the Republican party in his time. It is generally agreed among historians that it was Weed who was largely responsible for the presidential nominations of William Henry Harrison, Henry Clay, and Zachary Taylor.

Dutch family names dominated Albany life from the time of the Dutch Ascendancy and the rule of Holland. When New Netherland became New York and Fort Orange was renamed Albany, the power of the Hudson River squires—some still retaining the title of Patroon by courtesy—continued. (President Franklin D. Roosevelt's family was an example of this.) Early in the seventeenth century Kiliaen Van Rensselaer, a wealthy jewel merchant, was given a tract of land on the banks of the Hudson—Rensselaerwyck (part of which is the town of Rensselaer today). His holdings increased to more than a thousand square miles, extending twenty-four miles up and down the river and the same distance inland east and west. The last patroon to be so called was Stephen Van Rensselaer (1764–1839), who in 1824 founded the scientific school that grew to be Rensselaer Polytechnic Institute in Troy, New York. When Stephen, lieutenant governor of the state from 1795 to 1801, died, he was buried here.

Soldiers of all wars lie in the cemetery. Those of the Revolution and the War of 1812 who survived until the 1840s came naturally in the sequence of events. Those who died earlier were reburied here as the cemetery became increasingly popular. In 1862 the trustees decreed "that a sufficient and suitable piece of ground be set apart to inter the remains of officers and soldiers of the Army of the Union who have fallen, or may fall in endeavoring to suppress the present rebellion." Bronze plates bearing the names of 648 Civil War veterans buried here are affixed to the granite monument rising over the beautifully landscaped spot.

Tastes in cemetery art change. The extravagances of the nineteenth century fortunately remain among the simpler stones of today. They give the cemetery a great sense of character, of time, of place. Possibly only art historians or a historian of Albany's past remembers Erastus Dow Palmer, who died in 1904, aged eighty-seven years. Palmer, recognized as one of the leading sculptors of his day, was also for many years a trustee of the Albany Rural Cemetery. From 1846 on, he worked in his Albany studio, producing such works as *The Indian Girl* and *The White Captive* (which were shown at the Metropolitan Museum of Art in New York) and a relief called *Peace in Bondage* in the Capitol building in Washington, D.C. The grave of the Banks family is marked by Palmer's statue, *The Angel at the Sepulchre*. (He also did the one over the grave of William Learned Marcy.) The angel is young, and conveys a sense of eternal life as he sits in contemplation. His hands rest lightly on his knees, his gaze is toward infinity. He is truly an angel of the Resurrection among the rolling lawns and small forests of trees that meet the eye throughout the cemetery.

Thirty-two miles of winding roads carry the visitor past handsome mausoleums, small temples, Gothic chapels, obelisks, and broken pillars. There is a memorial over the grave of General Philip Schuyler (1733–1804), hero of the Battle of Saratoga and father-in-law of

Alexander Hamilton, and his family; the Saint Andrew's Society has a handsome monument for Scotsmen alone and friendless and far from their native heath, and there is an equally impressive one to the memory of General John Mills, killed at the Battle of Sackets Harbor in the War of 1812. A fountain in the cemetery's small, graceful lake is in memory of three members of the Werzinger family.

With the coming of twentieth-century encroachments to the land, the Albany Rural Cemetery guards this segment of the west bank of the Hudson River, a sentinel between Albany and Troy, protecting the memory of the men and women of its historic past. It has successfully endured for almost 150 years.

Major General Philip Schuyler monument. *Photograph by J. A. and R. H. Glenn*

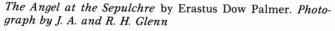

The Angel at the Sepulchre by Erastus Dow Palmer. *Photograph by J. A. and R. H. Glenn*

Soldiers and Sailors Plot. *Photograph by J. A. and R. H. Glenn*

The tomb of President Chester A. Arthur.

The Albany Masonic burial plat. *Photograph by J. A. and R. H. Glenn*

39. Forest Lawn Cemetery

BUFFALO, NEW YORK

BUFFALO, New York State's second largest city, in precolonial times was the home of a Seneca tribe of the Iroquois Confederation. Its first white settlement dates from 1758 when Chabert Joncaire, a fur trapper, established a post on the shores of Lake Erie.

Almost a century later, in 1849, Buffalo, then a growing city and a gateway to the West, could point with pride to Forest Lawn Cemetery, which was laid out in that year by Charles E. Clarke, who purchased eighty acres of land (at $150 an acre) for that purpose from the Reverend James N. Granger and his brother, Warren. The first burial, on July 12, 1850, was that of John Lay, Jr., a retired businessman. Lay, who lost much of his fortune in the crash of 1836, had taken an interest in Forest Lawn from its inception, and often visited the new cemetery. One day while there he pointed to a certain knoll and said he would like to be buried there. When death came, the liberal-hearted Clarke donated the spot to the Lay family.

Although Charles Clarke was the guiding genius behind Forest Lawn, by 1853 "it having been deemed desirable that the citizens should be more generally interested in it, and that its many interests and rights should not be committed to the care of one individual," a private corporation—Forest Lawn Cemetery Association of the City of Buffalo—was formed and secured the ownership and management of the cemetery from Clarke. By November 1864, a new organization—the Buffalo City Cemetery Association—began the development of the cemetery we see today (230 acres).

The setting on Conjockety Creek could not have been more suitable, with just enough variety in the terrain to ensure its eventual development. Forest and lawn, table and broken land, a succession of knolls running parallel with the creek from southeast to northwest, provided an approach not often found in cemeteries of the time.

In a burial ground filled with diverse monuments of varying interest, all Buffalo loves the one to Red Jacket (1758?–1830), the great Seneca chief. A fiery orator and a great egotist, Red Jacket opposed the American colonists in the Revolution, but afterward when the British sought to recover the Ohio Valley he refused to be a party to the contemplated war. President Washington presented him with a silver peace medal, which he wore proudly.

His statue, erected near his grave by the Buffalo Historical Society, has an example of his oratory on its base: "When I am gone and my warnings are no longer heeded, the craft and avarice of the white man will prevail. My heart fails me when I think of my people, so soon to be scattered and forgotten."

Another Indian of note, Ely Samuel Parker (1828–1895), lies not far from Red Jacket. Parker's father was a Tonawanda Seneca, his mother an Iroquois. Reared on a reservation and educated at a Baptist mission school, he studied law. Although he passed the New York State bar examinations, because of his ancestry he was never admitted to the bar. He did achieve success as a civil engineer and became a close friend of Ulysses S. Grant. When the Civil War broke out he was commissioned a captain, and rose to the rank of brigadier general. As Grant's military secretary, he transcribed the general's dictation of the articles of capitulation that Lee signed. When General Parker died in Fairfield, Connecticut, he was buried there, but in 1897 his body was returned to Buffalo and interred at Forest Lawn near Red Jacket, Tall Peter, Little Billy, Young King, Destroy Town, and Louis Bennett, known as Deerfoot. It seems just and fitting that he, said to be the only American Indian who could trace his ancestry to Hiawatha, is buried in ground where the nineteenth-century Indians held their council meetings.

Buffalo is linked with the presidency in several ways: Grover Cleveland was a resident of Buffalo when he ran for the office; William McKinley was assassinated here in 1901 when he attended the Pan American Exposition; and Theodore Roosevelt then took the oath of office in a private residence in the city. Earlier Millard Fillmore (1800–1874), a Buffalo resident, had succeeded Zachary Taylor. President Fillmore lived at 52 Niagara Square, and it was here on February 13 that he was stricken while shaving. He was soon paralyzed and died on March 8. His last words, on being offered something to eat, were: "The nourishment is palatable." President Grant came to Buffalo for his funeral three days later. Over his grave is a stark obelisk with his name and dates; it carries no words of eulogy.

In the move to develop the cemetery, and to create Buffalo's most important burial ground, those interred in the village burying ground on Franklin Square, in the Mathews, Wilcox, Delaware, and North Street grounds, were all reburied at Forest Lawn. Throughout are graves of historic interest: William G. Fargo (1818–1881), who helped found the American Express Company in 1850 and two years later was an organizer with Henry Wells of the first transcontinental express service (Wells, Fargo & Company); Sarah Hinson, the schoolteacher who founded Flag Day; and America Pinckney Peter Williams, great-granddaughter of Martha Washington. Beside her lies her husband, Captain William G. Williams, who was killed on September 21, 1846, while leading a charge at the Battle of Monterey in the Mexican War. The Tracy Memorial features a bronze relief plaque, the first work of Augustus Saint-Gaudens erected in Buffalo; Harriet Frismuth's bronze, *Aspiration,* was created for the William A. Rogers Memorial, and the monuments to the Grand Army of the Republic, to the soldiers killed in the Spanish-American War, and of World War I and II are of great interest.

Here too is the grave of Dr. Frederick A. Cook (1865–1940), often referred to as the "American Dreyfus of the Arctic." The first American to explore both polar regions, the first man to reach the summit of the North American continent, and the first with his Eskimo companions in the proximity of the top of the world, Dr. Cook was sur-

geon for Robert E. Peary's North Greenland Expedition in 1891. He later organized two expeditions of his own to the Arctic but returned on a relief expedition for Peary. In 1898 he was a member of the Belgian Antarctic Expedition and was knighted by Leopold II of Belgium. Later in 1906 he made the first ascent of Mount McKinley, the highest point in North America, and on April 21, 1908, he and two Eskimos reached the North Pole. After his death Dr. Cook's ashes were placed in the columbarium at Forest Lawn and his medals and decorations from American and European governments are on display in the chapel.

In keeping abreast of changes in cemeteries, Forest Lawn has set aside a burial area for World War I and II veterans and their families, an Urn Garden for the interment of those cremated, and a series of gardens: Garden of the Ten Commandments, Garden of Meditation, Garden of the Psalms, and Garden of the Eternal Light, as well as a modern community mausoleum.

40. Ferncliff Cemetery

HARTSDALE, NEW YORK

FERNCLIFF, situated on Secor Road in historic Westchester County, New York, was founded in 1903. In the more than seventy years since, the seventy-acre cemetery has had approximately fifty thousand burials. Many of these are from the world of the theatre, the motion picture, radio, and television.

David Warfield (1866–1951), who created the title role in *The Music Master,* was one of the most famous of the actors to be buried here, but when he died a new generation of theatregoers had come on the scene and most did not recall him. Others whose names lighted Broadway and Hollywood are Jack Donahue (c.1892–1930), often the dancing partner of the incomparable Marilyn Miller; Frances Heenan ("Peaches") Browning, who did not distinguish herself as an actress but whose courtship by and marriage to Edward ("Daddy") Browning kept America titillated during the 1920s and 1930s; Irene Bordoni (1894–1953), the French musical comedy star who charmed two continents; Ona Munson (1906–1955), best

remembered for her role of Belle Watling in *Gone With the Wind;* and Judy Garland (1922–1969). After an emotional and public funeral in the Hollywood manner, although she died in London and the funeral was held in New York, and despite the distinguished careers of the others buried here, Mickey Deans, Miss Garland's fourth and last husband, was told by the director of Ferncliff, according to Anne Edwards, one of Judy Garland's many biographers: "Your wife will be the star of Ferncliff. Jerome Kern rests here, and Moss Hart, Basil Rathbone, and Elsa Maxwell; but your wife will be our only star."

Jerome Kern (1885–1945), whose enduring melodies graced the musical theatre (*Show Boat, Roberta, The Cat and the Fiddle*) and make him more than a star, is not alone among the musicians. Sigmund Romberg (1887–1951), known for *Maytime, The Student Prince,* and *The Desert Song;* Béla Bartók (1881–1945), the great Hungarian who became an expatriate in New York; and Leopold Auer (1845–1930), the violinist, are here as well.

Others from the entertainment world include Ed Sullivan (1902–1974), newspaperman and television personality; Diana Sands (1934–1973), the actress who died before her full potential was realized; John Golden (1874–1955), the theatrical producer who was most proud of having written the lyrics for the song "Poor Butterfly"; Dona Fick ("Myrt" of "Myrt and Marge"); Jesse Crawford, long the organist of the Capitol Theatre, New York; and Sherman Billingsley (1900–1966), whose name means little to today's generation but who, before World War II, was the host of the Stork Club and a power to be reckoned with in New York; Hattie Carnegie (1889–1956), designer and couturier; T. V. Soong (1891–1971), financier, Chinese diplomat, and brother of Madame Chiang Kai-shek; and Lew Fields (1867–1941), that wonderful comedian (one-half the team of Weber & Fields), whom the spotlight followed through memorable routines in unforgettable Broadway musicals, all rest here.

The Ferncliff Mausoleum was constructed under the supervision of James Baird, builder of the Lincoln Memorial in Washington, D.C., and the Tomb of the Unknown Soldier in Arlington National Cemetery. In a 1934 advertisement in *Fortune* magazine, the mausoleum was presented in the most extravagant terms: "This is the entrance to Ferncliff. Within these portals the departed are laid to rest in dignity, cleanliness and perpetual security." Or, "a private room within Ferncliff . . . one of the most beautiful rooms which rival in splendor the most costly private mausolea." The would-be purchasers were assured: "Its advantages over dismal ground burial are obvious. Within immaculate marble crypts, the departed are safely laid to rest, forever secure, forever protected against the elements."

The Main Mausoleum has in excess of fourteen thousand crypts, in addition to three hundred private family memorial rooms, and fifteen thousand niches for cremated remains. (The cemetery handles approximately twenty-five hundred cremation services a year.) In 1957, with the demands for space increasing, Ferncliff began a new building, the Shrine of Memories, containing seventeen thousand crypts.

Ferncliff's handsome brochure assures the bereaved: "The Visitors' Reception Room and Lounge at the main entrance has been designed to suggest the atmosphere of home. Richly carpeted and handsomely furnished, the Lounge reflects the quiet good taste and sympathetic atmosphere which have become hallmarks of Ferncliff over the past four decades [the present management took over in 1925]." Visitors are comforted by the fact that "stained glass windows (many acquired from Old World chapels and castles) soften and warm Ferncliff's marble corridors and alcoves, while luxurious Oriental rugs muffle the tread of the bereaved. All this adds still further to the peace and calmness of this tranquil haven."

Ground burials—regular burial and the interment of ashes—"take place in an atmosphere of unbroken serenity." Bronze plaques mark the graves. Ferncliff maintains these give the "cemetery the appearance and calmness of a lovely verdant park," but the visitor longs for the cluttered, extravagant monuments of the nineteenth century that give the older cemeteries their own distinct character.

Standing starkly sentinel over these flat, tidy lawns is Ferncliff Pavilion, "an inspiring glass-enclosed chapel situated on the highest point of the cemetery. Of Georgian white-veined marble, it rests on steps of gleaming white granite and is frequently used by those who desire outdoor services. Surrounding this edifice are marble benches where visitors may also rest and reflect."

Of those buried in Ferncliff, perhaps none evokes greater emotion than John Gunther, Jr., the son of the foreign correspondent. His father wrote the well-known *Inside* books (*Inside U.S.A., Inside Europe*) but in a long and distinguished career nothing is more enduring than *Death Be Not Proud,* his tender memoir of his son. Johnny Gunther knew he was dying and with great courage and grace faced death. He rests here at Ferncliff. His father's words are his epitaph: "When Johnny died, nature took note."

The gate to the graveyard, about 1905. *Moravian Archives*

41. God's Acre

WINSTON-SALEM, NORTH CAROLINA

THE Moravian burial ground God's Acre in Winston-Salem is one of the most unusual and historic cemeteries in the United States. The name itself comes from the German *Gottesacher.* Quite simply, it is the acre, or field, dedicated to God; the bodies sown here are a declaration of faith awaiting resurrection.

The Moravian church, or the Renewed Church of the Brethren (Unitas Fratrum), arose in 1467 among the followers of John Huss, who died a martyr's death at the stake in 1415. During the Thirty Years' War the church all but disappeared, but there was a small band of the faithful who kept it alive for the next century until Christian David, by his preaching, provided the means for its awakening in scattered Moravian villages. In 1722 a number of the members took refuge in Saxony and found sanctuary on the estate of Nicolaus Ludwig, count von Zinzendorf (1700–1760), a remarkable man who in 1741 established a Moravian community at Bethlehem, Pennsylvania. Salem, North Carolina, was founded by a

group of Moravians in 1766. The purpose of these settlements was a desire to bring the teachings of Christ to the Indians.

"The way to God's Acre" is found on the proposed town plan drawn in 1765. In 1771, when the town was moved from the earlier settlement, Bethabara, God's Acre was established on a gently sloping elevation. Frederich William von Marshall and Christian Gottlieb Reuter, a surveyor, made a special journey from Bethabara to Salem on February 15, 1770, to locate the *allée,* or avenue, which borders God's Acre, and to "lay it off." Jacob Lung, who accompanied them, was a skilled gardener who brought a wagonload of cedar trees. These he carefully planted and thereby gave the *allée* the name of Cedar Avenue, which is still used, although the cedars fell victim to the ravages of time and the elements, and later were replaced by oaks.

The first burial took place on June 7, 1771, when John Birkhead, a Yorkshire-born tailor ("cloth maker"), one of the first to help with the construction of the early houses in Salem, was interred here. The early burials give as vivid a picture of the life and complexity of the town as written history can. Nine days later Peter Glotz, an apprentice yet in his teens who was born in Nazareth, Pennsylvania, followed Birkhead to God's Acre. Others at this time were John Wurtely, born in Wurtemberg; Johann Klein, a native of Waldeck who as Vorsteher, or business manager, of Salem was drowned in Little River; and the Reverend George Soelle (1709–1773). Soelle, born in Denmark and ordained a Lutheran minister, joined the Brethren's Church and was known in North Carolina as the "free agent of Jesus Christ," a home missionary.

A special feature of God's Acre—and peculiar to all Moravian graveyards—is the burial of the dead in "choirs." The choir system has been in use since the time of Count Zinzendorf. Each person is interred in the choir corresponding with his situation in life: married men, married women, single brothers, single sisters, widows, widowers, boys, and girls. This follows the Moravian precept of organizing the community into groups according to age, sex, and marital status for the purposes of worship, fellowship, and study. Similarly, the Moravians believe all men are equal in God's eyes, no matter what their station in life. Families are not buried side by side. Fathers are in one choir, mothers in another, children in still another. The explanation of this is that in reality all are in one family lot for the church is one family; hence the burial ground is a single family plot. They are one great brotherhood, all members equal before God.

This democracy in death is borne out by the markers, all similar and of a size. There are no elaborate mausoleums or imposing monuments here. Simplicity reigns. As early as 1778, the church board minutes mention the subject of the gravestones. In 1780 it was decreed they be of "equal size" and the stonecutter must "cut good letters and the inscriptions be in one language, not in German, English or Latin according to fancy or desire."

Present requirements state that "all gravestones shall be of white marble and shall be recumbent. All inscriptions shall be in plain characters. Raised lettering, or ornamentations of any kind, or anything objectionable will not be permitted. It is required that the stone be so lettered that the longest dimension of the stone shall be lengthwise with the grave. Sizes of stones shall be as follows. For four foot graves: 12 X 14 X 3 inches. For five foot graves: 14 X 16 X 3 inches. For six foot graves: 20 X 24 X 4 inches."

The Moravian view of death was, and is, that each man should look forward to the end of the earthly life and embrace the life hereafter. The word death is not used but the deceased are spoken of as "going home," "departed to the Saviour," "called to eternal joy," "transferred to the heavenly choir," or to have been "permitted to rest." There is no death, but only the expectation of resurrection; no sorrow or despair, only hope. Those who remain behind are cautioned not to weep or mourn.

The ritual formerly used in announcing deaths was a prescribed, time-honored one. From the belfry of the church the band played certain chorales. This was a notification of death and a reminder to the living of the intransigence of the earthly estate. In the eighteenth century a special chorale was selected for each choir, or group, and was played between the opening and closing numbers. The strains of "a pilgrim us proceeding" informed the community that death had occurred. The second chorale indicated whether the deceased was a man, woman, or child, or to what choir he or she belonged. This custom was discontinued about thirty years ago. In the burial ground itself, the Moravians followed a custom practiced by other denominations and banked the grave with greens and flowers to make it appear less grim.

There were, of course, early rules covering burial. The ground was reserved for Moravians, but an exception was made for non-Moravian boys and girls attending the boarding schools of Salem. By 1816 this was amended and a special plot was designated for "outsiders." These graves, however, were marked with stones corresponding to the Moravian custom.

Currently, interments are permitted the following classes.

> Communicant members of Salem Congregation whose annual contributions have been fully paid or provided for. Children under twenty-one years of age, of communicant members of Salem Congregation, who have not connected themselves with some other church. Non-communicant birthright and regularly contributing members, over 21 years of age whose contributions have either been paid or provided for as proportioned by the Trustees of the church with which they were affiliated. Individuals who have not affiliated themselves with Salem Congregation but whose wives or husbands are living members of Salem Congregation with their contributions fully paid or provided for. Former members of Salem Congregation who have transferred their membership to another Moravian Congregation provided their contributions to the Church to which they have transferred have been fully paid or provided for. This shall not include any other members of the family.

There are also exceptional cases that may be decided by the Central Board of Trustees and the Central Board of Elders.

The Easter Sunrise Service is one of the highpoints of the Moravian liturgical year and has been held in Salem without interruption since 1772. As many as thirty thousand people have gathered in God's Acre, waiting in darkness for the first streaks of dawn. Some four hundred musicians with wind instruments, seven hundred ushers, and church choirs all play important roles in the service. In other parts of the world Moravian congregations similarly gather for services so the world family is linked in a common expression of faith. (This practice has continued since April 12, 1732, when the young men of Herrnhut, on Count Zinzendorf's estate, "were of one mind" that they would go to "our resting place upon the Hutberg before the rising of the sun.") As early as 2:00 A.M. the musicians proceed to different sections of the city to call the faithful. The hymns peal forth, the townspeople gather in the square before the church, and are joined by the pastors, members of the Sunday School, and the minister. The first part of the Easter service is held in front of the church. The minister's voice proclaims: "The Lord is risen!" From the multitude the answer comes: "The Lord is risen indeed!"

The minister then leads the congregation to God's Acre for the second part. As the light of Easter dawns, the service continues here among the graves, the musicians and choirs blending their chorales with the song of the awakening birds. The voices of thousands, singing the Easter hymns, reaffirm joy in the Resurrection. Again there is no sorrow in God's Acre. There is no address, only the great confession of faith that is the liturgy for Easter morning. It begins with the admonition: "The day of resurrection, Earth, tell it out abroad." It closes with a triumphant hymn: "Sing Hallelujah, Praise the Lord!"

Today the graveyard is still used by the Moravian churches within the city limits of Winston-Salem and reflects the Moravian pride and concern for its burial ground. (Not all Moravian churches have their own graveyards, but some do; the Bethabara and Bethania graveyards are older than Salem's but smaller.) As in the streets, houses, and gardens of Old Salem—the eighteenth-century community that has been partially restored—the graveyard indicates a passion on the part of the Moravians for neatness, order, and respect for the dead.

As early as April 7, 1795, the church board of trustees' minutes read: "Before the new fence around the graveyard is set up we should see to it that the whole place is accurately surveyed once more.... In order to watch over the right order and position of the graves it was suggested that the boys in the school measure out some graves in advance." From the earliest time God's Acre was a place of repose and contemplation. It remains that today, and the gates, which are never locked, welcome the visitor to this historic spot.

Inside the graveyard in the mid-1880s. *Moravian Archives*

The south entrance to God's Acre. *Moravian Archives*

Spring Grove Cemetery Chapel, built in 1870. *Courtesy Spring Grove Cemetery*

42. Spring Grove Cemetery

CINCINNATI, OHIO

SITUATED where the Ohio River joins the mouth of the Licking River, Cincinnati was laid out in 1788 when Ohio, not yet a state, was part of the Western Reserve territory. When the city was a little more than a half century old—in the 1840s—Cincinnatians showed great concern for the twenty-three church cemeteries that were deteriorating in the basin area. In the 1830s and again in the early 1840s the citizenry was alarmed and saddened by a recurrence of the cholera epidemics of the past. As in other cities, such catastrophes brought about the establishment of a new cemetery.

In 1844 several members of the Cincinnati Horticultural Society who were prominent in civic and horticultural affairs formed the Cemetery Association. Among them was Salmon P. Chase (1803–1873), who was later senator from Ohio (1849–55, 1860) and chief justice of the United States. He had also been governor of Ohio and would serve as secretary of the treasury under Abraham Lincoln.

Cincinnati and the Cemetery Association planned well. These men traveled throughout the United States and Europe, visiting cemeteries known for their beauty and the excellence of their planning. They visualized something more grand than Père-Lachaise or those already formed in the eastern United States—Mount Auburn, Laurel Hill, and Green-Wood.

These plans materialized when on December 1, 1844, the sponsors applied to the Ohio legislature for a charter, which was granted by a special act on January 21, 1845. On August 28 of that year the 220-acre cemetery was dedicated and on September 1 the first interment was made.

In the more than thirteen decades since, Spring Grove —the largest nonprofit cemetery in the United States— has grown to 733 acres, of which 404.4 are landscaped and maintained; the remaining 328.6 are reserved for future development and ensure the permanence of the cemetery for hundreds of years. Too often a cemetery association will find that it has not planned wisely and there is no land set aside for further development. Cincinnati was not caught short.

Spring Grove's great beauty lies in its landscaping, and it is truly a masterpiece of the landscaper's art. Roads wind through the cemetery, forming gentle arcs and curves. If viewed from above, its roads bisect its acreage into hundreds of free circular shaped plots. A series of small lakes dramatize the greenery and give the visitor felicitous prospects to view. A woodland area, not devoted to grave sites, provides a huge copse near the center.

Spring Grove is not only beautifully landscaped, but it is an arboretum with 426 trees and shrubs listed in its inventory. The plan itself is masterly and the specimens exactly located and identified on the arboretum grounds according to the grid system. The visitor is given a map on which the letters A to X are used to designate 125-foot intervals, west to east on the grounds. The numbers 1 through 36 are used to designate 125-foot intervals north to south. To make their discovery even easier, each specimen on the arboretum handlist is followed by two pairs of coordinates. The first appears before the dash in the listing and gives the section number within the cemetery grounds. (These numbers may also be found on the trunks of trees as indicated on the Spring Grove map.) The second pair of coordinates gives a more specific location within that particular section. An example of this is the Katsura tree which is listed: Katsura . . . *Cercidiphyllum japonicum* 22–027. The system is ingenious and quite unique.

A special group of trees, designated Ohio Champions, are nineteen in number. Located in Spring Grove's arboretum, they are the largest trees of each species growing in Ohio. To determine which tree is the largest, the system followed is that used by the American Forestry Association: the sum of the circumference of the tree in inches, the height of the tree in feet, and one-fourth the average crown spread in feet. A boulder with an attached plaque has been placed at the base of each Ohio Champion for easy identification.

As in a cemetery of Spring Grove's age and vintage, the graves, the mausoleums, and the statuary are of the greatest interest. The largest and finest of all the monuments in Spring Grove is the Dexter Mausoleum, a Gothic triumph. Designed by James K. Wilson, it is a tribute to his mastery as an architect and a reminder of the Gothic Revival of the last century. It has all the romantic quality of nineteenth-century mausoleums, and appears to be a miniature cathedral with its turrets, pinnacles, and buttresses. The architect not only conceived a small masterpiece, but he placed it in a worthy setting. On one side it rises from the water, on the other is a green hill—a fitting location between earth and high heaven.

This Gothic look—so dear to the hearts of the Victorians and one that is being restudied and reappreciated today—is carried out in the Administration Building (1863) with its tower so indicative of Victorian grandeur. The chapel (1879–1880), on the other hand, is Norman in style.

Certainly one of the most striking of the monuments is the Fleischman Mausoleum, erected in 1913, and modeled after the Parthenon. It overlooks a lake with its own island. Throughout Spring Grove, obelisks, urns, and broken pillars—other reminders of an age past—can be seen among the trees.

Spring Grove has approached the late twentieth century and the consequent changes in burial practices with the same foresight that its founders showed over 130 years ago. A new five-thousand crypt Memorial Mausoleum—contemporary in feeling—has been opened in recent years and, in keeping with its development as an arboretum, the decorative theme of the Memorial Mausoleum is horticultural, which is carried out in the many wood and stone carvings and especially in the spectacular glass. Except for the ceremonial oak window, which was designed by Jean Barillet, all thirty-one stained and faceted windows in the mausoleum were created by Henry Lee Willet of Philadelphia, one of the nation's greatest artists in glass. Certain ones on the terrace are handcrafted in faceted glass. The windows depict such biblical stories, events, and parables as the Lilies of the Field (Matthew 6:28), The Sower (Matthew 13:3), and the Cedars of Lebanon (I Kings 5:6), the Gift of the Magi, Noah's Ark, Jesus Praying at Gethsemane, and A Grain of Mustard Seed. Others bear the titles of "The Legend of the Dogwood Tree" and "I Heard a Forest Praying" (inspired by Peter DeRose's song). A carillon towers over the mausoleum and the columbarium is located in the solarium.

In 1964 a memorial park section without upright monuments was developed. Providing a focal point in this section is a delightful sculpture, *Johnny Appleseed*, by Robert Koepnick. Johnny was in reality John Chapman (1774–1845), one of the most endearing of American folk heroes. A Swedenborgian missionary to the Indiana and Ohio frontier, he has been described as saintly in his own life, one who loved life in all its forms, and "had a joyous will to help the earth yield its fruits." The artist has depicted this legendary wanderer, Bible in hand, with a sack of seeds over his shoulder. In his other hand he holds an apple branch aloft, as he gazes heavenward.

In the more than a century since its opening, Spring Grove Cemetery has become an integral point of community life in Cincinnati. Because of the wisdom of its planners in developing an arboretum, Spring Grove is visited each year by hundreds of nature lovers, members of garden clubs, and out-of-city visitors. The flowering fruit trees, the carpet of daffodils, and the azaleas in spring; the roses and lilies in summer; the rich autumn foliage; and the evergreens in winter never fail to attract the faithful. Spring Grove is a testament to a tribute it received from an artist who said: "Only a place with a heart and soul could make for its dead a more magnificent park than any which exists for the living."

The Administration Building, erected in 1863. *Courtesy Spring Grove Cemetery*

The Fleischman mausoleum was modeled after the Parthenon. *Photograph by Paul Briol*

The waterfall and lake at Spring Grove Cemetery. *Courtesy Spring Grove Cemetery*

Johnny Appleseed by Robert Koepnick. *Courtesy Spring Grove Cemetery*

The Sullivan family lot. *Courtesy Spring Grove Cemetery*

The Dexter mausoleum. *Courtesy Spring Grove Cemetery*

Thousands of daffodils at Spring Grove. *Photograph by Paul Briol*

The 5,000-crypt mausoleum. *Courtesy Spring Grove Cemetery*

Benjamin Franklin's grave is marked by a flat stone at the end of the brick path. The table tomb behind it is that of David Hall, his partner in the printing business. *Jules Schick photograph*

43. Christ Church Burial Ground

PHILADELPHIA, PENNSYLVANIA

PHILADELPHIA, the focal point of the United States during the bicentennial, has some of the most beautiful and distinguished historic shrines in the nation. However, for most visitors to the city there are four: Independence Hall, the Liberty Bell, the Betsy Ross House, and Benjamin Franklin's grave.

The latter can be seen, just a few short blocks north of Independence Hall, in the old burial ground that was formally opened in 1719, just thirty-seven years after Philadelphia was founded by William Penn. Here at the corner of Fifth and Arch streets, opposite the United States Mint and the Free Quaker Meeting House, an opening in the wall on Arch Street exposes to view the graves of Franklin, his wife, Deborah, his family, and his partner, David Hall. Every year on January 19, the anniversary of Franklin's birth, wreaths and sprays of flowers are placed on the grave as one of the ceremonies marking Printing Week. Franklin—B. Franklin, Printer —is the patron saint of the industry in the United States.

The burial ground itself was established when it became evident that the churchyard surrounding Christ Church, three blocks away on Second Street, would soon not be adequate for the needs of the growing parish. At a vestry meeting held at the home of Enoch Story on June 23, 1718—at which the lieutenant governor, the Honorable William Keith, was present—the situation was discussed, and recorded in the minutes:

"The Vestry being Mett considered the unhappy circumstances of our Church Yard for a Burying place & Mr. Trent & Mr. Assheton are desired to find out a convenient purchase of Ground to add to the Church Yard and Report their proceedings at the next Meeting of the Vestry."

A little more than a year later—on August 7, 1719—the fine hand of the clerk recorded in the Minute Book: "Mr. Robert Assheton reported that pursuant to the Minutes of the 23 June 1718 he Hath Spake with Mr. Robinson about the Burying Ground therein mentioned but the

Title being precarious He treated with James Steel about a large Lott which lies very commodious and the same is now very well approved of and He is desired to inspect the Title and if it be good the Church Wardens are desired to compleat the Bargain with said Steel."

Benjamin Franklin, only thirteen in this year, had not yet left Boston to make his mark in Philadelphia. Had he known it, his burial in 1790 would give this plot of ground special meaning for visitors from all parts of the world.

The gravel walk from the gate passes through plots containing damaged stones, half-erased inscriptions, toppled monuments, weathered sandstone and slate. Some are propped up against the vagaries of the weather. Draped urns, broken pillars, and even a remarkable oval tomb—almost like a large patch box—here and there break up the simplicity of the burial ground. The path does pass, however, the graves of some of the most important men in United States history. In addition to Franklin, four other signers of the Declaration of Independence lie here, the greatest collection of signers in one burial ground. (Two others, Robert Morris and James Wilson, are in the churchyard of Christ Church.) Here are George Ross (1730–1779), a member of the Provincial Assembly as well as the Continental Congress and an uncle by marriage of Betsy Ross; Joseph Hewes (1730–1779), a Quaker merchant who left the Meeting and never returned after signing the Declaration for North Carolina, but devoted the rest of his short life to the arduous work of Congress; and Francis Hopkinson (1737–1791).

Hopkinson was certainly a man of many talents. In fact, he was almost as much the "compleat" eighteenth-century man as Franklin, but not as famous outside the country nor as well known to Americans today. He not only signed the Declaration, but he is credited with designing the first flag (although Betsy Ross is better known for having sewn it), representing New Jersey as a member of the Continental Congress, and he was the first native-born American composer ("My Days Have Been So Wondrous Free").

The other signer buried here is Benjamin Rush (1745?–1813), one of five doctors to have signed the historic document. He is known as the "father of American psychiatry," and his role during the disastrous yellow fever epidemic in Philadelphia in 1793 is legendary. He also inoculated Patrick Henry for smallpox. The other doctor of note (although not a signer) interred here is Philip Syng Physick (1768–1837), whom history has designated the "father of American surgery." Dr. Physick's name is still revered in Philadelphia, as is Dr. Rush's.

Leigh Hunt, the English poet, is more often associated with London or with Italy, where he was a member of the Byron-Shelley circle. However, Leigh Hunt's mother—Mary Shewell—was a Philadelphian and his parents were married in Christ Church on June 18, 1767. His father, a native of Barbados, came to Philadelphia to be educated at the College of Philadelphia (now the University of Pennsylvania). Isaac Hunt and his family moved to London in 1775, where Leigh was born nine years later. (He is buried in Kensal Green Cemetery.) However, six of his brothers and sisters were born in Philadelphia, and two of them—Eliza and Benjamin—are buried here. (Benjamin was named for a kindly neighbor who played the guitar!) Their graves are unmarked, but their interment here gives the burial ground a literary connection, albeit a rather remote one.

Edwin J. DeHaven (1816–1865), lieutenant, U.S.N., commanded the first Grinnell expedition to the Arctic in search of Sir John Franklin; and Colonel Edward Buncombe (1742–1778) gave his name to a word—"bunkum"—which has enriched the language. Colonel Buncombe died of wounds received at the Battle of Germantown on October 4, 1777. Buncombe County, North Carolina, was named for him in 1791.

Also in this ancient ground is Private John Ross, first husband of the celebrated Betsy. (She had three and is buried with her third husband just down the street in the garden of the Betsy Ross House.) John Ross was twenty-four and by trade an upholsterer. The son of the Reverend Aeneas Ross, an Episcopal cleric who was once assistant rector of Christ Church, Ross married Betsy in 1773. As a member of the Philadelphia militia, he was on sentry duty at a warehouse containing gunpowder and military stores. There was a gunpowder explosion, and Ross was badly injured and died shortly afterward at his home.

There has never been another funeral in the history of the burial ground to equal Franklin's. In fact, there has not been one like it in the city since. Some twenty thousand Philadelphians followed the cortege of the aged sage, whose death severed the link with the colonial era. Here he was laid next to Deborah, his wife, who had predeceased him; her father, John Read; and his infant son, Francis, who died in 1736 at the age of "4 years, 1 month, and 4 days." Here, beside him, lies David Hall (1714–1772), his partner in the printing business from 1748 to 1766. Later his daughter, Sarah (Sally), and her husband, Richard Bache, and generations of later Baches were to join them.

Children toss pennies on the grave through the grating in the wall and old men from the neighborhood later scurry to collect them. Franklin, who approved of thrift and preached its virtues, would not have looked kindly on this gesture on the children's part—even if it is for good luck—but would have nodded benignly at those poorer citizens. His spirit hovers over this burial ground as it does over his adopted city.

44. Mikveh Israel Cemetery

PHILADELPHIA, PENNSYLVANIA

ONE of the smallest burying grounds in the United States, and certainly one of the most historic, is the tiny graveyard of the Sephardic (Spanish-Portuguese) Jews on Spruce Street, between 8th and 9th streets. It stands opposite Pennsylvania Hospital, the oldest hospital in the United States (1751).

A high brick wall, broken only by wrought-iron gates, encloses this ground.

Nathan Levy, a shipowner who had come from New York to settle in Philadelphia (the *Myrtilla,* which he owned with David Franks, arrived in Philadelphia in August 1752, it is believed with the Liberty Bell for the State House), was the man responsible for the first Jewish burying ground in the city. In 1738, when one of his children died, he had the alternative of burying the child in either Christ Church Burial Ground or in the Strangers' Burying Ground. Neither was acceptable to Levy, a devout Jew.

Before a synagogue was built the Jews usually had a cemetery, for it was contrary to Jewish law to bury the dead in unsanctified ground. On September 20 he applied for a place to bury his child. Thomas Penn, the proprietor, granted Levy a small plot of ground on the north side of Walnut Street, between 8th and 9th, in the general area where the Walnut Street Theatre (the oldest in the English-speaking world) now stands. It was to be "enclosed with a Fence of Boards." Here he buried his child. Two years later he was able to secure a section of the present site—for the establishment of a permanent cemetery—from the proprietors (the Penns), and it is thought that the body of the child was reinterred here.

Benjamin Eastburn, the official surveyor of the province, made a sketch for the site. In 1740 the second Jewish burial took place in Philadelphia, this in Mikveh Israel Cemetery as we know it today. Although strict records were kept, there is no indication who was buried here first. It is thought that it too may have been another child, for infant mortality was high in those times. What had begun as a private family burial ground became a Jewish community cemetery. All Jews who died in Philadelphia in the colonial period were buried here.

By 1747 Levy again applied for additional ground, but this request was refused, which was unusual with the Penns, who were forbearing toward other faiths. However, five years later Levy was successful in obtaining additional ground and by 1765 Mathias Bush applied to and received from the proprietors an additional grant "for the Jewish nation forever."

During the troubled times of the Revolution, especially during the occupation of Philadelphia in 1777, the British were known to have shot deserters here, lining them up against the walls of the cemetery, a practice not unlike the later execution of the Communards against the walls of Père-Lachaise in Paris during the 1871 revolution.

David Franks, who was a Loyalist during the Revolution and consequently out of favor in the Philadelphia of the new nation, was asked to testify in 1791 on behalf of Mikveh Israel Synagogue—as the only surviving witness to the original application—"to establish the fact that it had been Nathan Levy's intention not only to provide sanctified ground for the burial of his family but also for 'the same to be a trust for the burial place for the interment of Hebrews' as such."

Although it is hallowed ground for the Jews, tradition tells us that a Negro, a non-Jew, was interred here as well. She was a cook for the Marks family and observed all the Jewish rites and holidays. When she died the family wanted her buried in Mikveh Israel but, of course, were refused. However, not to be deflected from their purpose, the family returned after nightfall and they buried her near the gate.

There is also the charming story concerning Dr. Benjamin Rush, the heroic doctor who not only signed the Declaration of Independence, but also bravely fought yellow fever in the epidemic of 1793. Dr. Rush had cared for Jacob M. Bravo of Jamaica, who was buried in Mikveh Israel in 1812. When the Widow Bravo, after the death of her husband, paid the doctor for his services, Rush was moved by this act to write in his *Commonplace Book:* "I did not expect the payment of this bill, having seldom, or perhaps never received the payment of a bill under equal circumstances. Mrs. Bravo was a Jewess. Blush Christians! who forget or neglect to practice similar acts of justice!"

Haym Salomon (1740?–1785), a Pole who contributed much of his personal fortune to the colonies during the Revolution and was never recompensed, lies in Mikveh Israel. Unfortunately, he is buried in an unmarked grave, but the fact is recorded on a memorial on the east wall. Salomon was one of the unsung heroes of the Revolution, and too few Americans know about him today. Aaron Levy, the founder of Aaronsburg, Pennsylvania, is also buried here.

More famous and legendary because of her beauty and the romantic aura that has grown up about her is Rebecca Gratz (1781–1869). Rebecca is buried here with twenty-four other members of her family, one of the most prominent in Philadelphia in the late eighteenth and nineteenth centuries. Her father, Michael Gratz, and his brother, Barnard, came to America from Silesia before the Revolution. They built a fortune in trade, acquired land in Kentucky, and were very much involved in the life of Philadelphia. In fact, the Gratz family—contrary to the precepts of the congregation—is the only one with a section of its own in the tiny cemetery. Rebecca's brothers, Hyman and Simon, later owned the Graff House in which Thomas Jefferson drafted the Declaration of Independence.

Rebecca Gratz fell in love with Samuel Ewing, the son of the provost of the University of Pennsylvania. He was a Christian and, although they were very much in love, she felt she could not wed outside her faith. She never married, although Ewing later did. Interestingly enough, his children were extremely fond of her, often visiting her, and called her "aunt." Rebecca's great friend Matilda Hoffman was the fiancée of Washington Irving. When Matilda died, Irving was bereft and never married. These two—Rebecca Gratz and Washington Irving—remained friends for the rest of their lives.

Later, when Irving was visiting Sir Walter Scott in Scotland, Scott told him of the difficulty he was having with the character of Rebecca in *Ivanhoe.* Irving, superb storyteller that he was, told Scott about Rebecca Gratz in Philadelphia, and she became the model for her namesake in the Scott novel. Years later, when writing to her sister-in-law, Rebecca asked: "Have you received *Ivanhoe?* When you read it tell me what you think of my namesake Rebecca." She lived to the age of eighty-eight, seeing several of her brothers, nieces, and nephews marry outside their faith. Charitable and loving, she never criticized their actions. She remained true to her own convictions and was interred here in 1869 alongside those family members who died before her.

There are no longer burials in Mikveh Israel Cemetery, and few of the thousands who pass here during the year realize the significance of this historic burial ground. A large gnarled butternut tree commands the center of the ground; in spring it is lacelike with green, in winter a skeleton outlined in snow. Small metal markers and flags note the graves of the veterans of the Revolution. An air of sadness hangs over the place; it houses ghosts of the past.

45. Gettysburg National Cemetery

GETTYSBURG, PENNSYLVANIA

IF any war can be said to be romantic, the Civil War—or the War Between the States, as it is often called—can. Despite the death and devastation, the sadness of brother against brother, the romantic vision of the Confederacy fighting a lost cause—in essence the last stand of chivalry—has reached us through the years. What has been referred to as the high mark of the Confederacy was the Battle of Gettysburg.

In the spring of 1863 General Robert E. Lee moved the Army of Northern Virginia, which he had reorganized into three infantry corps, westward from Fredericksburg, Virginia, and then slowly northward through Maryland into Pennsylvania. This band of brave men in gray had a rendezvous with destiny. President Lincoln ordered the Army of the Potomac to follow. They met by chance at Gettysburg.

The fighting raged three days (July 1–3). When the tide of battle receded, the smoke lifted, and the two armies withdrew—on July 5—from the tiny Pennsylvania town, they left over twenty-one thousand wounded and dying, and seven thousand dead. The dead lay where they fell or in hastily dug and covered shallow graves. Andrew G. Curtin, governor of Pennsylvania, journeyed from Harrisburg (where the sounds of cannon fired at Gettysburg were said to have been heard) to see that the wounded were properly cared for. The governor could hardly credit the appalling carnage. Because the dead had not been properly buried, he appointed David Willis, a local attorney, as his agent. It was Willis's mission to select and acquire the land for a Soldiers' National Cemetery.

Those Union states whose soldiers fell during the battle contributed funds, and Willis purchased 6.9 hectares (seventeen acres) of the battleground that adjoined the town cemetery (Evergreen Cemetery, established 1853). William Saunders, a landscape gardener, designed the cemetery's plan, and reburial of 3,512 bodies of Union soldiers began on October 27, a trememdous undertaking that took five months. The bitterness of the war itself prevented proper reburial for the 3,320 Confederates. They lay where they fell and were summarily buried. When the war itself was over and the nation began the difficult undertaking of Reconstruction, binding its wounds and trying to forget the ravages of four destructive years, the Confederate bodies were removed and reburied in Hollywood Cemetery, Richmond, Virginia, and in other southern burial grounds.

The dedication of the Soldiers' National Cemetery on November 19, 1863, has since been recognized as the most unforgettable cemetery dedication within memory. Edward Everett, one of America's renowned speakers, was selected to give the oration. And an oration it was in the florid manner of the time, rich with historical and classical allusions. It is forgotten today. Almost as an afterthought, but as a courtesy to President Lincoln as chief of state, he was invited—with members of the government.

Lincoln, who had requested that he be there, was asked to formally dedicate the ground with a "few appropriate remarks." His short speech of ten sentences lasted less than two minutes. Jotted on the back of an envelope, it synthesized the soldiers' sacrifice, the nation's grief, and the need to band together and unite once more. He captured the national spirit by giving meaning to the sacrifice of the dead and inspiration to the living. His touching words were: "That from these honored dead we take increased devotion to that cause for which they gave the last full measure of devotion."

In a unique way—no other cemetery can claim this—Lincoln's dedicatory address has achieved greater importance in the eyes of the world than the cemetery itself. Although visited by millions in the more than a century since the battle, others who have never seen the battlefield-cum-cemetery have read Lincoln's words. In 1895 a memorial to the Gettysburg Address was authorized by the Congress of the United States for placement in Gettysburg National Cemetery. Erected in 1912, it is the only known monument to a speech. The Soldiers' National Monument, the first monument placed on the battlefield (1869), on the site of the platform from which Lincoln delivered his memorable words, is the focal point for the great arc of graves. The plaque before it reads: "Kentucky honors her son, Abraham Lincoln, who delivered his immortal address at the site now marked by the Soldiers' Monument." The grave sites—twenty-two in number—contain the bodies of soldiers from Illinois, West Virginia, Delaware, Rhode Island, New Hampshire, Vermont, New Jersey, Wisconsin, Connecticut, Minnesota, Maryland, the United States Regulars, Maine, Michigan, New York, Pennsylvania, Massachusetts, Ohio, and Indiana, as well as three sections devoted to unknowns.

In 1872 the Commonwealth of Pennsylvania transferred the land to the United States, under the care of the War Department. Since 1933 Gettysburg National Cemetery has been administered by the National Park Service of the Department of the Interior. Veterans from other United States wars—24 Spanish-American, 71 World War I, 1,470 from World War II, 141 Korean, and 160 from Vietnam—lie about the Civil War burial plots. Some are buried in the five-acre annex donated in 1963.

The graves of the Civil War dead are marked by granite arcs almost flush with the grass. Each arc records the names of the fallen; if they were unidentifiable, the word "unknown" was cut in the granite, beside or between the names of the known soldiers. Before these arcs are small blocks of granite, bearing the states' names and the number of the dead: Massachusetts, 159 bodies; Minnesota, 52 bodies; Pennsylvania, 534 bodies; Maryland, 22 bodies; New York, 867 bodies; or Unknown, 411 bodies. The graves of the unknown are marked by tiny granite squares, containing only the number given the body.

The cemetery is an arboretum. Moss cypress, white pine, tulip trees, dogwood, Japanese maple, sugar maple, northern white cedar, the Kentucky coffee tree, and the fernlike Japanese split leaf maple abound. The ground is a carpet of violets and grass. Azaleas and dogwood are everywhere in the spring.

Simplicity is the watchword at Gettysburg. Other than the arcs marking the Civil War dead and the larger but uniform stones for those participants in the later wars, there are just four spectacular monuments—the Soldiers' Monument, one to Major General John F. Reynolds, the New York State Monument, and that to Lincoln's Gettysburg Address. The only others are a small one to Brevet Major General Charles H. T. Collis (1838–1902), "erected by survivors of his regiment and his friends," and an urn placed here by the surviving members of the First Regiment, Minnesota Infantry, to the memory of their late associates who "died on the field of honor." We are reminded that "all time is the millennium of their glory."

Cannon and stacked cannon balls placed strategically, and a handsome pair of entrance gates—surmounted by a pair of eagles flanked by urns—complete the cemetery. Otherwise, all is peace and tranquillity.

About the cemetery lie the town of Gettysburg, the Gettysburg National Military Park, and the rich, tidy Pennsylvania farmland that has remained generally unspoiled in spite of certain encroachments. The magic names associated with the battle—Culp's Hill, Spangler's Spring, Pitzer Woods, the Peach Orchard, Devil's Den, Little Round Top, and Cemetery Hill—encircle it. Monuments are seen here and there through the trees, at the bend of a road, deep in the woods, at the top of a rock formation. These man-made memorials in the fields and gardens of private homes, where fighting often took place, are reminders of those who died here in a fratricidal conflict. Today they sleep beneath the snows of winter and the blossoms of the orchards as they did almost 115 years ago. The dead are remembered throughout the cemetery by small tablets, each containing a four-line stanza, such as:

The neighing Troop, the flashing blade,
The bugle's stirring blast,
The charge, the dreadful cannonade,
The din and shout are past.

Minnesota memorial. *Photograph by the author*

<

Monument to Major General John F. Reynolds. *Photograph by the author*

>

New York State monument. *Photograph by the author*

Monument to "The Gettysburg Address." *Photograph by the author*

Above, left: Spanish-American War graves. *Photograph by the author*

Contemporary graves in Gettysburg National Cemetery. *Photograph by the author*

46. The Jewish Cemetery

NEWPORT, RHODE ISLAND

PERHAPS the best voice to listen to is that of Henry Wadsworth Longfellow, a New Englander reared in the Protestant ethic, who speaks for this ancient ground. In "The Jewish Cemetery at Newport," the publication of which was at the time courageous, according to Louis Untermeyer, the poet of Craigie House wrote:

> *How strange it seems! These Hebrews in their graves,*
> *Close by the street of this fair seaport town,*
> *Silent beside the never silent waves,*
> *At rest in all this moving up and down!*
>
> *The trees are white with dust, that o'er their sleep*
> *Wave their broad curtains in the south-wind's breath,*
> *While underneath these leafy tents they keep*
> *The long, mysterious Exodus of Death.*

It was, and is, one of the oldest Jewish burial grounds in the New World: The land itself was purchased in 1677. Rabbi A. P. Mendes, addressing the Newport Historical Society on June 22, 1885, remarked that the oldest inscription was that of Rachel Rodugues Rivera and bore the date May 1761. He continued:

This fact will at once strike you as being eminently remarkable. Here is a burial place opened 220 years ago, in continuous use by a large community for a century and a half, and yet, of the numerous interments which must have taken place between 1677 and 1761, not a trace is to be found. Whether the early Jewish settlers, contrary to the universal usage of their people, left the graves of their dead unmarked by any mortuary memorial; whether the material employed for that purpose was too perishable to survive the wreck of time; or whether the old monuments lie buried beneath the soil, among the debris of the lapsed age, are subjects for conjecture. The precise resting place of the Pacheicos, the Gutierezes and Campanals, who were prominent founders of the congregation, are now undistinguishable.

> *And these sepulchral stones, so old and brown,*
> *That pave with level flags their burial-place,*
> *Seem like the tables of the Law, thrown down*
> *And broken by Moses at the mountain's base.*
>
> *The very names recorded here are strange,*
> *Of foreign accent, and of different climes;*
> *Alvares and Rivera interchange*
> *With Abraham and Jacob of old times.*

The Touro Synagogue, named for an old Spanish family that came to Newport by way of the West Indies, was planned in 1759 and completed four years later. Jacob Rivera and Aaron Lopez, Sephardic Jews who were earlier arrivals from the Inquisition on the Iberian peninsula, were among Isaac Touro's compatriots who planned the synagogue. Stephen Birmingham in *The Grandees* tells us: "The building . . . contains an architectural detail that is a haunting reminder of the Marrano past of its builders, and the dangers their ancestors faced if they wished to practice their faith in Inquisitional Spain. The plans call for 'a few small stairs which lead from the altar in the center, to a secret passage in the basement'—for escape."

> *Closed are the portals of their Synagogue,*
> *No Psalms of David now the silence break,*
> *No Rabbi reads the ancient Decalogue*
> *In the grand dialect the Prophets spake.*

At the time Rabbi Mendes called Newport's attention to its historic treasure, there were thirty-nine monuments standing. One had no inscription; one was in three languages—Hebrew, English, and Portuguese; one in Latin and English; eleven in Spanish and English; one in English and Portuguese; three in English only; and the rest in Hebrew and English, so there appeared to be no set rule as to how they were marked.

> *"Blessed be God, for he created Death!"*
> *The mourners said, "and Death is rest and peace";*
> *Then added, in the certainty of faith,*
> *"And giveth Life that nevermore shall cease."*

The names are alien to our ears, yet many of the families were among the most distinguished in America at the time. Some names have been altered in the course of two centuries, others remain the same. We find Lopez, Polak, Alvarez, Seixas, Levy, Minis, and Hays among them. There is a charm in the wording of the inscriptions and epitaphs: "Here lieth the very honored and virtuous Mrs. Rachel Rodriquex"; "the burial place of the worthy woman, Mrs. Abigail, wife of Mr. Aaron Lopes"; "sepulchre of the venerated and honorable old man, Abraham Rodriquez Rivera"; and "Monument of the burial place of the modest virgin, Bilah, daughter of Benjamin, the Levite."

Gone are the living, but the dead remain,
And not neglected; for a hand unseen,
Scattering its bounty, like a summer rain,
Still keeps their graves and their remembrance green.

How came they here? What burst of Christian hate,
What persecution, merciless and blind,
Drove o'er the sea—that desert desolate—
These Ishmaels and Hagars of mankind?

The stones of the children—"the child Isaac Mendes Seixas, who was liberated for Paradise on the 6th day of Adar 546 [February 5, 1786]" and "Edwin, son of Leo and Mathilde Rosenstein, of New York. Born March 27th, 1866. Died July 23, 1866"—are poignant reminders of the high incidence of infant mortality then.

They lived in narrow streets and lanes obscure,
Ghetto and Judenstrass, in mirk and mire;
Taught in the school of patience to endure
The life of anguish and the death of fire.

All their lives long, with the unleavened bread
And bitter herbs of exile and its fears,
The wasting famine of the heart they fed,
And slaked its thirst with marah of their tears.

The Touro family for whom the synagogue is named are together in a plot to themselves. Reverend Isaac Touro (1738–1783) died in Kingston, Jamaica, at the age of forty-six, but although his remains are there, he is remembered on the monument as is his wife, Reyna, who died in Boston on September 28, 1787, at the age of forty-four. Their son Abraham erected "this tribute of filial piety." The epitaph on Abraham's monument, an obelisk surmounting a square pedestal, is in Hebrew and English. In Hebrew it says: "Monument of the Burial place of the worthy and esteemed Abraham, son of the Sweet Singer of Israel, Isaac Touro, of blessed memory." In English it tells that he "was suddenly taken from this transitory state in the 48th year of a useful and happy life." The irony is that Isaac, Reyna, and Abraham all died in their forties. Nearby lies Rebecca Touro Lopez, wife of Joshua, who lived until 1833, when she died at the age of fifty-four, slightly older than her parents and brother.

The most fascinating of the Touros was Judah (1775–1854), another son of Isaac. Judah left Newport—some said because of a broken romance with his cousin Catherine Hays—for New Orleans. He began his new life there as a commission merchant and by penury and a solitary existence (although he did have a mistress!) amassed a fortune of almost a million dollars. His will aroused great comment at the time for in it he left money to Jewish congregations in Albany, Baltimore, Buffalo, Charleston, Saint Louis, Cleveland, Cincinnati, Louisville, Memphis, Mobile, Montgomery, Philadelphia, Newport, New York, and Savannah, as well as bequests to hospitals, homes for indigent boys and orphan girls, and one to preserve the Old Stone Mill (the Newport Tower). The ground enclosing it is now known as Touro Park.

"Some striking points of divergence," according to Rabbi Mendes, "from general Jewish usage, are also observable in this cemetery. Ordinarily, on Jewish monuments, the dates of death and burial are expressed in a chronograph formed from some appropriate verse of Scripture, the letters of which taken in their numerical value, present the year of decease. Here, except in the solitary instance of Abraham Touro, where the date 522 is expressed in the verse, Eccles. VII. I, Hebrew numerals are employed in the ordinary manner, and the dates are curtly expressed, some in 'Liphrath gadol' or extended numeration, including the thousands, others in 'Liphrath Kattan' or abridged notation, limited to the hundreds."

The historian also noted that the word "died" was never used, but such phrases as "was gathered to his fathers," "went to his rest," "that his repose was glory," and "that he was liberated for Paradise." Judaism recognizes this world as a place of temporary abode to be succeeded by a reunion in another and higher sphere. This belief is emphasized in the lines that begin or terminate each epitaph, for example: "May his soul be bound in the hands of life." Some of the stones themselves are of the eighteenth-century slate variety, decorated with angels, the Hebraic legend below.

It was for Longfellow to pronounce the final benediction, to write the last epitaph:

But ah! what once has been shall be no more!
The groaning earth in travail and in pain
Brings forth its races, but does not restore,
And the dead nations never rise again.

47. Swan Point Cemetery

PROVIDENCE, RHODE ISLAND

A picturesque river provides the ideal setting for any cemetery. In Richmond, Virginia, the James establishes the prospect romantically for Hollywood Cemetery. In Providence, Rhode Island, the Seekonk River plays the same role in relation to Swan Point Cemetery. (The river rises as the Blackstone in central Massachusetts. Passing Worcester and Woonsocket as the Blackstone, it then assumes its Indian name at Pawtucket.)

Now an estate of some two hundred acres, Swan Point began modestly enough in 1846 on a sixty-acre tract of land bordering the so-called Neck Road and extending easterly to the riverbank. In the following year the Swan Point Cemetery Company was chartered. (It was rechartered in 1858 as a nonprofit corporation, The Proprietors of Swan Point Cemetery. It is also nonsectarian.)

In the mid-nineteenth century cemetery corporations or proprietors were generally civic-minded men who were desirous of developing a cemetery that would be a point of community pride. This was so in Providence and from time to time the cemetery acquired additional land between the Neck Road and the river. By 1862 expansion commenced westward with the purchase of farms and other properties and Swan Point extended as far as Hope Street.

During this time, the initial stages of development, which was to make it a handsome rural cemetery, began.

In 1886 to provide even easier means of access to the expanded property, the directors engaged a landscape architect, H. W. S. Cleveland of Chicago, and it was he who planned the layout of Blackstone Boulevard (constructed in 1894). Prior to its construction, the cemetery deeded the city a strip of land two hundred feet wide through its grounds. A mile and one-half boulder wall—one of the unique features of the cemetery today—was completed in 1900 along the east side of the boulevard, bounding the grounds on the west and north, and a new entrance established.

In an age that has bade farewell to the trolley car, it is pleasant to recall that the Butler Avenue trolley line was extended over Blackstone Boulevard to Swan Point in 1903, and a fieldstone shelter for riders erected opposite the cemetery entrance at the cemetery's expense. In that innocent age, Americans had not come to have the psychological fear of death they developed in the Age of Anxiety. It was a common family practice to visit the cemetery, pay homage to one's forebears, and then leisurely stroll about admiring the monuments and the vistas.

The landscaping at Swan Point is memorable: a pleasant combination of lawns and drives, growths of forest trees, and an equally luxurious undergrowth of laurel, rhododendron, azaleas, and other flowering shrubs.

(There are 255 different varieties of trees and shrubs.) Swan Point is noted for its tulip shows in the spring and its chrysanthemum shows in the fall, which were introduced by Francis H. Hamilton, who was in a management position for twenty years, beginning in 1952. Steep banks and ravines by the riverside provide striking contrasts to the open vistas of the surrounding countryside.

Swan Point is not only a horticulturist's paradise; it has a collection of superb monuments and memorials that reflect the attitudes of the city of Providence and its esthetic sensibilities in the Victorian age, as well as its wealth and confidence in its position.

Among the memorials that strike the visitor's fancy is one erected in 1850 on the First Congregational Society's ground, marking a spot quaintly known as "Pastors' Rest." Its inscriptions record much of interest concerning the early burial places of the society. Equally charming is the stone seat located on Rhododendron Path, designed by Norman M. Isham. Placed there in 1910, its inscription records: "This resting place for the people is erected as a loving tribute to Alfred Stone, F.A.I.A., in appreciation of his ability as an architect, his service as a citizen, and his character as a man, by his associates in the Rhode Island Chapter of the American Institute of Architects, May 1, 1910."

The Sayles family, plunged into grief at the death of a scholarly son, did not resort to the broken column, so popular at that time for one whose life was cut short early. Seated in a miniature temple is a bronze figure of the youth. He is reading, which is appropriate for one who was a student at Brown University at the time of his death.

Amasa Sprague, whose name is the only one inscribed in his family plot, was important in Providence: He was the father of one governor, the brother of another. (There are twenty-three former governors of Rhode Island buried here.)

In the past, members of a family visited a cemetery for familial reasons. In the twentieth century most cemeteries are places of pilgrimage for those who, in essence, form a cult. Those who admire a writer, artist, or statesman make the journey in an effort to achieve some communion with the long-revered deceased. H. P. Lovecraft (1890–1937), a pioneer in the art of science fiction, was for many years after his death an underground figure, one, like Anaïs Nin, whose work was known to the few but who has of late come into his own. The author of novels and short stories of a Gothic cast, which appeared in the pulp magazines during his lifetime, he is buried at Swan Point and was recently the subject of a full-length biography.

One should not fail to pause before the natural pond (acquired in 1862), which is among the graves. In 1878 two boulders were placed there. Through one a graceful spray of water, supplying the pond, emphasizes the cemetery's melding of earth, water, and sky. Water lilies complement the gentle jet that reaches heavenward.

About the same time (1876) the Pawtuxet Water System was extended to the cemetery. Not long afterward a fountain—a sculpture of a boy and girl beneath an umbrella, charmingly Victorian, unashamedly sentimental—was placed at Swan Point. It remained here until 1967 when it mysteriously disappeared. Providence missed the youthful pair beneath the umbrella and since then one similar to the original has been installed in a courtyard at the rear of the office complex.

Although it has served Providence for over 130 years now, Swan Point is as up to date as tomorrow. Two columbaria and a mausoleum, contemporary in design yet in complete harmony with their surroundings, have in recent years been added as have facilities for cremation. The mausoleum was designed with Weymouth granite end facings, and the exterior crypt fronts are red granite. The interior crypt fronts are of Perlatto marble from Italy.

In the older section near the river are many ancient stones marking the graves of generations of citizens originally interred in early Providence burial grounds. Many of these, more than a century older than Swan Point, were moved here when the newer cemetery opened. Three—the Union, Hope, and Manchester grounds—were acquired by Swan Point and the interred remains removed here between 1859 and 1882. The First Congregational Society (now the First Unitarian Society) transferred remains from the West Burial Ground (a group of private cemeteries), which had been owned by that society since 1785. These also included graves from an earlier burial ground established in 1722.

The boulder at the entrance—a New England landmark proclaiming to all that this is Swan Point Cemetery—typifies the strength of New England character, which is apparent in its smallest state.

The Chapel and Administration Building.

The Mausoleum, Swan Point Cemetery.

The Columbaria, Swan Point Cemetery.

48. Arlington National Cemetery

ARLINGTON, VIRGINIA

ARLINGTON'S history as recorded property extends back three hundred years. Few who admire the beautifully landscaped valhalla conceive that the land itself was originally part of a tract of six thousand acres granted in 1669 by the royal governor of Virginia, Sir William Berkeley, to Robert Howsing, a ship's captain. The grant itself was in gratitude for Captain Howsing's transporting settlers to the colony. Howsing, who evidently preferred the sea to land, soon sold his acreage to John Alexander for a mere six hogsheads of tobacco. However, it must be remembered that tobacco was a very salable commodity on the London wharves in the seventeenth century.

The Alexander family retained the property until 1778 when John Parke Custis, son of Martha Washington by her first marriage to Daniel Parke Custis, purchased 1,100 acres (the land now comprising Arlington Cemetery and the Fort Meyer Military Reservation). When John, aide-de-camp to Washington, died during the siege of Yorktown in 1781, two of his four children (Washington's step-grandchildren)—George Washington Parke Custis

and Eleanor Parke Custis—were adopted by George and Martha Washington. These are the children shown in the often-reproduced portrait by John Trumbull of the Washington family.

Following Martha Washington's death in 1802, George Custis (1781–1857) inherited Mount Vernon and the Washington memorabilia there. He, of course, also owned the Custis estate, which he first named Mount Washington. In order to house the mementos properly, in 1804 he began to build Arlington House overlooking the Potomac with a prospect of the new city of Washington in the distance. The name Arlington House was taken from the original property of the Custis family on the eastern shore of Virginia. (It, in turn, had been named for the Earl of Arlington, from whom the founder of the Custis family in America had received his original grant.)

The inheritance of the land is in itself an interesting chapter in American history, linking two of the nation's most historic families. George Custis and his wife, Mary Lee Fitzhugh, had only one child—Mary Ann Randolph

The amphitheatre at the Tomb of the Unknown Soldier. *American Airlines photograph*

Custis, born in 1808—who survived to maturity. Through her marriage in 1831 to Lieutenant Robert E. Lee, the Washington and Lee families became one. When George Washington Parke Custis died in 1857 he reverted to the English form of bequeathing property to succeeding generations. General and Mrs. Lee were given life tenancy to Arlington House and the estate; at their deaths it was to go to their son, George Washington Custis Lee. On the eve of the Civil War this then was the state of ownership of the Arlington property.

The house—a fine example of Greek Revival—had been a center of the gracious living associated with the Old Dominion in antebellum days. Robert E. Lee, although only a trustee of the estate, cherished it for its Washington associations. Lee, recognized as one of the most able young officers in the army (he was a graduate of West Point), was offered command of the Union army of the Potomac by the aged General Winfield Scott. Torn between his loyalty to his country and to his state, he refused, intending to serve neither. He returned to Arlington House on April 18, 1861. (On April 14 Fort Sumter

had been fired on.) Two days later he resigned his commission in the army, saying: "Save in the defense of my Native State, I never desire again to draw my Sword."

With war at hand and the Union armies just across the Potomac, the Lee family fled from Arlington House, removing their heirlooms—silver, furniture, paintings—to another estate they owned in Virginia. When Virginia—a border state and neutral until called upon to invade other southern states—withdrew from the Union in 1861, she did not immediately become part of the Confederacy. Later, when Virginia was drawn into the conflict, Robert E. Lee accepted command of the Confederate forces. Mrs. Lee was unable to unpack the Washington artifacts and once the house was occupied by Union forces looting began and many priceless Washington articles disappeared. Finally, in an effort to protect them, General Irvin McDowell deposited them in the Patent Office in Washington until the end of the war.

No member of the Lee family was to live in Arlington House again. The government took possession of the land under the "Act for the Collection of Direct Taxes in the Insurrectionary Districts within the United States" in 1862. The taxes on the estate were small—$92.07 and penalties. Mrs. Lee (who was living within Confederate lines) attempted to pay them through an agent. The commissioners appointed to collect the taxes were adamant, saying she must pay them in person. This she could not do, and on January 11, 1864, the commissioners bid in the estate to the federal government at an evaluation of $26,800 "for Government use, for war, military, charitable and educational purposes." Thus, Arlington House and its surrounding property became one of the spoils of war.

Its story—and fate—might have been different except for the jealousy of General Lee by Brigadier General Montgomery C. Meigs, quartermaster general. Secretary of State Edwin M. Stanton in 1864 instructed Meigs to select possible sites for a military cemetery. Meigs chose only one—Arlington House, knowing that once interments began it would be impossible for the Lee family to regain their estate.

Almost sixty years after George Washington Parke Custis began the building of Arlington House, this link with the Washington family was appropriated by the federal government and on May 13, 1864 the first burial took place—that of Private William Christman, Company G, 67th Pennsylvania Infantry. His, however, was not the first burial on the property. In 1828 Mary Randolph, a cousin of Mary Lee Fitzhugh Custis, was buried on the grounds as was the custom on southern estates. In time George Washington Parke Custis and Mary Lee Fitzhugh Custis joined her in this family burial ground.

Once a beginning had been made there was no turning the tide. Burials from the military hospitals in Washington and Alexandria began, and in an effort to ensure that the Lees could never return, Meigs permitted burials in the rose garden, practically to the doors of the house. (Ironically, Meigs is buried in Arlington.)

More than nineteen thousand Union dead were interred in Arlington. The bodies of others than those hospital deaths were gathered from the Virginia battlefields of Bull Run, Bristoe Station, Chantilly, and Aldie. Others were brought here from abandoned cemeteries of the District of Columbia, from other sections of Maryland and Virginia, and from the military post cemetery at Point Lookout, Maryland. An impressive monument by Sir Moses Ezekiel—himself interred in Arlington—was raised with money collected by the United Daughters of the Confederacy. The scars of war were healing, but they healed slowly. It has been said that the Confederate stones all came to a sharp point so that no Yankee could sit on them! As the custom of Memorial Day (Decoration Day) became more accepted nationally, both sides decorated the graves of their former enemies.

The Lees—in particular George Washington Custis Lee, to whom the estate had been left—were heard from once more, and with justification. Robert E. Lee died in 1870. (He is not buried at Arlington, but in the chapel of Washington and Lee University, Lexington, Virginia.) Mrs. Lee, daughter of George Washington Parke Custis,

died three years later. George Washington Custis Lee had been a major general in the army of the Confederacy. In 1877 he brought suit against the government to regain possession of Arlington, basing this claim on his grandfather's will. The case dragged on during five years of litigation and finally, in 1882, the Supreme Court declared George Washington Custis Lee the legal owner. The United States government was for all purposes a trespasser.

The situation was further complicated by the fact that during this time additional thousands had been buried at Arlington (and some of the estate had been developed as Fort Meyer). Arlington House (which had served as the office and living quarters of the cemetery superintendent) and the estate would never regain its former glory as a residence. Now its destiny lay not with the living but with the dead. George Washington Custis Lee resolved the situation when he accepted $150,000 as full compensation for the estate. Congress appropriated funds for the purchase on March 3, 1883. On March 31 Mr. Lee signed the deed and the government legally acquired title to the estate. The last connection with the Lee and Washington families was severed, and from that time on only memory would link Arlington National Cemetery with those two American families.

Arlington is the pantheon of United States heroes. Bodies of veterans of the Revolution, the War of 1812, and the Mexican War were brought here for burial alongside those of the Civil War. There is a Spanish-American War monument and one from the same conflict for the Spanish War Nurses. By Act of Congress, May 9, 1910, the mast of the U.S.S. *Maine,* the sinking of which in Havana harbor had precipitated the Spanish-American War, was raised and brought to Arlington to honor those who lost their lives in the explosion.

In the *Maine* section are the bodies of 229 men who died on the battleship—167 unknown and 62 known. Their names are inscribed on the memorial. Another hero—Ignace Jan Paderewski (1860–1941), pianist and premier of Poland—is buried at the base of the *Maine* monument. Technically, Paderewski is not buried here; he is lying in state, his body awaiting the day Poland is once again free. Then it will be returned to his homeland as was that of Manuel Quezon (1878–1944), first president of the Commonwealth of the Philippines, which once lay near Paderewski.

One of the most moving burials in Arlington was that of the Unknown Soldier of World War I, whose body was brought back from France in 1921 aboard the *Olympia,* Admiral Dewey's flagship at the Battle of Manila Bay. Sergeant Edward Younger, who had been wounded in the war, was chosen to select the body. He entered the City Hall at Châlons-sur-Marne, France, alone. There four caskets brought from the military cemeteries at Aisne-Marne, Meuse-Argonne, Somme, and Saint-Mihiel were side by side. Sergeant Younger, with a spray of white roses in his hand, after circling the caskets three times, finally laid the roses on one. The body of this unknown American was returned from France with the highest honors both nations could confer on it—a French government official pinned the Legion of Honor on the flag covering the coffin before *Olympia* moved out of the harbor of Le Havre. President Harding, General of the Armies John J. Pershing, and Americans from all walks of life gathered at Arlington on November 11, 1921, to honor their fallen comrade. The sarcophagus of white Colorado marble (erected in 1932) bears the eloquent inscription:

**Here Rests in
Honored Glory
An American
Soldier
Known But to God**

Since then an Unknown Soldier of World War II and one from Korea have joined him.

Some of the military and naval great who lie in Arlington include General Philip Sheridan (1831–1888); Admiral David Porter (1780–1843); Major Walter Reed (1851–1902), whose work on yellow fever was a landmark in the history of medicine; Rear Admiral Robert E. Peary (1856–1920), the first to reach the North Pole (1909); Admiral Richard E. Byrd (1888–1957), whose works in "Little America" at Antarctica was instrumental in the development of that polar continent; and those men whose names read like a roster of World War II: General of the Air Force Henry A. Arnold (1886–1950), Lieutenant General Claire Lee Chennault (1890–1958), General Jonathan M. Wainwright (1883–1953), Fleet Admiral William F. Halsey, Jr. (1882–1959), Admiral William D. Leahy (1875–1959), and General of the Army George C. Marshall (1880–1959). Here too are James V. Forrestal (1892–1949), first secretary of defense (1947–1949), and the astronauts Lieutenant Commander Roger B. Chaffee (1935–1967) and Lieutenant Colonel Virgil I. Grissom (1926–1967).

From the beginning Arlington had acceptance. Abner Doubleday (1819–1893), known as the creator of baseball but better known in his lifetime as a Civil War officer was interred here as were Robert Todd Lincoln (1843–1926), the only surviving son of Abraham Lincoln and himself secretary of war under President James A. Garfield, and Oliver Wendell Holmes, Jr. (1841–1935), the redoubtable Yankee from Olympus who was known as the "great dissenter" in his thirty years (1902–1932) as an associate justice of the Supreme Court.

William Howard Taft (1857–1930), twenty-seventh president of the United States and later chief justice of the Supreme Court, was the first chief executive to be buried at Arlington. In 1943 Helen Herndon Taft was buried beside her husband, the only First Lady to be interred here. Mary Roberts Rinehart (1876–1958), whose mysteries endeared her to several generations of Americans, and Dr. Anita Newcomb Magee, founder of the Army Nurses Corps, are two other women of note who lie in Arlington. The list is unending. Major Pierre Charles L'Enfant (1754–1825), the Frenchman who served as a private in the Revolution and whose plan was used for the city of Washington, is entombed in front of the Custis-Lee Mansion overlooking the city he planned. His tablelike monument was erected pursuant to congressional direction and appropriation of funds.

The shock of John Fitzgerald Kennedy's assassination on November 22, 1963 stunned the people of the United States and the world. It was Jacqueline Kennedy's decision to bury the fallen president in Arlington rather than in the Kennedy family plot in Massachusetts where the bodies of two of their children lay. (These were later reinterred in Arlington beside their father.) President Kennedy (1917–1963) lies in sight of the Custis-Lee Mansion, not far from the spot where the first burial took place. From the grave the Lincoln Memorial, the Washington Monument, and the dome of the Capitol can be seen in the distance over the Potomac. The president's grave area is paved with irregular stones of Cape Cod granite, which were quarried about 150 years ago near the site of the president's home, and were located by members of the Kennedy family. Fescue and clover have been planted in the crevices, which give the appearance of stones lying naturally in a Massachusetts field.

Before descending to the grave itself, the visitor finds himself on a plaza overlooking it. Bounding the plaza itself is a low wall on which are inscribed quotations from President Kennedy's inaugural address and other speeches.

The eternal flame lighted by Mrs. Kennedy on the day of the funeral burns from the center of a five-foot circular flat granite stone. Magnolia, crab apple, willow oak, hawthorn, yellowwood, American holly, and cherry trees have been judiciously planted in the 3.2-acre burial site. Nearby is the grave of the president's brother Robert F. Kennedy (1925–1968), who was also assassinated. His grave is marked with a simple white cross. South from the president's grave a path leads to a reflecting pool. The wall that forms the background of the pool contains quotations from the senator's speeches. The graves here are a testament to a nation's conscience, places of pilgrimage for citizens from all walks of life, from all nations of the world.

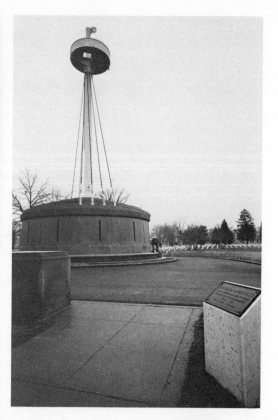

The Custis family plot.

Above, right: The U.S.S. *Maine* monument.

Another view of the *Maine* monument.

The grave of President William Howard Taft.

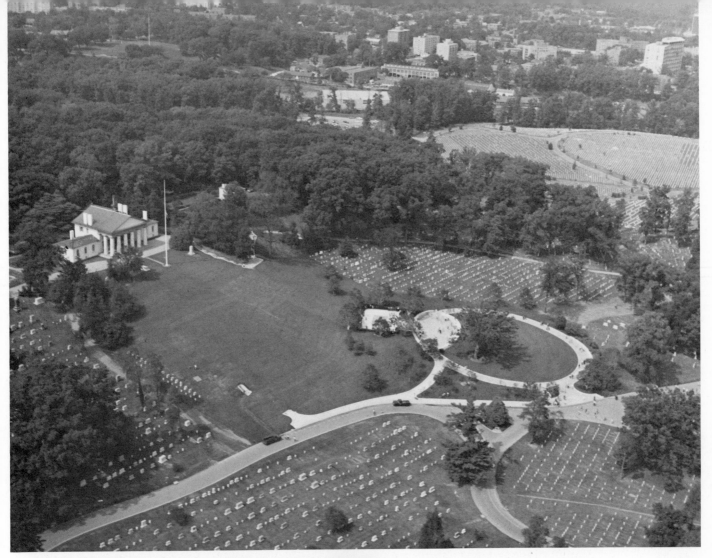

The grave of President John F. Kennedy with the Custis-Lee Mansion at left. *U.S. Army photograph*

Probably the most famous epitaph in the United States. *U.S. Army photograph*

49. Blandford Cemetery

PETERSBURG, VIRGINIA

ONE of the most beautiful of the Virginia cemeteries is adjacent to Old Blandford Church, erected in 1735. The little churchyard with its graves, surrounded by a wall, is approximately an acre of ground. In the English medieval tradition this was God's Acre (not to be confused with the Moravian concept of God's Acre). Within the little churchyard is a touching gravestone to a sailor, A. McConnald, his wife, Jane, and son, Daniel. The relief on the stone shows the seaman leading his family, who died soon after he did, into heaven. This, the highest elevation in Petersburg, known as Well's Hill, is adjacent to the larger Blandford Cemetery. It is known that at least one duel was fought here in the churchyard.

Major General William Phillips, the highest ranking British officer in the Revolution to lie on American soil, was buried secretly behind the church. Phillips, who died of natural causes if dysentery can be called a natural cause, was heard to murmur as Lafayette shelled the town: "Won't that boy let me die in peace?"

When Old Blandford Church was erected, Blandford was not even a town. It was not chartered until 1748, but later (1784), after the Revolution, it was absorbed into Petersburg. When a new Episcopal church was built in 1806, the old one was abandoned; in 1882 it was repaired by the city of Petersburg. It is now a memorial chapel and Confederate shrine in memory of thirty thousand Confederate soldiers buried nearby, and contains fifteen superb stained glass windows by Louis Comfort Tiffany. The Ladies Memorial Association of Petersburg was responsible for the renovation of the church, which began about 1901, and for its becoming a memorial chapel and shrine. (The ladies of the association solicited the money to install the windows.)

The cemetery itself dates to 1702 for in that year Richard Scarborough, aged eighty-seven, was interred here. His stone is the oldest extant today. Another is that of John Herbert, who died on March 17, 1704, at the age of forty. Many of the earliest gravestones are to colonists from Scotland, England, and Ireland. It is sad to note that few lived past middle age. One can find among these the coats of arms, crests, and mottoes of many old British families.

It was the nineteenth century that brought glory to Blandford Cemetery. An ornate monument to Captain Richard McRae honors the man who with the cockade-wearing Petersburg volunteers marched to Ohio in the War of 1812 and fought at the Battle of Fort Meigs. President Madison referred to Petersburg as the "Cockade of the Union" as a result of this exploit. Petersburg is still

called the "Cockade City." The ironwork fence about the monument is rich in ornament, with seventeen stars worked into it, one for each state then in the Union. The monument itself is surmounted by an American eagle. That in itself is not unique, but the fact that the eagle is covered with 23-karat gold is!

It is the Civil War, of course, which is remembered best here. There is a monument over the grave of Lieutenant Wayles Hurt, the youngest man—only sixteen years of age—killed in the battle on June 9, 1864. The city was besieged for ten months. On June 9, 1864, some 1,500 Union cavalrymen attacked and 129 old men and young boys kept them at bay until the city was saved. Here too is the mausoleum of General William Mahone, who in the Battle of the Crater (when Pennsylvania miners tunneled under southern fortifications and blew them up in a devastating explosion) led the Confederates and at his own request was buried in the midst of the thirty thousand men in gray at Blandford. There are two other Confederate generals here—Major General Cullen A. Battle (1829–1905) and General David Weisiger (1818–1899). The Washington Artillery of New Orleans has its own section in which crape myrtle is very much in abundance. (Petersburg has also been called the "Crape Myrtle City.")

One of the links with the Civil War period that is maintained today is the celebration of Petersburg's own Memorial Day, June 9. Nora Fontaine Maury Davison (1836–1929) on June 9, 1866—the second anniversary of the attack on the city—brought students here to decorate the Confederate graves. Earlier, in May of the same year, Miss Davison had brought her students on a day that the state of Mississippi had appointed to be observed as Confederate Memorial Day. On this earlier occasion they were observed by Mary Cunningham Logan, wife of General John A. Logan, then commander-in-chief of the Grand Army of the Republic. She was moved to write an article about this for a Washington paper. The Union general, inspired by his wife, issued the order that led to the present national observance of Memorial Day. The services held here each June 9 carry on that tradition.

Blandford's acres and rolling hills are also the burial place of some who had well-known associations, such as William Gordon McCabe (1841–1920), a friend of Matthew Arnold, Dickens, and Thackeray. Or Dr. Thomas Robinson, who fled Ireland and became a friend of Edgar Allan Poe. (There is an Irish harp on his stone.) Hiram Haines, editor of *The American Constellation,* died on January 15, 1844, at the age of thirty-eight and was bur-

The Jones family monument with a sculpture by Jacques Lipchitz. *Photograph by the author*

The monument to Captain Richard McRae. *Photograph by the author*

ied here. Poe and Virginia Clemm spent their honeymoon at the home of Haines. Dandridge Spotswood (1872–1939) is remembered because his former wife was Katharine Wolff, later the Baroness Kitty de Rothschild, mistress of Schloss Enzesfeld, the Austrian castle where former King Edward VIII waited patiently for Wallis Warfield Simpson's divorce to become final.

One of Blandford's most impressive monuments is a lifelike statue of Kate Compton of Lexington, Virginia, whose father was one of Stonewall Jackson's pallbearers. She married David Dunlop II, a tobacco manufacturer. Within thirteen months of her death he wed again, this time to Molly Johnston, who had been courted by his son. The statue of the first Mrs. Dunlop was ordered from Italy, and Petersburg legend has it that the ship bearing the work of art back to Virginia passed the one carrying the newlyweds to Europe.

One does not expect to find a sculpture by Jacques Lipchitz in Blandford Cemetery. Broken pillars, angels, and mourning figures yes, but hardly contemporary sculpture such as this one by Lipchitz on a small plinth over

the graves of Thomas Catesby Jones (1880–1946), Louisa Brooke Jones (1883–1967), and their son, Catesby Thomas Jones (1912–1967). The elder Jones, a New York admiralty lawyer, was a patron of modern art.

The Gothic ironwork—the cemetery boasts some fine examples—the landscaping, the gentle avenues, and the ornate monuments reflect its beauty, grace, and sense of history as does Old Blandford Church and the poem found on its walls in 1841. Some said it was written by Mrs. Schermerhorn, a daughter of Chief Justice Hening of the Virginia Supreme Court of Appeals. Others attributed it to Hiram Haines, the Petersburg journalist and friend of Poe. Most prefer to think its author was Tyrone Power, the Irish comedian and great-grandfather of the motion picture actor:

**The sun that shone upon their paths
Now gilds their lonely graves;
The zephyrs which once fanned their brows
The grass above them waves.**

The grave of Jane Stith Stanard, Edgar Allan Poe's "Helen." *Photograph by the author*

The monument to Nannie Euphemia Caskie, who died in Florence, Italy. *Photograph by the author*

50. Shockoe Cemetery

RICHMOND, VIRGINIA

IN use long before Hollywood Cemetery was planned, this well-kept burial ground at Hospital and 2nd streets is maintained—as all of Richmond's are—by the Richmond Bureau of Cemeteries. The care and restoration of headstones rests with the family of the deceased, but the grounds are maintained by the bureau. There are no hills, vales, and ravines here as in Hollywood, but flat, even greensward, with cedars, magnolias, tulip poplars, and wild cherry trees.

The lack of monotony is due to the fact that while there are the flat eighteenth-century-type gravestones, and some of the table variety, Shockoe was still in use when the flowering of nineteenth-century cemetery art was just beginning. There are rich and varied examples among the simpler stones.

Shockoe's most famous grave is that of Chief Justice John Marshall. His and those of his wife, Mary Willis (1766–1831), and his daughter, Mary Harvie (1795–1841), are within a wrought-iron fenced enclosure. Marshall's

tribute below the facts of his wife's birth and death is: "This stone is devoted to her memory by him who best knew her worth and most deplores her loss."

The Chief Justice died in Philadelphia, and it was during his funeral procession that the Liberty Bell cracked while tolling its mourning knell.

Lichen and the weather have all but obliterated Marshall's simple epitaph:

**John Marshall
son of Thomas and Mary Marshall
was born the 24th September 1759
Intermarried with Mary Willis Ambler
the 9th of January 1789
Departed this life
the 6th day of July 1835**

164

It is difficult not to discover memories of Edgar Allan Poe in Richmond. His mother's grave is in the churchyard of Saint John's Episcopal Church on Broad Street. Poe's stepfather, John Allan, a native of Ayrshire, Scotland, "who departed this life March 27, 1834, in the 54th year of his age," lies in Shockoe not far from Poe's "Helen," Mrs. Jane Stith Stanard, who died on April 28, 1824. The mother of a boyhood school friend of Poe, she was described by him as the "first purely ideal love of his soul." It was she who inspired his first really distinguished poem, "To Helen." Her kindness and sympathy were treasured by this sensitive, lonely fourteen-year-old boy. It is said that Poe haunted Shockoe after her death, visiting her grave often at midnight. A small marker at the foot of the grave quotes some of the lines from "To Helen."

Early Pattons are here, including John Mercer Patton (1797–1856), the great-grandfather of General George S. Patton. One of the most famous Virginia lawyers of his time, John Mercer Patton revised the Virginia Code (both civil and criminal) and was at one time acting governor of Virginia. And, although connected with another war than General Patton's, so is Elizabeth L. Van Lew (1818–1900) here. Elizabeth, a spy during the Civil War, rests beneath a handsome boulder from Capitol Hill in Boston, which was a "tribute from Massachusetts friends." The bronze plate on the boulder's face tells Elizabeth's story: "She risked everything that is dear to Man—Friends—Fortune—Comfort—Health—Life Itself —all for the one absorbing desire of her heart—that slavery might be abolished and the Union preserved."

This gives only the bare bones of Elizabeth's story. When the Civil War broke out, Elizabeth's sympathies lay with the federal government. Earlier she freed the family's servants and went so far as to purchase the freedom of others who were relatives of former slaves. As the war progressed, the Van Lew home was literally a hive of espionage activity. Elizabeth sent messages in code, hid papers in andirons and in the "double-bottom" warming dish (meant to hold hot water). She "romanced" Jefferson Davis; Provost Marshal General Winder; and Lieutenant Todd (half-brother of Mary Lincoln), keeper of Libby Prison, which held the captured Union troops. She also managed to thwart all efforts to entrap her. When Grant's troops were outside Richmond she was able to smuggle an American flag through the lines and hoisted the (thirty-four) stars and stripes above her home despite threats from an unruly mob. Perhaps Elizabeth's finest tribute came from General George Sharpe of the army intelligence bureau: "For a long, long time, she represented all that was left of the power of the United States government in the city of Richmond."

The stone over Peter Francisco's grave—which can be seen from Elizabeth's—has a marker on it, simply stating he was a "soldier of Revolutionary fame." Peter was set ashore at City Point (now Hopewell), Virginia, in 1765. He was a well-dressed child of five or six, wearing silver shoe buckles engraved "P.F." Adopted by Judge Anthony Winston, Patrick Henry's uncle, Peter grew to be 6 feet, 6 inches in height and weighed 260 pounds when he joined the Continental Army in 1776 at the age of sixteen. His strength was such that a normal-sized sword was of no use in his hands, and General Washington, who offered him a captain's commission (which Peter refused because he felt his lack of education ill fitted him to be an officer), had a five-foot sword hammered out for him. Francisco distinguished himself in engagements at Brandywine, Germantown, Monmouth, Stony Point, Camden, and Guilford Courthouse. He married three times, two wives predeceasing him. A friend of Lafayette, he named one of his children for the marquis. Following his death on January 16, 1831, the House of Delegates (where he was sergeant at arms) adjourned and joined the Senate, the governor, and the City Council in attending his funeral. He was buried with military and Masonic honors. The rest of the United States may know little of Peter Francisco, but Virginia remembers him with pride and affection.

Here also are Fanny Belle Butt; her mother, Pocahontas Stewart; her father, Boswell Beriah Butt; and her sisters, Cora Butt and Dixie Lee. And there is an angel with the word "Mizpeh" on the stone below it. This monument is in memory of Nannie Euphemia Caskie, who was born in Richmond and, like Elizabeth Barrett Browning, died far from home in Florence, Italy.

The peace of Shockoe is broken only by an occasional passing automobile or the sound of the lawn mower among the graves. Here among the iron railings, simple stones, and more elaborate monuments sleep the early Richmond dead.

President James Monroe's tomb. This photograph was taken in 1905 by the Detroit Publishing Company. *Reproduced from the collection of the Library of Congress*

51. Hollywood Cemetery

RICHMOND, VIRGINIA

IN a state filled with rich mementos of a romantic historic past, none preserves that quality more than Hollywood Cemetery at Cherry and Albemarle streets in Richmond, the first private cemetery in the city.

During the spring of 1847 two of the city's citizens—Joshua J. Fry and William H. Haxall—visited Mount Auburn. They returned filled with enthusiasm for the Cambridge cemetery and a desire to see a similar one in Virginia's capital. They, with William Mitchell, Jr., and Isaac Davenport, "purchased of Lewis E. Harvie ... for the sum of $4,675 ... 'a certain portion of the lots or parcels of land ... and contains by survey, forty-two

acres, three roods, but of which one rood, known as Harvie's burying yard or grave yard, with free ingress and egress to the said grave yard, is reserved.'"

A stock company was formed in August of that year and William A. Pratt, "architect and late superintending engineer of Green Mount Cemetery, near Baltimore ... very obligingly furnished the subscribers without charge a plan for their proposed Cemetery, prepared by himself after a careful topographical examination of the site." The board availed itself of a visit that John Notman, a native of Scotland but then a resident of Philadelphia, was making to Virginia "for the purpose of laying out the grounds at the Huguenot Springs" to engage him to prepare a more complete and precise plan than Pratt had furnished. (Notman also designed a number of Richmond's best-known churches and was afterward responsible for Capitol Square.)

Notman's labors were made infinitely easier by the site itself. Situated high above the James River, with a prospect of Richmond in the distance, and blessed with hills, gorges, ravines, and plateaus, no locale more epitomized the nineteenth-century concept of a cemetery. It is thought that Notman was influenced by landscape architect Andrew Jackson Downing.

In February 1848, Notman's plan was received, and the prevalence of holly trees on the grounds suggested the name to the architect.

What Notman achieved was the parklike appearance that earlier cemeteries such as Mount Auburn, Laurel Hill, and Green-Wood presented. The variety of plantings, the look of the arboretum that Hollywood gives, enables the visitor to contemplate the graves in a serene atmosphere.

The fact that two presidents of the United States are buried in Hollywood lends it unusual interest. (Arlington is the only other cemetery with two—William Howard Taft and John Fitzgerald Kennedy.) John Tyler (1790–1862), tenth president, succeeded William Henry Harrison a month after the inauguration when Harrison died of pneumonia. Elected with Harrison on the slogan "Tippecanoe and Tyler Too," Tyler returned to his native Virginia after his term, dying in Richmond in the first years of the Civil War. An imposing monument towers above his grave. Near him are his second wife, Julia Gardiner (1820–1889), and a number of his sixteen children (nine of his first marriage and seven from his second): Lyon Gardiner Tyler (1853–1935), Dr. Lachlan Tyler (1851–1902), R. Fitzwater Tyler (1856–1927), Pearl Tyler Ellis (1860–1947), and Julia Tyler Spencer, whose stone records that she "died the Second Monday in May, 1871, Aged 21."

By coincidence, both John and Julia Tyler died in the Exchange Hotel, Richmond. Mrs. Tyler, who was taken ill on a visit to the city, suffered a stroke. When someone in the room suggested she be given liquor, she replied, faintly, "tea." It was her last word. The former First Lady was a Roman Catholic and, although the president was not, they were buried together. At Tyler's funeral 150 carriages stretched for a quarter mile in the rain. The Tyler monument, topped by a bronze finial—a Greek urn supported between the spread wings of two American eagles—was dedicated by Pearl Tyler Ellis, the president's only surviving daughter, on October 12, 1915.

From the Tyler plot on President's Circle can be seen the Gothic cast-iron tomb of James Monroe (1758–1831). Designed by Richmond architect Albert Lybrock, it was cast in Philadelphia by the firm of Wood and Perot. The tomb looks like an openwork, latticed chapel. Inside can be seen the sarcophagus of Monroe, who died in New York City on July 1, 1831, and was buried in Greenwood Cemetery in lower Manhattan. At the centenary of his birth "by order of the General Assembly His remains were removed to this cemetery 5th July 1858 as an evidence of the affection of Virginia for her good and honored son." In the grass outside the crenellated monument are the graves of his wife, Elizabeth Kortright (1768–1830) and their daugher, Maria Hester Monroe Gouverneur (1804–1850). Their bodies were brought here in 1903 from the Monroe home, Oak Hill, in Loudoun County, Virginia.

Within the circle, which has been described as fashionable, accomplished, and select, although of lesser importance (but not to Richmond!) is the grave of Matthew Fontaine Maury (1806–1873), the American naval officer and hydrographer, often called "Pathfinder of the Seas." His valuable charts of the Atlantic Ocean were among the first of their kind and his *Physical Geography of the Sea,* published posthumously in 1885, was the first classic of modern oceanography.

Another president—the only president of the Confederate States of America (1861-1865)—rests in Davis Circle. The statue of Jefferson Davis over his grave, one hand resting lightly on a hip, the other holding his broad-brimmed Confederate hat, dominates the circle and the area, but a little more than a century after the Confederacy ceased to exist, his likeness seems more like that of a gentle than a forceful man, a true cavalier of a doomed cause.

The lines etched in the stone have a poignancy all their own:

Jefferson Davis
At Rest
An American Soldier
And Defender of the Constitution
(1808–89)

In the four years following his death and first burial in the Metairie Cemetery, the states of Mississippi, Kentucky, Georgia, and Virginia had each exhorted Varina Davis to permit his body to be transferred. Governor Fitzhugh Lee and Senator John Daniel had been the most persuasive and in May 1893, Jefferson Davis's body was returned to the capital of the Confederacy.

The train that carried the coffin from Metairie to Richmond stopped at stations along the way so the people of the South could pay their respects. At Beauvoir, his home in Mississippi, the tracks were strewn for a half mile with magnolia petals and other white blossoms. His funeral in Richmond was a military one and, appropriate to the fallen leader, he was then laid in the plot that would eventually hold the graves of Varina, his six children, his son-in-law, and several grandchildren.

To the right of Jefferson Davis's monument is that of Varina Anne, his daughter, erected in 1899 by the United Daughters of the Confederacy. A kneeling angel over Varina faces the statue of Davis in an attitude of genuflection. A companion sculpture on the left is reminiscent of Augustus Saint-Gaudens's *Grief*. Sculpted by George Julian Zolnay in 1911, it marks the grave of his daughter, Margaret Howell Davis Hayes, who died in 1908. The year before her death she erected the Zolnay monument to her father.

The Davis tragedy was not only the defeat of the Confederacy and the death of a dream, but the loss of so many children and grandchildren at an early age. Around the circumference of Davis Circle, the tiny graves dappled by sunlight and the shadows of the trees nearby, lie the Davis children: Samuel Emory Davis (1852–1854), Jefferson Davis, Jr. (1857–1878), Joseph Evan Davis (1859–1864), and William Howell Davis (1861–1871). The grave of Jefferson, Jr., is topped by a broken pillar, signifying a life sundered early, and the words on the stone record that he was the "last surviving and much beloved son of Jefferson and Varina Howell Davis."

Joe was four years old when he was killed, falling from a side balcony of the White House of the Confederacy to a brick-paved court thirty feet below. The funeral engendered great emotion, and an enormous crowd assembled along the river for the funeral. One thousand children wound up the hills of Hollywood and around the graves of Presidents Monroe and Tyler. They carried small bouquets of spring flowers and green sprays, which were placed on the burial site. Little Joe Davis's gravestone records that it was "Erected by The Little Boys and Girls of the Southern Capital."

Near the young Davis children are their nieces and nephews and the Davis grandchildren. In the circle are Jefferson Davis Hayes, who died on March 22, 1877, aged three months and three days; Elizabeth Frances Davis Hayes (1915–1916); and Jefferson Hayes Davis, Jr. (1911–1912). The graves are almost small cradles covered with ivy, a ring of descendants encircling the grave of their famous forebear. With them is Joel Addison Hayes (1848–1919), the president's son-in-law.

Across the road from the Davis entombment are the graves of a Grant family, but not *the* Grant whose name was anathema to the Davises. Walter Enders Grant (1856–1911) and his wife, Elize Augustine (1859–1917), are buried within sight of Jefferson Davis's standing figure.

Unusual too is the monument nearby to Tokukichiro Abe (1866–1907), who was born in Aktaken, Japan, and died in Richmond. The ever-present holly stands guarding the grave of this graduate (1892) of the Agricultural College of Tokyo University. He was a commissioner and official expert of the Imperial Tobacco Monopoly Bureau of Japan from 1897 to 1907. On the side of the monument, facing the Davis plot, is a fine example of Japanese calligraphy etched in stone, an incongruity in this historic Virginia burial ground.

Disparate sleeping citizens of Virginia abound in Hollywood. Major General James Ewell Brown Stuart, who —his stone records—died on May 12, 1864, aged thirty-one years, is interred in a grave atop a high hill, with a ravinelike meadow below. Beside him lies his wife, Flora Cooke (1836–1923), who, like many a southern woman, long outlived her husband.

Next to the J. E. B. Stuart plot is that of the Glasgow family. Here Ellen Glasgow (1874–1945), author of the Old Dominion novels, who won the Pulitzer Prize in fiction for *In This Our Life*, lies with her dogs Jeremy, a Sealyham, and Billy, a French poodle. Jeremy's death in 1929 was the occasion for an extended obituary of him in the Richmond *Times-Dispatch*, and Miss Glasgow received notes of condolence from England and New York as well as her Virginia friends. Such literary figures as Hugh Walpole, Radclyffe Hall, and Carl Van Vechten expressed their sympathy. These pet dogs were buried first in her garden (others had gone to the Pet Memorial Park in Richmond), and she left instructions that they be exhumed and their remains placed in the casket with her. In this way "Miss Ellen" created the greatest sensation of her long career. Her funeral procession was watched by the curious as it made its way from her home at One West Main Street to Hollywood.

Hollywood always had a strange and compelling fascination for Ellen Glasgow. As a small child she occasionally walked there with Lizzie Jones, a family servant who was said to have cooked dinner for Robert E. Lee the night before he surrendered. One of Ellen's biographers, E. Stanly Godbold, Jr., wrote of her: "The formless, the unknown, the mystery were embodied in memories of her childhood, in shadowy stones on a hill in Hollywood."

Among the stones in the Glasgow plot are those of her brother Francis T. and her brother-in-law George Walter McCormack, both suicides. She is said to have declared she would not be buried near her father, whom she hated, but her parents, brothers, and sisters are all about her. The stone above her is startling among the older, darker monuments of the past. Blazing white—almost stark—the slab bears her name and dates and the words from John Milton's *Lycidas*, which she selected herself: "Tomorrow to fresh Woods, and Pastures new." The stone, pristine, almost virginal, seems classic and fitting for Ellen Glasgow, who never married. On lower ground, not far from Ellen Glasgow's grave, is that of her friend and Richmond's other great literary figure, James Branch Cabell (1879–1958).

A cemetery of the magnitude of Hollywood must by definition be blessed with unusual graves. One that most fits this category is that of James E. Valentine, "killed in a collision, December 20, 1874, Aged 32 years." James met his end in a railroad accident. A train on the stone testifies to this. And there is a poem, reminiscent of the

Victorian verse of a century ago, to record his fate. It has begun to fade, and the sentimental details of James's demise are not legible for today's cemetery wanderers.

As in any cemetery in the South, no burial ground is worthy of its name without its complement of Confederate dead. There are eighteen thousand Confederate soldiers buried here, approximately eleven thousand unknown, many of them killed at Gettysburg and brought here a decade later. The pyramidlike monument—impressive because of its size and its dominance over the section in which it stands—is a cairn to those men in gray who gave their lives for a cause in which they believed—the Confederacy. The stones from the James River below are a testimony to the dead and to the dedication of those who gathered them and lived on.

The river, along which so much of early Virginia history was enacted, meanders below, at one point over a falls. Rocks, small islands, and formations pepper the flowing water, which is often white where it tumbles over the rocky juttings. The dead could not have a more appropriate resting place, with the timeless river rushing below and the towers of the new Richmond rising in the distance.

President John Tyler's grave. The square monument next to it is that of Matthew Fontaine Maury. *Department of the Army photograph*

The grave of Varina Anne Davis, daughter of Jefferson Davis. *Photograph by the author*

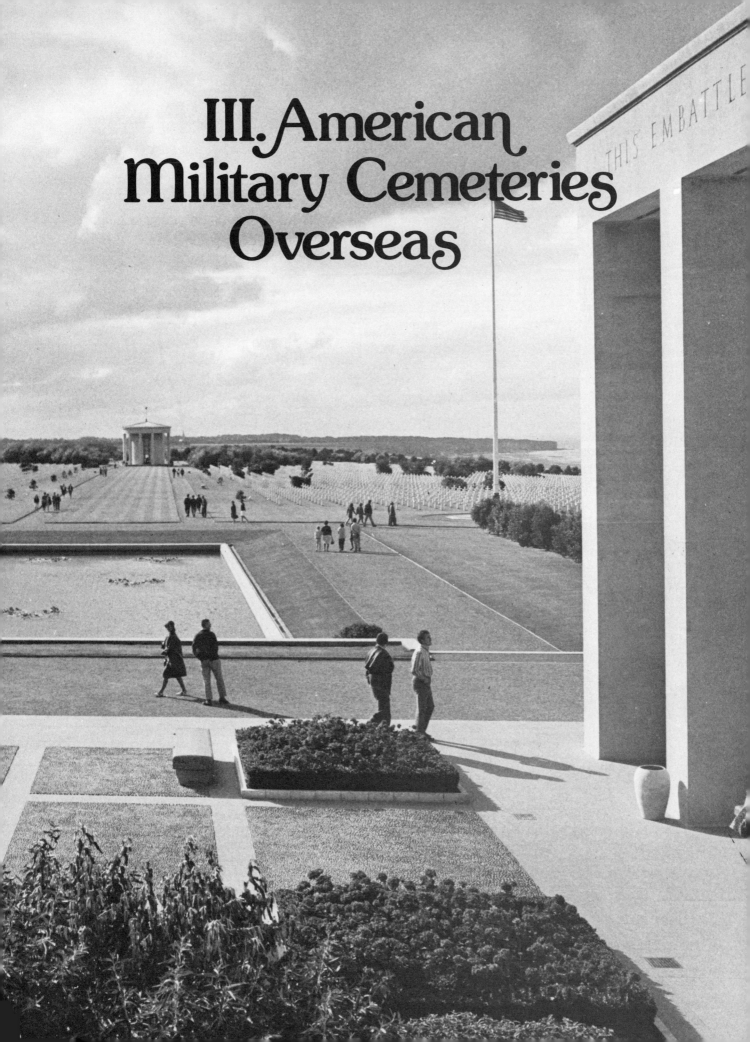

III. American Military Cemeteries Overseas

THIS EMBATTLE

52. Mexico City National Cemetery

MEXICO CITY, MEXICO

THE oldest of the overseas military cemeteries, this two-acre burial ground at 31 Calzada Melchoir Ocampo in Mexico's capital city was established in 1851. Small and uniform monuments signify the graves of the identified dead. A single monument marks the grave of 750 unidentified soldiers of the Mexican War of 1847, which was precipitated by the annexation of Texas in December 1845. (American troops entered Mexico City on September 14, 1847.)

There are 734 other graves in the cemetery, in which are buried 813 American veterans and others. The cemetery, which is filled and is closed to further interments, is easily accessible; it is about two miles west of the city's cathedral and about one mile north of the United States Embassy.

World War I Cemeteries

53. Flanders Field American Cemetery

WAREGEM, BELGIUM

In Flanders fields the poppies blow
Between the crosses, row on row,
That mark our place; and in the sky
The larks, still bravely singing, fly
Scarce heard amid the guns below.

THESE words, by John McCrae (1872–1918), touched the hearts of the Western world when they first appeared anonymously in *Punch* on December 8, 1915. A United States military cemetery now commemorates those who died on Flanders Field in World War I. The historic spot —a traditional battleground during the centuries, especially during the Napoleonic wars—again became a wartime setting when the Battle of Flanders began with the German invasion of the Low Countries on May 10, 1940, and ended with the Allied evacuation at Dunkirk on June 4 of that year.

In 1918 the 91st Division suffered severe casualties here in securing the nearby wooded area called Spitaals

The Memorial Chapel. *Photograph by Herman Manasse. American Battle Monuments Commission*

Bosschen. Before their entry into Belgium, the 91st and 37th divisions had been engaged in the fighting in the Meuse-Argonne region. Ordered to Belgium in October 1918, to join the French army there, on October 30 they took part in the beginning of the Ypres-Lys offensive; the 91st captured the Spitaals Bosschen and the 37th advanced to the outskirts of Cruyshautem. The Germans were in full retreat, the two divisions advanced rapidly to the Escaut (Scheldt) River, with the 37th succeeding in crossing under heavy fire on November 2. A German counterattack was repulsed two days later. The Group of Armies of Flanders, under the command of Albert I, king of the Belgians, held the position from November 4—when the two American divisions were relieved—until the Armistice on November 11.

Several interesting features concerning this, the smallest (six acres) of the permanent American military cemeteries on the European continent, deserve mention. It was not dedicated until August 8, 1937—practically the eve of World War II—and is the only American World War I cemetery in Belgium. No nation suffered more than this tiny one did during the Great War, nor did any rulers endear themselves more to their own and other peoples than King Albert and Queen Elisabeth. (She sold her jewels to aid the homeless and hungry, and lived at the front with the king.) As a gesture of gratitude to the American people, the Belgian government granted the use of the land free of charge or taxation in perpetuity.

While Colonel McCrae's poem was not written about the fighting here—he wrote it while serving at a medical station in Ypres—the cemetery at Flanders Field has always drawn a great many visitors because of the poem's appeal. (Colonel McCrae died of pneumonia, nine months before the large-scale fighting in the Flanders area. *In Flanders Field and Other Poems* was published posthumously in 1919.)

On May 30, 1927, just nine days after making his historic solo transatlantic flight, Charles A. Lindbergh flew over the cemetery to salute his fallen countrymen. From the *Spirit of St. Louis* he dropped poppies on the Memorial Day ceremonies being held below.

Handsome iron gates on the Waregem-Audenarde highway, leading from Courtrai to Ghent, are similar to those that might lead to some small ducal country estate. A short graveled lane, bordered by linden trees, leads to the memorial chapel and the graves beyond. Paul Philippe Cret, a Philadelphian, was the architect for the cemetery and the memorial. (He was involved in the architecture and planning of many European military cemeteries under the supervision of the American Battle Monuments Commission.)

The plantings—currant hedge, rhododendron, lilac, azalea, birch, ash, oak, elm, holly, maple, hydrangea, magnolia, spirea, and Japanese prune—are spectacular yet low key. Everywhere there is a sense of balance and order—and peace. The cast-bronze base of the fifty-foot flagpole on the terrace carries this communion with nature to an even finer degree. Designed by Egerton Swartwout, it features acanthus leaves, butterflies, seashells, oak leaves, acorns, and a circle of poppies where the staff and base meet. The other architectural ornaments in the cemetery were created by L. Bottiau of Paris.

The chapel itself is set in a sunken garden, which gives greater depth to the small area and allows the eye to be drawn even more to the pavilionlike building. Interdenominational in character, it forms a hub from which the radial paths and four rectangular grave plots spring. The entire concept is geometric in design and makes excellent use of the limited area. Flagstone paths lead from the chapel to steps at the four corners, beyond which are small secluded recesses, retreats for the contemplative, enclosed with trees. Each contains a decorative urn on a pedestal. The insignia of the four American divisions that fought in Belgium—the 27th, 30th, 37th, and 91st—are shown on the urns in sculptured form.

The graves, 368 in all, are evenly grouped so that 92 appear in each plot. Twenty-one of these are unknowns. Each bears the testimony: "Here rests in Honored Glory/ A Comrade in Arms/ Known But to God." They may be unknown, but they are not forgotten. Their graves are decorated from time to time with masses of flowers. Each of the four grave plots is framed by an English yew hedge and trees and shrubs.

The chapel is small, in keeping with the size of the cemetery, and appears almost as a beacon, drawing the walker along the path to its doors. Inscribed in the white Pouillenay stone over the bronze doors are the words: "Greet them ever with grateful hearts." On three of the outer walls inscriptions in English, Flemish, and French remind the visitor: "This chapel has been erected by the United States of America in memory of her soldiers who fought and died in Belgium during the World War. These graves are the permanent and visible symbol of the heroic devotion with which they gave their lives to the common cause of humanity." Beneath each are bas-relief figures, classical in concept, symbolizing Grief, Remembrance, and History.

Each of the chapels in the American cemeteries is distinctive, and the inscriptions, medallions, stained glass, and marble within chosen with care. That at Flanders Field is no exception. The altar is Grand Antique (black and white) marble. Above it carved on a rose-tinted marble panel is a crusader's sword outlined in gold. On the altar itself are the words: "I will ransom them from the power of the grave, I will redeem them from death" (Hosea, XII, 14). Flanking the altar are bronze candelabra and flagstaffs, bearing the flags of the United States, Belgium, France, Great Britain, and Italy. The side walls of rose Saint George marble bear the names of forty-three Americans who lost their lives in Belgium, but whose remains were never recovered or identified. Above the names are the Great Seal of the United States and the words: "In memory of those American soldiers who fought in this region and who sleep in unknown graves."

The cemetery—164 miles north of Paris and 50 west of Brussels—can be reached on the Lille-Ghent autoroute, which has an exit nearby. Visiting it is a moving experience. John McCrae's haunting words keep returning:

We are the Dead. Short days ago
We lived, felt dawn, saw sunset glow,
Loved and were loved, and now we lie
In Flanders fields.

Some 468 military dead lie beneath Surrey skies. *Photograph by Herman Manasse.*
American Battle Monuments Commission

54. Brookwood American Cemetery

BROOKWOOD, SURREY, ENGLAND

ITS unusual geographical location—within the civilian cemetery, which was founded by the London Necropolis Company—makes this 4½-acre burial ground entirely different from the other American military cemeteries abroad. Some 468 military dead lie here beneath Surrey skies, near the military cemeteries and monuments of the British Commonwealth and other Allied nations.

Within the American cemetery the crosses are arranged in four plots about a flagpole. Masses of shrubs and evergreen trees frame the white crosses and the classic-looking chapel. The white stone of the chapel's exterior contrasts with the tan-hued stone within. The chapel's walls are incised with the names of 563 missing who were lost at sea.

Brookwood Cemetery is easily accessible from London, twenty-eight miles away. A train from Waterloo Station takes less than an hour and the cemetery is just three hundred yards from the Brookwood railroad station.

Those who died at Belleau Wood lie here. *Photograph by Herman Manasse. American Battle Monuments Commission*

55. Aisne-Marne American Cemetery

BELLEAU, AISNE, FRANCE

BELLEAU Wood, before the battles and engagements of World War II, was as familiar to the average American, Frenchman, or Briton as Omaha Beach, Saint-Lô, or Dieppe were to a later generation. It was here that the Allies at great loss of life turned back the German offensive in the summer of 1918.

On May 27 the Germans had attacked in force on the Aisne front between Berry-au-Bac and Anizy-le-Château; the Allies responded by rushing reserves there from every quarter. A large salient had been driven into the Allied lines in the triangular area defined by Reims,

Château-Thierry, and Soissons. The Germans, in trying to widen their advantage, attacked toward Compiègne to secure that section of railroad between Compiègne and Soissons.

Unsuccessful, they prepared a major offensive on either side of Reims in the general direction of Épernay and Châlons-sur-Marne. Three German armies began their offensive on July 15. Under Marshal Foch's counterattack—the Allies having learned of the German plans beforehand—the enemy was halted. By July 18 the Allies launched a counterattack, on August 4 they reached the south bank of the Vesle River, and two days later the Allied high command could announce that a serious threat to Paris was removed and the railroad again freed for Allied use. Marshal Pétain, who drew up the Allied plans for meeting the German offensive, declared the counterattack could not have been successful without the aid of American troops.

The memory of those Americans who died during the ten-week period is honored in the Aisne-Marne American Cemetery at the foot of the hillside of Belleau Wood, 6½ miles northwest of Château-Thierry and just south of the village of Belleau on the road to Lucy-Le-Bocage. At first the ground was only considered a temporary cemetery, the American Expeditionary Forces' Cemetery Number 1764—Belleau Wood. In 1921 Congress authorized retention of the cemetery as one of eight permanent World War I military cemeteries on foreign soil. The following year an agreement was signed with the government of France, which granted its use as a military cemetery in perpetuity, free of charge or taxation.

Cram and Ferguson, Boston architects, laid out the 42½-acre cemetery in a T configuration, designing the graves area in two convex curved plots projecting from each side of a central mall at the foot of the hill of Belleau Wood. Here, near the scene of one of World War I's bloodiest battles—when the United States forces stopped the German advance—lie 2,288 military dead, most either from engagements in this area or from the Marne Valley in that fateful summer of 1918. The sounds of battle are forgotten now; few—except the very old—living in the area remember the death and destruction of that last year of the war. Each plot contains 13 rows of headstones and 1,144 graves. Of the 2,288 burials in the cemetery, 249 are unknown. An unknown from here was one of the four brought to Châlons-sur-Marne in 1921, one to be selected as the Unknown Soldier in Arlington Cemetery. These men represent the then forty-eight states and the District of Columbia. Multicolored shrubs, such as forsythia, laurel, boxwood, Japanese plum, deutzia, mock orange, and Oregon grape, frame the burial area, and the ever-present polyantha roses border the mall.

Distinguished by more traditional architecture than the World War II cemeteries (which are usually contemporary and more severe), the World War I cemeteries can be readily identified. The Aisne-Marne Cemetery is no exception. Its memorial chapel was erected over the front line trenches dug by the 2nd Division as part of the defense of Belleau Wood, following its capture by the division on June 25, 1918. Rising more than eighty feet above the hillside, the chapel—a striking example of French Romanesque architecture—has exterior walls, steps, and terrace of native Saint Maximin, Savonnières, and Massangis limestone. The carvings on the capitals of the three columns that flank each side of the chapel entrance depict scenes from trench warfare: soldiers preparing for a bayonet charge; automatic riflemen; artillery observers; a machine gun crew; and soldiers launching grenades.

Insignia of American corps and divisions that fought in the area and the United States coat of arms are carved on stone shields near the roof of the chapel. A crusader in armor, flanked by shields of the United States and France intertwined with branches of oak to symbolize the traditional unity of the two nations, graces the pediment. There is also a graphic reminder of World War II here as well. To the right of the chapel entrance is a hole in the stonework made in 1940 by a German anti-tank gun, which was firing at passing French tanks. It has been purposely left unrepaired as a reminder that no war is the last one.

Inside the large double doors of oak, ornamented with wrought iron, on the walls are recorded the names of 1,060 missing men whose remains were never recovered or identified, but who fought in the region and who lie in unknown graves. The visitor is immediately drawn to the apse, which holds an exquisitely carved and gilded altar of Italian marble, the color of peach blossoms. Across the altar's face is inscribed: "Peaceful they rest in glory everlasting."

At the top of the altar back are symbols to both nations, which form a frieze: an owl for wisdom; a crusader whose shield bears a lion device for fortitude; scales for justice; a Gallic cock symbolic of France; a pommée cross on an apple blossom with a serpent representing the Garden of Eden; a fouled anchor and lily to symbolize peace; a poppy for valor; and a passion flower—the Crucifixion and the Resurrection. Three of the five stained glass windows, high in the apse above the altar, depict Saint Louis, one of the great crusaders; Saint Michael triumphing over evil; and Saint Denis, patron saint of France.

Standing sentinel opposite the cemetery's entrance gates is a touching reminder of the American soldiers' feeling for the devastated French countryside. During the fighting the church in the village of Belleau was destroyed by American artillery fire. After the war a veterans' association of the 26th Division raised the funds to restore it. Sixty years after the Armistice, known as the 26th Division Memorial Church of Belleau, it stands as a tribute to Franco-American solidarity.

Looking toward the memorial. *Photograph by Herman Manasse. American Battle Monuments Commission*

56. Meuse-Argonne American Cemetery

ROMAGNE-SOUS-MONTFAUCON, MEUSE, FRANCE

VERDUN, twenty-six miles southwest of the Meuse-Argonne American Cemetery, was in 1916 the scene of the longest and bloodiest battle of World War I. Of the estimated two million men engaged, an incredible number—at least half—were killed. Although the fortresses of Douanmont and Vaux were taken by the Germans, Verdun itself repulsed all assaults. Marshal Pétain and General Nivelle were the commanders; the rallying cry:

"They shall not pass!" The city of Verdun with its battlefields and cemeteries is a French national sanctuary.

The small valley between Romagne and Cunel, the location of the cemetery, just to the rear of the German defensive position known as the Hindenberg Line, was also the area in which some of the hardest fighting by American troops occurred. Established October 14, 1918 —before the Armistice—by the American Graves Registration Service, the 130½ acres comprise the largest American military cemetery in Europe. The land was captured by the 32nd Infantry Division and was granted in perpetuity free of charge or taxation by the French government as an expression of its gratitude to the United States. This too was one of the four cemeteries from which the body of an unknown soldier was brought to Châlons-sur-Marne in 1921 so that one could be selected for interment in Arlington National Cemetery.

Generally rectangular in shape, the cemetery has three-quarters of its area devoted to the graves section and memorial. York and Sawyer of New York, architects, selected the plots in which lie 14,246 war dead (486 of whom are unknown), most of whom fell during the First Army operations from September 26 to November 11, 1918. Almost all units of the American Expeditionary Forces have burials here, among them many who fell in the Vosges Mountains beyond the Argonne Forest, in Germany, and in Russia. The great body of the military dead is represented by an immense array of crosses rising in long regular rows upward beyond the pool to the chapel that crowns the ridge under the skies of Meuse. In the distance is the Argonne Forest, whose name was in each correspondent's dispatch to the newspapers of the world in the fateful days at the close of the Great War.

To reach the graves area the visitor may enter either of two portals, which are, in turn, flanked by gatehouses surmounted by eagles. These lead to the grassy east-west entrance mall six hundred yards long that runs through the small valley across which the cemetery is located. He then takes a road bordered by a double avenue of beech trees, passes a circular pool with a fountain at the center, admires the goldfish and flowering lilies, and then turns and traverses another mall leading at a right angle from the pool through the graves area to the memorial. The entire effect is one of beauty and peace, far removed from the devastation of more than sixty summers ago. The grave plots are formed by square-trimmed linden trees, which are especially spectacular in autumn when their leaves turn color.

On the crest of the hillside at the end of the north-south mall, the living can pause before the memorial and contemplate the tragedy of war and death in battle. Romanesque in design, the memorial—a chapel and two flanking loggias—has exterior walls and columns of Eu-

ville Coquiller stone. The interior walls are Salamandre travertine.

The lintel over the chapel entrance holds the inscription: "In sacred sleep they rest." The tympanum encloses a bas-relief by L. Bottiau of Paris with figures representing *Grief* and *Remembrance*. The visitor then walks through the bronze filigree screen of the entrance, passing carved heads of American soldiers included in the design of the column capitals. Attention is immediately drawn to the apse, in the center of which stands the flag-banked altar. The stained glass windows memorialize the corps and divisions that fought here and create a subdued, soft light that seems to reflect the spirit of the chapel and the inscriptions on the arches over the door, apse, and windows: "God hath taken them unto Himself"; "Their names will live for evermore"; "Peaceful is their sleep in God"; and "Perpetual light upon them shines."

Outside, the loggias—in which one expects to find medieval nuns walking silently, telling their beads or reading their breviaries—contain an ornamental map of the Meuse-Argonne offensive and the incised names of 954 of the missing whose remains were never recovered or identified, including on a separate panel those of the missing from the Services of Supply, and those in the American expedition to northern Russia.

The floors of the pavilions at the ends of the loggias have directional arrows that point to prominent terrain features relating to the operations in the area. The arrows are instructive; the countryside is a reminder that fair is the land of France. In the distance can be seen the Montfaucon Monument, rising two hundred feet above the ruins of the former hilltop village of that name. Before its capture by the American 37th and 79th divisions on September 27, 1918, the site provided German forces with excellent observation.

The peace, the dead, the rows of stones standing serenely, do not tell of the storm of battle, the scene of death that has now become history. The names across the front and ends of the loggias are an echo of the American fighting in the region: Pont-Maugis, Bois-de-Cunel, Meuse, Cierges, Bois-des-Rappes, Consenvoye, Exermont, Grandpré, Meuse Heights, Barricourt-Heights, Gesnes, Montfaucon, Cornay, Bois-de-Foret, Stenay, Argonne, Cheppy, and Côte-de-Chatillon.

One of these graves is that of Joyce Kilmer, poet. *Photograph by Herman Manasse.*
American Battle Monuments Commission

57. Oise-Aisne American Cemetery

SERINGES-SUR-NESLES, FRANCE

IN that last summer of World War I, when the Allied troops were making what proved to be a last offensive, the 42nd Division succeeded in crossing the Ourcq River on July 28, 1918. North of the Ourcq stubborn fighting resulted with some points changing hands as many as four times. The 42nd captured Sergy and Seringes-sur-Nesles, where the cemetery is located, and fought on until relieved on August 3, a time when the enemy was being pursued toward the Vesle River.

During this week of fighting, the 42nd Division was assisted at times by the 47th Infantry Regiment of the 4th Division. When the 42nd was taken from battle it had

advanced seven miles. Its casualties—6,500—were enormous. Only three months remained until Armistice, but the weary men were not aware it was so close at hand. The 32nd Division had entered the line on July 30 on the right of the 28th, which had relieved a French division two days before. On July 30 these two divisions delivered a combined attack in which the 28th captured the Bois des Grimpettes. It then passed into reserve, while the 32nd continued in the offensive, covering both divisional fronts.

The tide of battle accelerated. The following day saw the taking of Cierges by the 32nd, and on August 1, after determined attacks, it captured an important position at Les Jomblets. It managed to hold it despite sustained and vicious counterattacks. By August 2 it was pursuing the German army, which had been forced to fall back to a line north of the Vesle River. The rhythm of pursuit and capture increased. Only two American divisions remained in line—the 4th and the 32nd. Fismes fell on August 4 and three days later the 32nd was relieved by the 28th Division. It had advanced eleven miles and lost almost 3,800 men.

And then began a campaign designed to allow the Germans no time to rest or reorganize. Allied operations were immediately planned against other portions of the front. The first of these—the Somme offensive—begun by the British on August 8 against the salient immediately east of Amiens was highly successful. By August 18 the French Oise-Aisne offensive in the vicinity of Noyon succeeded in forcing the Germans to abandon their positions on the Vesle and Aisne rivers. The 32nd Division, attacking from August 28 to September 1, captured the town of Juvigny in a brilliant assault, penetrating hostile positions to a depth of 2½ miles. When the division was taken out of the line on September 2, it had suffered 2,600 casualties. And when the 28th was relieved on September 8, its total losses on the Ourcq and Vesle were more than 6,700 officers and men. On September 16 the 77th was relieved, its casualties totaling nearly 4,800. The threat against Paris was removed and important railroads were freed for Allied use.

The fighting continued until November 5, six days before Armistice was declared, when the 370th Infantry of the 93rd Division reentered the battle and participated in the pursuit of the German army. The activity of this regiment concluded the American fighting in the Aisne-Marne region. The statistics give a graphic picture of the long and bloody campaign: a total American force of about 310,000 men served with the Allies and suffered losses of 67,000—almost one-fifth its complement.

When the sounds of battle ceased and survivors returned to the United States, a cemetery—the second largest World War I cemetery—was established about 1½ miles from Fère-en-Tardenois. The 36½ acres provide the last resting place for 6,012 military dead, including the graves of 591 unknown soldiers. Most of those buried here died in the fighting along the Ourcq River, which runs through Fère-en-Tardenois, and between here and the Oise River, approximately twenty miles north of Paris. Cram and Ferguson of Boston were the architects and the landscape architect was George Gibbs, Jr.

Handsome ornamental wrought-iron gates lead the visitor toward the burial area. Rows of trees line the central paths and in season beds of roses—in a sense signifying the blood spilled here—provide a border to the walkways. The chapel at the rear becomes a focal point and, as the wayfarer approaches it, the fields of white marble headstones constantly change pattern, the crosses arranging and rearranging themselves into a succession of symmetrical geometrical designs. They are, in essence, waves of Italian marble, undulating with the walker's pace, over the greensward.

Lying here—for sixty years now—is Sergeant Joyce Kilmer (1886–1918), poet and journalist, who reminded his and succeeding generations that a tree "may in summer wear/ A nest of robins in her hair." Kilmer lies with a French unknown soldier and several other nationalities attached to the American units at the time of their deaths. For a time Lieutenant Quentin Roosevelt (1897–1918) was one of the heroes buried here. A son of President Theodore Roosevelt, he was engaged in aerial combat on Bastille Day in the final year of the war. Shot down at Chamery, a village nearby, he was buried by the Germans where he fell. They marked his grave with the wheels of his plane and a rough cross, bearing the inscription: "Roosevelt, American Aviator." In September 1955, he was reburied in the cliffside Normandy Cemetery, overlooking Omaha Beach on the English Channel, beside his brother Brigadier General Theodore Roosevelt, Jr., who died in World War II.

Watching over the graves is the chapel—Romanesque in style, but modern in concept. Each front wall is decorated with the coat of arms of the United States, beneath a frieze of shields that display the insignia of branches of the army. Insignia of the American divisions that took part in the battles in this region are carved into the column capitals. Four medallions above the columns contrast the American doughboy of World War I with the medieval crusaders.

The 241 names of those who were declared missing from this region after the smoke of battle lifted are inscribed on the interior wall of the chapel. The altar bears a number of symbolic carvings: the olive tree for peace; a pelican feeding its young—the atonement of Christ's redemptive sacrifice; the oak tree for strength, faith, and virtue; the eagle flying—the Resurrection; the palm wreath and cross—the cross for Christian faith, the palm betokening the Christian's reward for his faith.

There is tranquillity here in the Oise-Aisne Cemetery, with lilac, Saint-John's-wort, hibiscus, and hydrangea planted to enhance the graves. In its framework (oak, birch, pine, fir, cedar, poplar, ash, and maple) of woodland, which gives the impression that the clearing has been hewn from an ancient forest, the words of the poet lying here—"But only God can make a tree"—seem more meaningful than on the printed page.

The memorial is classical in style. *Photograph by Herman Manasse. American Battle Monuments Commission*

58. Saint-Mihiel American Cemetery

THIAUCOURT, MEURTHE-ET-MOSELLE, FRANCE

THE Saint-Mihiel offensive of September 12, 1918—the first operation of World War I carried out by an American army under the separate and independent control of an American commander-in-chief (General John J. Pershing)—was a complete success and relieved the salient occupied by the Germans since 1914. The cemetery here is the last resting place of the Americans who died in this decisive action.

Though less important than the fortress of Verdun, Saint-Mihiel was one of the fortified towns guarding the strategic line of the Meuse on the approach to Paris from the east. The Germans, following their unsuccessful efforts in the first Battle of the Marne, occupied the Saint-Mihiel salient on the western front, a position that offered considerable defensive strength. It was roughly triangular in shape, running from Verdun on the north, south to Saint-Mihiel, and then east to Pont-à-Mouson on the Moselle River. Bordered by a line of trees known as the Heights of the Meuse, and a succession of lakes situated across deep ravines and dense forests, the salient also provided vital protection to the strategic rail center of Metz and the Briey iron basin—both vital to the Germans as a source of raw materials for munitions. It also permitted the Germans to interrupt French rail communications and constituted a constant threat against Verdun and Nancy.

It was at this stage—four years after the German occupation—that American aid was vitally needed to retake the salient before any large Allied offensive could be launched against Briey and Metz or northward between the Meuse River and the Argonne Forest.

When the smoke of battle lifted, the American Graves Registration Service established a temporary cemetery here in 1918, but after the war's end other temporary cemeteries in the area were discontinued. Those whose next of kin requested burial overseas were brought for permanent burial here, the third largest (40½ acres) of the eight permanent World War I American military cemeteries in Europe.

Thomas Harlan Ellett of New York, engaged as architect, developed the site into one of the most distinctive and unforgettable of all the American military cemeteries in Europe. A central mall, lined on each side by square trimmed European linden trees, leads from a formal entrance—with ornamental gates and fencing—to the memorial. In the center of the cemetery, at the intersection of the mall and transverse axis, is a sundial, a carved stone eagle gnomon on a round base surrounded by beds of floral annuals and bordered with a dwarf boxwood hedge. The shadow cast by the eagle on the Roman numerals indicates the time of the day and the truth of the inscription around its base: "Time will not dim the glory of their deeds."

From here the perspectives along the two axes can be seen—at the west end a figure by the sculptor Paul Manship of a youthful American officer in his field uniform before a stone cross. The figure, trench helmet in hand, with side arms and gas mask, is stopped in time and has caught the spirit of the words inscribed above him:

Il Dort
Loin des Siens
Dans la Douce
Terre de France

"He sleeps far from his family in the gentle land of France." Below the figure are the words: "Blessed are they that have the home longing for they shall go home." At the opposite end of the transverse axis from the doughboy (with the sundial between them) is an ornamental urn on a semicircular platform flanked by two beautiful yews.

Separated by the mall and transverse axis, the four sections of the graves area are the final resting place of the men who died in defense of France and Western democracy. The 4,152 headstones bear testimony to this.

Rather than the usual memorial building with pavilions or loggias as dependencies, the architect created the most classical of memorials—an open circular colonnade or peristyle of Rocheret limestone, with a chapel room to its left and a small museum room to the right. Here, on this slightly raised terrace, chestnut trees framing it, the peristyle becomes the simplest yet most effective of memorials. Behind are two large weeping willows.

Commanding the center of this classical structure is a rose granite urn, complete with carved drapery. It could be Roman in origin, some ancient funeral vase, or even nineteenth-century neoclassical in concept. Instead, it has the feeling of its own time within its classical frame. Pegasus, the winged horse, symbolizing the flight of the immortal soul to its final resting place in the afterlife, decorates the urn's face.

The chapel, its bronze doors decorated with stars and miniature soldier heads, is impressive with its large lighted bronze lamp, symbolizing an eternal flame, which dominates the Italian marble altar and draws the eye to the *Angel of Death* mosaic above the altar itself. The angel sheathes his sword as the doves of peace bear laurel branches aloft to meet the inscription: "I give unto them eternal life and they shall never perish." The museum houses the Wall of the Missing, the names of 284 American soldiers whose remains were never recovered or identified, beneath the inscription: "In memory of those American soldiers who fought in this region and who sleep in unknown graves."

The Picardy countryside enhances this small cemetery. *American Battle Monuments Commission*

59. Somme American Cemetery

BONY, AISNE, FRANCE

ANYONE with knowledge of English in the World War I years was familiar with Picardy through the words and music of the ballad "Roses of Picardy." Situated on a gentle slope, typical of the open rolling Picardy countryside, the fourteen-acre Somme American Cemetery contains the graves of 1,844 men, most of whom lost their lives while serving in American units attached to the British army, or in operations near Cantigny.

The headstones of the graves area are set in regular rows and are divided into four plots by paths that intersect at the flagpole near the top of the slope. The longer axis leads to the eastern end of the cemetery and the

chapel, a small building on whose outer walls are sculptured pieces of military equipment. Its entrance is a massive bronze door surmounted by an American eagle. On the interior walls are inscribed the names of 333 missing. Through a cross-shaped window of crystal glass, above the marble altar, the natural light from outside enters with a luminous radiance, touching the subdued interior and falling on the names incised on the walls.

The Somme American Cemetery, ninety-eight miles northeast of Paris, is southwest of the village of Bony, which is three-quarters of a mile west of highway N-44 bis from Saint Quentin to Cambrai and Lille.

President Woodrow Wilson dedicated this cemetery in 1919. *Photograph by Herman Manasse. American Battle Monuments Commission*

60. Suresnes American Cemetery

SURESNES, FRANCE

THE long shadow Napoleon cast remains at Suresnes American Cemetery just as it does at Père-Lachaise, although the first emperor of the French is buried in neither cemetery. In 1811 Napoleon confiscated the hill then known as Mont Valerian, which had earlier been called Mont Calvaire. It was Bonaparte's intention to build here a home for the orphans of the Legion of Honor, but during a subsequent visit he decided that it would be the ideal place for a fort. His defeat at Waterloo stopped work on the fort and Mont Valerian became a religious shrine, its original purpose.

In earlier years the mount was the site of a hermitage and was a place of pilgrimage for the religious. The hermits maintained gardens and vineyards here as well as a guest home that Thomas Jefferson often visited when he was ambassador to France from 1784 to 1789.

Its later history, before becoming a cemetery, is a grisly one. During the World War II German occupation the Fort of Mont Valerian (which was finally built in 1840 long after Napoleon's fall and death) was occupied by Nazi troops. They executed here 4,500 political prisoners and members of the Resistance. To honor those French men and women, the nation erected a monument to their memory along the south wall of the fort. This hill in Suresnes in the twentieth century became a symbol to the French of democracy's struggle for freedom and has again become a place of pilgrimage for both French and American people.

Established in 1917 by the Graves Registration Service of the Army Quartermaster Corps, Suresnes Cemetery contains, principally, the graves of World War I dead, the majority of whom died of wounds or sickness in hospitals located in Paris or at other places in the Services of Supply. Many were victims of the influenza epidemic of 1918–1919.

President Woodrow Wilson dedicated the cemetery at Memorial Day ceremonies in 1919, it was completed in 1932, and in 1934 its administration was taken over by the American Battle Monuments Commission. It is unique in that at the end of World War II it was decided that this particular cemetery should commemorate the dead of both wars. To achieve this, an additional grave plot was created for the remains of twenty-four unknowns from World War II and commemorative loggias were added to the original chapel. This new section was dedicated in 1952 with General George C. Marshall presiding and other dignitaries attending.

The three burial plots devoted to the graves from World War I contain a total of 1,541 graves—Latin crosses and the Star of David side by side, without distinction as to rank, race, or creed. There are seven nurses and a pair of brothers at Suresnes as well as a pair of sisters.

The 7½ acres of the cemetery are dominated by the chapel, which is classical in concept. Charles A. Platt, New York architect, designed the original chapel; his sons, William and Geoffrey Platt, performed the same service for the loggias and memorial rooms added after World War II.

Gilded wrought-iron entrance gates lead to an avenue of clipped lindens, at the end of which stands the chapel. Rhododendron and polyantha roses frame its setting. Having had longer to mature than those in the newer military cemeteries, the plantings at Suresnes are particularly lovely. Among the grave plots are beech, weeping willow, mountain ash, horse chestnut, and paulownia. Behind the chapel, the hillside becomes a curtain of pines, yews, acacia, and hornbeam.

The words "Peaceful is their sleep in glory" between the columns and pediment of its façade establish a tone of serenity for the chapel. Val d'Arion, a creamy French limestone, was used for the exterior walls and Rocheret, a limestone quarried in central France, for the interior. The principal decorative feature inside the chapel is the mosaic mural created by Barry Faulkner behind the altar. It depicts the Angel of Victory bearing a palm branch to the graves of the fallen. The Italian Levanto marble altar is itself inscribed: "I give unto them eternal life and they shall never perish."

The walls of the loggias commemorate the dead of both great wars: the left loggia those of World War I, that on the right those of World War II. Both are open on one side and give a view of the graves area and Paris in the distance. The bas-relief in the first portrays a group of soldiers carrying an empty bier, that on the opposite loggia a group bearing the shrouded remains of an unknown. The memorial rooms are dominated by works of art: *Remembrance,* a figure in Carrara marble by American sculptor John Gregory to those who died in 1917–1918; and *Memory* by the American Lewis Iselin to those who died between 1941 and 1945.

The names of 974 who were buried or lost at sea during World War I are tabulated on four large plaques. These, and those of their 1,565 fellows buried here, serve as reminders to a world fraught with wars and rumors of war. They fought to make the world safe for democracy.

The sculpture on the memorial was designed by C. Paul Jennewein. *Photograph by Herman Manasse. American Battle Monuments Commission*

World War II Cemeteries

61. Ardennes American Cemetery

NEUVILLE-EN-CONDROZ, BELGIUM

LIÈGE, the great commercial, industrial, and transportation center of Belgium, fell to the German invaders in 1914 and again in 1940. During the Battle of the Bulge (1944–1945), Liège and its surrounding area suffered heavily from bombardment by rocket weapons before it was finally liberated.

Ardennes Cemetery, near the southeast edge of the village of Neuville-en-Condroz, twelve miles southwest of

Liège, was liberated by the United States 1st Division on December 8, 1944, and was established as a military cemetery on February 8, 1945. Here, in 90½ acres of a slope that descends gently northward toward the village, are buried 5,279 American dead. If any spot can be said to be suitable for such a purpose—and military cemeteries have been chosen with the utmost care—it is the Ardennes Cemetery. Its south and east sides are framed in woodland in which red and white oak, beech, and ash predominate. Its west side is lined by an avenue of stately lindens and its north boundary by informal tree groups.

Architects Reinhard, Hofmeister & Walquist of New York worked within the framework of the contours of the land itself. The main gate is set within a plantation of white pine and its wing walls are backed by an evergreen hedge. An avenue bordered by horse chestnut trees leads for three hundred yards through the woods to a broad green mall bordered by massifs of prostrate yews.

Beyond this a memorial of English Portland Whitbed limestone stands austerely, guarding the graves area. One approaches a podium of Danube gray granite and after ascending seven steps reaches the memorial itself. An American eagle in high relief seventeen feet high decorates the south façade of the memorial. Beside the eagle are three figures symbolizing Justice, Liberty, and Truth—all designed by C. Paul Jennewein of New York and executed by Jean Juge of Paris.

At the far end, the north side facing the graves area, one finds the chapel entrance. To one side in the wall is the dedication, to the other a prayer somewhat abridged from one ascribed to Cardinal Newman. Beyond is the altar of Carrara marble. Above it, outlined in gilt metal against the white Carrara marble wall, an angel, designed by Dean Cornwell of New York and executed by Kersten-Leroy of Maastricht, The Netherlands, is illuminated through an oculus in the ceiling.

The north façade of the memorial facing the graves is decorated with the shoulder insignia of the major military units—colored mosaic set in Portland stone—grouped about a classic helmet. The legend beneath reads: "To the silent host who endured all and gave all that mankind might live in freedom and in peace." The names and particulars of 462 of the missing, engraved on twelve large slabs of gray granite, record their sacrifice. That of the 5,279 buried here—three-fifths of whom were airmen—is evident in the rows of crosses and the stars of David. Many died in repulsing the enemy's final major counteroffensive in the Ardennes in December 1944 and January 1945. Others gave their lives in the advance to the Rhine and across Germany, or in the strategic bombardment of Europe.

The gravestones in the four plots are arranged to form a huge Greek cross, but are separated by two broad intersecting paths. From the air or an elevation this pattern takes on an added poignancy. There are eleven instances of brothers buried side by side and three cases in which two identical airmen are buried in single graves. The inscription reads: "Here rest in honored glory two comrades in arms." Bronze plaques bearing their names and particulars are set in the ground before the headstones. The unknown graves are marked by 746 headstones.

The reentrants of the huge cross formed by the headstone pattern are planted with groups of oak, beech, hornbeam, and tulip trees, intended to extend the natural woodland enframement. The entire burial area is surrounded on four sides by wide borders of shrub roses. The burial area and its axial path gently slope down to the flagstaff and its platform at the north end of the cemetery. Groups of Canadian hemlock, Caucasian fir, and elm judiciously chosen by Richard K. Weber of Roslyn, New York, form the background. A transverse path leads westward to the linden avenue, which intersects the path at the head of the burial area.

At the end of the central transverse path stands the bronze figure by C. Paul Jennewein, which was cast by Bruno Bearzi of Florence, Italy. It typifies the spirit of American youth—so many of whom went east in the dark days of 1941–1945, and lie here in Ardennes.

A colonnade of twelve pairs of rectangular pylons in the classical tradition forms this memorial. *Photograph by Herman Manasse. American Battle Monuments Commission*

62. Henri-Chapelle American Cemetery

HENRI-CHAPELLE, BELGIUM

HIGH on the crest of a ridge just outside the village of Henri-Chapelle, on the much-traveled main highway from Liège, Belgium, to Aachen, Germany, the Henri-Chapelle American Cemetery guards the remains of almost eight thousand American military dead.

The site was liberated on September 12, 1944 by troops of the United States 1st Infantry Division; about two or three hundred yards to the north a spot was first used as a temporary cemetery on September 28 of that year. Because of its more attractive setting, affording wide prospects to the east and west, the present location was chosen as a permanent burial place. Most of those interred here gave their lives in the repulse of the German counteroffensive in the Ardennes, or during the advance into, and across, Germany during the autumn and winter of 1944 and the spring of 1945, or in air operations over the region.

To the west of highway N 18 (which crosses the property) is an overlook area. From its west end one has a view of the valley of the Berwinne streamlet (which lies in the sector of the advance of the United States 1st Infantry Division) and the ridge beyond. East of the highway lie the memorial and the graves area. The entire cemetery is in the shape of an open fan.

A bronze archangel bestowing the laurel branch on the dead guards the burial area. Designed by Donal Hord of San Diego, California, and cast by Battaglia of Milan, Italy, the dark archangel appears to be in suspension over the rows of white headstones. The eight plots, separated by a broad axial mall and by longitudinal grass paths, contain 7,984 headstones. The dead came from forty-nine states, the District of Columbia, Panama, and England. There are thirty-two instances here in which two brothers rest side by side, and one in which three brothers do. Ninety-four stones mark the graves of unknowns.

A colonnade of twelve pairs of rectangular pylons connects the chapel on one end and the museum on the other. Designed by Holabird, Root and Burgee of Chicago, and set within a framework of box hedges, the memorial has as its exterior stone Massangis limestone from the Côte d'Or region of France and the colonnade, chapel, and museum are paved with gray Saint Gothard granite from Switzerland. At each end are groups of weeping willows and on the north and south sides are groups of Servian spruce and Norway spruce mixed with hawthorns. The paths of the approach to the memorial are lined with pink and scarlet polyantha roses and geraniums.

On the forty-eight faces of the colonnade are engraved the names and particulars of the 450 missing, and also the seals of the wartime forty-eight states, three territories, and the District of Columbia. The austere chapel with its altar of Belgian blue and French vert d'Issorie marble is hung with the flags of the Air Force, Armor, Christian Chapel, Jewish Chapel, Engineers, Field Artillery, Infantry, and Navy Infantry Battalion. The walnut pews were fabricated in Holland and with the cross over the altar were purposely designed to be off-center (with off-center lighting), thus balancing each other.

Built into the museum's west interior wall of English Portland Whitbed stone is a map of Swedish black granite, designed by Sante Graziani of Worcester, Massachusetts, and fabricated by Enrico Pandolfini of Pietrasanta, Italy. It portrays military operations in northwestern Europe from the Normandy landings to the war's end. A similar but somewhat smaller map by the same artist on the south wall is entitled *Aachen and the Advance to the Roer,* illustrating military operations in this region.

Franz Lipp of Chicago, landscape architect, took into consideration the broad and picturesque valley when choosing the trees and shrubs. Within the graves area birch, hornbeam, and yew were planted and free growing box massed in groups against the surrounding walls. The central mall terminates in a wall-enclosed flagpole plaza, backed by a copse of oak and spruce trees. Beyond the wall are groups of rhododendron, chestnut, and Norway spruce.

The graves area holds 3,811 headstones in seven curved grave plots. *Photograph by Herman Manasse. American Battle Monuments Commission*

63. Cambridge American Cemetery

CAMBRIDGE, ENGLAND

OFTEN called the "flower of English cities," Cambridge, the ancient market town that is the home of the university, is situated on the Cam River, which flows slowly through the fens toward the North Sea. It has special meaning for Americans. One of the university's seventeenth-century graduates, John Harvard (Master of Arts of Emmanuel College), emigrated to Massachusetts. His benefactions led the newly formed college to change its name to Harvard and Newetown was rechristened Cambridge in honor of the English university. At that time it

had educated about seventy leaders of the Massachusetts Bay Colony.

Cambridge itself dates before the Norman Conquest. In the first century B.C. it is known that Belgic invaders covered fifteen acres of Castle Hill with oval enclosures, and later in A.D. 43 the Romans had a garrison there and appropriated about twenty-eight acres on the same promontory. In 1284, under the terms of Hugh de Balsham's will, the first of the Cambridge colleges, Peterhouse, was formed. Since then Cambridge has become one of the great centers of learning, and is architecturally superb. Of all the places of beauty in Britain, none other could be more desirable for an American cemetery.

Established in 1943 on land donated by the University of Cambridge, the American Cemetery of 30½ acres is located three miles west of the city on the main highway (A45) to Saint Neots. It is situated on the north slope of a hill, where the prospect is superb. On clear days Ely Cathedral, fourteen miles distant, can be seen. The cemetery is framed by woodland on the west and south. In the beginning it was one of several temporary military cemeteries in Britain, but was later selected as the only permanent World War II military cemetery in the British Isles.

The architects—Perry, Shaw, Hepburn and Dean of Boston—were faced with the problem of using a small area fully, yet creating an effect of great space. In resolving this, they created two malls, each meeting the other at a 90-degree angle. The west mall stretches from the seventy-two-foot flagpole, just inside the entrance gates; the great mall from the flagpole to the memorial. About the flagstaff is a quotation from *In Flanders Fields* by John McCrae:

To you from failing hands we throw
The torch; be yours to hold it high

The great mall, with its reflecting pool bordered by polyantha roses, stretches eastward, and along its south side is the Wall of the Missing, recording the names and particulars of 5,125 missing in action, lost, or buried at sea. The names of twenty-four unknowns interred in the cemetery are probably included among those on the wall of Portland stone. Four statues carved by English craftsmen, representing a soldier, a sailor, an airman, and a coast guardsman in typical uniform, are stationed along the wall itself.

The fan-shaped graves area holds 3,811 headstones in seven curved grave plots. Among the stones aligned in rows of concentric arcs are two that represent burials of two and three servicemen respectively, whose names are known but could not be separately identified. Their remains are buried together; bronze tablets over the graves record their names. Viewed from the north edge of the flagpole platform, the graves pattern is evident—the stones are aligned like the spokes of a wheel. Each plot is enclosed with a boxwood hedge, with tulip trees, catalpa, beech, oak, and sweet gum. It is in its own way one of the most unusual formations of graves to be found in any cemetery.

About 39 percent of the temporary burials made in England and Northern Ireland during the war are interred in this permanent cemetery. A high proportion of the American servicemen and women were crew members of British-based American aircraft. Most of the others buried here died in the invasion of North Africa and France, in the training areas of the United Kingdom, and in the waters of the Atlantic.

In selecting Portland stone for the memorial, the architects had historic precedent to follow. Saint Paul's Cathedral and many other monumental buildings in the British capital are of this stone quarried on the south coast of England. Above the five pylons on the north face is the inscription: "Grant unto them O Lord eternal rest." Below the bronze rope railing on the north face balcony is written: "In grateful tribute to their sacrifice and in proud memory of their valor."

The entrance with its teakwood doors on the west end is framed with two pylons. Above them on the pediment are the words: "To the glory of God and in memory of those who died for their country 1941–1945." Facing the garden, a map executed by English artist David Kindersley depicts each location in the United Kingdom where an American unit of battalion or larger size was stationed during World War II, the principal land and sea routes to Great Britain from the United States, and the invasion routes to North Africa in 1942 and to Normandy in 1944.

The memorial's interior is separated into a large museum room and at the far end a small devotional chapel. Another impressive map, this one designed by the American artist Herbert Gute and entitled *The Mastery of the Atlantic—The Great Air Assault,* dominates the museum. Seals of the war and navy departments and their individual decorations are depicted in the glass panels.

Simplicity is the theme of the tiny chapel. Over the teakwood doorway bronze characters proclaim: "Into Thy hands O Lord." And the words "Faith" and "Hope" in bronze letters are set into the chancel rail. A cloth of mail is spread over the Portland stone altar on which rests a large bronze cross. Flanking the altar are two large ornamental candelabra embellished with mosaic.

Francis Scott Bradford created a mosaic depicting the Archangel trumpeting the Resurrection and the Last Judgment, which covers the wall above the altar and continues across the entire ceiling of the memorial. Ghostly aircraft, accompanied by mourning angels, make their final flight. A nimbus surrounds each of the single-engine, twin-engine, and four-engine aircraft, separating them from earthly forces while they carry the souls of the men who perished in the skies. The ship and aircraft depicted above the altar are in memory of the members of the naval sea and air forces who are buried or commemorated at the cemetery. The Latin crosses and the Star of David symbolize those buried under them.

The visitor should not begin his examination of this lovely spot without first reading a small bronze tablet on the wall of the Visitors' Building. It is a reminder of the affection the British people have for the Americans. The grateful citizens of Cheshunt and Waltham Cross placed it there to honor the members of an American bomber crew who sacrificed themselves in order to avoid abandoning their disabled aircraft over these English villages.

From the tower, in clear weather, Mont-Saint-Michel can be seen fifteen miles away.
Photograph by Herman Manasse. American Battle Monuments Commission

64. Brittany American Cemetery

SAINT JAMES, MANCHE, FRANCE

ON the border between Brittany and Normandy, two departments of France whose countryside has often been ravaged by war, the twenty-eight-acre Brittany American Cemetery stands just outside the village of Saint James, Manche, twelve miles from Avranches on the channel coast.

Following the Allies' assault landings on the Normandy beaches on June 6, 1944, a beachhead was estab-

lished extending roughly along the east-west line through Saint-Lô, some forty miles to the north of the cemetery. By July 25, while the British held the enemy in the eastern portion of the beachhead toward Caen, the American forces broke out at the west end and captured Avranches on July 31. With these strategic points theirs, the American Third and First armies advanced in different directions—westward toward Brest, southward toward Loire, and eastward toward the Seine.

Familiar hedgerows so characteristic of the region border the highways that reach the cemetery, which is on land that once lay in the sector of the 8th Division and was liberated on August 2, 1944. Here rest 4,410 Americans, representing 43 percent of those who were originally buried in temporary cemeteries in the region extending from the beachhead westward to Brest and eastward to the Seine. The cemetery, with its stone chapel at one end of the mall and cenotaph at the other, can be thought of as either bell-shaped or shield-shaped with sixteen burial plots, eight on each side of the central mall. Ninety-five of the headstones mark graves of unknowns; two of these graves each contained the remains of two unknowns who could not be separately identified. In twenty instances brothers are buried side by side.

The plantings here are extraordinary and were planned by landscape architects Shurcliff and Shurcliff of Boston. The cemetery is surrounded by a hawthorn hedge with an interior hedge of boxwood enclosing the grave plots. In the broad grass walks dividing the plots are flowering crab apple, double hawthorn, pagoda tree, goldenrain tree, and yellowwood tree. Elsewhere are found both evergreen and deciduous trees: Giant sequoia, white fir, Norway spruce, Scotch pine, holly oak, tulip tree, purple beech, and the European varieties of oak, chestnut, hornbeam, and elm. The Brittany Cemetery is an arboretum. Reservoirs for the cemetery have been constructed nearby.

The memorial, designed by William T. Aldrich of Boston, housing the museum and chapel, consists of a nave and tower of local La Pyrie granite and is strongly reminiscent of the ecclesiastical architecture typical of the region. On entering, beyond the antechamber, is the memorial room hung with flags. A map—*The Break-Out from the Beachhead and Advance to the Seine*—dominates the north wall and opposite it is a similar one—*Military Operations in Western Europe*. Extracts from General Eisenhower's final report to the combined chiefs of staff and an extract from Franklin D. Roosevelt's D-day prayer on the occasion of the invasion of Normandy are cut deep into the stone.

Separated from the museum by a granite screen and wrought-iron gates, the chapel is graced by an altar of French Hauteville Perle limestone from the Juras. Below the stained glass window, with the seal of the United States as its motif, and above the altar is a blue and gold damask hanging. Above and encircling the window are the words from Exodus: "In the morning ye shall see the glory of the Lord." Just outside the window on the east end of the memorial can be seen the sculptural group *Youth Triumphing Over Evil* by Lee Lawrie of Easton, Maryland, which was executed by Jean Juge of Paris. Lawrie was also responsible for the sculptural group over the main door on the west end—an eagle, shield, stars, laurel, and arrows taken from the Great Seal of the United States. The other sculpture—the cenotaph at the lower end of the mall—is also of La Pyrie granite and was designed by Lawrie. Along the curved retaining wall of the terrace the names of 498 of the missing are incised.

It is suggested to visitors that they ascend the ninety-nine-foot tower to the lookout platform sixty-three feet aboveground. From this aerie the Breton and Norman countrysides are spread before the eye in all their beauty and peace, the stately pattern of headstones below takes on a particular pathos, and on clear days Mont-Saint-Michel, the medieval abbey of the Benedictines that is one of the great treasures of Gothic architecture, can be seen fifteen miles in the distance. Henry Adams, especially, would have appreciated the view.

Malvina Hoffman did the decorative sculptures on this memorial. *Photograph by Herman Manasse. American Battle Monuments Commission*

65. Epinal American Cemetery

EPINAL, VOSGES, FRANCE

EPINAL, a town of somewhat over twenty thousand people, lies in the mountainous French department of Vosges in the region of Lorraine. This pastoral area, which also has the largest iron fields in Europe, is a remnant of the ancient kingdom of Lotharingia (from which the name Lorraine is derived). The region suffered heavily in both World Wars: Verdun being the center of the fighting in 1916–1918; Metz and Vosges in 1944.

The Epinal Cemetery, forty-eight acres in extent, lies on a plateau a hundred feet above the Moselle River in the foothills of the Vosges Mountains, four miles south of Epinal, approximately 231 miles east of Paris, 46 from Nancy, and 55 from Belfort. Liberated by troops of the

United States 45th Division on September 21, 1944, the site became a battlefield cemetery on October 6 during the fighting to force the passage of the Vosges Mountains.

Here in eastern France near the borders of Luxembourg, Germany, and Switzerland lie 5,255 American military dead. They represent 42 percent of the burials originally made in the region, most of whom gave their lives during the advances across central France and up the Rhone valley, the fighting in the Vosges, in the Rhine valley, and across Germany beyond the Rhine.

The cemetery, designed by architects Delano and Aldrich of New York, is shaped like an amphitheatre, with its entrances leading circuitously to a central oval, then to a memorial and Court of Honor. Before this a central rectangular mall bisects the two burial areas. Here the 5,252 headstones, all in regular alignment in straight rows upon the smooth green lawn, harmonize with the dignified effect of the rectangular lines of the memorial and Court of Honor.

Perhaps the overlying theme for these victims of the god Mars is found in the words inscribed on the walls of the Court of Honor: "This is their memorial—the whole earth their sepulchre." Recorded on the walls are the names of 424 missing. In each of two graves are the remains of two known dead who could not be separately identified. Sixty-nine headstones mark the graves of unknowns and one—poignantly—contains the remains of two of these comrades-in-arms. In fourteen instances brothers are buried side by side. Use of the site, granted in perpetuity by the French government, includes a right of way 550 yards long, leading from highway N-57 to the cemetery.

The memorial, which houses the chapel and the museum, has on its south face toward the mall two bas-reliefs by American sculptor Malvina Hoffman, representing *The Crusade in Europe* and *The Resurrection,* as well as an eagle on the face of the attic. Above the altar within the chapel Miss Hoffman created an *Angel of Peace* to fit the inscription from Saint Luke, which accompanies it: "Give light to them that sit in darkness and guide our feet into the way of peace." The rear wall is decorated with two rondels—one with a cross and another with the tablets of Moses.

The mosaic wall map, designed and fabricated by Eugene Savage of Branford, Connecticut, dominating the museum, depicts the American and Allied military operations from the landings on the southern coast of France on August 15, 1944 to the junction on September 11 at Sombernon, near Dijon, with the Allied forces coming from Normandy.

Homer L. Fry of Austin, Texas, landscape architect, planted the wide mall separating the two grave plots with rows of sycamores. Beyond, immediately to the south, is a natural woodland of oak, spruce, and beech. Flanking the memorial are two cedars of Lebanon and informal masses of flowering quince, rhododendron, azalea, forsythia, and Scotch broom. This beautiful combination of trees and flowering shrubs complements the magnificent view of the Moselle valley and the wooded slopes beyond the cemetery, one of the most unforgettable in France.

The rectangular memorial is sixty-seven feet high. *Photograph by Herman Manasse.*
American Battle Monuments Commission

66. Lorraine American Cemetery

SAINT AVOLD, MOSELLE, FRANCE

THE largest World War II American military cemetery in Europe (113½ acres), this final resting place of 10,489 military dead is three-quarters of a mile north of the town of Saint Avold, which is twenty-eight miles east of Metz and seventeen miles southeast of Saarbrücken. The town of Saint Avold was named for a Roman Christian soldier (whose name is often spelled Saint Nabor), who was martyred about A.D. 303 in the reign of the Emperor Maximilian.

An American military cemetery was first established in the area on March 16, 1945, about a half mile to the south. The area itself had been liberated by the 80th Infantry Division on November 27, 1944. Later when a permanent cemetery was planned the present site was selected becasue of its location and outstanding prospects.

The overall design, by architects Murphy and Locraft of Washington, D.C., is unlike that of any of the military cemeteries abroad. Rather, it is like one of the nineteenth-century rural, or garden, cemeteries, consisting of nine plots laid out about the axis in a symmetrical pattern, divided by gracefully curved paths. When it is viewed from the air, one sees a large oval, circled by a path. The eight other plots, all curved to a degree, abut this central plot.

One enters the main entrance gates at the west end of the cemetery and proceeds along a linden-lined avenue to the memorial crowning the hill. From here the graves —of men who gave their lives in the advance to the Rhine and across Germany in the final spring of the war in 1945—stretch in straight lines in each of the plots, and represent 41 percent of the burials originally made in this region. One hundred and fifty mark the graves of unknowns, in twenty-six cases brothers are buried side by side, and one stone marks the burial site of three men whose names are known and who were buried together. A bronze tablet covers the grave and records their names. Beyond the graves area—about 350 yards from the memorial—the ground rises to a gentle knoll upon which is an overlook. From this vantage point the visitor is afforded a prospect of the entire cemetery—a moving experience—as well as the countryside for miles to the west.

The tall rectangular memorial tower, sixty-seven feet high, flanked by massive hedges of European beech backed by lindens, is built of Euville limestone from the region of Commercy near the Meuse River, seventy miles to the southwest. The west façade of the tower bears a rondel of the obverse of the Great Seal of the United States. Toward the top are three superimposed angels of victory, each bearing a laurel wreath, which were designed by Walter Hancock of Gloucester, Massachusetts. Above the entrance on the east side is an exciting sculpture by Michael Lantz of New Rochelle, New York, de-

picting Saint Avold, his hands raised in the act of blessing the dead. It is one of the finest pieces of sculpture to be found in any military cemetery—heroic in size, bold in concept, suspended between earth and sky.

This same excitement generated in stone extends to the interior where Lantz created five sculptured figures, representing the eternal struggle for freedom, typified by a youthful center figure. Flanking him—two to each side —are religious and military heroes who embraced this struggle: King David, Emperor Constantine, King Arthur, and George Washington. They form the background over the altar of French green Antique Patricia marble, bearing the text from Saint John X, 28: "I give unto them eternal life and they shall never perish." The altar complex is bathed with light that streams through the window facing north.

Maps of colored glazed ceramic, designed by Pierre Bourdelle of Oyster Bay, New York, and Georgette Pierre of Paris, portray military operations in Northwest Europe from the Normandy landings until V-E Day and the fighting in the Saint Avold region from the Moselle to the Rhine.

Outside the Walls of the Missing, flanking the tower, are reminders of the 444 men who gave their lives but whose remains were not recovered or identified. It faces the graves area, beautifully landscaped by Allyn R. Jennings of Oley, Pennsylvania, with informal groups of English oak, honey locust, red and white flowering hawthorns, and the pagoda tree. Hibiscus, hydrangea, and lilac flowers in the open areas complement this. The total effect seems to echo the sentiment found in the words on the wall between the altar and the five freedom figures that hang above it:

Our fellow countrymen—enduring all and giving all that mankind might live in freedom and in peace. They join that glorious band of heroes who have gone before.

The Spirit of American Youth Rising from the Waves soars over the cemetery as a swimmer emerging from the depths. *Photograph by Herman Manasse. American Battle Monuments Commission*

67. Normandy American Cemetery

SAINT LAURENT-SUR-MER, FRANCE

IN the museum at Bayeux, preserved now for almost nine centuries, the celebrated Bayeux Tapestry records a channel invasion, in this instance that of William I of England. William's forces sailed for England in 1066 and defeated Harold, the last Saxon king, at Hastings. Since that time invasions from the English side of the channel have not been infrequent.

In preparation for the massive assault on Normandy on June 6, 1944, Allied air forces disrupted transportation between the Seine and the Loire rivers and conducted strategic air bombardment deep into enemy territory in an attempt to keep the German air force occupied and on the defensive, and to isolate landing areas.

In the early morning hours, protected by a cover of

darkness, the Allied invasion, known to all men as D day, began when three airborne divisions—the British 6th and the United States 82nd and 101st—were dropped to the rear of the beach areas to cover deployment of the seaborne assault forces. Utah Beach was taken with relatively light casualities. In contrast, Omaha Beach's terrain was a major obstacle and in fighting to achieve the plateau at the head of the steep sandy bluffs the loss of life for Allied forces was heavy. Before the day was over the United States 1st Division took the high ground on which the cemetery now stands.

Once the Normandy beaches were taken, Cherbourg, Caen, Saint-Lô, Coutances, and Avranches were liberated and the road to Paris open. Those who died in this memorable and terrible assault were buried in temporary cemeteries. On June 7 (known to the military as D+1) the Army's Graves Registration Service established the first temporary American World War II cemetery in France. This, and others, continued in operation until permanent ones were ready. When the temporary cemeteries were disestablished by the army, the remains of the dead whose next of kin requested permanent interment overseas were moved to one of the permanent sites on foreign soil, usually the one closest to their temporary graves.

High on the bluffs and looking toward Britain, from where the landing craft started their fateful rendezvous with destiny, the 172½-acre American Cemetery is one of the largest military cemeteries overseas. It is northwest of Saint Laurent-sur-Mer, a mere ten miles from the ancient city of Bayeux. Farther on is Saint-Lô, a scene of great destruction during the assaults. It is rectangular in shape, its main paths laid out in the form of a Latin cross. A little more than three-quarters of the cemetery is devoted to grave sites in which 9,386 servicemen and women, 307 of whom are unknown, lie.

Harbeson, Hough, Livingston & Larson of Philadelphia, architects, planned the rectangle to include ten burial plots, five on each side of a central mall. Two Italian granite (Baverno) figures, representing the United States and France, rise above the graves area at the western end of the central mall. The chapel, about one-third of the way along the mall toward the western end, is complemented on the east by a memorial at the head of a reflecting pool. Landscape architect Markley Stevenson, also of Philadelphia, chose heavy masses of Austrian pine, interplanted with whitebeam, Russian olive, sea buckthorn, Japanese rose, and French tamarisk to frame this burial area so close to the sea.

Those buried here include men and women from all fifty states and the District of Columbia, as well as from England, Scotland, and Canada. Buried here side by side are a father and his son, and in thirty instances brothers. Two of these were especially well known to an earlier generation of Americans when their father, Theodore Roosevelt, was in the White House. The Roosevelt children brought a sense of gaiety and hilarity to that formal atmosphere. Quentin even rode his pony into the historic presidential mansion.

Brigadier General Theodore Roosevelt, Jr. (1887–1944), died during the taking of France and was buried here. In 1955 the remains of First Lieutenant Quentin Roosevelt (1897–1918), who was shot down near the village of Chamery in the last months of World War I, were transferred from the Oise-Aisne American Cemetery and re-interred next to his brother.

Several structures of interest rise above the masses of white crosses. The circular chapel is almost like an elegant tent in concept. Constructed of Vaurion limestone (except for the granite steps), it is surmounted by a bronze finial with an armillary sphere, which appears to be a weather vane but serves as a lightning arrester. An inscription in English and French tells us: "This chapel has been erected by the United States of America in grateful memory of her sons who gave their lives in the landings on the Normandy beaches and in the liberation of northern France. Their graves are the permanent and visible symbol of their heroic devotion and their sacrifice in the common cause of humanity."

The chapel lintel bears the words: "These endured all and gave all that justice among nations might prevail and that mankind might enjoy freedom and inherit peace." Above is an engraved replica of the congressional Medal of Honor.

"I give unto them eternal life and they shall never perish" is engraved in the black and gold Pyrenees Grand Antique marble of the altar. It sits on a two-tiered platform of travertine limestone quarried in France and is flanked on both sides by flags of the United States, France, Great Britain, and Canada. The translucent amber window behind it frames a star of David with a dove in the center of the star and a slender Latin cross of teak. The inscriptions chosen here are ones of hope. On the north and south walls can be read: "Think not only upon their passing. Remember the glory of their spirit" and "Through the gate of death may they pass to their joyful resurrection."

The most unusual feature of the chapel is its colorful mosaic ceiling, designed and executed by Leon Kroll of New York City. Symbolizing America blessing her sons as they depart by sea and air to fight for freedom, it also depicts a grateful France bestowing a laurel wreath upon American dead who gave their lives to liberate Europe's oppressed peoples.

To the east facing the chapel, a semicircular colonnade of Vaurion limestone from the Côte d'Or embraces loggias at each end (with blue ceramic tile ceilings by Gentil et Bourdet of Paris), housing bronze maps. In keeping with the character of the memorial, pebbles from the invasion beach below have been embedded in mortar for the floor of the open area.

A heroic statue, *The Spirit of American Youth Rising from the Waves* by Donald De Lue (he also designed the urns in the loggias), soars from its pedestal as a swimmer gracefully emerging from the depths. The arms of the figure seem to embrace the wide Norman sky. Encircling the pedestal on the floor are the opening words of "The Battle Hymn of the Republic," the inspiring poem by Julia Ward Howe. The sculpture, silhouetted against the colonnade and reflected in the pool, symbolizes the credo carved on the lintel: "This embattled shore, portal of liberation, is forever hallowed by the ideals, the valor and the sacrifice of our fellow countrymen."

The Normandy landings, the development of the beachhead, the air operations (March-August 1944), the amphibious assault landings, and military operations in western Europe from D day to V-J Day are depicted on the loggias' maps (designed by Robert Foster and executed by Maurice Schmit of Paris) engraved in the stone and embellished with enamel. Behind the memorial, the Garden of the Missing, with its semicircular wall containing the names of 1,557 missing in the region, is a remembrance of those whose remains were never recovered or if recovered not identified.

The landings at Normandy are history now. What was once a scene of bitter strife is one of serenity and peace.

An overlook on a small jut of land just north of the memorial affords an excellent view of Omaha Beach and the English Channel. An orientation table shows the various beaches and forces involved in the Normandy landings. The imaginative can visualize the action, hear the sounds of gunfire, sense the scene of carnage. A future generation will open on June 6, 2044 the time capsule in which were sealed reports of the June 6, 1944 landings. Affixed to the center of the slab is a bronze plaque adorned with the five stars of a general of the army and engraved with the following inscription:

In memory of GENERAL DWIGHT D. EISENHOWER and the forces under his command this sealed capsule containing news reports of the June 6, 1944 NORMANDY LANDINGS is placed here by the newsmen who were there. June 6, 1969.

The Angel of Peace decorates this memorial. *Photograph by Herman Manasse.*
American Battle Monuments Commission

68. Rhone American Cemetery

DRAGUIGNAN, VAR, FRANCE

SEVERAL features distinguish the Rhone American Cemetery from other American military burial grounds in France. Lying within the city of Draguignan (most others are outside cities and towns), the Rhone Cemetery is also the southernmost in France. The others are found in the north where casualties were high following the Normandy landings, or in central and eastern France where so much of the savage fighting of World War I and II took place.

In other characteristics such as form, a large twelve-acre oval, it seems even more distinctive. The shape was determined by its architect, Henry J. Toombs of Atlanta, Georgia, as its plantings were by A. F. Brinckerhoff of New York, landscape architect. Situated near the eastern edge of Draguignan, the cemetery occupies an area at the foot of a hill clad with the characteristic cypresses, olive trees, and oleanders of southern France. Just to the west of it is the cemetery of the city of Draguignan.

On the night of August 16, 1944, elements of the 1st Airborne Task Force entered Draguignan, the first United States troops to do so. They were joined by units of the United States 36th Division the following day. Just three days after the city was liberated the Rhone American Cemetery was established, and today 861 dead lie here, representing 39 percent of the burials originally made in the region. Most of these died during the operations incident to the landings on the southern coast on August 15, 1944 and the subsequent advance northward. The name is derived from the Rhone River, whose watershed was the scene of these operations.

The cemetery is entered on the north side of highway D59. Often the memorial is encountered first in these military cemeteries with the graves area lying beyond. The design is reversed here to great effect: The four burial plots are situated about a central oval pool that is set at the intersection of the axes of the cemetery. Sixty-two of the stones mark the graves of unknowns and in two instances brothers are buried side by side. Oleanders and ancient olive trees are planted among the headstones.

Outside the oval wall, and on the transverse axis of the cemetery, are charming small gardens. At the east is an intimate enclosure with a small circular pool, which has a background of tall Italian cypresses. Surrounded with beds of broad-leafed evergreens, including oleanders, crepe myrtle, and seasonal plants, it is entered by a small iron gate. The west garden is somewhat smaller; its pool is octagonal in form and set in brick pavement in contrast to the east garden's green lawn. All is enclosed by a high sheared hedge of evergreen Japanese privet. Both invite contemplation.

After the serenity of the graves area and the intimacy of the small gardens, the memorial seems more in keeping with those generally found in other military cemeteries, but it too is distinctive. Before it, flanked by two flagstaffs 66½ feet high, a bronze relief map, fabricated by Bruno Bearzi of Florence, Italy, portrays the military operations south of here and the subsequent advance up the valley of the Rhone. These forces, which joined with those from Normandy at Sombernon near Dijon, isolated the enemy in southwest France and freed the port of Marseille for incoming troops, equipment, and supplies. The Wall of the Missing records the names of 293 of these men.

The memorial itself is dominated by the heroic sculpture of the Angel of Peace, designed by Edmund Amateis of Brewster, New York, and carved by Georges Granger of Chalon-sur-Saône. Through bronze grilles one enters the chapel, much of which is decorated with mosaics designed and fabricated by Austin Purves of Litchfield, Connecticut. An altar of Vert des Alpes marble from the valley of Aoste in the Italian Alps is engraved with a cross and the tablets of Moses, and covered with a cloth of Florentine leather. The mural behind it symbolizes the sacrifice of the dead and the dedication of the modern crusade in Europe that culminated in the Allied victory. One of the mural's components shows the figure of Saint Louis of France (King Louis IX), an earlier crusader who set sail from a port in this region, standing on the walls of the city of Aigues-Mortes. Behind him is Saint Chapelle, built in Paris to enshrine the relics of his crusade. His credo—"My faithful friends, we shall be unconquerable if we remain united in charity"—is inscribed below.

Outside, the terrace is lined with a double row of closely planted Italian cypresses that form a green curtain behind the chapel and across the ends of the terrace. The areas at the two sides are enclosed with low formal hedges and are planted with a few redbud and strawberry trees.

Provence—this ancient province noted for its troubadours and the cold, dry mistrals that sweep over it from the Mediterranean coast sixteen miles away—had listened to the drums of Napoleon's armies and heard the footfall of the Roman legionnaire before the coming of American troops. The memory of these modern crusaders is forever enshrined here.

The Tuscan hills provide a background for the graves. *American Battle Monuments Commission*

69. Florence American Cemetery

FLORENCE, ITALY

THE long arduous campaign up the Italian peninsula, beginning with the Allied landing at Salerno in September 1943, continued into the next year. Rome fell on June 4, 1944, and after this the Allies pursued the enemy northward toward the Po River and the Alps. For the first time since the Salerno landings the enemy was in full retreat. In June and July the Allies advanced rapidly north from Rome. Leghorn fell to United States troops of

the Fifth Army on July 18, Pisa on the 23rd, and Florence on August 4. By this time the Allies had crossed the Arno and reached the outposts of the Gothic Line, the last enemy defensive system in Italy.

Although in September the Fifth Army and the Eighth reached Rimini, the outset of winter delayed the final thrust until the following spring. The offensive northward was resumed on April 9, 1945. Bologna fell on the

21st, Milan was reached on April 29. On May 2 the enemy troops in northern Italy surrendered and the Allied conquest of Italy was complete.

Such fighting—much of it in the foothills and mountains over difficult terrain—increased the number of fatalities. A number of temporary burial sites were used by the United States Armed Forces until peace, and a period of reconstruction brought about consideration of a permanent site. A survey of those in northern Italy revealed that there was at least one major objection in every instance for retention of any except that in Florence, as a permanent cemetery.

Located 7½ miles south of Florence on the Via Cassia, a main highway connecting the Tuscan capital with Siena and Rome, the American Cemetery is graced with entrances about 250 meters apart. The setting, a site liberated on August 3, 1944 by the South African Sixth Armoured Division, later became part of the zone of the United States Fifth Army. The seventy acres are astride the Greve "torrente," with the entrances, parking areas, offices, and Visitors' Building on the east bank.

The architects—McKim, Mead and White of New York—conceived the cemetery on both banks of the river —the entrances and aforementioned buildings on one side; the graves area, framed by the wooded hills that rise to a height of several hundred feet, on the west bank. A bridge provides the link between the two areas of the cemetery.

A central grassy mall, flanked by a double row of Oriental plane trees, leads from the bridge to the memorial through eight sections (four on each side) devoted to the graves. Here 4,398 headstones tell their own tale of death in wartime. Radiating in gentle arcs from a memorial pylon and curving inward slightly, they contribute to a harmonious relationship between the graves area and the memorial. These graves are of identified servicemen and women (4,402 are buried here). Two stones mark the graves of unknowns whose remains could not be separated; another marks the grave of three who were found in this state. As in other American military cemeteries abroad, five pairs of brothers are buried here side by side, a reminder that war shows no mercy to families. The burials represent 39 percent of the temporary burials originally made between Rome and the Alps. Most of those died in the fighting that occurred after the capture of Rome and include the casualties from the heavy fighting in the Apennines.

In keeping with Italian tradition the memorial consists of two open atria, or courts. A connecting wall with the names of the missing from the region joins the atria. Between both, a stele on an open terrace, surmounted by the sculptured figure *The Spirit of Peace*—created by American artist Sidney Waugh—stands as a beacon. The atria themselves are paneled in Baverno granite from

quarries at the north end of Lake Como. Each inner wall panel of the south atrium bears an inscription. Three are from A. E. Zimmern's translation of Pericles's *Praise of the Dead,* as recorded by Thucydides; one is taken from a prayer of Cardinal Newman; one from the Episcopal prayer book; and another from the 44th chapter of Ecclesiastes.

From the atria bronze doors, fabricated by the Fonderia Marinelli of Florence, and surmounted by Sidney Waugh's sculpture *The Spirit of American Youth,* lead to the chapel. Directly opposite the entrance stands the altar of Belgian black marble, with a mosaic behind it designed by Barry Faulkner of New York and executed by Fabrizio Cassio of Rome. It depicts Remembrance standing on a cloud, holding the lilies of Resurrection and contemplating a crocus-strewn field of marble headstones. The trees in the background show the first buds of spring, symbolizing new life. The walls are of Rosso Collemandino marble from Versiglia; the floor is paved with Verde Serpentino marble from Sondrio, and the pews are of walnut.

The north atrium houses two military operations maps that recall the achievements of the American forces in the region; they were designed by Bruno Bearzi of Florence. The larger depicts northern Italy and operations at the end of the war from the vicinity of the cemetery northward. The smaller, an insert in the larger, illustrates the broad outline of military operations in Sicily and Italy, beginning in July 1943. It was executed in scagliola by another Florentine, Emilio Martelli. Texts on the walls in English and Italian explain each. Six other key maps record the development of the war against Germany and that against Japan.

The Wall of the Missing contains the names of 1,409 from every state in the Union (except Hawaii and Alaska), the District of Columbia, and Canada, who were missing in action in the region or lost at sea. The names themselves are testimony of the historic struggle that took place here in the last year of World War II. As if these were not reminders enough, there is a frieze of escutcheons on which are embossed the names of the ground and air battles in which Americans participated: Gela-Palermo-Troina; Salerno-Altavilla-Volturno; Magnano-San Pietro-Rapido; Cassino-Anzio-Cisterna; Rome-Leghorn-Arno; Futa-Santerno-Radicosa; Serchio-Bologna-Po Valley; Ploesti-Vienna-Munich; and Regensburg-Budapest-Brenner.

The words of General Eisenhower, from his book *Crusade in Europe,* on the north atrium's wall, are a litany: "Freedom from fear and injustice and oppression is ours only in the measure that men who value such freedom are ready to sustain its possession, to defend it against every thrust from within or without."

Roman travertine from the quarries of Tivoli was used in the memorial. *American Battle Monuments Commission*

70. Sicily-Rome American Cemetery

NETTUNO, ITALY

ALONG the coast that borders the ancient Tyrrhenian Sea, between Rome and Naples and just north of Nettuno, which is immediately south of Rome (thirty-eight miles), lies the Sicily-Rome American Cemetery.

Established originally on January 24, 1944, following the first landings on the Anzio beaches two days earlier, the cemetery rises in a gentle slope from the Via della Rimenbranza. A small stream, the Fosso dei Tinozzi, runs near it to the north. Lying in the zone of advance of the 3rd Division, the site of seventy-seven acres contains the graves of 7,862 military dead who gave their lives in the long, bloody fight against the Germans entrenched on the Italian peninsula—from the July 10, 1943 landing on the south and east shores of Sicily, the later assault of the Salerno beaches, the taking of Naples, the crossing of the Volturno River, the landings at Anzio, and the victorious march on the Eternal City, which was liberated on June 4, 1944.

The architects—Gugler, Kimball & Husted of New York—conceived the cemetery as almost bell-shaped with a central mall connecting the memorial with a circular pool. This divides the ten burial plots, five to each side of the mall. Beyond the handsome bronze entrance gates and fence—worthy of the most elegant Roman villa —one comes first upon the pool. It is utterly Italian in concept, with a tiny island in its center, which can be termed an Isle of the Dead. A cenotaph of "bronze" travertine stone, flanked by formal groups of Italian cypresses, lends a feeling of classical antiquity to a contemporary setting. It could well be the tomb of Vergil, Propertius, Ovid, or Juvenal.

A mass of evergreen oak trees beyond the pool frames the vista up the mall to the distant memorial. To either side, in gentle arcs that sweep across the broad green lawns, are the 7,860 headstones, reminders of the heavy toll taken in the eleven months when the Allied troops inched their way northward. Each grave plot is surrounded by a Pittosporum hedge, while the grass paths between the plots are lined by rows of characteristic Roman pines. A few of the stones record that some of these soldiers were born in Canada, Eire, Finland, Scotland, Spain, and Sweden. Stones mark the graves of unknowns (488 stones for 490 graves) and in twenty-one instances two brothers lie side by side.

North and south gardens of great formal beauty flank the memorial: a chapel, peristyle, and museum. They are built of Roman travertine brought from the quarries of Tivoli east of Rome, and the Roman feeling for classical forms and beautiful marble has been observed throughout. The peristyle is particularly memorable because of the sculpture *Brothers in Arms* by Paul Manship, which stands on a pedestal of "bronze" travertine within its colonnade. Idealized American youth, two young men bare to the waist, dressed in trousers and shoes, walk toward the future, arms about each other's shoulders.

Symbolizing the American soldier and sailor shoulder to shoulder, they stand heroically as does the single Roman pine beside them.

Manship is also represented by a sculptural panel in relief entitled *Remembrance* on the east face of the chapel and one entitled *Resurrection* on the east façade of the museum. The bronze chapel doors (cast by the Marinelli Foundries of Florence) lead to an interior purposely designed without windows. (Should natural lighting ever be needed, two bronze panels of the west wall may be swung open.) These walls serve as the Wall of the Missing, recording 3,094 names of those in the army, air force, and navy who were unaccounted for.

Paul Manship also designed the triptych of Serravezzo white marble from the Carrara region, which dominates the altar of golden Broccatello Siena marble. The archangel Michael on the central panel, the text from *The Greek Dead at Thermopylae* by Simonides, and a quotation from the Eighth Psalm carry out the religious and classical approaches to death and burial. The eye is carried naturally from the altar adornments to the ceiling dome, twenty-two feet in diameter, designed by the architects but executed by Manship and Bruno Bearzi of Florence. Using the medieval signs of the zodiac to represent the constellations, the artists have stopped Mars, Jupiter, and Saturn in the relative positions they occupied at two o'clock in the morning of January 22, 1944— that never-to-be-forgotten moment when the first wave of American and British troops landed on the beaches near Anzio.

The inscription on the base of the dome—"O ye stars of heaven bless ye the Lord, praise Him and magnify Him forever"—captures this spiritual feeling. The words on the panel of the triptych from Simonides speak for the dead:

"Nobly they ended high their destination. Beneath an altar laid, no more a tomb, where none with pity comes or lamentations but praise and memory, a splendor of oblation. Who left behind a gem-like heritage of courage and renown, a name that shall go down from age to age."

More than five thousand military dead lie here in the Grand Duchy of Luxembourg, including General George Patton. *Photograph by Herman Manasse. American Battle Monuments Commission*

71. Luxembourg American Cemetery

LUXEMBOURG

THE tiny Grand Duchy, whose then-ruler, the Grand Duchess Charlotte, sought refuge in the United States with her family during World War II, was unknown to most Americans before 1941 except through the melodies of Franz Lehár's fanciful operetta *The Count of Luxembourg.* Yet, here in this Graustarkian country—one of Europe's most charming monarchies—lie many who were unfamiliar with the nation that had been raised to the rank of a Grand Duchy after the Congress of Vienna (1814–1815).

The cemetery—50½ acres—lies within the limits of the capital city. The glade framed by spruce, beech, oak, and other trees was liberated by troops of the United States 5th Armored Division on September 10, 1944. On December 29 of that year the battlefield cemetery was established, which now contains the graves of 5,076 military dead, representing 43 percent of the burials that were originally made in this and other cemeteries of the region. In gentle waves, almost semicircular in form, are row on row of simple white crosses marking the burial places. Most of these men gave their lives in the Battle of the Bulge, fought some miles to the north of the city, and in fighting eastward to the Rhine, and beyond, during the winter of 1944 and the spring of 1945.

The Grand Ducal government granted to the United States government in perpetuity the use of the site. Dominating it, almost as a stage (with the cemetery becoming an amphitheatre), is the memorial—a columnar square building containing the chapel, which is set upon a podium and reached by two short flights of steps. Before this lies a terrace flanked by two pylons. The chapel and terrace in effect survey the burial area beyond.

Great care was exercised by architects Keally and Patterson of New York in the design of the chapel. It is in a wooded setting, and a forest of trees provides a rich background. The French white Valore stone was brought from the Jura Mountain region. Rising fifty feet above the podium, it is ornamented on its east façade with the obverse of the Great Seal of the United States carved in high relief. Below it is the inscription:

1941–1945
In proud remembrance
of the achievements of her sons
and in humble tribute
to their sacrifices
this memorial has been erected by
the United States of America

The west façade bears the coat of arms of the Grand Duchy of Luxembourg and a French translation of the dedicatory inscription.

The Angel of Peace surmounted by a dove, a figure designed by Leo Friedlander, rises twenty-three feet above the chapel door. Carved in Swedish Orchid Red granite, its right hand raised in benediction, the statue floats above the inscription on the lintel: "Here is enshrined the memory of valor and sacrifice." The bronze door, also designed by Friedlander, contains eight panels symbolizing the military virtues of physical fitness, proficiency, valor, fortitude, fidelity, sacrifice, family ties, and faith.

Within, a sense of serenity is maintained by the use on the walls of Hauteville Perlé stone from the French Jura region. The west wall, inscribed "Grant us grace fearlessly to contend against evil and to make no peace with oppression," is surmounted by a roundel containing a cross. The east wall bears the inscription "Take unto thyself O Lord the souls of the valorous that they may dwell in thy glory," and it in turn is surmounted by a roundel with the tablets of Moses. Over the door are the words: "Some there be which have no sepulchre. Their name liveth for evermore."

The altar itself—of Bleu Belge marble from southern Belgium—is graced with the words of Saint John (X, 28): "I give unto them eternal life and they shall never perish." As in all memorial chapels under the supervision of the American Battle Monuments Commission, the finest modern stained glass predominates. A narrow window designed by Allyn Cox contains the insignia of the five major American military commands that operated in this region. The mosaic ceiling carries to an even finer degree the feelings of spirituality. In the center the Holy Spirit is represented by the dove on a background of clouds, and the sun's rays, within a nimbus held by four angels. At their feet is a running inscription, which becomes the circumference of the circle.

Every detail in this house of prayer reflects honor on the living who erected it to the memory of the dead. The pews and prie-dieu are of ebony-stained birchwood and were made in Rome. The light fixtures are of bronze and the floor is a triumph of different marbles from Italy in which has been set a bronze nimbus with the thirteen stars of the Great Seal of the United States, wreathed in oak, pine, and laurel.

The burial area, divided into nine plots and separated by two radial malls and two transverse grass paths, holds the graves of the simple soldier and the world-famous leader. The most prominent is that of General George S. Patton (1885–1945), who lies here among the men who were under his command. His grave is separate, close to the memorial terrace. The 5,076 headstones, arranged in parallel arcs across the broad green lawn, mark the burial places of the dead of fifty states and the District of Columbia. Humanely, the United States government in twenty-two instances buried brothers side by side.

The memory of the battles fought here is recorded on the pylons at the foot of the terrace. On the outer faces there is the inscription: "Here are recorded the names of Americans who gave their lives in the service of their country and who sleep in unknown graves." Beneath are the names of 370 missing from the army and air force.

On the inner faces of the pylons are two maps—an overall map and a regional one—showing the military operations that led to V-E Day. That on the west portrays military operations in northwestern Europe from the landings in Normandy until the end of the war; on the east pylon are the operations in the immediate area of Luxembourg, including the Battle of the Bulge, with the subsequent fighting to clear the west bank of the Rhine, and the crossing of that river at Oppenheim.

Inscriptions in English and French on the west pylon tell of the June 6, 1944 landing of Allied forces on the coast of Normandy, the subsequent push into French territory, the liberation of Brest, the fall of Metz, the Allied occupation of the Saar, the halting of the German counteroffensive in the Ardennes, the seizure of the Remagen bridge, and the surrender on May 8, 1945. The regional map on the other pylon recounts the push from December 16, 1944 through March 22, 1945, when the Third Army crossed the Rhine at Oppenheim.

These battles in the last months of World War II exacted a terrible toll, and many of those who fell now rest in the Luxembourg American Cemetery. The wooded area surrounding the cemetery has been planted liberally with horse chestnut. A hedge of beech and a broad band of *Cotoneaster horizontalis* encircle the chapel, which is flanked with plantings of Japanese holly chosen by Alfred Geiffert, Jr., landscape designer. Other plantings of yew link two flagpoles. Roses bloom along the paths in summer, and during spring rhododendron lend their own special hue to the landscape.

Those who lie here are best eulogized in the words from General Dwight D. Eisenhower's dedication of the Golden Book in Saint Paul's Cathedral in London. They are set in bronze letters in the pavement of the terrace:

All who shall herafter live in freedom will
be here reminded that to these men and their
comrades we owe a debt to be paid with grateful
remembrance of their sacrifice and with the
high resolve that the cause for which they
died shall live eternally.

The only American military cemetery in The Netherlands was established in 1944.
Photograph by Herman Manasse. American Battle Monuments Commission

72. Netherlands American Cemetery

MARGRATEN, THE NETHERLANDS

ON the continent of Europe the greatest concentration of American military cemeteries is in France, where so many of the battles of both world wars took place. Holland has but one, situated in the village of Margraten, six miles east of Maastricht on the main highway to Aachen, Germany.

Here, in the gently rolling farmland near the southeast border of this maritime nation, 65½ acres of a site liber-

ated on September 13, 1944 by troops of the 30th Infantry Division was set aside as a battlefield cemetery, one of the first to be used for the interment of American soldiers who fell on German soil. The cemetery was established here on November 10, 1944 by the United States Ninth Army.

Sixteen plots, evenly divided on each side of a central mall, are the burial ground for 8,301 Americans who died in World War II. In forty instances—an unusually large number—two brothers lie side by side, and one of the 8,300 headstones marks the common grave of two unknowns. The parallel arcs of the stones sweep across the lawn toward the memorial at the end of the mall. The landscape architects—Clarke, Rapuano and Halleran of New York—suggested that American tulip poplars line the mall. Beds of rhododendron, which produce their wealth of blossom just before Memorial Day each year, are prominent throughout the cemetery. Hawthorn hedges as well as forested areas of oak, maple, and hawthorn, and wide curved borders of polyantha roses framed within a coping of dwarf box backed with a holly hedge, add to the beauty of the cemetery.

The Court of Honor with its reflecting pool leads naturally to the chapel and tower. On the north and south walls of the court are recorded the names of 1,722 men who gave their lives in this region but were declared missing. They came from every state (except Alaska) and the District of Columbia. On the north wall are the words of John McCrae from "In Flanders Field":

**To you from failing hands we throw
The torch; be yours to hold it high!**

Shepley, Bullfinch, Richardson and Abbott of Boston, architects, were responsible for the chapel and tower. The bronze sculptured group standing before the tower —the mourning figure of a woman, doves, and a new branch growing from a war-destroyed tree—was designed by Joseph Kiselewski of New York and cast by the Battaglia foundries of Milan. The inscription at its base proves an accurate description of the work itself: "New life from war's destruction proclaims man's immortality and hope for peace."

The tower rises 101 feet above the Court of Honor and can be seen from great distances over the flat Dutch countryside. On its exterior walls which, like those of the Court of Honor, are of English Portland stone, a free translation of Pericles's oration as recorded by Thucydides is inscribed on its west face: "Each for his own memorial earned praise that will never die and with it the grandest of all sepulchres: not that in which his mortal bones are laid, but a home in the minds of men." An observation platform within, reached by 149 steps, affords a wide panoramic view of the burial area.

Exquisitely designed doors by H. H. Martyn of Cheltenham, England, bearing in outline a Tree of Life, lead to the chapel. The doors themselves are not only distinctive but of such beauty that the visitor must stand and admire them before entering.

Once within, this beauty is extended to all elements of the interior. Suspended from the ceiling (the chapel is fifty-two feet high) is a handsome lighting fixture, a gift of the Dutch people. It is celestial and resembles a constellation of lights or jewels. A royal crown surrounded by tiny lights recalls the firmament above. It is gossamer, iridescent, and unforgettable. The silver vase on the altar, inscribed *Pro mundi libertate mortuis* (To those who died for a free world), and the wrought-iron candelabra next to the altar were also gifts of a nation that has never failed to voice its gratitude for American help during the war. A tablet near the door records in English and Dutch: "The lights and altar ornaments are the generous gifts of the government of The Netherlands and the administration and people of the province of Limburg."

These are tangible reminders, as are the 8,300 white stones, of the savagery of war. On the walls flanking the tower are other reminders—the names of the battles fought in the region: Maastricht, Eindhoven, Grave, Nijmegen, Arnhem, Jülich, Linnich, Geilenkirchen, Krefeld, Venlo, Rheinsberg, Cologne, Wesel, and Ruhr.

The hemicycles seemingly embrace the Memorial Court. *American Battle Monuments Commission*

73. Manila American Cemetery, Manila

REPUBLIC OF THE PHILIPPINES

IN the long war in the Pacific, from the bombing of Pearl Harbor to the fall of Japan, thousands of servicemen and women died in New Guinea, the islands of the Central Pacific, in Southeast Asia, and in the final assault on the Philippine Islands. At the war's end, after major objections were found to all the temporary cemetery sites that had been established during World War II, the government of the Philippines on April 1, 1948 granted permission to the United States to establish a memorial cemetery on part of the former United States reservation of Fort William McKinley, about six miles from the center of the city.

It is here—the largest in area (152 acres) of the cemeteries built and administered by the American Battle Monuments Commission—that 17,208 military are buried, representing 40 percent of the burials that were originally made in temporary cemeteries in New Guinea, the Philippines, and other islands of the Southwest Pacific area, and also in the Palau Islands of the Central Pacific. Most of these men and women died in the defense of the Philippines and the East Indies in 1941 and 1942, or in the long return of the American forces through the vast island chain.

Designed by Gardner A. Dailey of San Francisco (who

was also responsible for most of the landscape development), the graves area is arranged in concentric circular rows on gently rising ground around the high point on which the memorial stands. The prospect is unforgettable: Mount Arayat to the north, over Laguna de Bay toward Mount Makiling to the southeast, and Tagaytay Ridge to the south.

The burial area itself consists of eleven plots of varying sizes and, in addition to the markers for the known dead, there are 3,660 for the graves of 3,744 unknowns, two bronze plaques for the graves of four known dead who could not be separately identified, and four plaques that mark the graves of twenty-four others who met death together. In twenty instances, two brothers lie side by side. These men and women came from every state, the District of Columbia, Panama, Guam, the Philippines, Puerto Rico, Australia, Canada, China, England, Mexico, Costa Rica, Honduras, Finland, Jamaica, Burma, and Peru.

A long mall lined with mahogany trees leads from the main gate and pool at the north to the memorial—two hemicycles that focus on a tower, all faced with travertine limestone quarried near Tivoli, east of Rome. The tower containing the chapel and the hemicycles that embrace the memorial court are approached from the mall by a monumental staircase. At the head of the stairs in the pavement, the Great Seal of the Commonwealth of the Philippines (authorized for use during World War II until the republic was established) meets the eye.

Here the eye is also directed to the twenty-four pairs of fin walls upon the four faces of which are inscribed the names and particulars of 36,279 missing (including Philippine scouts who shared in the defense of the archipelago), those lost either in the jungles or in the waters of the Pacific. In front of the steps is the chapel —a reminder to all that this is United States territory in the obverse of the Great Seal of the United States carved in the travertine pavement. The tower's façade is decorated with sculpture in high relief by Boris Lovet-Lorski of New York and executed by Filippo Cecchetti of Tivoli, depicting a series of superimposed groups: the young American warrior symbolized by Saint George fighting his dragon, the enemy in the jungle. Above them are representations of Liberty, Justice, and Country. Columbia, with the child symbolizing the future, stands at the zenith.

Beyond the bronze grille doors of the chapel, the entrance is lined with blue glass mosaic. From The Book of Common Prayer, inset in gold tesserae, are the words: "O God who are the author of peace and lover of concord, defend us thy humble servants in all assaults of our enemies that we surely trusting in thy defense may not fear the power of any adversaries." Opposite is an abridged prayer by Cardinal Newman: "O Lord support us all the day long until the shadows lengthen and our work is done. Then in thy mercy grant us a safe lodging and a holy rest and peace at the last."

These lead to the altar of Perlato di Sicilia marble. The entire wall behind the altar is decorated with mosaic—complementing the entrance—on a predominantly blue background. Above the inscription—"To their memory their country brings its gratitude as flowers forever living"—a madonna figure scatters flowers.

The hemicycles themselves serve as memorials, and each houses a fascinating collection of maps, designed by Margaret Bruton of Carmel, California, and fabricated by the P. Grassi American Terrazzo Company of San Francisco. They are of tinted concretes with brilliant colored fine aggregates; the military data is expressed by mosaic or ceramic inserts and the borders and compasses recall the art patterns of the Pacific Islands. The entire spectrum of the war in the Southwest Pacific and Southeast Asia is reflected in the subjects in each of the four map rooms.

One room depicts the defense of Luzon, of Southeast Asia, the Battle for Leyte Gulf, the return to the Philippines, the Luzon campaign, the reoccupation of Manila, and the liberation of the Philippines. Another records the Battle of the Coral Sea, the China-Burma-India Theater, the American Air Ferry routes and the supply to the U.S.S.R., the United States submarine operations in the Pacific, the Marianas (June 15–August 10, 1944), the Battle of Midway, and the Battle of the Philippine Sea.

Others are devoted to the general strategy in the Pacific, 1942–1945; Guadalcanal (August 7, 1942–February 9, 1943); fast carrier strikes in the Pacific; the air assault on Japan, Okinawa (March 26–June 22, 1945), and Iwo Jima (February 16–March 16, 1945). Still others illustrate the war against Germany, supply routes across the Pacific, New Guinea (July 21, 1942–May 11, 1945), the Northern Solomons (March 6, 1943–March 27, 1944), and the invasion of the Palau Islands.

Visualizing a parklike background, which would assure a rotation of bloom, Gardner A. Dailey achieved a large botanical garden with stately stretches of broad lawns and magnificent vistas, using flowering trees, shrubs, palms, and foliage plants of the Philippines, the East Indies, and the warmer climates of southern Asia, Africa, and tropical America. There is a special bit of the United States—like Rupert Brooke's line, "That there's some corner of a foreign field/ That is for ever England" —in the Manila American Cemetery. The grass covering most of the cemetery is Zoysia Matrella and all of it has been propagated from two square yards of sod shipped in 1951 from the United States Department of Agriculture Experimental Station at Beltsville, Maryland.

The entire cemetery reflects the dedicatory inscription on the façades of the hemicycles:

In proud remembrance of the achievements of her sons and in humble tribute to their sacrifices, this memorial has been erected by the United States of America. 1941–1945.

One of the four fountains and pools of Roman travertine. *American Battle Monuments Commission*

74. North Africa American Cemetery

TUNIS, TUNISIA

CARTHAGE! The name alone evokes visions of the city said to have been founded by Phoenicians from Tyre in the ninth century B.C. Once a great Mediterranean city-state, its ruins can be seen today outside Tunis.

After the end of World War II a survey made jointly by representatives of the secretary of war and the American Battle Monuments Commission revealed that all sites of temporary cemeteries in North Africa established dur-

ing the war had disadvantages. It was determined in 1948 to establish a permanent cemetery on the outskirts of Tunis. The twenty-seven acres selected lay in the sector of the British First Army, which liberated the Tunis area in May 1943.

Near the towns of Amilcar and Gammarth, the cemetery occupies a section of a plateau lying between the Mediterranean and the Bay of Tunis. It is near the site of

Carthage (destroyed by the Romans in 146 B.C.) and lies over part of what was once Roman Carthage. Just two hundred yards to the east are remnants of Roman houses and streets. Vestiges endure of the Carthaginian civilization and the Roman. It is an odd juxtaposition in time: the American dead who sleep here from the battles of World War II and about them the bones of another, earlier civilization and war.

Moore and Hutchins of New York, architects, were faced with certain problems peculiar to the terrain and not encountered at most other military cemeteries abroad. The land is flat here, so there was not the question of adapting to its rise and fall, of following certain contours of hill or river. Water, always a factor in any desert country, was a consideration, and provision was made for it in order to maintain the cemetery's green look.

Generally rectangular in shape, the graves area is divided into nine plots arranged in rectangular lines harmonizing with the composition of the memorial and of the cemetery. Here there is no central mall as in so many other military burial grounds, but in the burial area there are four fountains and pools of Roman travertine which, with their surrounding plantings of rosemary, oleander, and pink geraniums, form small and welcome oases in this frequently hot climate.

The 2,840 dead represent 39 percent of the burials originally made in North Africa and Iran. A high proportion gave their lives in the landings in, and occupation of, Morocco and Algeria and the subsequent fighting that resulted in the liberation of Tunisia. Others died of accident or sickness in these and other parts of North Africa or while serving in the Persian Gulf Command in Iran.

Landscape architect Bryan J. Lynch selected rows of eucalyptus and ornamental India laurel fig trees for the forecourt just inside the gates. This becomes an extension of the highway to Tunis, which runs parallel to the mall and is also bordered by eucalyptus. Beds of Tobira, scarlet hibiscus, English ivy, cassia floribunda, orange berry, and other shrubs and vines add color to the sun-drenched landscape. A reservoir beneath the green plot in the center of the forecourt stores the much-needed water for the cemetery, as well as the pumps for the sprinkler system. (All water comes from a storage area some miles south of Tunis.)

The mall follows the line of the highway rather than bisecting the graves area. The Wall of the Missing, 364 feet long, is of local stone—Nahli limestone with Gathouna limestone copings. Panels of Trani limestone set within it record the names of 3,724 of the missing, who died either in air or land engagements or at sea in the waters surrounding the African continent.

The memorial is low, blending into the landscape. The Court of Honor takes the form of a cloister and within it ceramic maps (designed and fabricated by Paul D. Holleman of Roxbury, Massachusetts) tell the dramatic story of Allied military operations in Morocco, Algeria, and Tunisia from the initial "Torch" landings on November 8, 1942 to the Axis surrender on May 13, 1943. Descriptions are in English, French, and Arabic.

Various works of art enhance the whole. Near the pool on the mall is the figure of *Honor* about to bestow a laurel branch; farther along the Wall of Memory are *Memory,* a Madonna-like figure, and *Recollection,* holding a book with the inscription *Pro Patria.* Within the cloister is a rectangular stone of remembrance—black diorite d'Anzola from northwest Italy with an inscription from Ecclesiasticus XLIV. Within the Visitors' Building, a Roman mosaic discovered in the region was donated by President Bourguiba of Tunisia to Ambassador G. Lewis Jones, who, in turn, presented it to the cemetery. A Neptune-like figure in his chariot holds the reins as a pair of mythological horses cavort. He could be a god of war or a peaceful Neptune. It seems well that he has returned permanently to grace this ancient spot.

The chapel is entered through bronze doors fabricated by the Morris Singer Company of London (who also did the windows). The altar is of white Carrara marble, the wall behind it of polished Rosso Porfirico marble from Udine near the Austrian border. An inscription from Shelley's "Adonais" (written in memory of Keats)—"He has outsoared the shadow of our night"—balances the sculpture *Sacrifice* by Henry Kreis, which hangs from the wall near the altar. The ceiling is of Moroccan cedar.

Here lie many Americans who died under the same African skies two thousand years after the ancient Carthaginians watched their ships depart for distant harbors, where they plotted the Punic wars, and where Scipio Africanus Minor finally destroyed the city.

IV. A Selection of Other Interesting Cemeteries

THESE cemeteries are of interest either because they are historic in their own right or because they contain one or more graves of the famous. This is not intended to be a list of all *cemeteries in a country or state, and the selection has been arbitrary on the author's part. In no way does it pose as an objective selection, but it is given to show the diversity and interest of these burial grounds.*

ARGENTINA

BUENOS AIRES. RECOLETA CEMETERY.

Strongly suggestive of those in New Orleans (but, with the exception of Metairie, much better cared for), the cemetery occupies the same place in the hearts of the citizens of Buenos Aires as Père-Lachaise does for those of Paris. In 1821, administered by a religious order, the cemetery became the central cemetery on the outskirts of the city, then a small river port. Among the early arrivals was Antonio, described as a "black slave of Felix Gironbein." He was eighteen years old when he was buried here on November 13, 1836.

As Buenos Aires grew to be the large cosmopolitan center it is, Recoleta changed as well. In 1881 it was remodeled, declared nonsectarian, and became the charge of the municipal authorities.

The most famous of those buried here is Luis Angel Firpo (1896–1960), the "wild bull of the Pampas," who in 1923 fought Jack Dempsey for the heavyweight boxing championship of the world and lost. Before his tomb a larger-than-life statue of Firpo stands, attired in trunks and robe. Lesser known is Philadelphia-born Guillermo Carlos Wright (1807–1868), one of the countless soldiers of fortune who went to Argentina in the nineteenth century.

Often referred to as the "cemetery of the aristocrats," Recoleta now stands in one of the most fashionable districts of the capital, and tombs are passed down from generation to generation. Occasionally, less well-to-do Argentinians rent space for a short time in a Recoleta mausoleum (and are later transferred elsewhere) so that the deceased's family will have a sense of status. Often an heir of Recoleta property will raze a large mausoleum, subdivide his property and sell half, then erect a smaller tomb on his remaining half.

A handsome tomb marks the burial site of President Pedro Aramburu, who in 1970 was kidnapped and murdered by Peronistas. His body was later stolen from the tomb and the ransom demanded for its return was that the body of Eva Peron, second wife of dictator Juan Domingo Peron, be given in exchange. Eva died of cancer in 1953 and was embalmed, it was reported, at a cost of $100,000. After Peron was deposed in 1955, Eva's body was stolen and secretly buried in an Italian cemetery. When it was recovered, Peron brought it to the home in Spain he shared with Isabel, his third wife. When Peron returned to Argentina, so did Isabel—and Eva! It was then that Aramburu's body was returned to Recoleta.

Eva did not find eventual shelter in Recoleta. Her body was kept at the presidential residence and a chapel built for it. Eva's sisters brought suit against Isabel (before her fall from power) to recover the body for eventual reburial in Recoleta, where Eva's sisters own a crypt.

Only twelve acres in size, Recoleta contains more than 5,500 mausoleums, which are extremely well cared for. It has been impossible to estimate the number of burials. The cemetery has been called a "sea of mausoleums" and is second only to the cemetery in Milan.

AUSTRIA

SALZBURG. SAINT PETER'S CHURCHYARD.

The present churchyard dates from 1627 and is the oldest Salzburg cemetery still in use. The Chapel of the Cross, Romanesque in concept and dating from 1170, is now used principally as a mortuary chapel. In 1614 it was converted by Konrad Asper into a mausoleum for Prior Anton, count of Lodron, who died the following year. It was restored in 1960–1961.

The arcades house numerous family vaults. Number 16 contains the bones of Lorenz Hagenauer, the Mozart family's landlord, and Number 39 is of Sigmund Haffner, to whom the composer dedicated his Haffner Symphony. Near the entrance to the catacombs is a general vault. Among those interred within it are Marianne Mozart, Michael Haydn, and Andreas Nesselthaler, a court painter. Saint Peter's Churchyard has been called a "model of urbane peace and calm."

BERMUDA

HAMILTON. SAINT ANNE'S CHURCHYARD.

This old church, surrounded by flowering shrubs and tall cane grass, dates from 1616 and the earliest grave in the churchyard from almost a half century later. The oldest stone bears the line: "MD, December 24, 1668." The tombs at Saint Anne's are typical of those elsewhere on the island. Of limestone and oblong in shape—almost coffinlike—they are whitewashed. This is the limestone that is indigenous to the island, composed of skeletons from hundreds of sea creatures. Each tomb is made to hold eight coffins and its top is in four sections. At the time of burial each section can be moved aside to allow entrance of the coffin. Many of the tombs have only a number on them, although an occasional name can be found. There are, of course, the graves of foreign seamen and others who drowned as a result of boating accidents. Where traditional tombstones are found, they are usually ones brought here from England by ship.

CZECHOSLOVAKIA

PRAGUE. STRASCHNITZ CEMETERY.

Czech novelist Franz Kafka (1883–1924) and his parents Hermann Kafka and Julie Löwy are buried near one of the main gates of this Jewish cemetery. Kafka, dying of tuberculosis of the larynx, called to his doctor—Klopstock—as he left his bedside to clean a syringe: "Don't leave me." The doctor reassured him he would not. It was then that Kafka replied: "But I am leaving you."

ENGLAND

GRASMERE. GRASMERE CHURCHYARD.

In this Cumberland churchyard are the graves of William and Mary Wordsworth. William (1770–1850), a Lake Poet, moved to the Lake District in 1799 and occupied Dove Cottage until 1808. The stone over his grave states simply: "William Wordsworth 1850." Below are the words "Mary Wordsworth 1852." The graves of their son, daughter, and two children who died in infancy are here, as well as that of his sister, Dorothy (1771–1855). William Watson immortalized the churchyard in a poem entitled "Wordsworth's Grave." In "Memorial Verses," Matthew Arnold wrote:

Keep fresh the grass upon his grave,
O Rotha, with they living wave!
Sing him thy best! for few or none
Hears thy voice right, now he is gone.

GRAVESEND. SAINT GEORGE'S CHURCHYARD.

This is the burial place of Pocahontas (1595?–1617), daughter of Powhatan. She supposedly saved the life of Captain John Smith at Jamestown, Virginia. She married John Rolfe, an English colonist in Virginia, visited England, and as an Indian princess caused a sensation there. She died on shipboard as she and Rolfe were preparing to return to America. The church burned in 1727 and a new one was built over it. After the fire the bodies buried in the church were put into a common grave and all attempts to identify the bones of Pocahontas have failed.

JORDAN'S GRAVEYARD, BUCKINGHAMSHIRE.

This graveyard adjoining Jordan's Meeting, where William Penn (1644–1718) and other Quakers met, dates from 1671 and contains the bones of Penn, the founder of Pennsylvania, his first wife, Gulielma Springett, his second wife, Hannah Callowhill, his son, John, and his daughters, Margaret Freame and Letitia Aubrey. Mary Springett Penington, Gulielma's mother, and Isaac Penington, her stepfather, are buried here as well.

LONDON. ABNEY PARK CEMETERY, STOKE NEWINGTON CHURCH STREET.

Dating from 1840, some thirty-five acres in size, this nineteenth-century cemetery is of interest because of the Egyptian Revival lodges and entrance gates, and a Gothic chapel that captures the Victorian spirit. The architect for the cemetery was William Hosking (1800–1861). The plantings are "now a delight, and a lesson to us how well the nineteenth century understood the juxtaposition of trees and monuments." Buried here are

William Booth (1829–1912), founder of the Salvation Army, and his wife, Catherine Mumford (1829–1890), as well as Bridget Fleetwood (died 1662), elder daughter of Oliver Cromwell. A handsome monument honors Isaac Watts (1674–1748), composer of hymns, who once resided in a house on this site, but who is buried in Bunhill Fields.

BROMPTON CEMETERY, OLD BROMPTON ROAD OR FULHAM ROAD.

This Kensington cemetery was one of the first of the great metropolitan cemeteries that evolved when cemetery reform was beginning, a time when the movement to close the older and smaller churchyards was afoot. Founded by the West of London and Westminster Cemetery Company, it first attracted Londoners in advertisements as early as 1836, but was not consecrated until 1840. Later that year the first burial, that of Mrs. C. Boyle Shaw, took place.

About forty acres were purchased from Lord Kensington and plans were originally made for it to be developed on a grand scale. Laid out on a strong axis from Old Brompton Road to Fulham Road, the cemetery's gate on Old Brompton Road led to a long tree-lined avenue that in turn terminated in a Great Circle. The initial plan was to have the octagonal Anglican chapel on the circle, facing the avenue and the Old Brompton Road gate. Facing each other from opposite sides of the circle were to be the Roman Catholic chapel and that for the Dissenters. These two were never built.

Poor management, a change of architects, and rising building costs plagued Brompton Cemetery in its early years. Despite this, a number of interesting and important Londoners managed to find their way here. Among them are: "Gentleman" John Jackson (1769–1845), champion of England from 1795 to 1803 who later taught Lord Byron the manly art in his boxing school on Bond Street; Henry Brinley Richards (1819–1885), composer of the song "God Bless the Prince of Wales"; Sir Francis Pettit Smith (1808–1874), inventor of the four-bladed screw propeller for steamships; Brandon Thomas (1850–1914), author of the popular farce *Charley's Aunt* (1892); actor William Terris (1847–1897), who was murdered as he entered the Adelphi Theatre in London; Emmeline Pankhurst (1858–1928), the energetic suffrage leader who founded the Women's Social and Political Union; and Richard Tauber (1891–1948), the monocled Austrian tenor who thrilled Europe and America with such songs as "Yours Is My Heart Alone" and "Vienna, My City of Dreams."

The athletes have impressive monuments. "Gentleman" John Jackson's is guarded by a recumbent lion atop it, and that of Robert Coombes (1808–1860), a champion sculler who died in an insane asylum, has an upturned sculling shell on top. His epitaph reads: "Fare thee well my trim-built wherry, oars, coat and badge, farewell." At the time it was erected it was termed "bad

and vulgar, so ugly as a whole, so execrable in the details." Actually, it holds great interest for us today, and is one of the most fascinating and distinctive in Brompton Cemetery.

The classical arch, the lodges at the entrance on Old Brompton Road, the catacombs stretching as arms around the Great Circle, the bell tower, the Victorian monuments, and the density of burial here among the shrubbery, which has taken firm hold, make a visit to Brompton Cemetery an intriguing glimpse into Victorian London.

LONDON. BUNHILL FIELDS, CITY ROAD, FINSBURY.

What makes Bunhill Fields unique is that it is the place in which most nonconformists—Quakers, Methodists, Baptists, and Independents—were laid to rest between 1685 and 1854. These were the men and women who opposed the established church, the Church of England.

Bunhill is a corruption of "Bone Hill," where the bones removed in 1547 from Saint Paul's by Edward Seymour, duke of Somerset, were deposited. The entrance itself is Grecian in character. The dramatis personae of Bunhill Fields reads like an introduction to English literature. Daniel Defoe (1659?–1731), author of *Robinson Crusoe, Moll Flanders,* and *The Journal of the Plague Year,* dissenter and pamphleteer, is here. John Bunyan (1628–1688), whose fame rests on *Pilgrim's Progress,* lies beneath a recumbent effigy on his tomb, a practice more often reserved for royalty, members of the peerage, and the clergy. William Blake (1757–1827) and his wife, Catherine (1762–1831), lie here, although not beneath the monument to their memory. Mystic, artist, and poet, Blake was drawn to the teachings of Emanuel Swedenborg.

Others here are Charles Fleetwood (died 1692), who married Oliver Cromwell's daughter, Bridget, and three later descendants of the Lord Protector—Henry, Richard, and William Cromwell. In the cemetery too is Susannah Wesley, mother of Charles and John, leaders of the Methodist movement. John (1703–1791) is interred in the center of a small burial ground behind the John Wesley Chapel, which stands just outside the City Road gate to Bunhill Fields. The opposite gate is on Bunhill Row, where John Milton spent the last twelve years of his life, finishing *Paradise Lost* and writing *Paradise Regained.* On Whitecross Street, Bunhill Row, is buried George Fox (1624–1691), founder of the Society of Friends (Quakers).

LONDON. NORWOOD CEMETERY, NORWOOD HIGH STREET, LAMBETH.

Established first as the South Metropolitan Cemetery, it was consecrated in 1837 by the Bishop of Winchester. The architect, Sir William Tite (1798–1873), is interred in the vaults. Designed with wide, spacious lawns, clumps of trees, and winding drives, it was developed from forty acres in Lambeth Manor, which had once belonged to Lord Thurlow. Originally an Anglican chapel (demolished in 1960) and one for Dissenters, with catacombs beneath each, stood here. Both were damaged during the bombing in World War II, but a great many splendid Victorian monuments remain.

Mrs. Beeton (1836–1865), born Isabella Mary Mayson, was a household name in nineteenth-century England for her books on housekeeping and cooking. Her husband, Samuel Orchart Beeton (1831–1877), who published the first English edition of *Uncle Tom's Cabin,* lies beside her. Others of interest at Norwood are Sir Henry Bessemer (1813–1898), discoverer of the Bessemer process for making steel inexpensively from pig iron; Sir Henry Doulton (1820–1897), of the pottery family, who developed sgraffito ware; General Sir William Napier (1785–1860), historian of the Peninsular War; and Sir Henry Tate (1819–1899), whose bequest founded the Tate Gallery in London.

Within the northeastern corner of Norwood lies a Greek cemetery, founded in 1842 by the Brotherhood of the Greek Community in London. One of its more spectacular bits of architecture is a chapel, designed as a Doric temple by John Oldrid Scott, erected by Stephen Ralli in memory of his son.

In 1847 the parish of Saint Mary-at-Hill acquired a small portion of Norwood as a parish burial ground, and in 1966 the cemetery was taken over by the Lambeth Borough Council.

LONDON. SAINT BRIDE'S CHURCHYARD, FLEET STREET.

Any church by Sir Christopher Wren attracts even the uninitiated. One does not have to be an architectural historian to revel in the beauty of Wren architecture. The first church erected on this site was built in the thirteenth century. In 1680, after the Great Fire, Wren rebuilt it with the tallest Wren steeple in London. During World War II the church was damaged badly as were many others in this section of the city.

In the old churchyard on the south side are a number of notable Londoners. Although she is known only to scholars today, Mary Monckton, countess of Cork and Orrery (1746–1840), cut an eccentric figure during her long life. She lived during five reigns—George II, George III, George IV, William IV, and Victoria—and it is thought that Dickens immortalized her in *Pickwick Papers.* The late Annette Joelson, the South African writer, wrote of her as *A Lady of Quality With Lions.* Lady Cork, or "Corky," was a bluestocking and entertained such lions as Lord Byron, "Prinny" (George IV when Prince Regent), Sir Walter Scott, and the playwright Richard Brinsley Sheridan.

Also here is Samuel Richardson (1689–1761), the father of the novel. *Pamela* was published in 1740 and was followed soon afterward by *Clarissa Harlowe.* His two wives and two of his sons are buried in the churchyard too. An early printer, Wynkyn de Worde (died 1534?), who printed *Morte d'Arthur* and the *Canterbury Tales* is

here as well. Remembered only by historians is Thomas Sackville, 1st earl of Dorset (1536–1608). It was he who in 1586 informed Mary Stuart that she was to be beheaded.

LONDON. SAINT GILES CHURCHYARD, CRIPPLEGATE.

The section of the city known as Cripplegate dates from 1010, the year in which the body of King Edmund the Martyr was carried into London through this entrance. The church (the first was probably built in ancient times in the reign of King Canute) did survive the Fire of London, but was burned during World War II. In 1960 the restored church was reopened. Today the churchyard is visited because John Milton (1608–1674), the poet whose *Paradise Lost* is one of the masterpieces of the language, lies in Saint Giles. His father, John, was buried here in 1647. Here too is the grave of navigator Martin Frobisher (1535?–1594), who searched for the Northwest Passage and commanded the *Triumph* against the Spanish Armada.

LONDON. SAINT JOHN'S CHURCHYARD, CHURCH ROW, HAMPSTEAD.

This is another Hampstead burial ground that contains graves of interest to the contemporary cemetery visitor. Of course, Hampstead has always been part of London that has attracted artists, writers, and actors, so it is only natural that this churchyard should. John Constable (1776–1837), that superb portrayer of the glories of the English countryside, is buried beside his wife, Maria Bicknell (1786–1828). Salisbury Cathedral is probably more familiar because of his painting than through thousands of photographs. Joanna Baillie (1762–1851), Scottish poet and playwright, is also here. Although her plays are forgotten today, the Kembles and Mrs. Siddons appeared in them during the dramatist's lifetime.

In the extension to the churchyard, the ashes of George du Maurier (1834–1896) were placed. The French-born artist lived in Hampstead and his novels *Peter Ibbetson* (1891) and *Trilby* (1894), and the latter's transferral to the stage, brought him international fame. Gerald du Maurier, the actor, was his son, and his granddaughter is novelist Daphne du Maurier. Sir Herbert Beerbohm Tree (1853–1917), actor-manager and half-brother of Max Beerbohm, is here as well as Kay Kendall (1927–1969) and Anton Walbrook (1900–1967), stage and film stars. A familiar figure to the British and Americans, Hugh Gaitskell (1906–1963), chancellor of the exchequer (1950–1951), will be remembered also as a leader of the Labour Party from 1955 to 1963.

LONDON. SAINT JAMES'S CHURCHYARD, PENTONVILLE ROAD, FINSBURY.

There are two buried here who deserve to be remembered. Richard Parkes Bonington (1801?–1828), one of England's finest watercolorists, died too young, but his paintings are treasured by connoisseurs. The other is Joseph Grimaldi (1779–1837), actor, pantomimist, one of the great clowns of the theatre who by his art lighted the stages of Drury Lane, Sadler's Wells, and Covent Garden. The church, built in 1787 by Aaron Hunt, became in 1791 a Chapel of Ease to Clerkenwell Parish Church. It has been a parish church since 1854.

LONDON. SAINT MARY'S ROMAN CATHOLIC CEMETERY, KENSAL GREEN.

This cemetery of twenty-six acres adjoins the larger, better-known Kensal Green Cemetery and has been used since the first half of the nineteenth century. It has been a place of pilgrimage especially because of the grave of Francis Thompson (1859–1907), the poet best known for "The Hound of Heaven." Thompson, who studied first for the priesthood, then medicine, died of consumption. The lettering on his gravestone was done by sculptor and wood engraver Eric Gill (1882–1940). Alice Meynell (1847–1922), the poet who helped care for Thompson during his addiction to opium, is buried here too, as is Sir John Barbirolli (1899–1970), conductor of the New York Philharmonic and the Hallé Orchestra.

One Bonaparte gives Saint Mary's an imperial cast. Prince Louis-Lucien (1813–1891), son of Lucien, Prince Canino, Napoleon's younger brother, lies here. He was born in London, lived much of his life in Bayswater (dying in Paddington), wrote or edited two hundred volumes, and was awarded a pension by Gladstone because of his contributions to science and literature. At his death, "his coffin was so designed that having been placed in the sarcophagus, its sides and lid could be removed, and the Prince revealed in court dress, lying on a mattress of violet satin fringed with gold. His chest was aglitter with orders."

Lesser figures buried here include Sir Anthony Panizzi (1797–1879), principal librarian of the British Museum and the man responsible for the idea of the Reading Room; several members of the family of Marie Tussaud (founder of Madame Tussaud's Wax Museum), and Christine Granville (1915–1952). Christine was born Countess Krystyna Skarbek in Warsaw. She was a member of the French Resistance during World War II and aided many Allied soldiers and airmen to escape. Awarded the Order of the British Empire, the Croix de Guerre avec Palmes, and other honors, she recieved more decorations for her wartime service than any other woman. Her death was an ironic one after her miraculous survival of the war. She was murdered in London by a former lover.

LONDON. SAINT NICHOLAS'S CHURCHYARD, CHISWICK MALL.

A church has occupied this site since the fifteenth century. All that can be seen of the early church today is the old tower. The present one dates from 1884. Of interest are two artists who worked over a century apart. William Hogarth (1697–1764), the painter and engraver known for his series *The Rake's Progress* and *Marriage à la Mode* (his father-in-law, Sir James Thornhill, is here as well), lies here, as does James Abbott McNeill Whistler (1834–1903), the American-born painter who became a London dandy and painted some unforgettable scenes of the city and the river. More flamboyant than either was Barbara Villiers, countess of Castlemaine and duchess of Cleveland (1641–1709). Mistress of King Charles II, she was known as the "Royal Whore," and bore the king at least five children.

LONDON. WEST HAMPSTEAD CEMETERY, FORTUNE GREEN ROAD, HAMPSTEAD.

Not as old as Kensal Green or Highgate, West Hampstead Cemetery, established in 1876, has many graves that interest the curious visitor. There is also a period chapel and lodge, designed by Charles Bell, in this rural cemetery on the outskirts of the city of London. Kate Greenaway (1846–1901) is here. Author and illustrator of *The Tailor of Gloucester* and other favorites of children the world over, she was joined over sixty years later by another writer—Pamela Frankau (1908–1967), novelist and daughter of writer Gilbert Frankau (1884–1952).

The theatre is best represented here. In fact, it would be of interest to know what prompted Gladys Cooper (1888–1971), stage and screen actress; Marie Lloyd (1870–1922), music hall and musical comedy singer; and Fred Terry (1863–1933), brother of Ellen and Kate who appeared with Irving, and his wife, Julia Neilson Terry, to choose this quiet cemetery as their last resting place. Henry Broadribb Irving (1870–1919), son of Sir Henry Irving (whose ashes are in Westminster Abbey), was an actor (and a barrister), although never as famous as his father.

Others in West Hampstead Cemetery are Joseph Lister, 1st Baron Lister (1827–1912), father of antiseptic surgery; and Grand Duke Michael of Russia (1861–1929), and his morganatic wife, Sophie, countess de Torry (1868–1927).

MORTLAKE. MORTLAKE CATHOLIC CEMETERY, NORTH WORPLE WAY.

Here is one of the most extravagent tombs to be seen, and it suits a bizarre and romantic character. Sir Richard Burton (1821–1890), the explorer who journeyed through Moslem lands in various disguises and was able to enter Mecca and Medina, is buried in this cemetery. He also translated the *Arabian Nights,* which was in keeping with his life and career. He and his wife are buried beneath a concrete, life-size Arab tent, decorated with Christian and Moslem symbols.

SCARBOROUGH. SAINT MARY'S CHURCHYARD.

In this small burial ground beneath the guardian castle above lies Anne Brontë (1820–1849), author of *Agnes Grey* and *The Tenant of Wildfell Hall,* youngest of the three sisters writing in the parsonage at Haworth, Yorkshire. (Her sisters, Charlotte and Emily, and their brother, Branwell, are buried in the church of Saint Michael and All Angels, Haworth.)

STOKE POGES, BUCKINGHAMSHIRE.

This small churchyard—in the heart of England—inspired Thomas Gray (1716–1771) to pen what is the greatest tribute to any burial ground, "Elegy Written in a Country Churchyard."

> *The curfew tolls the knell of parting day,*
> *The lowing herd winds slowly o'er the lea,*
> *The plowman homeward plods his weary way,*
> *And leaves the world to darkness and to me.*

It was a copy of this poem that General James Wolfe carried with him to the Battle of Quebec, which would end so tragically for him on the Plains of Abraham. He is reported to have said: "I would rather have been the author of that piece than beat the French tomorrow." Wolfe was victorious over the French, and one of the poem's verses could well have been his own epitaph:

> *The boast of heraldry, the pomp of power,*
> *And all that beauty, all that wealth e'er gave,*
> *Awaits alike the inevitable hour:*
> *The paths of glory lead but to the grave.*

FRANCE

CANNES. PROTESTANT CEMETERY.

Maxine Elliott (1868–1940), the legendary American-born actress who was the toast of two continents, is buried here.

FONTAINEBLEAU. PROTESTANT CEMETERY AT AVON.

The grave of Katherine Mansfield (1888–1923), the New Zealand-born short story writer, is here. On her gravestone are these words from Shakespeare:

But I tell you, my lord fool, out of this nettle, danger, we pluck this flower safety.

PARIS. CIMETIÈRE DE MONTPARNASSE, BETWEEN THE BOULEVARD EDGAR QUINET AND THE RUE FROIDEVAUX.

One of the great cemeteries of Paris, although it has been overshadowed by Père-Lachaise. Charles Baudelaire (1821–1867), author of *Les Fleurs du Mal* (*Flowers of Evil,* 1857); Charles-Augustin Saint-Beauve (1804–1869), the most celebrated of critics; Guy de Maupassant (1850–1893), master of the short story; Jules Barbey d'Aurevilly (1808–1889), critic and novelist; César Franck (1822–1890) and Camille Saint-Saëns (1835–1921), composers, are all here.

PARIS. CIMETIÈRE DE MONTMARTRE.

Here are buried Louis Hector Berlioz (1803–1869), Jacques Offenbach (1819–1880), Léo Delibes (1836–1891), composers, and Émile Zola (1840–1902), novelist.

VERSAILLES. CIMETIÈRE DES GONARDS.

Edith Wharton (1862–1937), the American novelist of manners, is buried in a double plot she purchased near the grave of her great friend, Walter Berry. At her funeral an honor guard of World War I veterans and others from Saint Brice, which she had befriended, attended. Other than her name and dates, her simple stone has only the Latin words *Ave Crux Spes Unica,* which she selected herself.

IRELAND

DRUMCLIFFE CHURCHYARD, COUNTY SLIGO, ON THE SLIGO-BUNDORAN ROAD.

James Plunkett in the *The Gems She Wore* writes: "Some miles from Sligo town the road to Lissadell rides high above the magnificent sweep of Drumcliffe Bay, passing as it goes the entrance to the churchyard at Drumcliffe, where Yeats himself is buried." William Butler Yeats (1865–1939), one of Ireland's greatest poets, died at Cap Martin, France, and during the war his body was temporarily in the cemetery at Roquebrunne. It was this remote churchyard that Yeats designated as his final resting place. He himself wrote his simple epitaph:

Cast a cold eye
On life, on death
Horseman, pass by!

Ben Bulben rises nearby. Between the mountain and Drumcliffe, the Battle of the Books between the followers of Saint Colmcille and Saint Finian took place in A.D. 561. The round tower (Yeats's great-grandfather was a clergyman here a century before the poet's death) dominates the churchyard and a Celtic cross seems more than appropriate here. Not far from Drumcliffe Church is Lissadell, home of the Gore-Booth family. Yeats often visited there and was an intimate of the sisters Eva and Constance (Countess Markievicz), the latter a fervent Irish patriot.

ITALY

Florence. Il Cimitero degli Allori. Opened in 1878, after the closing of the Cimitero degli Inglesi three years before, it contains the graves of many expatriates such as Charles A. Loeser (1864–1928), who bequeathed to the city a collection of objets d'art; his fellow American Herbert Percy Horne (1864–1916), translator of *Tales of Botticelli*; Francesca Alexander (1837–1916), author of *Roadside Songs of Tuscany* and friend of John Ruskin; and artist Arnold Boecklin (1827–1901). However, Carlo Steinhauslin (1893–1951), Swiss consul in Florence for twenty years, is the one best remembered by Florentines. During World War II, especially in the war's last two years, he stood in for the mayor and the city council because these men were either bearing arms, in prison, or had disappeared. The responsibility for the city's safety fell to him and in order to save it from Allied or German bombardment, he was in constant communication with both sides. Later he was made a "citizen of honor" of Florence.

MAURITIUS

SAINT MARTIN. ANGLICAN CEMETERY.

There is a little-known but touching story concerning the Christian cemetery in this small hamlet just outside Port Louis, the capital. Between 1941 and 1945 more than fifteen hundred Jews from Central Europe found their way to this island, one of the Mascarene Islands that were then the possession of Great Britain.

Mainly Zionists, the voyagers set out for Palestine (as Israel was then called) in various vessels, but were denied residence there and were deported. One such group, originally from Czechoslovakia, was seventeen days en route from Palestine to an unknown destination, which proved to be Mauritius.

Their reception at Mauritius was more cordial than at Palestine, but the only accommodation available was an old jail at Beau Bassim. Here they were permitted relative freedom, for the doors remained open. The immigrants succeeded in organizing certain cultural and business activities during their enforced residence.

During the four years they remained on Mauritius, 124 of the group died, all of natural causes. The Jews, having organized a Chebra Kaddisha, obtained a section of the Christian cemetery, consecrated it, and buried their dead in this small corner of this tiny island in the Indian Ocean. Over the gate they inscribed the words "Blessed Be the True Judge." Separated from the main cemetery by a stone wall, the Jewish burying ground was enclosed with a green hedge. Here through the years, the 124 stones were erected in orderly rows, each bearing the name of the deceased, the birth and death dates, the place from which he or she emigrated, and sometimes the occupation. Today the stones bear witness to their flight: they came from Warsaw, Vienna, Danzig, and cities in Czechoslovakia. A larger, more elaborate stone marks the grave of Bernhard Friedmann (1889–1943), from the free city of Danzig, who came to die on this tropical island five hundred miles off the coast of Madagascar.

RUSSIA

LENINGRAD. PISKAREVSKOYE CEMETERY.

This cemetery on the northern edge of the city contains the graves of many victims of the World War II siege of Leningrad. It is staggering to contemplate but some eight hundred thousand are buried here. There are long rows of grass-grown mounds containing the bodies of heroic people who died defending their city. On the wall at the end of the cemetery is a lament by Olga Berggolt. Its lines are a threnody: "Be aware . . . that no one is forgotten, and nothing is forgotten."

SCOTLAND

GLASGOW. CARMUNNOCK CHURCHYARD.

Carmunnock has been described as the "kind of a place one imagines as a child, and has long since forgotten and only now remembers." Here the "stairs are so fine that the houses wear them outside for show." It is an area of steep little hills and many blind corners "for Carmunnock is designed more for a rumbling farm horse and cart or a homeward-bound hay wain with its gently swaying load."

The old church also wears its stairs outside. It has been here from before the Reformation, the first incumbent since that schism being "John Ramage, Exhorter and Reader, 1569." Another was the Reverend Matthew M'Kail, a relative of Hugh M'Kail, the Covenanter, who was taken prisoner after the disastrous Pentland Rising and tortured with the iniquitous "Boot." It was said when he stood on the scaffold, there was not one spectator in all the crowd of hardened onlookers who was not weeping.

In the churchyard are the graves of Arthur Mackie Morrison and Agnes Brysson Inglis, both descended from families that go back into the mists of Scotland's early history. They were the parents of a remarkable family of writers—often compared to the Brontës—March Cost (Margaret Mackie Morrison), and Mary, John, N. Brysson, and T. J. Morrison. The latter best described this churchyard, the town (now absorbed into Glasgow), and the atmosphere when he wrote: "Here you walk seven hundred feet above sea-level, with the wheeling peewits over your head. If you are very fortunate you may even hear a far-away whaup utter its wild, sad God-gifted cry.... Your face is turned to the Renfrewshire hills, where the scattered white-washed farm houses lie, catching and reflecting the sunshine like rain-washed pebbles. Behind these hills the peaks of Arran rise, blue and ethereal."

INCHMAHOME, LAKE OF MENTEITH, PERTHSHIRE.

On this island in the only "lake" in Scotland (the others are lochs) is buried R(obert) B(ontine) Cunninghame Graham (1852–1936), Scottish poet, horseman, traveler, and man of letters. Descended in the direct line from King Robert II, he was regarded by antiquaries such as Andrew Lang as the "uncrowned king of Scots" (because of the alleged illegitimacy in the Stewart line). He was the author of *Thirteen Stories* and *Rodeo*.

SAINT ANDREWS. CATHEDRAL BURIAL GROUNDS.

Saint Andrews is to Scotland as Mecca is to the Mohammedan world or Constantinople to Byzantium. The city was founded in 1140 under a charter granted by King David I of Scotland. Twenty years later the cathedral itself was founded and consecrated in 1318. At that time it was the largest in Scotland—355 feet in length. Its historic associations are numerous: Robert the Bruce returned here to give thanks for his victory at Bannockburn in 1314, and it was the scene of the marriage of the parents of Mary Queen of Scots, James V of Scotland and Mary of Guise, in 1538. The cathedral was sacked by the mob in 1559 after an inflammatory sermon by John Knox, leader of the Reformation in Scotland. After the fall of the Roman Catholic Church in Scotland it fell into disuse, and through the years masons of Saint Andrews took the dressed building stone for other purposes so that all that remains are a few ruined walls.

The gravestones nearby are scattered in the cathedral grounds and are not necessarily all of ancient vintage. One unique one from the last century is that of Tom Morris, Jr., who won the British Open Golf championship three times, in 1868, 1869, and 1870. He died at twenty-six and there is no telling how many more he would have won had he lived longer. The white gravestone shows Morris in golfing stance, a tam-o'-shanter on his head. It reads that it is in memory of "Tommy."

This magnificent stone in the cathedral grounds of Saint Andrews was erected to Thomas Morris by golfers from all over the world. *Photograph courtesy of James K. Robertson*

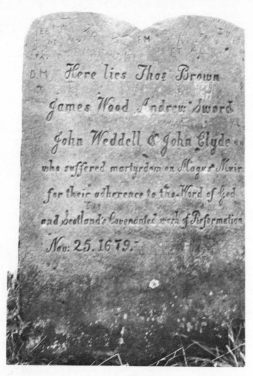

The little-known tombstone of five Covenanters who were implicated in the assassination near Saint Andrews of Archbishop Sharp. The stone was erected near the spot where the archbishop was dragged from his coach and stabbed to death before his daughter. *Photograph by G. M. Cowie, courtesy of James K. Robertson*

Rising above the burial ground, Saint Rule's tower is a landmark for all at sea, as is Saint Andrews Castle (first built in 1200). It was Saint Rule (or Regulus) who, carrying the bones of Saint Andrew from Patras in Greece, was shipwrecked at the foot of the cliffs where the tower stands.

The town's official guidebook says that a "famous Scottish judge has said there is no place in this country over which the genius of antiquity lingers so impressively as Saint Andrews." This is nowhere more evident than in the ruins of the cathedral and the burial grounds.

SPAIN

CÓRDOBA. CITY CEMETERY.

Here lies Manuel Laureano Rodríguez y Sánchez (1917–1947), more familiarly known as Manolete, the idol of Spain's aficionados who throng the *corridas*. Manolete brought the art of the matador to even greater heights, a finer degree of grace and execution during his short lifetime. His death plunged Spain into national mourning. Generalissimo Francisco Franco bestowed on him Spain's highest civilian decoration—La Cruz de la Beneficencia. His grave is recognizable at once because of his full-length marble figure on his sarcophagus. His dress cape beneath his shoulders, he lies at the foot of a large crucifix. Barnaby Conrad in *The Death of Manolete* says: "Some poets, referring to the days when Córdoba belonged to Rome, spoke of Manolete as a fallen Caesar and compared his glories to those of the ancient Seneca and Lucan, fellow Córdovans."

SWITZERLAND

ZURICH. FLUNTERN CEMETERY.

In this Swiss cemetery far from the Ireland he celebrated, James Joyce (1882–1941), novelist and short story writer—*Ulysses* and *Dubliners*—was buried. On January 15 his simple wooden coffin was lowered into the grave without any religious service, as was his wish. As it was winter, one of the few tributes was a green wreath with a lyre as an Irish motif. The cemetery adjoins the zoological gardens and Nora Joyce—remembering her husband's affection for lions—remarked that she liked to think of him near the savage beasts, hearing them roar. Nora died in 1951 but because of her nonchalance in such matters, the space next to Joyce was filled and she was buried elsewhere in the cemetery.

UNITED STATES

ALABAMA

MONTGOMERY. OAKWOOD CEMETERY, RIPLEY AND LOWER WETUMPKA ROAD.

The spot has become a tourist attraction because Hank Williams (1923–1953), the folk singer, is buried here. (His wife, Audrey, was buried beside him in 1975.) A guitar is cut on the tombstone; on its reverse is a poem that begins:

Thank you for all the love you gave me.
There could be no one stronger.
Thank you for the many beautiful songs.
They will live long and longer.

ARIZONA

TOMBSTONE. BOOT HILL CEMETERY.

This is probably the most widely known cemetery in the state and has been celebrated in story, song, and motion picture. It was largely restored through the efforts of Emmett Nunnelley, who was buried here, and his wife, Lela. Most of the 250 graves are unidentified, and burials date chiefly from the 1880s, the earliest having been in 1878 and the latest in 1953. Some of the colorful individuals buried here have equally colorful names: Dutch Annie (died 1883), sometimes known as Queen of the Red Light District; Indian Bill; Six-Shooter Jim (died 1884), who was shot by Burt Alvord; Kansas Kid, a cowboy killed in a stampede; Red River Tom and Bronco Charley, both shot by a man named Ormsby; Stinging Lizard, shot by Cherokee Hall; and Margarita, who was stabbed by Gold Dollar, another dance-hall girl, in a quarrel over a man.

CALIFORNIA

LAWNDALE.

In this community, eight miles from San Francisco on the peninsula, is a series of cemeteries that dot the hills on each side of the highway. There is a Japanese, Chinese, Italian, Greek Orthodox, and a Serbian cemetery, as well as Cypress Lawn Cemetery, which is interdenominational.

SAN FRANCISCO. MISSION DOLORES, DOLORES STREET BETWEEN 16TH AND 17TH STREETS.

The mission was founded in 1776 by Junípero Serra, and the old cemetery adjoins the church. Many inscriptions are in Spanish and there are over 5,500 Indians here,

Above, right: Mission Dolores Cemetery. *Kerrigan photograph. Historic American Buildings Survey. Reproduced from the collection of the Library of Congress*

>

Mission Dolores Cemetery. Monument to Don Luis Antonio Argüello. *Kerrigan photograph. Historic American Buildings Survey. Reproduced from the collection of the Library of Congress*

buried between 1777 and 1848. Many early distinguished Californias lie here as well. A statue of Padre Serra stands guard over the burial ground and there is a particularly impressive "grotto of Lourdes." A redwood cross within is inscribed with the words: "Dedicated to the Neglected and Forgotten Who Rest Here."

SAN FRANCISCO. NATIONAL MILITARY CEMETERY, INFANTRY TERRACE AND LINCOLN BOULEVARD.

This lovely twenty-five-acre spot overlooking the Golden Gate is banked with laurel, cypress, and eucalyptus trees. Pauline Cushman Tyler (1835–1893), an actress who served as a Union spy in the Civil War, lies here. (She was later given the honorary commission of brevet major.) Unknown soldiers of World War II—408 of them—are buried in a heart-shaped plot dominated by a granite monument. The dead from certain abandoned military cemeteries—Fort Klamath, Oregon; Fort Colville, Washington; the Modoc Lava Beds in California; Old Camp Grand, Arizona—were transferred here. Some sixteen thousand of these men are buried here now.

SANTA MONICA. WOODLAWN CEMETERY, MICHIGAN AVENUE BETWEEN 14TH AND 15TH STREETS.

Originally known as Ballona Township Cemetery, it has been managed by the city since 1898 and is thought to have been privately owned by the Carrillo family and donated to the city in lieu of unpaid taxes. We do know that in 1886 it was nine acres; today it is twenty-six. The remains of early Spanish families—Machados, Higueras, Lugos, and Talamantes—are found here as well as the family plot of the Vawter (Vater) family. Williamson Dunn Vawter (1815–1894), who was born in Madison, Indiana, was a founder of the city's First Presbyterian Church. There are twenty-two graves in the family plot, making it the largest in the cemetery.

A few celebrities are here, the most famous being Leo Carrillo (1881–1961), best known for his portrayal of the Mexican general in *Viva Villa!* and later for his role of Pancho, Cisco Kid's companion in adventure. Irene Ryan, the Broadway, Hollywood, and television actress whose best-known role was that of "Granny" in *The Beverly Hillbillies* television program, is interred in the mausoleum as is Janos Prohaska (1919–1974), known for his role of "Cookie Bear" on the Andy Williams television hour.

An unusual touch in the mausoleum is an urn with a medal won for swimming atop it. What better place for a trophy than gracing the urn containing the man's ashes? The mausoleum itself is particularly fine, with interior walls of Italian Vermont marble and Colorado yule, another marble. California scenes—the Pacific Palisades, Monterey cypress, the redwoods, desert flowers, and Yosemite Falls—are depicted in the stained glass. Purchase of graves is limited to persons who have lived in Santa Monica at least five years, or who have a relative, by either blood or marriage, interred here.

CONNECTICUT

BRIDGEPORT. MOUNTAIN GROVE CEMETERY, NORTH AVENUE AT DEWEY STREET.

Here are the graves of Phineas T. Barnum (1810–1891), showman extraordinary, impresario, and the man who introduced Jenny Lind to America, and another of his protégés, General Tom Thumb (1838–1883). Until recently the grave of the most famous midget of all time (whose real name was Charles S. Stratton) was marked by an impressive monument. As recently as 1974 it was vandalized.

COVENTRY. NATHAN HALE CEMETERY.

A memorial to Nathan Hale (1755–1776), the patriot schoolmaster who was hanged by the British as a spy, dominates the cemetery. We remember him for his words: "I only regret that I have but one life to lose for my country." The Hale family plot is nearby.

DANBURY. WOOSTER CEMETERY, ELLSWORTH AVENUE.

Notable for the grave of Charles Ives (1874–1954), a native of Danbury, who was a successful insurance executive and, as an avocation, a composer. Today, belated recognition is his, for the works themselves and the vitality and originality he brought to composition.

GUILFORD. ALDERBROOK CEMETERY, BOSTON STREET.

The cemetery is of interest because it contains the grave of Fitz-Greene Halleck (1790–1867), poet and one of the group known as the "Knickerbocker Wits."

LEBANON. TRUMBULL CEMETERY, ROUTE 207.

William Williams (1731–1811), a signer of the Declaration of Independence, lies here among the graves of many other Revolutionary War soldiers.

MOHEGAN. FORT SHANTOK INDIAN BURYING GROUND.

Located in Fort Shantok State Park is the site of the burial grounds of the Mohegan Indians, immortalized by James Fenimore Cooper in *The Last of the Mohicans.*

NEW HAVEN. GROVE STREET CEMETERY, 227 GROVE STREET.

Originally opened in 1797, the cemetery is notable for its Egyptian Revival gate (1848), considered one of the finest extant examples of this style. The architect was Henry Austin (1804–1891). There are a number of graves here that should be seen, those of Lyman Beecher (1775–1863), Protestant minister and father of both Harriet Beecher Stowe and Henry Ward Beecher; Timothy Dwight (1752–1817), author and president of Yale University; Charles Goodyear (1800–1860), originator of rubber vulcanization; and Noah Webster (1758–1843), the lexicographer.

The grave that should not be overlooked, however, is that of Roger Sherman (1721–1793), the only man to sign all four fundamental documents on which the United States government is based: the Articles of Association in 1774; the Declaration of Independence in 1776; the Articles of Confederation in 1778; and the Constitution in 1787. Also here is Jehudi Ashman (1794–1828), first colonial agent to Liberia; General David Humphreys (1752–1818), revolutionary diplomat, pioneer industrialist, and the first to introduce Merino sheep into America; and Theodore Winthrop (1828–1861), novelist and one of the first officers killed in the Civil War. There are nine presidents of Yale University here, including Timothy Dwight.

Egyptian Revival gate at Grove Street Cemetery. *Goode photograph. Historic American Buildings Survey. Reproduced from the collection of the Library of Congress*

<

The grave of Lady Alice Fenwick (died 1648) at Saybrook Point, Connecticut. *Albert G. Robinson photograph. Reproduced from the collection of the Library of Congress*

NORWICH. OLD NORWICH TOWN CEMETERY, OLD CEMETERY LANE.

Samuel Huntington (1731–1796), signer of the Declaration of Independence, president of the Continental Congress, and governor of Connecticut, is buried here with other members of his family.

Oak Hill Cemetery and chapel. *Jack E. Boucher photograph. Historic American Buildings Survey. Reproduced from the collection of the Library of Congress*

DISTRICT OF COLUMBIA

OAK HILL CEMETERY, 3001 R STREET, N.W. (GEORGETOWN).

This nineteenth-century cemetery (chartered in 1848), in an area known as "The Rock of Dumbarton," has become a place of great interest to architectural historians and preservationists, because of its collection of highly individual monuments, the chapel designed by James Renwick (1818–1895), and the gatehouse, the work of architect George de la Roche (1791–1861).

The chapel, erected in 1850, is the one example of Renwick's Gothic Revival church design still standing in the District of Columbia. A miniature Gothic gem, the chapel sits on the highest ridge of the cemetery. The gatehouse, a handsome Victorian building in the Italianate style (erected about 1850), forms an impressive entry into the wooded grounds of Oak Hill, which is itself located on the highest point of ground in Georgetown.

William Wilson Corcoran (1798–1888), who is interred here and who gave the city the art gallery bearing his name, purchased the land for the cemetery that was to eventually be the last resting place of Edwin M. Stanton (1814–1869), secretary of war in Lincoln's cabinet; John George Nicolay (1832–1901), Lincoln's private secretary; and Margaret O'Neill (1796–1879), whose marriage to

John Henry Eaton, secretary of war (1829–1831) in Andrew Jackson's administration, helped disrupt the cabinet. Peggy was said to have been intimate with Eaton before their marriage, and this and her humble birth caused cabinet members and their wives to look upon her with disapproval. The marriage caused a rift between the President and Vice-President John C. Calhoun, whose wife was one of the leaders of Washington society.

John Howard Payne (1791–1852), whose song "Home, Sweet Home" is the only memory to have survived from his opera *Clari, or, the Maid of Milan* (London 1823), lies here in his second grave. Payne, a not-too-successful actor and playwright, was appointed consul at Tunis by President Tyler (at the suggestion of Daniel Webster). He was recalled in 1845 by President Polk, but returned there again in 1851 by President Fillmore, and it was at Tunis he was first buried. Thirty-one years after his death, Corcoran, an admirer of the song that made Payne famous, had his body returned here for reburial. President Chester A. Arthur and General William Tecumseh Sherman were present at the ceremonies.

Of the mausoleums, the one that is most evocative of the past is that of John Peter Van Ness, once representative in Congress from New York. Earlier it had been erected in a small cemetery at H Street between Ninth

The Van Ness mausoleum in Oak Hill Cemetery. *Historic American Buildings Survey. Reproduced from the collection of the Library of Congress*

Old Huguenot Cemetery, Saint Augustine, in 1904. *Detroit Photographic Company. Reproduced from the collection of the Library of Congress*

and Tenth streets, but was moved here in 1872. Modeled by architect George Hadfield after the Temple of Vesta in Rome, it lends a classical air to this cemetery of ravines and woodland, which contains more than seventeen thousand graves.

FLORIDA

JACKSONVILLE. EVERGREEN CEMETERY.

This is the burial spot of Cora Crane (1868–1910), wife of Stephen Crane, American novelist. Ironically he is buried in a cemetery of the same name in Hillside, New Jersey. Cora died after helping push a car that was stalled in the sand, a rather sad ending for a notorious and romantic figure in American literature.

SAINT AUGUSTINE. OLD HUGUENOT CEMETERY, JUST NORTH OF THE CITY GATES IN OLD SAINT AUGUSTINE.

This, the city's oldest Protestant burial ground, was opened in September 1821, shortly after Florida became a territory of the United States. Saint Augustine was

given its name on September 8, 1565, and is the oldest permanent settlement in America.

The cemetery, part of the land owned by the Reverend Thomas Alexander, was deeded by him in trust to the Presbyterian Church "for the use of the Protestant inhabitants of Saint Augustine." In Spanish colonial times, it is recorded that this spot (one-half acre) had sometimes been used as a potter's field and as a burial place for criminals and excommunicates.

Many of the city's leading citizens were buried here during the nineteenth century, but no burials have taken place in recent years. An annual Service of Remembrance is held, usually on Palm Sunday, by the Protestant churches in memory of Saint Augustine's Protestant pioneers as well as Florida's first settlers, the French Huguenots (Huguenot was a term often used then to mean Protestant), who, under Jean Ribault, suffered death for their faith near Saint Augustine in 1565.

SAINT AUGUSTINE. OLD TOLOMATO CEMETERY.

This land was first used as a cemetery in 1777 by the citizens of Saint Augustine, but in 1799 when called upon to settle a dispute over the rights to the property, Don Miguel O'Reilly, the parish priest, wrote that "since time immemorial" the ground had been used for burials, citing that in the early Spanish days it was used to bury Christian Indians of the town of Tolomato and continued as such until the British occupation of the province. In 1777 the British governor, Patrick Tonyn, granted the land for cemetery use without remuneration.

The names here are a mixture of Spanish—Solano, Hernandez, Sanchez, and Oliveros—and Anglo-Irish—Masters, Mayne, Wilkinson, Crosby, and O'Reilly. Don Juan McQueen, one of East Florida's heroic figures, who died on October 11, 1870, lies in an unknown grave. The last recorded burial was that of Robert P. Sabate, who died on January 11, 1892.

Bishop Agustin Verot (1805–1876) is buried in the mortuary chapel. At the time of his interment the chapel already contained the remains of Cuban patriot-priest Félix Francisco José Maria de la Concepcion Varela (1788–1853). Father Varela was born in Havana and in 1821 was elected to the Spanish Cortés (Parliament), but his advocacy of Cuban rights so angered Spain that he was forced into exile. On his last visit to Saint Augustine he died there. In order to make a place for Bishop Verot's body, the bones of Father Varela were put into a pillow and moved to one end of the vault. In 1911 they were removed to Cuba, to be enshrined in a monument erected to him as a national hero.

Bishop Verot, named head of the new vicariate of Florida in 1858, was a strong supporter of the Confederate cause. His stand marked the first time an American bishop entered national politics on an issue that did not directly affect Catholicism. He was known in the North as the "Rebel Bishop."

Lindbergh's simplicity in his approach to life, and his constant desire to withdraw from the limelight, dictated his choice of burial spot. The "Lone Eagle," first to fly the Atlantic alone (1927), would have been welcome in Arlington. Instead, he chose this spot on the island of Maui in the Hawaiian chain that stretches across miles of the Pacific.

Charles and Anne Morrow Lindbergh built a simple rustic home at Hana and for a part of each year they retreated here. Because of their love for it, in his last illness Colonel Lindbergh asked to be flown here to die. He instructed his physician, Milton M. Howell, not to use any extraordinary measures to keep him alive. He made the arrangements beforehand for his funeral: local carpenters made his simple wooden coffin, he was dressed in ordinary work clothes, no announcement of the funeral was made beforehand, and only Mrs. Lindbergh and a few friends attended the simple rites.

A grove of old trees shields the cemetery. The church itself is almost unseen beneath the protection of a huge spreading banyan tree. The small cemetery is filled with graves, their stones washed smooth and round by mountain streams (before their use as gravestones) and the rains that move in from the sea and often lash the island.

Since Lindbergh's death, more and more visitors have driven the eleven miles of winding road that climb tortuously through valleys and along cliffs from Wailuku over the windward slopes of Haleakala to Hana, and then to Kipahulu. Before Lindbergh's death the church register showed about fourteen hundred names of visitors for the previous year. In the first year following his funeral eight thousand names were recorded.

The pilot of "The Spirit of St. Louis," who typified the modern adventurer, the conqueror of new frontiers for those coming of age in the 1920s and 1930s, lies in a grave around which grow yellow plumeria plants. His name and dates are on the marble marker, and also the prophetic words:

**... If I take the wings of the morning,
and
dwell in the uttermost parts of the sea ...**

HAWAII

KIPAHULU, MAUI. PALAPALA HOOMU CONGREGATIONAL CHURCH CEMETERY.

The graves of the famous often focus attention on an otherwise-unknown burial ground. The decision on the part of Charles Augustus Lindbergh (1902–1974) to be buried in this lovely, peaceful spot brought it to the attention of the world.

ILLINOIS

CHICAGO. ROSEHILL CEMETERY, 5800 RAVENSWOOD AVENUE.

This, the largest nonsectarian cemetery in the Chicago metropolitan area, was chartered in 1859. One of its incorporators was Major John H. Kinzie, son of the first white settler who is also referred to as the "father of Chicago." Another incorporator was Dr. Levi D. Boone, great-nephew of Daniel. Dr. Jacob W. Ludlam, Jr., from whom the property was purchased less than a year earlier, was to be the first interred here—on July 11, 1859.

A number of unusual monuments greet the visitor's eye, but none is more striking than that over the grave of George S. Bangs, designer of the first railway car. It is a small-scale reproduction of the car itself, carved in granite, and set alongside a sheltering tree trunk, also hewn from granite. Bangs's invention carried forward the work of George Buchanan Armstrong, founder of the United States railway mail service, whose monument is also at Rosehill. Another monument, colossal in size, as was the man who selected it, is the obelisk erected by the city's twenty-first mayor, "Long" John Wentworth. During the last months of his life Wentworth, who was 6 feet, 6 inches tall, determined that his monument would be the largest in the west. He ordered it from the Hallowell Granite Company in Maine. Its huge base weighed fifty tons and its shaft rose to a height of seventy-two feet, reportedly costing an estimated $38,000.

Others here are General Charles Gates Dawes (1865–1951), vice-president in the Coolidge administration (1925–1929); Lyman J. Gage (1836–1927), secretary of the treasury in the cabinet of William McKinley; Frederick Stock, conductor of the Chicago Symphony Orchestra; and General Thomas Edward Greenfield Ranson, of whom Ulysses S. Grant said: "He has always proved himself the best man I have ever had to send on expeditions."

Leonard W. Volk, sculptor of Lincoln, is buried here. A life-size statue (his own work) of Volk marks his grave (he also executed other monuments at Rosehill), and there are graves of veterans of every United States war from that of "William Duval, Veteran of Revolutionary War, age 75" to Vietnam.

IOWA

NEW LIBERTY. PARKER PIONEER CEMETERY, JUST NORTH OF THE TOWN.

This small cemetery is of greater interest because of a trust fund that benefits education than for the graves in it. The land was originally granted to Asa Haile by the government in 1840 and deeded to the trustees of Liberty Township for a cemetery in 1855. It was named the Parker Cemetery because many buried here were members of that family who arrived in New England in 1625 and settled in Iowa in the 1840s. They were ancestors of Bessie Dutton Murray, who, with her husband, John, spent time and money improving the cemetery during the 1930s. Both the Murrays are buried here and a $40,000 trust fund, established by Mrs. Murray (who died in 1945) in memory of her husband, ensures the cemetery will be well cared for. The cemetery is located in Scott County and is northwest of Davenport.

KENTUCKY

COVINGTON. LINDEN GROVE CEMETERY, HOLMAN STREET BETWEEN 13TH AND 15TH STREETS.

This is one of Covington's oldest cemeteries. Among those buried here are John Griffin Carlisle (1835–1910), secretary of the treasury (1893–1897) in the second administration of President Grover Cleveland. He was a lawyer, legislator, lieutenant governor, congressman, and speaker of the House of Representatives. Also here are the graves of Revolutionary War soldiers and those from most other United States wars.

FORT KNOX. MILL CREEK CEMETERY, SOUTH OF THE TOWN OFF US 31W.

Of interest because here are the graves of Bersheba Lincoln, Abraham Lincoln's paternal grandmother, and her daughters, Mary Lincoln Crume and Nancy Lincoln Brumfield.

MAINE

ANDOVER. ANDOVER CEMETERY.

The grave of Molly Locket is of special interest in this small burial ground. Molly, an Indian, was so greatly in demand as a midwife by white settlers that she became a legend in the area during her lifetime. Her second husband was said to have been Chief Sabattus. There is some question concerning the statement on her gravestone that she was the last of the Pequawkets, because local tradition has it that two of her daughters married white settlers. Her inscription reads:

Mollocket baptised Mary Agatha
Catholic, died in The Christian Faith
August 2, A.D. 1816
The Last of the Pequawkets

BANGOR. MOUNT HOPE CEMETERY, STATE STREET.

Hannibal Hamlin (1809–1891), vice-president in Abraham Lincoln's first administration (1861–1865), is buried here. The cemetery is modeled after Mount Auburn.

BRIDGETON.

The small cemetery near the Glines neighborhood contains the grave of Captain John Haywood, who distinguished himself at Bunker Hill. The slate over his grave records the familiar New England caution of the eighteenth century:

Pause stranger, ere you pass by
As you are now, so once was I.
As I am now, soon you'll be,
Prepare for death, to follow me.

It was Haywood, then a private, who seized his captain's sword as he fell. Inspiring his men, he directed them and emerged from the battle a hero. He survived the Revolution, returning to his native town, North Bridgeton, to die.

BUXTON. OLD TORY MEETING HOUSE BURYING GROUND AT BUXTON LOWER CORNER.

A memorial to Kate Douglas Wiggin (1856–1923), author of *The Birds' Christmas Carol, Mother Carey's Chickens,* and *Rebecca of Sunnybrook Farm,* stands in the small cemetery, although she is not buried here. Her ashes were scattered on the Saco River.

GRAY. GRAY CEMETERY.

The famous are not here, but an unknown lad in gray is and thereby hangs a tale. In September 1862, Amos and Sarah Colley were informed that their son Lieutenant Charles H. Colley had been killed in the Battle of Cedar Mountain during the Shenandoah Valley campaign in Virginia. He was a member of Company B, 10th Maine Volunteers, one of eight thousand Union soldiers who attacked twenty thousand Confederates.

Amos and Sarah were told that when they had sent money for preparation of the body, and for the cost of shipping it, Lieutenant Colley would be returned to Gray. When the coffin arrived, and the body was examined, it was found not to be Colley's but that of a Confederate soldier in full uniform.

Although feeling in the North ran high—especially in New England, which was strongly abolitionist—the Colleys and the townspeople buried the unknown soldier with full honors. The simple white stone reads:

STRANGER
A Soldier
of the late war
died 1862
Erected
by the Ladies of Gray

Several weeks after The Stranger's burial a second coffin arrived for the Colleys; this time their son's body was in it. He was buried close to The Stranger.

The Ladies Relief Corps of the Grand Army of the Republic promised to care for the grave. For over 115 years now, on Memorial Day, flowers have decorated the grave of The Stranger and a small flag of the Confederate States of America is always placed there, the only one to be seen in Gray, Maine. The Stranger is among friends.

PORTLAND. EASTERN CEMETERY, CONGRESS STREET.

One would expect a port such as Portland to have maritime and naval memories in its cemetery, and the city does not disappoint the visitor in this nor does the cemetery. Commodore Edward Preble (1761–1807), who led the United States fleet against the Barbary pirates in the war against Tripoli, is here. He was the commander of the U.S.S. *Constitution* ("Old Ironsides"). Two who commanded opposing vessels in a naval engagement and died on September 5, 1813 during the War of 1812 lie side by side in Eastern Cemetery. Lieutenant William Burrowes was twenty-eight years old and commander of the *Enterprise;* his opponent was the twenty-nine-year-old Briton Captain Samuel Blyth, commander of the *Boxer.* The battle over and both commanders dead, the American *Enterprise* towed the captured *Boxer* into Portland harbor. All ships at anchor saluted the fallen warriors who were buried here. Burrowes's stone records it was placed there by a "passing stranger." Blyth's was erected by the "surviving officers of his crew."

There is a memorial to Lieutenant Henry Wadsworth (uncle of Henry Wadsworth Longfellow), who was killed in 1804 at Tripoli when the *Intrepid* was blown up to save it from capture. The cemetery has been used for nearly three hundred years and for more than two hundred it was the only one within city limits. It is six acres in size and the oldest stone extant dates from 1717.

MARYLAND

ANNAPOLIS. OLD CHURCH YARD.

Annapolis, the only colonial capital (1694) that still continues as a state capital, is the proud owner of many old burial grounds, notably the Old Church Yard. As the town grew, the burial ground was soon filled and the cemetery itself moved farther along Northwest Street. A number of old and distinguished early Marylanders lie here, including Sir Robert Eden, the last colonial governor. When the Revolution began, Sir Robert returned to England, but aferward he longed for America and realized how he loved it, so he returned here to die.

BALTIMORE. LOUDON PARK CEMETERY.

The Mencken family plot holds the ashes of H. L. Mencken (1880–1956), the enfant terrible of American letters, and his wife, Sara Haardt (1898–1935). In her youth Mrs. Mencken said she wanted her ashes scattered on the Alabama River where they would be borne out to sea. Her husband, noted for his public advocacy of the single state, placed them here beside those of his family. Mencken once penned an epitaph for himself (which was not used): "If after I depart this vale, you ever remember me and have thought to please my ghost, forgive some sinner and wink your eye at some homely girl." Associated Press correspondent R. P. McHugh went him one better, after observing his funeral: "As I watched I couldn't help but think what an unlikely vehicle a hearse was for a doughty old warrior like Mencken. In my view, they ought to have carried him away on a shield."

BALTIMORE. WESTMINSTER PRESBYTERIAN CHURCHYARD, FAYETTE AND GREEN STREETS.

One of the most historic and Gothic churchyards in Baltimore, this is best known because Edgar Allan Poe (1809–1849) is buried here. A large monument, just inside the gates, bears a medallion of Poe and marks his grave.

Behind the church itself is a monument to David Poe, Sr., the author's grandfather, who was born in Londonderry, Ireland, in 1743 and died in Baltimore in 1816. There is also a marker that states that Edgar Allan Poe's burial place was here from October 9, 1849 until November 17, 1875. It reads: "Mrs. Maria Clemm, his mother-in-law, lies upon his right and Virginia Poe, his wife, upon his left under the monument erected to him in this cemetery." Six small square markers, all with the letter P on them, block out the boundaries of the Poe family plot.

James McHenry, M.D. (1755–1816), a signer of the Constitution of the United States, and eighteen generals of the Revolution and the War of 1812 lie here, as do many others with the family names of Henderson, Boyd, Finley, Ramsay, and Falconer, which indicate the congregation's Scottish Presbyterian origins.

The ground itself originally belonged to John Eager Howard, who served as governor of Maryland for three terms. About 1782 he deeded the plot to the First Presbyterian Church for approximately $700. By 1849 there was a city ordinance prohibiting the establishment of cemeteries within the limits of Baltimore and banishing those already in use to the outskirts of the city. The Westminster churchyard was allowed to continue because it was attached to a church.

The present church was built over the cemetery on brick stilts in 1852, and during the Civil War people actually lived in the vaults below it.

No visitor should leave without seeing the Egyptian Revival tombs to the rear of the church. They are rare in American burial grounds, having been designed by Maximilian Godefroy, who also was responsible for the Baltimore Unitarian Church, the Battle Monument, and the chapel of Saint Mary's Shrine. They are monumental in size, brooding in appearance, overpowering, truly sepulchral. One built for John O'Donnell (who owned a section of the city named Canton) is decorated with exotic caryatids and the entrance doors have handles with special combinations—probably long since forgotten. O'-Donnell was one of the founders of the Rosicrucians in America.

CHESTERTOWN. SAINT PAUL'S CHURCHYARD.

Tallulah Bankhead (1903–1968), the Alabama-born stage and screen actress, is buried here in this old churchyard. She is in a corner by herself, far from the other Bankheads in Alabama, except for her nephew, Brock Bankhead, who is also interred here.

ROCKVILLE. SAINT MARY'S CEMETERY.

F. Scott Fitzgerald (1896–1940), the novelist of the twenties and thirties, and his wife, Zelda (1900–1948), were moved here in 1975 to graves beside Fitzgerald's father and mother. They had earlier been buried in Rockville Cemetery (Old Union Cemetery) because, at the time of his wife's and his death, the Catholic Church would not permit them to be buried there because he was not a practicing Catholic and "his writings were undesirable."

MASSACHUSETTS

AMHERST. WEST CEMETERY, TRIANGLE STREET.

The cemetery is old—dating back to the eighteenth century—but it is the grave of Emily Dickinson (1830–1886), the reclusive poet, that attracts visitors from all corners of the world. Emily died about six o'clock in the evening of May 15. Thomas Wentworth Higginson, her "dear preceptor," wrote: "Emily Dickinson's face a wondrous restoration of youth—she ... looked 30, not a grey hair or a wrinkle, the perfect peace of the beautiful." Shortly before her death she wrote her cousins, the Norcross sisters: "Little cousins,—called back. Emily." The words "Called Back" are on her tombstone. At her funeral Higginson read Emily Brontë's poem "No Coward Soul Is Mine," which could have been written by Emily Dickinson.

Emily Dickinson's gravestone in West Cemetery, Amherst. *Photograph by Clive E. Driver*

A gravestone in the Boston Central Cemetery. *Photograph by Clive E. Driver*

BOSTON. CENTRAL BURYING GROUND, ON BOSTON COMMON NEAR BOYLESTON STREET.

One is always happy when examining this burial ground that it is on the Common, for its location probably accounts for its preservation. However, although Bostonians know it is here, they generally hurry past without stopping in. Established in 1756, because both Granary and King's Chapel burying grounds were becoming crowded, it had earlier been known as the South Burying Ground and the Common Burying Ground. Gilbert Stuart (1755–1828), the portrait painter who irritated Boston when he referred to Philadelphia as the "Athens of America," is buried here, but there is doubt about the exact location of his grave. A slate marker states that in 1895 the remains of approximately 1100 adults were found in the vicinity, so the burying ground must have been larger than the one we see today.

BOSTON. COPP'S HILL BURYING GROUND, HULL STREET.

On one of the highest hills in Boston, overlooking the harbor and Charlestown beyond, is one of the most appealing burial grounds to be found in America. It is not far from Old North Church and Paul Revere's house; the Boston silversmith looked this way as he waited in Charlestown for the signal light to appear in the church tower that was to start him on his ride.

The burying ground was first established here in 1660. The stones are timeworn and weathered, many of the inscriptions dim or not legible at all. The most famous graves are those of the Mather family, a colonial dynasty that ruled church and school and is still spoken of with reverence in Boston. Increase Mather (1639–1723), son of the Puritan clergyman Richard, was a conservative exponent of Puritan theocracy; his son, Cotton (1663–1728), the most famous of all the family, succeeded his father

King's Chapel burying ground. *Photograph by Clive E. Driver*

as pastor. He is best remembered for his role in the Salem witch trials of 1692. His son, Samuel (died 1785), is here as well.

In 1976, when workmen were installing an electric light pole and underground wiring on Charter Street on the north slope of Copp's Hill, they accidentally broke into a tomb and were confronted by three skeletons. One was that of Edward Chamberlin, who died on January 10, 1807, another of Henry W. Gould, who died at the age of six weeks on September 5, 1830. The other remained unidentified. *O tempore, O mores!*

Copp's Hill, as in the case of Père-Lachaise and other cemeteries, was violated in time of war. A tablet reminds the visitor that "on this ground were planted the British batteries which destroyed the Village of Charlestown during the Battle of Bunker Hill, June 17, 1775."

BOSTON. FOREST HILLS CEMETERY, FOREST HILLS AVENUE, JAMAICA PLAINS.

This rural cemetery (although now part of the city) was established in the nineteenth century and is evidence that not *all* good Bostonians go to Mount Auburn when they die. Among those buried here are Eugene O'Neill (1888–1953), the greatest playwright America has produced (*The Emperor Jones, Mourning Becomes Electra*); Edward Everett Hale (1822–1909), author of *The Man Without a Country* (1863); William Lloyd Garrison (1805–1879), the abolitionist who founded (1831) the *Liberator* and fought against slavery for the next thirty-odd years; and E. E. Cummings (1894–1962), American poet. Worth seeing too is Daniel Chester French's bronze relief *Death Staying the Hand of the Sculptor* on the Milmore Memorial.

BOSTON. KING'S CHAPEL BURYING GROUND, TREMONT STREET.

The oldest cemetery in Boston (1630) surrounds King's Chapel and is near three other Boston landmarks, the old State House, the Parker House, and the old City Hall. It contains the grave of Governor John Winthrop (1588–1649), and is one of the few repositories of seventeenth-century graves in the United States. There is a handsome obelisk in memory of the Chevalier de Saint Sauveur, a French naval officer who aided the colonists during the Revolution.

CAMBRIDGE. CITY OF CAMBRIDGE CEMETERY, 76 COOLIDGE AVENUE.

Although Mount Auburn is *the* cemetery in Cambridge and one of the great ones of the world, this particular cemetery should not be ignored and is of interest because two giants of American literature, William Dean Howells (1837–1920) and Henry James, are buried here.

James died in London and the group that gathered at his funeral in Chelsea Old Church was a celebrated one to bid farewell to "The Master." John Singer Sargent, Edmund Gosse, Rudyard Kipling, Ellen Terry, and Dickens's daughter Mrs. Perugini were among the mourners. James was cremated at Golders Green and his ashes returned to America by Mrs. William James. Actually, they were smuggled in because Mrs. James did not dare risk trouble with customs officials in wartime.

The urn was buried beside his father, Henry (1811–1882), student of religious and social problems and follower of Swedenborg; his mother; his sister, Alice (1848–1892); and his brother, William (1842–1910), philosopher and psychologist. James's biographer Leon

Edel wrote: "He stood there in 1904 and looked at the Medusa-face of life and cried 'Basta, basta!'" The stone over his grave reads:

Henry James, O. M.
Novelist-Citizen
of Two Countries
Interpreter of his
Generation on both
Sides of the Sea.
New York April 15, 1843
London February 28, 1916

Memento mori, in Concord Hill Cemetery.
Photograph by Clive E. Driver

CHARLESTOWN. PHIPPS STREET BURYING GROUND.

It is the grave of John Harvard (1607–1638), chief founder of Harvard University, who left half his fortune and his library to the then-college, that has brought most visitors to this old seventeenth-century graveyard not far from the Bunker Hill Monument. In this, Greater Boston's second oldest cemetery, is a monument to Harvard, but it now appears that no one is quite certain where he is buried. A town historian explains that at his death Harvard was buried near his home in the Town Hill section of Charlestown. When the British looted Charlestown, his original gravestone was damaged and lost. As the town grew and new buildings were erected near his

grave site, the location became even more mysterious and lost for all time. By 1828 students of Harvard College contributed money for a monument to be erected over his grave, only to discover that no one knew where it was. With the logic learned at Harvard, they decided to place the monument in the cemetery nearest to where he was believed to have been buried!

PITTSFIELD. PITTSFIELD CEMETERY, WAHCONAH STREET.

Originally called Pontoosuc Plantation, Pittsfield was not given its present name until 1761. The early settlers, who buried their dead "in scattered locations, generally chosen for being high and dry," in 1753 voted to create a public cemetery but it was not until 1768 that Pittsfield's first burial ground came into general use. This particular cemetery was filled by 1830 and a new one established; in 1840 it was decided to remove the bodies in the old one and transfer them to the new ground.

Let it not be said that Pittsfield accepts change without questioning it. The spirit of the New England town meeting prevailed. Work proceeded on the transferral of the graves until 1849 when Dr. Joel Stevens (1818–1871) protested. He, when notified that the remains of his ancestors were to be reinterred in the new cemetery, maintained it would be too small, would soon be overcrowded, then obsolete. He reasoned that the remains of his family would eventually be moved again. He called for a cemetery that would last for hundreds of years. At a town meeting in the autumn of 1849 it was decided to buy the 130-acre George W. Campbell farm on Wahconah Street and create a new Pittsfield cemetery.

Dr. Oliver Wendell Holmes, physician and poet, was present on September 9, 1850 for the dedication. The autocrat of the breakfast table celebrated the occasion in verse:

Angel of death! Extend thy silent reign!
Stretch thy dark sceptre o'er this new domain!
No sable car along the winding road
Has borne to earth its unresisting load;
No sudden mound has risen yet to show
Where the pale slumberer folds his arms below;
No marble gleams to bid his memory live
In the brief lines that hurrying time can give;
Yet, O destroyer! From thy shrouded throne
Look on our gift; this realm is all thine own!

Soon afterward graves in the older cemeteries were moved to the Pittsfield Cemetery. The oldest stone is that of Sarah Root (1762–1763), but the first monument (Pittsfield marble) placed here was for Lemuel Pomeroy

Stephen D. Budrow rubbing a stone in Pittsfield Cemetery.

(1778–1849), which was hauled rough and carved at the site; the first granite monument was cut in Brooklyn, New York, and erected for Professor Charles E. West.

While there are no nationally known figures buried here, those that are in the cemetery reflect the fabric of the town. There is Colonel William Williams (1710–1785), one of the first settlers of Pontoosuc Plantation. He married three times (two of his wives are here) and fought in the French and Indian War. Through his influence with Governor Bernard, the town in 1761 was renamed Pittsfield in honor of the English statesman William Pitt, earl of Chatham.

Major Butler Goodrich (1768–1863)—they lived to advanced ages in Pittsfield—was an ardent Federalist in politics. Charles Goodrich (1720–1815), another nonagenarian, came to Pontoosuc in 1752 and built the first house two years later. William Francis Bartlett (1840–1876) fought in the Civil War, lost his leg, was wounded several times more, and captured. Mustered out as a major general, he was not yet twenty-five years old. The Reverend Thomas Allen (1743–1810)—"The Fighting Parson"—served as chaplain to three Berkshire regiments during the Revolution, and was at Ticonderoga and the Battle of Bennington. His grandson, Thomas Allen (1813–1882), published a newspaper, *The Madisonian,* in Washington, D.C., became a congressman from Missouri, and built at his own expense the Missouri Building at the Centennial Exposition in Philadelphia in 1876. He was returned to Pittsfield for burial

beneath an obelisk of red granite (larger than his grandfather's) from the Allen quarries in Missouri. It was his bequest that provided the cemetery's gateway of gray stone, built in 1884.

True, these men were not world famous, but they were of importance in Pittsfield. For instance, in the home of John Chandler Williams (1755–1831) we learn that the "first carpet covering a whole floor in the Village of Pittsfield was laid in the Williams parlor." It was Gordon McKay (1821–1903) who, financially, left his mark on the town—to the tune of twenty-five million dollars, which he bequeathed to Harvard University. McKay invented a shoe-nailing and shoe-lasting machine, and greatly improved a shoe-sewing machine. (Massachusetts is a center for shoe manufacture.) These inventions revolutionized the industry and brought him millions. His mausoleum, designed by a woman—Mary E. Tillinghast —which at the time was most unusual, was constructed ten years before his death. Built of Lee marble, it is 20½ feet high and the walls are 15 inches thick. The cathedral windows were exhibited at the Chicago World's Fair of 1893 before being installed in the mausoleum.

The urn and the willow, death's head and crossbones, Father Time and the hourglass, and the hand pointing to heaven are in evidence on the tombstones throughout the cemetery. They reflect the fascination with death and its symbols that so delighted the New England character and conscience.

Although his words seem extravagant to present-day

readers, Holmes's lines evoke a time past when Pittsfield was young, when its cemetery was beginning its role in the life of the community:

Fair is the scene; its sweetness oft beguiled
From their dim paths the children of the wild;
The dark-haired maiden loved its grassy dells,
The feathered warrior claimed its wooden swells,
Still on its slopes the ploughman's ridges show
The pointed flints that left his fatal bow,
Chipped with rough art and slow barbarian toil,—
Last of his wrecks that strews the alien soil!

MISSOURI

ASH GROVE. NATHAN BOONE HOMESTEAD.

Near the house built by Colonel Boone in 1837 is a family cemetery. Boone, youngest son of Daniel Boone, and his wife, Olive van Bibber, lie here.

HANNIBAL. MOUNT OLIVET CEMETERY.

Samuel Langhorne Clemens (1835–1910), better known as Mark Twain, spent his childhood here, the scene of both *Tom Sawyer* and *Huckleberry Finn*. Many family members are in this cemetery, including his parents, John Marshall Clemens (1798–1847) and Jane Langhorne Clemens (1803–1890) his brothers, Henry (1838–1858) and Orion (1825–1897), and Orion's wife, Mary E. (1836–1904).

INDEPENDENCE. MOUNT WASHINGTON MEMORIAL CEMETERY.

Trapper, fur trader, scout, and legendary frontiersman, James Bridger (1804–1881) is buried here. A native of Virginia, Jim came West with his parents in 1812, and was identified with the development of the Northwest Territory. He was the first white man known to visit Great Salt Lake (1824).

KANSAS CITY. UNION CEMETERY, WARWICK STREET.

Established about 1858, this burial ground contains an estimated fifty thousand graves. Best known are those of George Caleb Bingham (1811–1879), American genre painter, and Alexander Majors (1814–1900), originator of the Pony Express. Fifteen Confederate soldiers who died while prisoners of war in Kansas City were interred here and their graves marked by a ten-foot monument. There are approximately twelve hundred other soldiers here as well.

SAINT CHARLES. SAINT CHARLES BORROMEO CATHOLIC CEMETERY.

Buried here is Jean Baptiste Point de Sable, the first permanent resident of Chicago. Rebecca Younger (1826–1850), wife of Coleman Younger, outlaw of the 1860s, is also here.

SAINT LOUIS, CALVARY CEMETERY, 5239 WEST FLORISSANT AVENUE.

The largest in the city (476 acres), it is a Roman Catholic cemetery and was founded in 1864. Among those interred here are René Auguste Chouteau (1749–1829), one of the founders of Saint Louis who began to clear the land for the city as a lad of fourteen; General William Tecumseh Sherman (1820–1891), whose "March to the Sea" desolated Georgia during the Civil War; Thomas Biddle, a Philadelphia army officer killed in a duel with Congressman Spencer Pettis in 1831; and Alexander McNair, Missouri's first governor.

SPRINGFIELD. NATIONAL CEMETERY.

Established in 1869, it is the burial place of 2,347 Union and 569 Confederate soldiers. What makes it distinctive is that it is the only spot in the United States where a Union and a Confederate cemetery adjoin. Some years ago a gate between the two was opened, but not without great opposition. The two are now one.

NEW HAMPSHIRE

CONCORD. OLD NORTH CEMETERY, NORTH STATE STREET NEAR BOUTON STREET.

Here are Franklin Pierce (1804–1869), fourteenth president of the United States, his wife, Jane Appleton (1806–1863), and their sons, who died in childhood. Also interred nearby is the Reverend Timothy Walker (1705–1782), his daughter, Sarah Walker Rolfe Thompson (1739–1792), first wife of Sir Benjamin Thompson, Count Rumford (1753–1814), Massachusetts-born scientist. Their daughter, Sarah Thompson, Countess Rumford (1774–1852), the first woman to be ennobled by a European court (Bavaria), is buried nearby.

JAFFREY CENTER. OLD BURYING GROUND, LOCATED BEHIND THE ORIGINAL MEETING HOUSE.

The graves of Amos Fortune, a slave born in Africa, and his wife, Violate, are here. An exceptional man in every way, Fortune has been the subject of many books. He bought his own freedom, then purchased Violate's, and married her. He died in 1801 at the age of ninety-one, she the following year, aged seventy-three. Also buried here is Willa Cather (1876–1947), Virginia-born and Nebraska-bred. She chose this spot as her final resting place and on the stone itself are the words from her novel *My Ántonia:* "That is happiness, to be dissolved into something complete and great."

NEW JERSEY

BEDMINSTER. BEDMINSTER CHURCHYARD.

Originally the First Dutch Reformed Church (built in 1759) stood here on land granted by a prominent banker, Jacob Vanderveer. The church has since disappeared, but among the graves is that of the infant Julia Knox, who died on July 2, 1779. Julia is forgotten today although her father, General Henry Knox (1750–1806) of the Continental Army, and later secretary of war (1785–1794), is at least remembered by historians. At the time of the child's death the general was quartered in the Vanderveer house.

Earlier, Jacob Vanderveer's insane daughter was refused burial in the churchyard because in the eighteenth-century scheme of things she was "possessed by the devil." Her father, rather than risk church censure, buried her in an enclosure on his land adjacent to the churchyard. The elders were a strict, adamant lot and when Julia died she too was refused burial on church property because her father, a Boston man, was a Congregationalist and not a member of the Dutch Reformed Church.

The patriotic Vanderveer, who earlier had suffered at the hands of narrow-minded churchmen, provided burial space for Julia in the enclosure beside his own daughter. Time changes everything, even the feelings of strict churchmen. Many years later the church accepted the Vanderveer land as part of the churchyard, the fence separating the two lonely graves was removed, and they were included in the churchyard proper.

CAMDEN. HARLEIGH CEMETERY, HADDON AVENUE AND VESPER BOULEVARD.

Walt Whitman (1819–1892), American poet, is buried here in a simple vault of rough stone, which he designed himself. A triangle above the entrance bears the poet's name. It is not a mausoleum in the accepted sense, but a tomb sunken, and hidden by trees. It was inspired by William Blake's *Gates of Paradise.*

CHERRY HILL. COLESTOWN CEMETERY, CHURCH ROAD AND KING'S HIGHWAY.

The sign before the gates reads "burials since 1690," but recently historians have traced the burial of a woman to 1683. Legend has it she died en route from Burlington to Salem on the Old Salem Road. The cemetery encompasses the old Saint Mary's Episcopal Cemetery on Church Road, and it has been estimated there have been nine thousand people buried here, and that there is space for an additional five thousand graves.

In 1858 the cemetery, which had been exclusive and was used by the old Camden County families, opened to the general public. In that year the stone gatehouse was built at a cost of $4,263. It is a landmark in the area and has been included in the National Register of Historic Places. The gatehouse includes a chapel (recently restored), which, in the nineteenth century, was used for funerals. Graveside services were rare, and once the service in the chapel was over, mourners departed and the burial was private.

Among those buried here—early merchants, financiers, landowners, and religious leaders—are numerous Lenni Lenape Indians.

FRENEAU. FRENEAU FARM NEAR MATAWAN.

Here lies Philip Freneau (1752–1832), one of the earliest American poets, often called the "Poet of the American Revolution." A marble shaft marks his grave on a knoll overlooking the valley. In his later years Freneau was more attuned to spirits than verse, and after a night in the local tavern he died in the snow just before Christmas 1832.

GREEN BANK. TOWN CEMETERY.

It is not far from Batsto, the eighteenth-century Pinelands town that has been restored, and is on the banks of the Mullica River (named for Eric Molica, or Mullica, an early Swedish settler). One of the most touching monuments is that to Rachel M. (1860–1883), daughter of Dr. Charles and Sarah J. Ridgway. The largest monument in the family plot, it is the traditional broken pillar with vine leaves encircling it, symbolizing a life cut short. Beneath the statistics of Rachel's short life is the inscription: "Her last words, 'I am almost home.'"

HACKENSACK. FIRST DUTCH REFORMED CHURCHYARD.

Northern New Jersey was settled soon after New York and the older burial grounds contain stones dating from the Dutch Ascendancy. This one contains the graves of early Dutch settlers, some stones dating from the mid-seventeenth century. The burial yard contains the graves of nineteen soldiers of the American Revolution, among them Brigadier General Enoch Poor, who died in 1790. General Poor commanded the New Hampshire Brigade of the Continental Army and fought at the Battles of Saratoga, Monmouth, Stillwater, and Newton. George Washington and the Marquis de Lafayette attended his funeral in the church (built in 1696, rebuilt in 1728, and enlarged at various times until 1869).

HILLSIDE. EVERGREEN CEMETERY.

The grave of Stephen Crane, author of the classic *Red Badge of Courage,* is here. He died in Germany of tuberculosis. His burial place is marked by a simple granite slab, recording: "Stephen Crane—Poet—Author—1871–1900."

MORRISTOWN. FIRST PRESBYTERIAN CHURCH BURIAL GROUND, 65 PARK PLACE.

The church, unfortunately, was erected in 1893 and is not the original built in 1742, which served as a hospital for the Continental Army. Many pre-Revolutionary graves of those prominent in Morristown history are here, the earliest stone dating from 1732. There are also approximately 150 graves of Revolutionary soldiers, including General John Doughty, third commander in chief of the army.

NEWARK. FAIRMOUNT CEMETERY.

Here lies Clara Maass (1876–1901), a remarkable nurse who gave her life so that more might be known about yellow fever. When the Spanish-American War began, Miss Maass volunteered as a nurse but the short-lived war was over when she was dispatched to the 7th Army Corps in Florida. When William Gorgas issued a call for volunteer nurses to help with yellow fever victims in Cuba in 1900, she answered the call and was eventually stricken with the disease, but recovered. Later she was infected again and died. She was first buried in the Colon Cemetery in Havana, but in 1902 her body was returned to Newark and buried with full honors. Newark has a hospital named for her and in 1976 the government issued a postage stamp with her likeness on it.

PENNSAUKEN. ARLINGTON CEMETERY.

The grave of Peter J. McGuire (1852–1906) is here. At his urging in 1882 Labor Day was named a national holiday in the United States. His dying words were: "I've got to get to California. The boys in Local 22 need me."

PRINCETON. PRINCETON CEMETERY, WITHERSPOON AND WIGGINS STREETS.

A burial ground since the eighteenth century, the earliest grave, that of Margaret Leonard, is dated 1760. The cemetery contains the graves of all the presidents of Princeton University except three. Aaron Burr (1756–1836), vice-president in Jefferson's first administration, is buried at the foot of the graves of his father, Aaron Burr, and his grandfather, Jonathan Edwards. Paul Tu-

lane, founder of Tulane University, is here among the Princetonians.

Grover Cleveland (1837–1908), the twenty-second and twenty-fourth president, is interred here as is his wife, Frances Folsom Cleveland (1864–1947), several members of the Colonial Assembly and the Continental Congress, the Senate, the House, and officers who served in the Continental Army during the Revolution.

Not far from Grover Cleveland—in fact, with only the stones of Cleveland's father-in-law and mother-in-law between them—is the grave of John O'Hara (1905–1970), novelist and short story writer whose works influenced a generation of American writers. His stone reads:

**Better
Than Anyone Else
He Told The Truth
About His Time
He Was
A Professional
He Wrote
Honestly and Well**

There are other writers in this small cemetery, and one who was a friend of many. Henry Van Dyke (1852–1933), author of *The Other Wise Man* and a much-admired essayist, and Sylvia Beach, daughter of a Presbyterian clergyman, are here too. Miss Beach, who is buried with her family, published *Ulysses* by James Joyce at her Paris bookshop, Shakespeare and Company. It was the gathering place on the Left Bank of most writers of note during the 1920s and 1930s.

TRENTON. OLD FRIENDS BURIAL GROUND, EAST HANOVER AND MONTGOMERY STREETS.

George Clymer (1739–1813), signer of the Declaration of Independence, Governor Richard Howell, and other prominent early citizens are buried here.

TRENTON. RIVERVIEW CEMETERY, 870 CENTRE STREET.

The historic-minded come here because Major General George B. McClellan (1826–1885), the Civil War leader, is buried here, but for the more curious its history goes back to the seventeenth century. Tradition has it that the spot was an Indian burial ground and there may be some truth to this assumption because the ground has yielded a number of Indian relics.

A small portion of the present cemetery was originally a burial plot called Lambert Burying Grounds and was acquired from John Lambert by the Society of Friends in the late seventeenth century. The minutes of the Chesterfield meeting state that the first burial here in 1685 was that of John Brown, one of the original colonists. The ancient Quaker plot contains the remains of others among Trenton's earliest settlers; probably included is Mahlon Stacy, who was buried on April 5, 1704. Only a few are marked by stones as it was not the Quaker custom to identify graves. Two adjoining slabs indicate the spot where John Bainbridge and his wife lie. They both died in 1732. The Quaker burial ground continued until 1858 when the property became the Riverview Cemetery. At that time adjoining lands were purchased and expansion began. At the present time the cemetery embraces about fifty acres, and part of it was once an estate known as Pine Grove and owned by Joseph Bonaparte.

John A. Roebling (1806–1869), the German-born designer and builder of the Brooklyn Bridge; Thomas Maddock, one of Trenton's earliest potters; and Dr. Charles Conrad Abbott, author and naturalist, are among the well known at Riverview Cemetery. Dr. Abbott's tombstone is inscribed: "In this neighborhood Dr. Abbott discovered the existence of Paleolithic man in America."

A section for Civil War veterans was provided and deeded to the city by Chancellor Henry Woodhull Green in 1862, and the Mercer County Board of Freeholders has since added to the plot. General McClellan's monument, erected in 1903, is an imposing granite shaft surmounted by an American eagle.

TRENTON. SAINT MICHAEL'S PROTESTANT EPISCOPAL CHURCHYARD, 140 NORTH WARREN STREET.

The church was erected in 1819, replacing an earlier one that had stood since 1748. In the churchyard lies Pauline Joseph Ann Holton, the illegitimate daughter of Joseph Bonaparte, king of Spain, and Annette Savage, a Philadelphia Quaker girl.

NEW MEXICO

TAOS. KIT CARSON CEMETERY, AT THE END OF DRAGOON LANE EXTENDING NORTH FROM KIT CARSON AVENUE.

Christopher (Kit) Carson (1809–1868), the Indian fighter and scout who acted as guide for John C. Frémont's Western expeditions of 1842, 1843, and 1845, is buried in this cemetery, which bears his name. The Masons erected the stone over Carson's grave in the 1880s and the state of New Mexico purchased the cemetery and nineteen additional acres in 1952 to establish Kit Carson Memorial Park. Here too is Padre José Martínez, who came to Taos in 1826 and for forty years championed the cause of the Spanish-Americans and sought to educate them. At one point Bishop John B. Lamy (the prototype of Father Latour in Willa Cather's *Death Comes for the Arch-*

bishop) excommunicated Padre Martínez because of his political activity as well as his opposition to church authority.

NEW YORK

HAWTHORNE. CEMETERY OF THE GATE OF HEAVEN, STEVENS AND BRADHURST AVENUES.

Reached from New York City by the scenic Taconic State Parkway, this 250-acre cemetery in Westchester County is owned and operated by the trustees of Saint Patrick's Cathedral in New York. The property was purchased in 1917 from the Fairlawn Burial Association. Charles Wellford Leavitt, a New York architect who designed the cemetery's original plan, envisioned a rural cemetery with formal gardens, cathedral-type buildings, and large landscaped areas. He also designed the cemetery's Gothic bridge, which spans the lake, and the receiving vault known as "The Tower."

Anna Held (1873?–1918), the French-born musical comedy star who was the first wife of Florenz Ziegfeld, was one of the first of the famous to be buried here. Her burial plot attracted others who wished to be interred near the famous star. George Herman ("Babe") Ruth (1895–1948), the well-known home run king of baseball ("Sultan of Swat"); James J. Walker (1881–1946), mayor of New York (1926–1932), whose style made him enormously popular with the electorate; radio comedian Fred Allen (1894–1956); and a number of well-known journalists—Dorothy Kilgallen (1913–1965), Fulton Oursler (1893–1952), Westbrook Pegler (1894–1969), and Bob Considine (1906–1975)—all lie here, as does "Dutch" Schultz, gangland figure of the 1930s, and Mrs. Harry Houdini, widow of the magician and escape artist.

About 180 acres are developed. The Garden Crypt (completed in 1969 as were the office and chapel) provides 3,542 crypts and the chapel has floor-to-ceiling sloping windows of faceted glass designed by Benoit Gilsoul.

IRVINGTON. OLD DUTCH CEMETERY.

The graves of this cemetery, founded in 1697, are mostly of Dutch settlers. The land was part of Philipse Manor, a Dutch estate that stretched thirty miles along the Hudson River from the Bronx to Croton. The Dutch headstones were generally made of sandstone and brought by barge from Connecticut. Washington Irving (1783–1859), author of the most appealing tales ever written about the Dutch in the Hudson Valley, is buried here. What better spot for the author of *Rip Van Winkle* than this quiet churchyard on the other side of the river from High Tor?

Monument erected on Hart Island. *Photograph by Robert Hendrickson*

NEW YORK. CITY CEMETERY, HART ISLAND (MANHATTAN).

On a map of New York City in that area of water just north of the confluence of the East River, where it enters Long Island Sound, lies Hart Island. It is just off the Bronx, south of New Rochelle, and opposite Sands Point. Thus, surrounded by land and water of the city, its Potter's Field is both isolated and an integral part of the five boroughs. Its position in relation to New York is somewhat akin to that of the cemetery island of San Michele to the city of Venice.

This island was once owned by Oliver DeLancey, a Loyalist during the Revolution, and was known as Spectacle Island or Little Minnefords. It is thought to have received its present name from John Hart, a New York City policeman and Civil War hero who saved the Union flag at Fort Sumter.

Hart Island was purchased by the city in 1868. Before that time many of New York's well-known locations—Washington Square, City Hall Square, Madison Square, and the site of the present New York Public Library at 42nd Street and Fifth Avenue—were Potter's Fields. Louisa Van Slyke, an orphan who died at the Old Charity Hospital, was the first to be buried in Potter's Field in 1869. In little more than a century, almost three-quarters of a million bodies have been buried here.

Victims of many of the city's disasters have found their last resting place here. In 1904, when the excursion boat *General Slocom* sank off Hell Gate, the bodies of 1,030 victims were interred here. The victims of the Triangle Shirtwaist Factory fire (which brought about sweatshop reform) and those from the Malbone Street subway crash joined them.

The sixty-six-acre cemetery (the island itself is 103 acres) has received ten thousand bodies an acre and all sixty-six acres have been used at least twice for burials. The graves are opened and reused every twenty-five years—the remains placed in single coffins and reinterred. The statistics of mass graves are awesome. They consist of trenches 140 feet long, 16 feet wide, and 8 feet deep with room for 1,200 coffins. The loss of identity of the dead, and the consequent lack of mourners, enables the city to leave the trenches open until they are filled.

Inmates from the prison on Riker's Island—called the "Ghoul Squad"—are the gravediggers in this modern equivalent of Aceldama, the barren piece of ground near Jerusalem where Judas Iscariot hanged himself and was buried. In this lonely burial ground, without even the sterile identity that modern bronze markers give others, stands a small granite cross erected by a mission society in 1902. It reads: "He calleth His children by name."

NEW YORK. FIRST CEMETERY OF THE CONGREGATION OF SHEARITH ISRAEL, SAINT JAMES PLACE BETWEEN JAMES AND OLIVER STREETS (MANHATTAN).

This small plot is all that remains of this early Jewish cemetery, which once covered all of Chatham Square. One final section was taken from it about a hundred years ago so that New Bowery could be cut through as a thoroughfare. A marker at the entrance puts its dates from 1656 to 1833, but some historians claim the land was purchased in 1682 by a group of Spanish and Portuguese Jews who fled to New Amsterdam after the Inquisition. Others say the Jews arrived from Brazil. The oldest stone bears the date 1682, making this burial ground the oldest Jewish one in New York City, even if it is not the one granted in 1656. Among those interred here are Jews who served in the Continental Army during the Revolution.

NEW YORK. MARBLE CEMETERY (MANHATTAN).

This burial ground, dating from 1830, can be seen through the alley that runs between 41 and 43 Second Avenue. It consists of a lawn and a few small trees surrounded by a high wall. Beneath the lawn are 156 marble vaults without individual identification; the sole identifying mark being marble plaques set in the surrounding wall. The last interment was over fifty years ago.

NEW YORK. OLD SAINT PATRICK'S CATHEDRAL CHURCHYARD, MOTT AND PRINCE STREETS (MANHATTAN).

This is the burial place of Pierre Toussaint, once a slave and a well-known figure in post-Revolutionary New York. In the church Bishop John Neumann, now canonized, was ordained in 1836.

NEW YORK. SAINT MARK'S-IN-THE-BOUWERIE (MANHATTAN).

The present church (1795–1799) is on the site where Peter Stuyvesant (1592–1672), director general of the Dutch West India Company and the last governor of New Amsterdam, built his family chapel in 1660. Stuyvesant was buried under the chapel in the family vault, his widow, Judith, beside him in 1687. In her will she bequeathed the chapel to the Dutch Reformed Church of New York with the provision that the Stuyvesant family vault be preserved. The chapel fell into disuse and deteriorated, but on the side of the present church in the East Yard is a stone with Stuyvesant's name—he is called Petrus on it. In addition to Peter Stuyvesant and seven generations of his descendants, the graveyards (on each side of the church) are the burial site of many notable Americans. Not so notable but possessed of a charming name was "Mangle Minthorne, who departed this life on the 20th day of April 1821."

Daniel D. Tompkins (1774–1825), governor of New York from 1807 to 1817 and vice-president of the United States (1817–1825) under President Monroe; Philip Hone, mayor of New York (1826); William Harris, an early rector of Saint Mark's and first president of Columbia College (now Columbia University), are here as is Commodore Matthew Calbraith Perry (1794–1858), the American naval officer who visited Japan (1853–1854) and opened it to the West. He was interred in the Slidell vault.

At the entrance to the East Yard is a bust of Stuyvesant by Dutch sculptor Toon Dupuis, presented by Queen Wilhelmina. A statue of Tompkins stands at the entrance to the West Yard. Solon Borglum sculpted the statues of the two American Indians and that of the Indian *Prayer for Rain.*

In 1975 one of the annual Bard Awards for excellence in New York architecture was given Saint Mark's for the conversion of its rundown graveyard. Now a peaceful, graceful landscaped area for public recreation—the extant gravestones are still in evidence—the changes were made by 150 schoolchildren, working under the direction of architects Edelman & Salzman.

NEW YORK. THE SECOND CEMETERY OF THE CONGREGATION OF SHEARITH ISRAEL, 11TH STREET BETWEEN FIFTH AVENUE AND THE AVENUE OF THE AMERICAS (MANHATTAN).

This tiny plot between numbers 70 and 78 11th Street is all that remains of the cemetery established here in 1805 when there was no more allotted space in the old burial ground at Chatham Square. In 1830 the city, acting under the power of eminent domain, acquired a portion of the property for the cutting through of 11th Street. The congregation was left with only a small triangular lot on the south side of the street, since the property ran on an extreme bias on what is now the bed of 11th Street. A low masonry wall mounted by a low fence encloses the cemetery. A gate at the center gives access to the little graveyard, which still has some of the original tombstones, including a small stone obelisk. It is at the rear of the New School for Social Research.

NEW YORK. TRINITY CHURCH CEMETERY, 153RD TO 155TH STREET BETWEEN AMSTERDAM AVENUE AND RIVERSIDE DRIVE (MANHATTAN).

Established in 1842, when Trinity Churchyard on lower Broadway began to have less space for graves, this cemetery contains the graves of Alfred Tennyson Dickens (1843–1912), son of Charles Dickens and godson of Alfred Lord Tennyson; Clement Clarke Moore (1779–1863), author of *A Visit from St. Nicholas;* and Eliza B. Jumel, second wife of Aaron Burr, vice-president under Thomas Jefferson.

NEW YORK. MACHPELAH CEMETERY, GLENDALE (QUEENS).

This cemetery is of interest because it contains the grave of Harry Houdini (1874–1926), the magician. A life-size bust of the necromancer, placed there by the Society of American Magicians, was destroyed in 1975 by vandals.

NEW YORK. ASBURY CHURCH OF THE NAZARENE, BULLS HEAD (STATEN ISLAND).

Here is the grave of Colonel Ichabod B. Crane. Washington Irving, author of *The Legend of Sleepy Hollow,* which made the character of Ichabod Crane internationally famous, met the actual Colonel Crane when both were in military service during the War of 1812. Irving felt the name was one of the most unusual he had heard, and he used it for the character in his story. The six-foot marble headstone to the old soldier had fallen into disrepair and lay in four pieces until restored in 1976 by student members of the Staten Island Community College's Veterans' Advisement Center.

NEW YORK. MORAVIAN CEMETERY, RICHMOND (STATEN ISLAND).

The ownership of this beautiful old cemetery goes back to the Stuart kings and the earliest days of New York. Deeds, documents of transaction and sales, and historic records show that a crown patent was issued in May 1684. On March 31, 1687, the council confirmed the patent of a grant of land to John Palmer and on April 16 of that year, after about a fortnight's ownership, Palmer and his wife, Sarah, conveyed the tract to Governor Thomas Dongan.

Governor Dongan died childless and the land eventually passed to his great-nephew Thomas, who, with his wife, Magdalene, sold 285 acres to John Beatty in 1760 for £720.14.9. It was Beatty who sold the original plot upon which the first Moravian Church was built in 1763 when 5½ acres were transferred to the church for the equivalent of $124.08½.

From the earliest days, before its ownership by the Moravian Church, a portion of the land was used for burial. Some of the more ancient stones remain and there is one to "Coll. Nicholas Britten Decd. ye January 12, 1740." Next to it, "Here lyes ye Body of Frances, wife of Coll. Nicholas Britten, aged 66 years. Decd. May ye 7, 1748." There are bodies of British soldiers here, those who died when the army was stationed on Staten Island during the colonial period.

In the beginning burials were made "indiscriminately and at convenient spots, where there were no trees or obstructions to cause the sexton undue labor in opening the graves. The only rule of burial was the placing of the body with the feet toward the East." No charge, either for the ground or the sexton's work, was made, and many island families discontinued interments on family farms. About 1819 the trustees resolved to charge one dollar for opening a grave for a nonchurch member and in 1823 instituted a three-dollar charge, half to support the church, half to go to the sexton for his labor.

By 1861 and 1862 the trustees of the church purchased three acres for the enlargement of the original tract, and in 1865 Commodore Cornelius Vanderbilt, who is buried here, presented the church with 8½ acres. Three years later the commodore made an additional gift of forty-five acres of contiguous land. The interest of the Vanderbilts continued with a gift in 1882 from Cornelius's son, William, of four acres and a dwelling house (for the use of the superintendent). Today it is over eighty acres and one of the most beautiful spots on Staten Island.

MENANDS. SAINT AGNES CEMETERY.

This cemetery was incorporated on May 9, 1867, and consecrated ten days later by Bishop John J. Conroy. Among the citizens of Albany buried here are Patrick Hughes (1820–1896), of Mount Charles, Donegal, and his wife, Catherine Martin (1835–1885), of Paisley, Scotland, and their daughter, Ellen Hughes (1854–1936), and her husband, John H. McCarthy (1850–1919), great-grandparents and grandparents of the author. It was here he began his cemetery quest.

RIVERHEAD. RIVERHEAD CEMETERY.

This old burial ground has one of the most unusual tombstones on Long Island. Seven feet tall, the stone is in memory of Captain James Fanning, who died in 1776 at the age of ninety-three. It recounts James's descent from Dominicus Fanning, his being taken prisoner at the Battle of Drogheda, and his beheading by Cromwell. The family's emigration to America is recounted, the marriages and descendants, and in some cases the extent of their careers. It was erected in 1850 and is a curiosity for those who live in the immediate area.

ROCHESTER. MOUNT HOPE CEMETERY.

The land on which the city is located was purchased by Colonel Nathaniel Rochester, Major Charles Carroll, and Colonel William Fitzhugh, who paid $17.50 an acre for a hundred-acre tract in 1803. Thirty-five years later on October 3, 1838, the Reverend Parcellus Church dedicated the cemetery with the words: "We have come to consecrate a home for the dead in which they may rest secure from the encroachments of industry and avarice till the last trumpet calls them to a judgment." The first burial that year was of William Carter.

There are many buried here who were instrumental in Rochester's development, but two who lie here left their mark on American history. Susan B. Anthony (1820–1906) was a leader in woman suffrage and a founder of the Daughters of Temperance. With Elizabeth Cady Stanton, she secured the first laws in New York, giving women rights over their children and property. Frederick Douglass (1817?–1895), the son of a slave mother who in 1838 escaped and took his surname from Sir Walter Scott's *Lady of the Lake,* fought for his race when it was not popular to do so.

Also here are Colonel Rochester, his wife, Sophia, their five sons and five daughters; the first mayor, Jonathan Child, and his wife, Sophia Eliza (daughter of the Rochesters); and George Selden, who claimed to be the inventor of the gasoline automobile; Jacob H. Meyer, inventor of the voting machine; and Johnny Baker, sharpshooter with Buffalo Bill.

WATERVLIET. ANN LEE CEMETERY, SHAKER ROAD.

Mother Ann Lee (1736–1784), born in England, formed the first Shaker settlement in America in Watervliet in 1776. She is buried here with others of the sect, which now has dwindled to a few surviving members.

WEST POINT. WEST POINT CEMETERY.

Nothing runs more parallel to the history of the United States than that of the United States Military Academy at West Point. Although the academy was founded in 1802, fortifications (some remnants of those of the Revolution are still visible), barracks, and other buildings already existed at the time, for the site had been occupied as a military post since January 20, 1778. It was its hoped-for betrayal to the British that brought about the hanging of Major John André in 1780 and the flight to England of Benedict Arnold.

The government purchased eighteen hundred acres from Stephen Moore in 1790. The infant republic realized there was a need for a system of training officers, for during the Revolution American leaders had been forced to rely upon foreign drillmasters, artillerists, and trained engineers. The international political situation in 1801–1802 was such (in the aftermath of the French Revolution, Napoleon was rising to the height of his power) that public opinion had moved toward more energetic national government and better-trained armed forces.

Burials began here in the eighteenth century—the oldest grave is that of Ensign Dominick Trant, who died in November 1782. However, there are some graves in the northeast section of the cemetery marked "unknown" for Revolutionary War soldiers. Although these graves are located here, the cemetery itself has only been in its present location since the latter part of the last century. Prior to that it was located near the library, and many of the older graves, including those of the Revolutionary War soldiers, were scattered about the military reservation. The Old Cadet Chapel, which has great meaning for those who have attended the academy, was moved piece

West Point Cemetery. *Department of the Army, U.S. Military Academy*

by piece in 1911 to its present location at the entrance to the cemetery, after standing near the library for seventy-five years.

The names on the graves provide a chronicle of American history: General Winfield Scott (1786–1866), known as "Old Fuss and Feathers," hero of the War of 1812, the Black Hawk, Mexican, and Civil Wars; General George Armstrong Custer (1839–1876), who with two hundred of his men died at the hands of the Indians in the Battle of Little Big Horn and thereby achieved immortality; General Egbert L. Viele, engineer in chief of the construction of Central Park in New York City; Major General George W. Goethals (1858–1928), builder of the Panama Canal; and Lieutenant Colonel Edward H. White (1930–1967), the American astronaut who became the first man to walk in space.

More than four thousand men and women are buried in the cemetery, including officers and men who died in battle in every war in which the United States took part, including Vietnam. Seventeen graves are here of former superintendents (fifteen served in the nineteenth century), including that of Sylvanus Thayer, fifth holder of the office, who is often referred to as the "father of the Military Academy." Margaret Corbin, New York's "Molly Pitcher," was given that name when her husband was killed in the Hessian attack on Fort Washington and she took his place in the firing line. After the war she received a soldier's pension and was the first woman to be interred here.

Burial in the West Point Cemetery is now limited to

graduates of the academy; members of the armed forces of the United States, including cadets who were on active duty at the academy at the time of their death; members of the armed forces who were on active duty at the academy at the time of their retirement or whose last duty station was the academy at the time of their retirement; wives, husbands, widows, widowers, minor children, and dependent unmarried children of those military personnel who are eligible for interment; and persons having bona fide reservations assigned by the superintendent under previous regulations and policies. When the cemetery is finally filled, officials expect to open another, or an annex to the present one, elsewhere on the post.

NORTH CAROLINA

ASHEVILLE. RIVERSIDE CEMETERY, BIRCH STREET.

Two men who left their mark on American letters are buried here in the shadow of the Great Smoky Mountains. William Sydney Porter (1862–1910), who wrote under the pseudonym O. Henry, is here. (His second wife was Sarah Lindsay Coleman of Weaverville, nine miles distant.) Thomas Wolfe (1900–1938), whose *Look Homeward, Angel* scandalized Asheville when it was published, achieved international recognition, and the city forgave him before he died. He is in the family plot with his father, mother, and brothers. One of the honorary pallbearers at his funeral was his editor, Maxwell Perkins.

Governor Zebulon Baird Vance's grave is marked by a rough block of granite. His brother, General Robert B. Vance (1828–1899), commander of the military district of North Carolina for the Army of the Confederacy, is nearby. Another Confederate, Brigadier General Thomas L. Clingman (1812–1897), who is buried here, served in both houses of Congress.

Eighteen interred German sailors who died of typhoid fever at the United States Hospital, Kenilworth, are remembered with a monument erected by the Kiffin Rockwell post of the American Legion and other legionaries throughout the state.

BEAUFORT. OLD BURYING GROUND.

This cemetery is not only old by American standards—it is thought to date to 1709—but is has some wonderfully bizarre burials associated with its colorful history. Beaufort, located near the sea islands that form the Outer Banks, was one of the earliest settlements in the state.

The Old Burying Ground was deeded to the town in 1731 by Nathanael Taylor and has always been public property. The earliest legible tombstone date is that of 1756 (it contains only the initials A.P.), but it is certainly not the oldest grave. The north corner was used first for burials, but because there was no native stone available at that early time only an occasional marker is seen in that section today. The gravestones here are turned to the east in order that the occupants will be facing the sun on Judgment Day. The granite tomb of Captain Otway Burns is surmounted by a cannon taken from his privateer *Snap Dragon.*

It is thought that some of the unmarked graves are those of victims of the Indian wars and massacres. Colonel William Thompson, the highest ranking officer from Beaufort to serve in the Revolution, lies here. A native of County Down, Ireland, he was a New Bern merchant. There is a British officer here too, who died aboard ship in the town harbor. Not wanting to be buried "with his boots off," he was accorded the singular honor of being buried standing up.

There are Civil War veterans: Captain Josiah Pender, who wrested Fort Macon from Union forces in 1861; Jechonias Willis, who was killed when the fort was retaken in 1862; and Captain Matthew Gooding, who successfully penetrated the federal blockade with the runner *Nashville.* Captain Pender was the grandfather of Mrs. George C. Marshall, widow of the general.

Although not well known or remembered in their own right, the graves of Mary and Robert Chadwick should not be passed by. Robert, the collector of customs at the port of Wilmington (North Carolina), and Mary Chadwick were told by a ship's captain of a young Chinese stowaway aboard his ship. To save the boy from deportation, the Chadwicks took him into their home and educated him at Trinity College (now Duke University). He—Soong Yao-ju, or Charles Jones Soong—returned to China as a Methodist missionary. His daughters—the famous Soong sisters—became Mme. Chiang Kai-shek, Mme. Sun Yat-sen, and Mme. H. H. Kung.

There is a child buried here in a keg of rum—she died at sea on a voyage from England to Beaufort; another—the Dill child—was first buried in a glass-topped casket. Unfortunately, vandals exhumed it, the body disintegrated, and it was reburied.

By 1825 the graveyard was filled and declared a "closed cemetery," but Beaufort residents would have none of this and continued to bury their dead here until the early part of this century when Ocean View Cemetery was opened. The early records were lost during the Revolution, when the Anglican church rector fled to Canada, taking the records with him. The Purvis Chapel African Methodist Episcopal Zion Church (1820), the Ann Street Methodist Church (1854), and the First Baptist Church Educational Building (1960) overlook this ancient coastal cemetery.

HENDERSONVILLE. OAKDALE CEMETERY, 6th AVENUE.

Here, not too far from Asheville, is Tom Wolfe's angel,

the one that inspired Wolfe to write *Look Homeward, Angel.* His father, William Oliver Wolfe, a tombstone cutter and sculptor, created the angel that made such a deep impression on his son. Here too is the tomb of the "Sunshine Lady," Mrs. Charles B. Hansell, who died of tuberculosis. Before her death she requested that she be buried so the sun would always shine upon her. Placed in the top of her tomb were lenses through which the sun would shine (and the skeleton be seen!) until it was covered in 1939.

OCRACOKE.

A small burial ground here maintains the memory of four British seamen, all crew members of H.M.S. *Bedfordshire,* which was torpedoed by a German submarine off the North Carolina coast in 1942. Four bodies washed ashore three days after the *Bedfordshire* sank. Two were identified as Lieutenant Tom Cunningham and Stanley Craig, a telegraphist. The other two were unidentified. A white picket fence was erected around the graves and to it affixed a plaque with the oft-quoted lines of Rupert Brooke:

If I should die, think only this of me:
That there's some corner of a foreign field
That is forever England.

The state purchased the cemetery near the small island village and in 1976 leased it to Great Britain in perpetuity. The National Park Service will provide maintenance equipment, and the Coast Guard the manpower. For many years the Coast Guard has daily raised the Union Jack over the tiny cemetery to honor these men who were protecting the coast of North Carolina—and the United States—during World War II.

SALISBURY. NATIONAL CEMETERY.

The graves of 11,700 federal soldiers who died in the Civil War lie here, including that of Robert Livingstone, son of David Livingstone, the African missionary. In all, there are the graves of more than twelve thousand soldiers here, including those from later wars.

WILMINGTON. OAKDALE CEMETERY, 15TH STREET.

One of the South's great heroines, Rose O'Neill Greenhow (c. 1817–1864), lies here. She warned the Confederates of McDowell's advance on Manassas and thereby enabled them to win the first Battle of Bull Run. She was later arrested by Allan Pinkerton and imprisoned for a time. She was returning from England aboard the Confederate blockade runner *Condor,* when the ship was grounded off New Inlet, near Wilmington. When she put out for shore in a small boat, it capsized and she was drowned.

Henry Bacon, designer of the Lincoln Memorial in Washington, D.C., is also buried in Oakdale. He admired honeysuckle buds while traveling in Egypt, and his brother, who designed his gravestone, incorporated the pattern into the stone.

Southern cemeteries attract unusual burials. In Oakdale there are several. Captain William A. Ellerbrook is buried with his dog, Caesar, in the same casket. Caesar died trying to rescue his master from a burning building. The community felt so strongly about this act of sacrifice and loyalty that it erected a monument to Ellerbrook and his dog. Nancy Martin, on the other hand, died at sea in 1857. Her homecoming was rather bizarre. Her father seated her body in a chair and enclosed both in a cask of rum (a popular way of preserving bodies after death at sea).

WILMINGTON. SAINT JAMES'S CHURCHYARD, THIRD AND MARKET STREETS.

The church, which dates from 1839, was built near the site of an earlier one (1751). In the churchyard is the grave of Thomas Godfrey (1736–1763), author of *The Prince of Parthia,* produced in Philadelphia in 1767. It was the first drama written by a native American and produced professionally. Also here is Cornelius Harnett (1723–1781), who had the distinction of being a member of thirteen colonial assemblies, the deputy provisional grandmaster of the Masonic order in North Carolina, and was a delegate to the Continental Congress.

PENNSYLVANIA

BAUMSTOWN. EXETER FRIENDS BURYING GROUND.

Actually the burial ground is outside Baumstown, near the George Boone House, built in 1733 by Daniel Boone's grandfather. The Friends Meeting House was erected in 1730 and in the burial ground are ancestors of both Daniel Boone and Abraham Lincoln. The rear half of the ground is about two feet higher than the rest because of an additional layer of graves in that section.

BETHLEHEM. MORAVIAN CEMETERY, CHURCH STREET AND HECKEWELDER PLACE.

This cemetery was used as a burial ground from 1742 until 1910. The site was selected and consecrated by Count von Zinzendorf (1700–1760), who was responsible

Moravian Cemetery, Bethlehem, Pennsylvania, circa 1910. *Reproduced from the collection of the Library of Congress*

for many Moravian settlements in this part of the state. The stones, all similar in size and shape, connote that all buried here are equal. The dead are of various nationalities and races. Some of the stones are charmingly cut with decorative eighteenth-century lettering, such as that of Catharina Haidt, who was born "July 4, 1700 at London. Departed Sept. 14, 1782." Others show that those buried here came from Norway; Stockholm; Saint Johns, Canada; Germany; and even Staten Island. One proclaims "Eve of the Mohican nation, Wife of Nicodemus. Departed at Nain, November 18, 1758." Every year at dawn of Easter day a trombone choir plays in the cemetery.

BETHLEHEM. NISKY HILL CEMETERY, CHURCH AND CENTER STREETS.

There are two graves of particular interest here: those of Jessie Woodrow Sayre (1887–1933) and Hilda Doolittle (1886–1961). Jessie Wilson, one of the three daughters of Woodrow and Ellen Axson Wilson, married Francis Bowes Sayre, an Episcopal clergyman, while her father was in the White House. She was buried in the Sayre plot, although her husband (who before his death was rector of the cathedral) is buried in the National Cathedral in Washington, D.C., where the twenty-seventh president is also entombed.

Hilda Doolittle, born in Bethlehem, gained fame as H.D., the imagist poet. After her marriages and a life lived principally abroad, her body was returned to the Doolittle family plot for burial.

This small cemetery, on the bluff overlooking the Lehigh River, has a Civil War section where veterans are buried together around a mounted cannon. Metal markers with stars bearing the G.A.R. insignia mark their graves.

BIGLERVILLE. BENDER'S LUTHERAN CHURCH BURIAL GROUND.

This graveyard adjoining the church (the first was built in 1811) is located one mile outside the sleepy town of Biglerville (Adams County) in Butler's Township on Bender's Church Road. What makes this churchyard worth visiting is the large collection of stones in an excellent state of preservation. Some are in German and bear such seldom-used names as Lebricht, Catherie, Magdaleon, and Maria Charlotta. Many record family names still familiar in the county: Rex, Bender, Shriver, Houch, Deatrick, Trostle, Pensyl. Soldiers of the Revolution and the Civil War are buried here; many of the stones are of slate; and some are cut with stars or a Pennsylvania Dutch flower motif. Many are no more than a pointed edge, the stone having broken in the decades since. There is a preponderance of willows—the weeping variety so popular in memorials of the late eighteenth and nineteenth centuries—repeated on many stones, and even lilies sculpted on the top edge of several. One tiny lamb records the death of a child. Another stone is for Peter L. Riegle, who died in February 1819, at the age of "sixty-three Y 10 Ms & 4D." He is memorialized by the words: "God's finger touched him and he slept."

BOALSBURG. ZION CHURCHYARD.

This tiny village nestled in Center County, several miles

from State College, the home of Pennsylvania State University, has the distinction of being the birthplace of Memorial Day. Other towns—many in the South (notably Petersburg, Virginia)—have claimed the honor but it seems to be Boalsburg's.

In 1864 two village girls—Emma Hunter and Sophie Keller—gathered flowers on an October day and walked to the cemetery to decorate the grave of Emma's father, Dr. Reuben Hunter, who had been killed at Annapolis the month before.

As they walked through the village streets, their arms heavy with flowers, several Boalsburg women asked what they were about. The women joined them, others followed, and by the time they reached the cemetery there was a good-sized gathering. They decorated the graves of those who served in the War of 1812 and the Mexican War, Dr. Hunter's, and then, not wanting to show partiality, all the others.

Each year following, a day was set aside to decorate the graves and hold a memorial service. Through the years the custom grew and now the observance of Memorial Day is the most important event on the town's calendar.

In 1868 Memorial Day was designated as May 30 and one by one the states adopted it as a legal holiday. Eventually, the names Decoration Day and Memorial Day became one.

CARLISLE. OLD GRAVEYARD, SOUTH STREET BETWEEN HANOVER AND BEDFORD STREETS.

Here is the grave of Mary Ludwig (c. 1754–1832), more familiarly known as "Molly Pitcher." A domestic servant, Molly came to Carlisle from New Jersey in 1769, married John Hays (Heis), a barber. He, in 1775, enlisted as a gunner in Proctor's Artillery of the Continental Army. He reenlisted in 1777, was at Valley Forge in 1777–1778, and took part in the Battle of Monmouth. Mary carried water to the Continentals while the battle was in progress, thus earning her sobriquet. She also took her husband's place as cannoneer beside the cannon when he was wounded. After the war was over, Mary became a washerwoman in Carlisle; the state eventually granted her a pension. Each Memorial Day her grave is decorated with flowers by the children of the town. The oldest grave in the cemetery is that of Charles Robb (died May 2, 1757), and there are a number of soldiers from the Revolution here.

CHESTER. OLD SAINT PAUL'S CEMETERY, THIRD AND WELSH STREETS.

A place of special interest because it is the oldest Swedish burial site in the United States. Unfortunately, the graves are not marked, but the original stones—if any—were probably crude at best. John Morton (1724?–1777), signer of the Declaration of Independence, lies in a grave marked by a marble shaft.

DARBY. MOUNT LAWN CEMETERY, 84TH STREET AND HOOK ROAD.

Bessie Smith (1894–1937), the blues singer, is buried in grave 3, range 12, lot 20, section C. There was no stone on the grave for many years because after paying the funeral expenses the family found that nothing remained. Thirty-three years after Bessie's death, a black woman, Mrs. Barbara Muldow of Philadelphia, wrote to a local newspaper, pointing out that the grave was unmarked. Singer Janis Joplin, an admirer of Bessie Smith, and Mrs. Juanita Green of Philadelphia, a former maid of the singer, purchased a stone. It was unveiled on August 7, 1970.

DOUGLASSVILLE. SAINT GABRIEL'S CHURCHYARD.

The chapel, a charming stone building reminiscent of English ones, dates from 1801, but the churchyard has been here since 1720. A number of Revolutionary soldiers lie here, the Douglass family for whom the town was named, as well as Anthony Sadowski (died 1736), a Polish pioneer who in 1712 settled in the area.

EPHRATA. GOD'S ACRE NEAR THE CLOISTERS.

The buildings were erected in 1730 by the Seventh-Day Baptists, a German monastic community. The graves of Johann Konrad Beissel, its founder; Peter Miller, the second superintendent of the Cloisters; and other early leaders of the sect are here.

EPHRATA. MOUNT ZION CEMETERY, NEAR GOD'S ACRE.

This cemetery contains graves of many Revolutionary soldiers who fought at the Battle of the Brandywine in 1777.

GETTYSBURG. EVERGREEN CEMETERY.

This old cemetery adjacent to the National Cemetery is the burial place of Marianne Moore (1887–1972), American poet. It is fitting that Miss Moore's body was returned to Pennsylvania for burial, although she spent much of her life in New York. This plot was purchased at the time of her grandmother's death, which resulted from nursing typhoid victims during the Civil War.

JOHNSTOWN. GRANDVIEW CEMETERY, WESTMONT STREET.

More than five hundred unidentified victims of the Johnstown Flood (May 31, 1889), when the Conemaugh River overflowed, are buried here in orderly rows. A large monument was erected to the memory of all, but it is a marker such as the one to Mary Elizabeth Davis, aged three days, that is a reminder of the poignancy and horror of the tragedy.

Shreiner's Cemetery, Lancaster, Pennsylvania. *Collection of Eugene E. Smith*

KENNETT SQUARE. UNION HILL CEMETERY.

This cemetery, far from the glamour of Hollywood, provides the final resting place of Linda Darnell (1921–1965), the beautiful motion picture star of the 1940s and 1950s. Miss Darnell died as the result of burns suffered in a fire in Glenville, Illinois, and her ashes remained in a Chicago cemetery for nine years before being transferred here for reburial in 1975.

LANCASTER. SHREINER'S CEMETERY, CHESTNUT AND MULBERRY STREETS.

Thaddeus Stevens (1792–1868), who fought against slavery, is buried here. His epitaph speaks for itself and for the man.

LANCASTER. WOODWARD HILL CEMETERY, 511 SOUTH QUEEN STREET.

Originally owned (from the middle of the nineteenth century) by the Lutheran Church of Lancaster, it was established as a nonprofit corporation in 1851. James Buchanan (1791–1868), fifteenth president of the United States and the only bachelor president, is buried here, beneath a tombstone decorated with sculptured oak leaves; as well as Edgar Fahs Smith, former provost of the University of Pennsylvania; James Shulze, once governor of the state; Clement B. Grubb, ironmaster during

the American Revolution; Gotthilf Henry Muhlenberg, pioneer botanist; and Jacob Eicholtz (1776–1842), portrait painter.

LINGLESTOWN. BLUE MOUNTAIN.

About 1½ miles from the town, atop the mountain, are stones marking the graves of slaves, ones who evidently escaped north. Dr. C. H. Smith, who was certainly concerned with their welfare, erected the stones, which tell their own story. One is to an "unknown," who died in 1853. The legend on the stone speaks of "one whose life was filled with pathos and suffering and who had a tragic end. He had the North Star as a guide to liberty, yet in a fitful moment for fear of betrayal, he took the deadly cup to free himself from bondage by his fellow men."

The other is to George Washington, who died on April 8, 1868. The stone reminds us that "his virtues are related by all who knew him." And the admonition, as apt today as then: "Looking into the portals of eternity teaches that the brotherhood of man is inspired by God's word; then all prejudice of race vanishes away."

LITITZ. MORAVIAN CHURCH CEMETERY, EAST MAIN STREET.

The grave of John A. Sutter (1803–1880), the German-born immigrant on whose property (Sutter's Mill on the banks of the Sacramento River) gold was discovered in 1849, is here. After being one of the wealthiest men in California, he became impoverished after the Gold Rush. He lived in Lititz from 1871 until his death, which occurred in Washington, D.C.

NORTHUMBERLAND. RIVERVIEW CEMETERY.

Burial place of Joseph Priestley (1733–1804), the English-born scientist who emigrated to America and spent the last years of his life in this Pennsylvania town.

PHILADELPHIA. FAIRHILL FRIENDS BURIAL GROUND, GERMANTOWN AVENUE AND CAMBRIA STREET.

The Meeting was founded in 1703, one of the earliest in the area. Among the stones—which are uniform, as in all Quaker burial grounds—lies Lucretia Mott (1793–1880). Born on Nantucket Island, she was a friend and confidante of William Ellery Channing, William Lloyd Garrison, and other abolitionists. Mrs. Mott's was an eloquent voice against slavery, and it was because she was refused a seat at the antislavery convention in London in 1840 (although she was a duly elected delegate from the United States) that she, and Elizabeth Cady Stanton, convoked the Women's Rights Convention at Seneca Falls, New York, in 1848.

PHILADELPHIA. GLORIA DEI CHURCHYARD, NEAR FRONT AND CHRISTIAN STREETS.

The church, popularly called Old Swedes', is the oldest in Pennsylvania, having been built in 1700. (Originally it was Swedish Lutheran; now it is Episcopal.) However, a marker informs us that a blockhouse church stood here in 1677 so burials must date from that time. Most famous of those buried here is Alexander Wilson (1766–1813), father of American ornithology. A native of Paisley, Scotland, he emigrated in 1794 and died of the fever at the age of forty-seven. The newly cut stone over his grave was paid for with contributions by schoolchildren in his native city.

There is a "Revolutionary Corner," containing the graves of soldiers of the War for Independence, including that of James Peale, painter. Originally these stones were in the now-defunct Ronaldson's Cemetery and were moved here after it closed. The tallest monument among these marks the grave of the "Scottish Stranger."

PHILADELPHIA. GREENWOOD CEMETERY, ADAMS AVENUE AND ARROTT STREET.

Because of putting the cemetery's perpetual care funds into poor investments (the now-bankrupt Pennsylvania Railroad), the sixty-acre cemetery has little money for its upkeep and is sadly neglected. The Shackamaxon Society of Philadelphia does maintain the graves of James L. (1841–1913) and Kate Dunkenfield (1855–1925), parents of W. C. Fields. The stone over James has on it the comedian's tribute to his father: "A Great Scout." On Kate's are the words "A Sweet Old Soul."

PHILADELPHIA. HOLY TRINITY CEMETERY, 6TH AND SPRUCE STREETS.

The church building itself was opened in 1789 by a German Catholic congregation. The tiny churchyard in the shadow of a large high-rise apartment house seems lost in the city. Stephen Girard (1750–1831), the French immigrant who became a merchant prince, was first buried here, but his body was later transferred to Girard College, which was established with funds left in his will for that purpose. It is interesting that Girard, who by his will forbade clergymen to hold services at Girard College, was married in an Episcopal church and buried in a Roman Catholic churchyard. A number of Acadians, who fled Nova Scotia and New Brunswick in 1755 when the French relieved the British of Canada, are buried here. This is the "little Catholic churchyard in the heart of the city" in which the lovers of Longfellow's poem *Evangeline* are said to be buried.

PHILADELPHIA. MOUNT MORIAH CEMETERY, 62ND STREET AND KINGSESSING AVENUE.

The cemetery came into national prominence in December 1975, when the bones of Elizabeth Griscom Ross Ashburn Claypoole (1752–1836), the most popular seamstress in American history, and those of her third husband, John Claypoole, were moved. Betsy Ross, who according to tradition sewed the first American flag, was buried first in the Free Quaker Cemetery at Fifth and Locust streets in Philadelphia. When that ground was abandoned in 1857 the remains of the Claypooles were moved to Mount Moriah. With bicentennial fervor, some of her descendants obtained a court order to have the bones disinterred and reburied in the garden of the Betsy Ross House at 239 Arch Street. An anthropologist from the University of Pennsylvania was engaged to supervise the exhumation, but the first day's digging brought only consternation. No bones could be found. Because of the high acid content of the soil the anthropologist considered it likely that nothing remained of Betsy. Eventually, a coffin was discovered that seems likely to be Betsy's and John's and it was duly reburied in the garden on Arch Street.

Somewhat different was the funeral of Lew Smith, who ran a towing service in Philadelphia for illegally parked cars. Smith, who could never understand why he was universally disliked, was buried in Mount Moriah. Although he was carried in proper fashion to his grave in a hearse, his cortege included a line of freshly washed tow trucks!

Mount Moriah Cemetery. *Photograph by Ruth Branning Molloy*

PHILADELPHIA. OLD PINE PRESBYTERIAN CHURCHYARD, SOUTH FOURTH AND PINE STREETS.

The Third Presbyterian Church, familiarly known as "Old Pine," was built in 1768 and altered in 1837 and 1857. During the American Revolution the British used the last of the pews and woodwork for firewood; the church was commandeered as a stable by the dragoons. One hundred Hessians are buried in a common grave along the east wall of the church. William Hurry (1721–1781), whose fame rests on the fact that he rang the Liberty Bell at the first public reading of the Declaration of Independence, and Jared Ingersoll (1749–1822), signer of the Constitution, are buried here.

PHILADELPHIA. OLD SAINT MARY'S CEMETERY, SOUTH FOURTH STREET BETWEEN LOCUST AND SPRUCE STREETS.

The church was founded in 1763, the present structure enlarged in 1810. Among those buried here are Commodore John Barry (1745–1803), "father of the American Navy"; Thomas Fitzsimons (1741–1811), signer of the United States Constitution and member of the Continental Congress and the first three United States Congresses; General Stephen Moylan (1737–1811) of the American Revolution in which he was an aide-de-camp to Washington; Mathew Carey (1760–1839), founder (1785) of Lea & Febiger, the oldest book publishing house in the nation; and George Meade, grandfather of the Civil War general of the same name. Since the presidency of John F. Kennedy, most visitors are drawn to the graves of Jacqueline Kennedy Onassis's forebears. Michel Bouvier (1792–1874), an emigrant from France and a distinguished Philadelphia cabinetmaker, was the former First Lady's great-great grandfather. He, his wife, and many of their descendants are buried along the wall on the Locust Street side.

PHILADELPHIA. SAINT JOHN THE EVANGELIST CHURCHYARD, 13TH STREET BETWEEN MARKET AND CHESTNUT STREETS.

A double row of vaults, many with the names of Philadelphia's oldest Catholic families on their covers, is on the north side of the church. Of particular interest is vault number nine, that of Maria Huarte de Iturbide, first empress of Mexico (1822–1823), who occupied the throne forty years before the ill-fated Carlotta became the country's second empress. She was the consort of Agustín de Iturbide (1783–1824), who was executed by the Republicans. She and their children eventually came to Philadelphia to live. During the Mexican War of 1845–1846 the former empress appealed to President James Knox Polk to intervene with Mexican authorities to see that her pension was continued. She died on March 21, 1869, at the age of seventy-nine. A son, Agustín, a daughter, Sabina, and two other children brought from Mexico for reburial in 1849 lie beside their mother.

Saint Peter's Churchyard. *City of Philadelphia, Office of the City Representative*

PHILADELPHIA. SAINT PAUL'S EPISCOPAL CHURCHYARD, SOUTH THIRD STREET AT WILLINGS ALLEY.

The church, built in 1761, is no longer used except as headquarters for the Episcopal Community Services of the Diocese of Pennsylvania. In the small churchyard is the grave of Edwin Forrest (1806–1872), the great tragedian known for his Spartacus and other dramatic roles.

PHILADELPHIA. SAINT PETER'S CHURCHYARD, SOUTH THIRD AND PINE STREETS.

The church itself was erected in 1761 and is one of the three eighteenth-century churches in America that have not been changed structurally. The most famous grave here is that of Stephen Decatur (1779–1820), hero of the War of 1812, who was killed in a duel with Commodore James Barron at Bladensburg, Maryland. Others here are Charles Willson Peale (1741–1827), the portrait painter who limned so many of the Founding Fathers; Dr. William Shippen (1712–1801) and Dr. Adam Kuhn (1741–1817), eighteenth-century physicians who were influential in American medicine; Colonel John Nixon (1731–1808), who first read the Declaration of Independence to the people of Philadelphia in the State House yard on July 8, 1776; and seven Indian chiefs who died in 1793 of smallpox. The churchyard is a full city block long and provides a garden for the neighborhood. Among the trees can be seen the tallest monument, that of Admiral Decatur. A granite pillar surmounted by an eagle marks the hero's grave.

PHILADELPHIA. WEST LAUREL HILL CEMETERY, BELMONT AVENUE ABOVE CITY LINE AVENUE.

Among those buried here is Anna Jarvis (1864–1948), founder of Mother's Day. She is buried beside her mother, Anna Reeves Jarvis, who died in 1905. After her mother's death, Miss Jarvis began her campaign to have Mother's Day recognized. Finally in 1914 Woodrow Wilson signed the congressional resolution and declared the second Sunday in May to be observed as Mother's Day.

PHILADELPHIA. WOODLANDS CEMETERY, 40TH AND WOODLAND AVENUE.

This is one of the two green enclaves on the lower Schuylkill River. (The other is the John Bartram House and garden.) Industrial blight and urban sprawl have desecrated most of the river's banks, but Woodlands Cemetery remains on oasis in the city.

The Woodlands, the eighteenth-century home that gave the cemetery its name, still stands and is now occupied by the superintendent. It was built by William Hamilton in 1788, incorporating an earlier and simpler house his grandfather, Andrew Hamilton, had erected. That Andrew—called Andrew the First—purchased three hundred acres in Blockley Township in 1735. (It did not become part of Philadelphia until 1854.) It was he who defended John Peter Zenger that year in New York in a trial that became a landmark in the preservation of freedom of the press. (He is also credited with being one of the two architects of Independence Hall, although this has never been completely proven.)

After the death of Andrew the First's grandson, "William of the Woodlands," the estate eventually became Woodlands Cemetery, the burial place of some of Philadelphia's oldest families—the Stotesburys, Drexels, Newbolds, Prices, and Da Costas.

Perhaps the most distinguished Philadelphian buried here is Thomas Eakins (1844–1916), the artist who is now recognized as one of the giants of American painting. *The Gross Clinic* is considered one of the great paintings of the nineteenth century, second only to Rembrandt's *Anatomy Lesson* as a tribute to the medical profession. Dr. Samuel D. Gross (1805–1884), the subject of the painting, is at Woodlands too. Also here is Frank R. Stockton (1834–1902), author of such recognized American classics as *The Lady or the Tiger?* and *The Casting Away of Mrs. Lecks and Mrs. Aleshine;* S. Weir Mitchell, M.D. (1829–1914), distinguished physician and man of letters whose novels *Constance Trescott, The Red City,* and *Hugh Wynne, Free Quaker* were popular with Americans seventy years ago; and Commodore David Porter (1780–1843). The naval hero's remains were returned from Constantinople and first interred in a cemetery on the grounds of the Old Naval Home, later transferred here, and in 1945 to Arlington National Cemetery. The largest monument is to Dr. Thomas William Evans (1823–1897) and his wife, Agnes Doyle (1822–

1897). He was the founder of the Thomas W. Evans Museum and Dental Institute, now part of the University of Pennsylvania School of Dentistry.

RADNOR. OLD SAINT DAVID'S CHURCHYARD.

This is one of the most beautiful churchyards to be found in this part of the state, the new extending naturally from the old over the undulating ground. It has every appearance of being English. Just inside the gate is the grave of "Mad Anthony" Wayne (1745–1796), who lived at Waynesborough, his estate at nearby Paoli. One of his feats was the capture of Stony Point, New York (1779). He died at Erie, Pennsylvania, and some years later his son went to collect his remains and moved them here. The story is rather grisly for the body was boiled to remove the flesh, and the bones packed in saddlebags for the return journey. Here historians disagree. There is one story that the saddlebags were stolen en route, so that no one knows where Anthony's bones are. The other is that they were returned to Old Saint David's.

READING. CHARLES EVANS CEMETERY, 1119 CENTRE AVENUE.

Named for its founder Charles Evans (1768–1847), a Philadelphia-born Berks County lawyer, the original twenty-five acres of ground and $2,000 endowment were given by Evans in 1846. To this he left $10,000 outright and three-quarters—or almost $67,000—of the residue of his estate.

The first burial was that of Harriet Norton (1797–1847). Among others buried here are Captain Anthony Kanalassy (1822–1853), exiled from Hungary because he fought for its independence; Matilda Edwards Strong (died 1851), who jilted Abraham Lincoln and married another; Captain Peter Nagel (1750–1834), who was with George Washington at the siege of Boston (1776); and several Union officers in the Civil War: Major James McKnight (1820–1888), Major General David McMurtrie Gregg (1833–1916), General Alexander Schimmelfennig (1824–1865), and Brigadier General Simon Snyder (1839–1913).

The brownstone arched gate is particularly handsome, and just inside is a full-length statue of Evans. A spectacular sphinx—a reminder of the Egyptian Revival—guards the graves of the Rake family. A pyramid over F. Lauer is another example of this once-popular style. The cemetery is beautifully landscaped and is a fine example of the rural, or garden, cemetery.

WEST CHESTER. OAKHILL CEMETERY.

Here, in the country he loved and where he lived so many years, Joseph Hergesheimer (1880–1954), author of

Three Black Pennys, Java Head, and other novels, is buried.

SOUTH CAROLINA

CHARLESTON. SAINT PHILIP'S CHURCHYARD.

This lovely old churchyard in the heart of this historic port city has as its most famous grave that of John C. Calhoun (1782–1850), representative from South Carolina (1811–1817), secretary of war (1817–1825), vice-president of the United States (1825–1832), and senator (1832–1843, 1845–1850). When, during the Civil War, it was thought that Union troops might take the city, the sexton and his assistant exhumed the body of Calhoun and reburied it by night beneath the church. They feared Yankee troops might desecrate it. After the war the remains were returned to the original grave. At Calhoun's funeral two of the bearers were Henry Clay and Daniel Webster, and in keeping with the solemnity of the occasion even the palmetto trees were swathed in black.

Also here are Edward Rutledge (1749–1800), signer of the Declaration of Independence and delegate to the first and second Continental Congress, and Colonel William Rhett (1666–1722), captor of Stede Bonnet, the notorious pirate, and his fellows, who were hanged. Charles Pinckney (1757–1824), signer of the Constitution, is with them, but it is Maria Gracia Dura Bin who is of particular interest. Daughter of a Greek merchant from Smyrna, she was the first Greek woman to settle in North America. With her husband, Dr. Andrew Turnbull, she established the colony of New Smyrna, Florida, in 1768 before settling in Charleston in 1782.

CHARLESTON. SAINT MICHAEL'S CHURCHYARD.

Saint Michael's church is older than Saint Philip's, although the latter is the older parish. Built in 1752, Saint Michael's bells, clock, and organ came from England, and its churchyard contains the graves of many early Carolina families—Rhett, Waring, Hayne, Izard, Pringle, and Petigru. Revolutionary soldiers lie among them as do two signers of the Constitution—Charles Cotesworth Pinckney (1746–1825) and John Rutledge (1739–1800).

SOUTH DAKOTA

DEADWOOD. BOOT HILL BURYING GROUND.

Located on Mount Moriah are the fenced-in graves of some of the Old West's most colorful and legendary characters. They cannot be called heroes in the true sense of

the term for they were often on the other side of the law, or took it into their own hands.

Calamity Jane, in reality Martha Jane Burke (Canary) (1852?–1903), rests here after an adventurous life and a busy one too, with twelve husbands to her credit. (Later in life she entered show business.) It is said her intemperate actions sent eleven of the twelve husbands to early graves. Then there is "Potato Creek" Johnny Perrett, last of the old-time prospectors, and Seth Bullock, organizer of the Rough Riders.

As colorful as any was Preacher Smith, killed by the Indians while endeavoring to spread the Gospel. Ever optimistic, even in the wild frontier of his day, Smith left a note pinned to his cabin door just before being ambushed. It read: "Gone to Crook City, and if God is willing, will be back at 2. p.m."

The cemetery also contains the grave of James Butler ("Wild Bill") Hickok (1837–1876), the legendary marshal in Kansas who was known as an expert marksman in encounters with outlaws. Hickok, called the "Prince of Pistoleers," was a handsome devil—one of the finest looking men in the West—and was one of the quickest, if not the most accurate, shots in his heyday. It is known he dispatched at least twenty-seven men (there were thirty-six notches on his gun). In his later years he drifted north to Deadwood. What he did not realize was the Deadwood miners feared his appointment as town marshal. To de-

A gravestone in Saint Philip's Churchyard, Charleston, South Carolina. *Photograph by Marjorie R. Maurer*

Calamity Jane at "Wild Bill" Hickok's grave, circa 1903. *Reproduced from the collection of the Library of Congress*

feat this, they hired a gunman, Jack ("Crooked Nose") McCall, gave him $300 (and saw that his courage was bolstered by cheap whiskey). He stole into the No. 10 Saloon while Wild Bill was playing poker and put a bullet through the back of his head.

The story didn't end there. Legend has it that Wild Bill's last poker hand held aces and eights—since known as the "dead man's hand." McCall was first freed by a packed jury, but later a United States court found him guilty of murder, and he was hanged.

Calamity Jane, dressed in men's clothing (as was her custom), is said to have viewed Hickok, long hair to his shoulders, in his plain pine coffin and commented: "It's the purtiest corpse I ever done seen." Later she was photographed standing jauntily before his grave (she was later buried near him). Not the Calamity Jane portrayed by the beautiful Jean Arthur that most motion picture audiences remember!

VERMONT

ARLINGTON. SAINT JAMES'S CHURCHYARD, ROUTE 7.

Mary Brownson, first wife of Ethan Allen, is interred here. (Allen is in Greenmount Cemetery in Burlington, and his second wife in the Elmwood Avenue Cemetery in that town.) There are many fine eighteenth- and nineteenth-century monuments and tombstones here.

BARNARD. BARNARD CEMETERY.

Dorothy Thompson (1894–1961), one of America's most distinguished journalists, is buried here with Maxim

Kopf, Czech painter, who was her third husband. (The Nobel Prize winning novelist Sinclair Lewis was her second.)

BARRE. HOPE CEMETERY, MAPLE AVENUE.

The gigantic monuments here are among the most unusual to be found anywhere in the United States today.

A realistic sculpture. *Photograph by Clive E. Driver*

Hope Cemetery. *Photograph by Clive E. Driver*

Representations of those buried here, as they appeared in life, are on a heroic scale, and in some cases bizarre in treatment. William and Gwendolyn Halvosa are portrayed in bed together. Their portraits are on what would be the bed's headboard. The bed and counterpane themselves provide the flat stone over the grave. Another shows a couple comforting one another in grief (or are they just being affectionate?). That of Elia Corti, a stonecutter, has him seated before a massive granite rock, wearing his dress suit, and a bow tie. His chin is propped on one hand as he gazes pensively at the world. Corti was accidentally shot to death during a riot in 1903, and his fellow stonecutters erected this distinctive monument to his memory. Hope Cemetery in itself is a monument to the granite produced in Vermont and to the ingeniousness of its craftsmen.

BENNINGTON. OLD BENNINGTON CEMETERY, ROUTE 9, ONE MILE WEST OF THE TOWN CENTER.

The cemetery is one of the most charming in the state and its most famous grave is that of Robert Frost (1874–1963). His epitaph is typical of this simple, yet complex poet: "I had a lover's quarrel with the world." Frost rests surrounded by historic dead: British and American soldiers who died at the Battle of Bennington (1777), and Isaac Tichenor (1754–1838), a member of the Vermont legislature who was an agent to the Continental Congress between 1782 and 1789.

BURLINGTON. GREENMOUNT CEMETERY, COLCHESTER AVENUE.

Ethan Allen (1738–1789) and many of his Green Mountain Boys are buried here. Allen's grave is marked by a forty-two-foot Tuscan marble monument, which was dedicated in 1873. Topping it is an eight-foot statue of him by Peter Stephenson, which was cut in Carrara, Italy. It depicts Allen demanding the surrender of Fort Ticonderoga (1775). A marker bears the legend: "The mortal remains of Ethan Allen, fighter, writer, statesman and philosopher, lie in this cemetery beneath the marble statue. His spirit is in Vermont now."

PLYMOUTH. NOTCH CEMETERY, ON ROUTE 100-A.

Calvin Coolidge (1872–1933), thirtieth president of the United States, and his wife, Grace Goodhue (1879–1957), are buried here. Coolidge, Vermont's only president, was here on a visit when notified of President Harding's death. His father administered the oath of office by the light of a kerosene lamp. The family Bible was used, and the scene has become as much a part of American folklore as of history.

VIRGINIA

GLENDALE. GLENDALE NATIONAL CEMETERY, ON VIRGINIA STATE HIGHWAY 156, APPROXIMATELY 15 MILES SOUTH AND EAST OF SEVEN PINES NATIONAL CEMETERY.

The national cemeteries near Richmond are all visible reminders of the savage fighting that occurred here in the siege of the Confederate capital. General George B. McClellan's cry was "on to Richmond" and his forces scourged the land as they thrust forward, then retreated back to the James River and the protection of Union gunboats. There was bitter and hotly contested rearguard action at Savage Station, White Oak Swamp, and Glendale (Frayser's Farm) as McClellan strategically retreated. Finally, there was a battle at Malvern Hill on July 1, 1862, the culmination of the Seven Days' campaign. McClellan's peninsula campaign was a failure and Union forces moved down the James to Harrison's Landing.

Although Richmond was saved, the cost in lives was frightful. Union casualties totaled 1,734 killed, 8,062 wounded, and 6,053 missing, out of an army of 91,169 men. The Confederate forces were smaller—85,000 men. Of these, some 3,478 were killed, 16,261 wounded, with 875 missing.

The cemetery land, a little more than two acres in area, was appropriated for this use in 1866 and purchased by the federal government in 1869 and 1873. Located within two miles of the site of the Battle of Malvern Hill, it is within the area of battlefield interments of the many casualties resulting from the final period of the Seven Days' campaign. There were hasty burials under combat conditions and in 1866 many reinterments were made. As of March 31, 1961, the interments in Glendale National Cemetery totaled 1,209 and of these 960 are unknown.

HOPEWELL. CITY POINT NATIONAL CEMETERY, 500 NORTH 10TH AVENUE.

During the last six months of 1864 and in the early ones of 1865, when the final tragic act of the Civil War was being played, Ulysses S. Grant was making every effort to secure Petersburg, a vital communication center, and —once that city fell—Richmond, the prize long sought. Robert E. Lee and the now-legendary Army of Northern Virginia desperately and stubbornly defended this last bastion of the Confederacy.

At City Point, where the James and Appomattox rivers meet, the Union army established a large supply depot for receipt of troops and vast quantities of all manner of war materiel in preparation for another thrust at Richmond. The action at the various battles leading up to the fall of Richmond necessitated the establishment of an army general hospital at City Point to care for the sick and wounded. The death rate from disease and wounds

was high and many of the combatants were interred in burial grounds near the hospital.

City Point National Cemetery, its land appropriated in 1866 and purchased by the United States in 1872, contains that hospital burial ground on the bank of the Appomattox River. Other bodies not originally buried here were recovered from another burial ground at City Point, from Point of Rocks in Chesterfield County, and from Harrison's Landing in Charles City County.

The City Point National Cemetery differs from the five other national cemeteries in the general Richmond area, which were established in 1866, in that the number of identifiable remains exceeds the number of unknowns buried here. Initially, 3,753 known and 1,403 unknown were interred at City Point. As of March 31, 1961, some 5,561 interments had been made, 4,107 known and 1,454 unknown.

There is a latter-day footnote to the history of the region when in 1955 the remains of seventeen unknown soldiers of the Civil War were discovered during the excavation of some vacant lots in Hopewell (apparently the site of an abandoned cemetery). Buttons from both Union and Confederate uniforms were found in the graves. These and the bodies of two other Union soldiers recovered in 1959 from shallow graves in the path of Interstate Route 95 were reinterred in City Point National Cemetery, which contains a total of 118 Confederate bodies.

Today the cemetery is part of the city of Hopewell. Included within its boundaries is a white marble monument, approximately twenty feet high, erected in 1865 to the memory of the dead of the Army of the James by direction of Major General B. F. Butler, commander of that army from April 1864 to January 1865.

JAMESTOWN. OLD CHURCHYARD.

This spot, truly ancient for the United States, is situated on the banks of the James River, up which the Virginia colonists sailed to establish Jamestown in 1607. So much of Jamestown is gone, and the only remnants of the seventeenth-century settlement are some excavations of the original house of burgesses, the old church tower, and the graves beside it. The tower is thought to have been built after the completion of the first brick church, sometime between 1639 and 1647.

The churchyard served as a burial ground for many decades during and after the century (1607–1699) that Jamestown was Virginia's capital. (The capital was moved to Williamsburg in 1700.) Today, only a few of the graves are marked with stones, and even the location of most has been lost. There is a fragment of the stone marking the grave of Lady Frances Berkeley, wife of Sir William, who was twice governor of the colony. Another is believed to mark the tomb of Sir George Yeardley, a leader of Jamestown from 1609 and several times governor of the colony. He was knighted by King James I in 1618 and died at Jamestown on November 12, 1627. The tomb has inlaid brasses, unique for an American colonial site.

Elizabeth Drummond's gravestone tells that she died at Greenspring in 1699 and was the daughter of William Drummond, the first governor of North Carolina, who took sides in Bacon's Rebellion (a popular uprising precipitated by Governor Berkeley's failure to defend the frontier against Indian attacks) and was executed on January 20, 1676. A large tree has split the graves of Mrs. Sarah Blair (1670–1713) and the Reverend James Blair (c. 1656–1743). Inside the church some of the early citizens of Jamestown were entombed. Their graves are now marked by stones in the floor.

Walking from the churchyard, seeing these remnants of an interpid band of settlers, it is difficult to realize that 370 years have passed since the *Susan Constant, Godspeed,* and *Discovery* sailed bravely up the James to allow 105 men to land and found a New World.

RICHMOND. COLD HARBOR NATIONAL CEMETERY, VIRGINIA STATE HIGHWAY 156.

Located about nine miles east of Richmond, and established as a national cemetery in 1866, this small burial ground is a mute testimony to the men who fell in the defense of Richmond, and those who sought its fall. In a sense Cold Harbor is a battlefield cemetery. It was the scene of action for a portion of two Union campaigns to reach Richmond. The Seven Days' battles of June 26-July 2, 1862 virtually brought General George B. McClellan's Peninsula Campaign to a state of collapse. The engagement at Gaines's Mill (Cold Harbor) on June 26–27 has often been described as the most costly and vicious of the Seven Days' battles because of the heavy losses sustained by both the Union and Confederate forces.

The second encounter took place June 1–3, 1864, when the armies under Ulysses S. Grant and Robert E. Lee met at Cold Harbor—a strategic crossroad guarding the approaches to Richmond. Grant's army was superior in numbers, but the men in gray managed to stave off the fall of Richmond for another ten months. The casualties on both sides were great and Lee, according to Douglas Southall Freeman, "had won his last great battle in the field."

The price of victory and defeat was tremendous. Nearly two thousand graves—1,313 of them those of unknown soldiers—bear witness to this. With the war's end and the establishment of the National Cemetery, a search was made for the bodies of the fallen. More than a twenty-two-mile area was covered in the search, hastily dug graves uncovered, and the bodies brought here.

To honor these men several monuments have been erected in the wall-enclosed cemetery. The United States government in 1877 erected a large white sarcophagus.

Its legend reads: "Near this stone rest the remains of 888 Union soldiers gathered from the Battle Fields of Mechanicsville, Savage Station, Gaines Mills and the vicinity of Cold Harbor." In 1909 the Commonwealth of Pennsylvania had a tall granite monument bearing the figure of a soldier at parade rest placed here. It records: "To all Pennsylvania Regiments which participated in the operations from May 31st to June 12th 1864 incident to and during the Battle of Cold Harbor, Virginia, June 1–3, 1864." That same year the New York State Monuments Commission placed still another in the National Cemetery. It bears a bronze plaque listing the names of 219 members of the Eighth New York Heavy Artillery who were killed or died of wounds received in the Battle of Cold Harbor on June 3.

RICHMOND. FRANKLIN STREET BURYING GROUND, 21ST AND FRANKLIN STREETS.

Established in 1791 by Isaiah Isaacs, this was a cemetery for the Richmond Jewish community. There are no stones remaining, but the grass is well kept and there are three trees and an especially fine pair of iron gates.

RICHMOND. HEBREW CEMETERY, HOSPITAL AND 5TH STREETS.

Opened in 1816, it is located next to a nursing home, a building erected in 1860, which served as a Confederate hospital. The Confederate section of the cemetery is marked by a cast-iron fence of stacked rifles and crossed swords.

RICHMOND. OAKWOOD CEMETERY, 9 MILE ROAD AND 31ST STREET.

The first burials took place here in 1855. The antebellum cemetery contains one of the largest burial plots of Confederate dead. A memorial reads: "This ground is the last bivouac of 17,000 Confederate soldiers slain in defense of the South." The grounds are well kept and there is a charming bandstand, an inevitable adjunct to any Civil War cemetery.

RICHMOND. RICHMOND NATIONAL CEMETERY, 1701 WILLIAMSBURG ROAD.

During the four years from 1861 to 1865 of the Civil War, when often members of families were fighting each other on opposing sides, Richmond was a prime target of Union troops. Seven major drives were launched against the city. As the pace of war accelerated, and especially during the final ten months, the capture of Richmond (only 110 miles from the federal capital in Washington) became a symbol, a prime psychological objective, and, in essence, a crusade. After it was captured, the expression "as Grant took Richmond" crept into the language.

In 1866 the site of the present cemetery was appropriated by the United States government (the enactment of legislation in 1862 initiated the establishment of national cemeteries in the United States) and the ground was purchased in 1867, 1868, and 1906. Once the inevitable search for the remains of Union dead and reinterments from Oakwood and Hollywood cemeteries in Richmond began, others followed from the cemetery of the Belle Island Confederate prison and from the battlefields of Cold Harbor and Seven Pines. Transferrals were made from other locations in Chesterfield and Hanover counties, and the situation became stable. More than seventy locations within a maximum distance of twenty-five miles of the cemetery were searched so the boys in blue could be returned for burial to a national cemetery.

By 1868 there were 6,326 interments but only 822 of these had been identified. In more than a century since the opening of the 9.74-acre cemetery, the dead of other wars—the Spanish-American, World War I, and World War II—have found a final resting place here. As of March 31, 1961, there had been 8,348 interments; of these 2,644 were known and 5,704 unknown.

RICHMOND. SAINT JOHN'S CHURCHYARD, BROAD AND 24TH STREETS.

The church was erected in 1741 and the name changed to Saint John's about a century later. The oldest grave dates from 1751. Of interest here are the graves of George Wythe (1726–1806), signer of the Declaration of Independence, who was the first professor of law in the United States and numbered among his pupils Thomas Jefferson, John Marshall, and John Randolph; James Mercer (1736–1793), member of the Continental Congress; Dr. James McClurg, one of Virginia's delegates to the Constitutional Convention in 1787, and Elizabeth Arnold Poe (1787–1811), mother of the poet. Mrs. Poe's monument was erected in 1927 by the Raven Society of the University of Virginia, with the cooperation of Actors Equity Association and the Edgar Allan Poe Shrine of Richmond. A handsome medallion by Elbert McSprann Jackson of Mrs. Poe, who was an actress, is on one side of the monument and an excerpt on the reverse from an article by Poe in *The Broadway Journal* for July 19, 1845, citing his mother's devotion to the drama. Although we are principally interested in the churchyard, it was in Saint John's Church on March 23, 1775, in the presence of Washington, Jefferson, and other members of the Virginia convention, that Patrick Henry made his speech in which he said: "If this be treason, then treason it is, but give me liberty or give me death."

SANDSTON. SEVEN PINES NATIONAL CEMETERY, AT THE JUNCTION OF VIRGINIA STATE HIGHWAY 156 AND U.S. HIGHWAY 60.

This, like so many southern Civil War cemeteries, was a battlefield. In the early months of the long and disastrous war—toward the end of May 1862—Union forces under General George B. McClellan advanced from Fort Monroe up the York-James rivers peninsula to a point almost in sight of Richmond, the Confederate capital.

Union observers sent aloft in balloons were able to see the church spires of the city from their mobile observation points. General Joseph E. Johnston, the Confederate commander, believing that McClellan planned to remain north of the James River, decided to attack. McClellan, curtailed by geography and the inclement spring weather in Virginia, established his main line of defense at the junction of the Nine Mile Road and the Williamsburg Road. It was here that the armies met and Johnston attacked on the morning of May 31, 1862. This in the chronicle of Civil War engagements began the Battle of Fair Oaks (Seven Pines). The outcome was inconclusive. General Johnston was wounded and the Confederate forces repulsed. However, Union troops also suffered heavy losses and this made McClellan even more cautious. Richmond remained safe for a time.

One important and historic result of this little-known battle was that Jefferson Davis, president of the Confederate States of America, appointed Robert E. Lee to succeed the wounded Joseph E. Johnston as commander of the forces. This noble band became the legendary Army of Northern Virginia.

With the cessation of hostilities, Lieutenant Colonel James M. Moore of the Quartermaster Corps was authorized by Washington to select a site for a permanent national cemetery in the area, so that the remains of the dead might be reinterred.

In 1866 (the year Cold Harbor National Cemetery and others were authorized), the present site of Seven Pines National Cemetery was appropriated as a cemetery, and in 1867 one and three-tenths acres were purchased. In 1875 a small additional strip was added. The bodies of the valiant were removed from the battlefields of Seven Pines and Savage Station (and from farmyards and fields where they had been hastily interred soon after the smoke of battle lifted) in a four-mile area surrounding the present cemetery. Then 1,358 bodies were reburied here (1,208 unknown). As of 1961—a century after the opening guns of the Civil War sounded—a total of 1,427 bodies were reinterred here, but only 190 have been identified. It is one of the sorrows of this fratricidal conflict that so few of the dead were identifiable.

WILLIAMSBURG. BRUTON PARISH CHURCHYARD.

The church, designed by Royal Governor Alexander Spotswood, was completed in 1715 upon the site of an earlier one built in 1674. The church and the churchyard are not a part of the Colonial Williamsburg Foundation.

Edmund Pendleton (1721–1803), Revolutionary patriot and early Virginia jurist, is buried within the church. Washington, Jefferson, Monroe, Patrick Henry, John Marshall, and John Tyler all worshiped here. The burial ground is of interest for its association with the church and its communicants, rather than for the famous buried here. The stone over Thomas Ludwell (born in Bruton, Somerset, England), secretary of state to Governor Berkeley, bears the date 1678, making it the oldest marked grave. There were earlier ones that were either unmarked or whose stones have long since disintegrated with time and weather. Most of the stones are of the tablelike variety and were brought over from England as ballast, because there was no stone indigenous to this part of Virginia that would retain an inscription. Tariffs on tombstones were high, so only the well-to-do could afford them.

WINGINA, NELSON COUNTY.

On the extensive grounds of Union Hill, an estate that was the Cabell family home, is one of those charming family burial grounds that can still be seen in rural areas of the United States, especially in New England, the South, and parts of the Midwest. Colonel William Cabell (1730–1798), the son of Dr. William Cabell, who emigrated from England about 1723, built his home at Union Hill between 1774 and 1778. In this one family cemetery there are over fifty known graves, beginning with that of Colonel Cabell. Many of the family members were influential in Virginia's history in the eighteenth and nineteenth centuries, among them Patrick Henry, Jr., who married Elvira Cabell but died within the year.

What is forgotten—especially in the North—is that slaves were often buried in the family cemetery. Mayo Cabell (1800–1869), a successful farmer, owned about 150 slaves, and his treatment of them must have been kind for many stayed on even after Emancipation and died on the property. Edward Marshall Cabell remembered that many of the favorite slaves were interred in the family graveyard. Some of the slave graves are marked with "river" stones and some not at all.

VIRGIN ISLANDS

CHARLOTTE AMALIE, SAINT THOMAS. JEWISH CEMETERY, KRONPRINDSENS GATE.

The oldest grave in the cemetery dates from 1837 (5597 on the Jewish calendar), which is the year the cemetery chapel, Beth Chaim (House of Life), was erected. The chapel and the cemetery are of the Sephardic rite and are owned by the Saint Thomas Jewish Congregation of Blessing and Peace and Acts of Piety. Prior to the congregation's use of the cemetery, it used one at Silke Gade and Jøde Gade. A wall of brick and stone rubble, laid in lime, borders the cemetery, which lies just outside the area included in the Hingelberg map of Charlotte Amalie of 1836–1837.

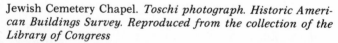

The grave of Alexander Hamilton's mother at Estate LaGrange, Fredericksted, Saint Croix, Virgin Islands. The stone was erected by author Gertrude Atherton. *Von Scholten Collection, Enid M. Baa Library, Charlotte Amalie*

Jewish Cemetery Chapel. *Toschi photograph. Historic American Buildings Survey. Reproduced from the collection of the Library of Congress*

Bibliography

Bailey, Conrad. *Harrap's Guide to Famous London Graves.* London: George G. Harrap & Co., Ltd., 1975.

Bliss, Harry A. *Memorial Art Ancient and Modern.* Buffalo, New York: Harry A. Bliss, 1912.

Blythe, Ronald. *Akenfield.* New York: Pantheon Books, 1969.

Brod, Max. *Franz Kafka.* New York: Schocken Books, 1960.

Curl, James Stevens. "The Architecture and Planning of the Nineteenth-Century Cemetery." *The Journal of the Garden History Society,* Summer 1975, III, 3.

————. *The Victorian Celebration of Death.* Detroit: The Partridge Press, 1972.

Ellmann, Richard. *James Joyce.* New York: Oxford University Press, 1959.

Forbes, Harriette Merrifield. *Gravestones of Early New England.* Princeton: The Pyne Press, 1974.

Gilchrist, Agnes Addison. *William Strickland. Architect and Engineer. 1788–1854.* New York: Da Capo Press, 1969.

Gillon, Edmund V., Jr. *Victorian Cemetery Art.* New York: Dover Publications, Inc., 1972.

Gunther, John. *Death Be Not Proud.* New York: Harper & Brothers, 1949.

Hedley, Olwen. *Cambridge. The City and the Colleges.* London: Pitkin Pictorials, Ltd., 1971.

Jones, Barbara. *Design for Death.* New York: The Bobbs-Merrill Company, Inc., 1967.

Kull, Andrew. *New England Cemeteries. A Collector's Guide.* Brattleboro, Vermont: The Stephen Greene Press, 1975.

Ludwig, Allan I. *Graven Images. New England Stonecarving and Its Symbols.* Middletown, Connecticut: Wesleyan University Press, 1966.

Morley, John. *Death, Heaven and the Victorians.* Pittsburgh: University of Pittsburgh Press, 1971.

Morrison, T. J. "Carmunnock and Its Church. An Old-World Village on the City's Borderland." *The Evening Citizen* (Glasgow), June 25, 1927.

Plunkett, James. *The Gems She Wore.* New York: Holt, Rinehart and Winston, 1973.

Spiegl, Fritz, ed. *A Small Book of Grave Humour.* London: Pan Books, Ltd., 1971.

Tegg, William. *The Last Act: Being The Funeral Rites of Nations and Individuals.* London: Wm. Tegg & Co., Pancras Lane, Cheapside, 1876.

Toynbee, J. M. C. *Death and Burial in the Roman World.* Ithaca, New York: Cornell University Press, 1971.

ALBANY RURAL CEMETERY

"Albany Rural Has Well Observed the Ideals of Its Founding." *American Cemetery,* April 1966.

ARLINGTON CEMETERY

Andrews, Peter. *In Honored Glory.* New York: G. P. Putnam's Sons, 1966.

Gurney, Gene. *Arlington National Cemetery.* New York: Crown Publishers, Inc., 1965.

Hinkel, John V. *Arlington. Monument to Heroes.* Englewood Cliffs, New Jersey: Prentice-Hall, Inc., 1970.

BERMUDA

Kotker, Norman. "Encounter: 'Heaven Smiles, But Even Here the Smile Fades.'" *The New York Times,* February 23, 1975.

BLANDFORD CEMETERY

Nichols, Janet Bernard. *Sketch of Old Blandford Church.* Petersburg, Virginia, 1957.

BUNHILL FIELDS

Piper, David. *The Companion Guide to London.* New York: Harper and Row, 1965.

CALIFORNIA

Hansen, Gladys, ed. *San Francisco. The Bay and Its Cities.* Originally compiled by the Federal Writers' Project of the Works Progress Administration for Northern California. New Revised Edition. New York: Hastings House, 1973.

Ripton, Ray. "In Beginning, Woodlawn; Then Came Santa Monica." *Los Angeles Times,* October 5, 1975.

CENTRAL CEMETERY

Baedeker's Austria-Hungary. 11th Edition revised and augmented. New York: Charles Scribner's Sons, 1911.

Barkan, Hans, trans. and ed. *Johannes Brahms and Theodor Billroth. Letters from a Musical Friendship.* Norman, Oklahoma: University of Oklahoma Press, 1957.

Creed, Virginia. *All about Austria.* New York: Duell, Sloan & Pearce, 1950.

Lo Bello, Nino. "Vienna's More-or-Less Happy Hunting Ground." *The Philadelphia Inquirer Magazine,* February 16, 1969.

CHICAGO

Connely, Willard. *Louis Sullivan as He Lived. The Shaping of American Architecture.* New York: Horizon Press, 1960.

Graham, Jory. *Chicago. An Extraordinary Guide.* Chicago: Rand McNally & Company, 1967.

CIMITERO DEGLI INGLESI

Bigland, Eileen. *The Indomitable Mrs. Trollope.* Philadelphia: J. B. Lippincott Company, 1954.

Morton, H. V. *A Traveller in Italy.* New York: Dodd, Mead & Company, 1964.

CIMITERO DI SAN MICHELE

Brion, Marcel. *Venice. The Masque of Italy.* New York: Crown Publishers, Inc., 1962.

Bruning, Leslie D. "L'Archiconfraternità di S. Cristoforo e Compagnia della Misericordia." *American Cemetery,* January 1976.

Grundy, Milton. *Venice Recorded.* London: Anthony Blond, 1971.

Holiday Magazine Guide to Venice, A. New York: Random House, 1962.

Honour, Hugh. *The Companion Guide to Venice.* New York: Harper and Row, 1966.

Symons, A. J. A. *The Quest for Corvo.* Baltimore: Penguin Books, 1966.

CIMITERO DI STAGLIENO

Camposanto di Genova. Genoa: Fratelli Lichino, n.d.

O'Faolain, Sean. *A Summer in Italy.* New York: The Devin-Adair Company, 1951.

Origo, Iris. *A Measure of Love.* New York: Pantheon Books, n.d.

CONGRESSIONAL CEMETERY

Barzman, Sol. *Madmen and Geniuses. The Vice-Presidents of the United States.* Chicago: Follett Publishing Company, 1974.

Cleaves, Freeman. *Old Tippecanoe. William Henry Harrison and His Time.* New York: Charles Scribner's Sons, 1939.

Goebel, Dorothy Burne. *William Henry Harrison. A Political Biography.* Indianapolis, Indiana: Historical

Bureau of the Indiana Library and Historical Department, 1926.

Oman, Anne H. "Congress Authorizes $230,000 for Historic Cemetery." *The Washington Post,* October 14, 1976.

CROWN HILL

Nicholas, Anna. *The Story of Crown Hill.* Indianapolis, Indiana: Crown Hill Association, 1928.

DISTRICT OF COLUMBIA

Goode, James M. *The Outdoor Sculpture of Washington, D.C. A Comprehensive Historical Guide.* Washington: Smithsonian Institution Press, 1974.

Jacobsen, Hugh Newell, ed. *A Guide to the Architecture of Washington, D.C.* New York: Frederick A. Praeger, 1965.

Shandler, Philip. "D.C.'s Neglected Cemeteries Are in Search of New Life." *The Washington Star-News,* November 4, 1974.

Shuster, Alvin, ed. *Washington, D.C. A Guide to the Nation's Capital.* Washington, D.C.: Robert B. Luce, 1967.

Truett, Randall Bond, ed. *Washington, D.C. A Guide to the Nation's Capital.* Originally compiled by the Federal Writers' Program of the Works Progress Administration. New Revised Edition. New York: Hastings House, 1968.

FOREST LAWN, BUFFALO

Griffis, William Elliot. *Millard Fillmore. Constructive Statesman, Defender of the Constitution, President of the United States.* Ithaca, New York: Andrus, 1915.

Rayback, Robert J. *Millard Fillmore. Biography of a President.* Buffalo, New York: Henry Stewart, Inc., for the Buffalo Historical Society, 1959.

FOREST LAWN, LOS ANGELES

Art Guide of Forest Lawn with Interpretations. Introduction by Bruce Barton. Glendale, California: Forest Lawn Memorial Park, 1941.

Pictorial Forest Lawn. Forest Lawn Memorial—Parks. Glendale, Hollywood Hills, Cypress, Covina Hills. Glendale, California: Forest Lawn Memorial—Parks Association. Second Revised Edition, 1970.

Turan, Kenneth. "The Immaculate Merger of Show Biz and Death." *The Washington Post,* September 10, 1976.

Waugh, Evelyn. *The Loved One.* Boston: Little, Brown and Company, 1948.

GLASGOW NECROPOLIS

"Ancient and Honorable Cemeteries of Scotland, The." *American Cemetery,* June 1975.

Curl, James Stevens. *The Cemeteries and Burial Grounds of Glasgow.* Glasgow: Parks and Botanic Gardens Department, Corporation of Glasgow, 1974.

GLASNEVIN CEMETERY

Dublin. Official Guide. Dublin: Irish Tourist Association, n.d.

Marreco, Anne. *The Rebel Countess. The Life and Times of Constance Markievicz.* Philadelphia: Chilton Books, 1967.

Shelburne Hotel Guide to Dublin, The. Dublin 1891.

GOD'S ACRE

Blair, William A. *The Moravian Graveyard. Salem, N.C.* Winston-Salem, North Carolina, n.d.

GREEN MOUNT CEMETERY

Aronson, Theo. *The Golden Bees. The Story of the Bonapartes.* Greenwich, Connecticut: New York Graphic Society, 1964.

Beirne, Francis T. *The Amiable Baltimoreans.* New York: E. P. Dutton, 1951.

"Green Mount Beyond the Wall, The." *The Baltimore Sun (The Sun Magazine),* May 16, 1976.

Green Mount Cemetery. One Hundredth Anniversary 1838–1938. Baltimore, Maryland: The Proprietors of the Green Mount Cemetery, privately printed, 1938.

Hill, Michael. "Green Mount Cemetery. History, Poetry and Tranquility." *The Evening Sun* (Baltimore), May 18, 1976.

———. "Green Mount Cemetery's Narrow Roadways Are Ideal for Walking." *The Evening Sun* (Baltimore), September 3, 1976.

Kelly, Jacques. "Green Mount Cemetery: Where History Comes Alive." *The News American* (Baltimore), May 2, 1976.

Ruggles, Eleanor. *Prince of Players. Edwin Booth.* New York: W. W. Norton & Company, Inc., 1953.

Windsor, Wallis, Duchess of. *The Heart Has Its Reasons.* New York: David McKay Company, Inc., 1956.

GREEN-WOOD CEMETERY

Blackmore, John. "Sung and Unsung Share Green-Wood Resting Place." *The Phoenix* (Brooklyn), July 1, 1976.

Clines, Francis X. "Where the Dead Live On." *The New York Times,* October 27, 1976.

Lockwood, Charles. "As Near to Paradise as One Can Reach in Brooklyn, N.Y." *Smithsonian,* April 1976.

Morris, Rebecca. "The Gates of Heaven." *The New York Sunday News,* November 9, 1975.

GREYFRIARS CHURCHYARD

Hay, George. *The Kirk of the Greyfriars. A Short History and Guide to the Kirk and Kirkyard.* Edinburgh: T. and A. Constable, Ltd., 1959.

Stevenson, Robert Louis. *Edinburgh: Picturesque Notes.* London: Rupert Hart-Davis, 1954.

HAWAII

Bowman, Pierre. "Below Smooth Stones a Simple Hero Rests." *The Honolulu Star-Bulletin,* August 26, 1975.

Packwood, Mary P. "On the Road to Kipahulu into Lindbergh Country." *The Sunday Bulletin* (Philadelphia), February 1, 1976.

HIGHGATE CEMETERY

Brown, Ivor. *Winter in London.* London: Collins, 1951.

Curl, James Stevens. "The Plight of Highgate Cemetery." *Country Life,* April 1, 1976.

Doughty, Oswald. *A Victorian Romantic: Dante Gabriel Rossetti.* London: Frederick Muller, 1949.

Hughes, Catharine. "Gothic Highgate." *The New York Times,* October 6, 1974.

Zaturenska, Marya. *Christina Rossetti: A Portrait with Background.* New York: The Macmillan Company, 1949.

HOLLYWOOD CEMETERY

Chitwood, Oliver Perry. *John Tyler. Champion of the Old South.* New York: D. Appleton Century Company, 1939.

Godbold, E. Stanly, Jr. *Ellen Glasgow and the Woman Within.* Baton Rouge, Louisiana: Louisiana State University Press, 1972.

Historical Sketch of Hollywood Cemetery. From the 3rd of June, 1847, to 10th July, 1889. Richmond, Virginia: The Baughman Stationery Company, Printers, 1893.

Morgan, George. *The Life of James Monroe.* Boston: Small, Maynard and Company, 1921.

Strode, Hudson. *Jefferson Davis. Tragic Hero. The Last Twenty-Five Years, 1864–1889.* New York: Harcourt, Brace & World, Inc., 1964.

JEWISH CEMETERY, NEWPORT

Birmingham, Stephen. *The Grandees. America's Sephardic Elite.* New York: Harper and Row, 1971.

Mendes, Reverend A. P. "The Jewish Cemetery at Newport, R.I." *The Rhode Island Historical Magazine,* October 1885, vol. 6, no. 2.

JEWS' BURIAL GROUND, NEVIS

Stern, Malcolm H. "A Successful Caribbean Restoration." *American Jewish Historical Quarterly,* September 1971, LXI, 1.

KENSAL GREEN CEMETERY

Iremonger, Lucille. *Love and the Princesses.* New York: Thomas Y. Crowell Company, 1958.

St. Aubyn, Giles. *The Royal George.* London: Constable, 1963.

LAUREL HILL CEMETERY

Guide to Laurel Hill Cemetery Near Philadelphia with a List of Lotholders. Philadelphia: For Sale at the Cemetery and by the Treasurer, 1854.

Kane, Harnett T. *Spies for the Blue and Gray.* Garden City, New York: Doubleday & Company, Inc., 1954.

Rules and Regulations of the Laurel Hill Cemetery of Philadelphia. Philadelphia: Office of the Company, No. 45 S. Seventeenth Street, 1892.

Sculpture of a City. Philadelphia's Treasures in Bronze and Stone. New York: Walker Publishing Company, 1974.

Smith, R. A. *Smith's Illustrated Guide to and through Laurel Hill Cemetery.* Philadelphia: Willis P. Hazard, 1852.

MAINE

Bearsley, Ray, ed. *Maine. A Guide to the Vacation State.* Second Edition. Revised. Boston: Houghton Mifflin Company, 1969.

MARYLAND

Franklin, Ben A. "'Happy Thought'; Fitzgerald Reburied." *The New York Times,* November 8, 1975.

Mayfield, Sara. *The Constant Circle. H. L. Mencken and His Friends.* New York: Delacorte Press, 1968.

MASSACHUSETTS

Amory, Cleveland. *The Proper Bostonians.* New York: E. P. Dutton, 1947.

Craig, Barbara. "Some of Boston's Historic Shrines Don't Even Exist." *The Philadelphia Inquirer,* March 7, 1976.

Marchand, Earl. "Workmen Accidentally Open Ancient Tomb with 3 Skeletons." *Boston Herald-American,* July 17, 1976.

Williams, Melvin G. "Graveyard School of Art." *Antiques & Auction News,* December 27, 1974.

MIKVEH ISRAEL CEMETERY

Davidson, Joe. "Memorial Site for Colonial 'Hero' Hits Snag." *The Evening Bulletin* (Philadelphia), May 27, 1975.

Elmaleh, Reverend L. H. and Samuel, J. Bunford. *The Jewish Cemetery.* Philadelphia: privately printed, 1906. Revised and enlarged by Reverend Leon H. Elmaleh. Philadelphia, 1962.

Wolf, Edwin, 2nd, and Whiteman, Maxwell. *The History of the Jews of Philadelphia from Colonial Times to the Age of Jackson.* Philadelphia: The Jewish Publication Society of America, 1957.

MISSOURI

Missouri. A Guide to the "Show Me" State. Compiled by workers of the Writers' Program of the Works Projects Administration in the State of Missouri. New York: Hastings House, 1954.

MOUNT AUBURN CEMETERY

McVicar, Douglas. "The View from Mount Auburn." *Yankee,* May 1971.

Wyman, Donald. "Trees of Mount Auburn." *Horticulture,* June 1964.

NEW JERSEY

"Irishman Who Started Labor Day, The." *The Shamrock News* (Philadelphia), September 1, 1976.

New Jersey. A Guide to Its Present and Past. Compiled and Written by the Federal Writers' Project of the Works Progress Administration for the State of New Jersey. New York: Hastings House, 1959.

Reichenbach, Bob. "Colestown: Tombstones of History." *The Courier-Post* (Camden), November 1, 1975.

Sama, Dominic. "U.S. to Honor Heroic Nurse from N.J." *The Philadelphia Inquirer,* August 15, 1976.

"Walk Traces Hackensack's Past." *The New York Times,* May 3, 1976.

NEW MEXICO

New Mexico. A Guide to the Colorful State. Compiled by workers of the Writers' Program of the Works Progress Administration in the State of New Mexico. New and Completely Revised Edition by Joseph Miller. Edited by Henry G. Alsberg. New York: Hastings House, 1962.

NEW ORLEANS

Bartlett, Larry. "Architecture for All Souls." *The Times-Picayune (Dixie Magazine),* October 27, 1974.

Huber, Leonard V., McDowell, Peggy, and Christovich, Mary Louise. *New Orleans Architecture.* Volume III, *The Cemeteries.* Gretna, Louisiana: Pelican Publishing Company, 1974.

Kane, Harnett T. *Queen New Orleans. City by the River.* New York: William Morrow & Company, 1949.

"New Orleans' Famed Metairie Offers All Forms of Burial." *American Cemetery,* June 1965.

Pope, John. "A Fight to Save the 'Cities.'" *The States-Item* (New Orleans), May 1, 1975.

Reed, Roy. "Deterioration of Quaint Old Tombs Provokes New Orleans Controversy." *The New York Times,* February 15, 1975.

Strode, Hudson. *Jefferson Davis. Tragic Hero. The Last Twenty-Five Years, 1864–1889.* New York: Harcourt, Brace & World, Inc., 1964.

NEW YORK

Devlin, John C. "U.S. May Honor Jews' Cemetery." *The New York Times,* July 21, 1964.

Fowler, Glenn. "Bard Awards Honor 8 Examples of Good Urban Design." *The New York Times,* June 12, 1975.

Hendrickson, Robert. "Journey to Potter's Field." Unpublished.

NORTH CAROLINA

Robinson, Blackwell P., ed. *The North Carolina Guide.* Chapel Hill, North Carolina: The University of North Carolina Press, 1955.

NOVO-DEVICHY CEMETERY

"Soviet Forest Lawn." *Parade,* August 18, 1974.

Wren, Christopher S. "A Monument Is Raised to Khrushchev." *The New York Times,* September 3, 1974.

———. "Neizvestny, Sculptor, Leaves Soviet Union." *The New York Times,* March 11, 1976.

OLD BURIAL HILL

Bessom, Frank L. *Guide to the Old Burial Ground Containing Many Quaint Inscriptions.* Marblehead, Massachusetts: Oldstone Press, 1972.

"Burial Hill Restored." *Daily Evening Item* (Lynn), July 16, 1976.

Lord, Priscilla Sawyer, and Gamage, Virginia Clegg. *Marblehead: The Spirit of '76 Lives Here.* Philadelphia: Chilton Book Company, 1972.

OLD JEWISH CEMETERY, PRAGUE

Old Jewish Cemetery, Prague. Prague: The State Jewish Museum in Prague, n.d.

PENNSYLVANIA

Campisi, Gloria. "A Burial Stone Gathers No Ross." *The Philadelphia Daily News,* December 16, 1975.

Gillespie, John T. "Betsy Ross Kin Ask Court to Switch Graves to Center City." *The Evening Bulletin* (Philadelphia), May 15, 1975.

Lewis, Barbara. "Remains of Betsy Ross Being Moved." *The Evening Bulletin* (Philadelphia), December 16, 1975.

Lichten, Frances. *The Art of Rural Pennsylvania.* New York: Charles Scribner's Sons, 1946.

Lowry, Joseph F., and Morrison, John F. "Hunt for Betsy Ross Digs Up Little." *The Evening Bulletin* (Philadelphia), December 17, 1975.

McGeer, William J. A. *Reproducing Relief Surfaces. A Complete Handbook of Rubbings, Dabbing, Casting and Daubing.* Concord, Pennsylvania: Minuteman Press, 1972.

Marion, John Francis. "Center County Town Held Memorial Day Birthplace." *Grit,* May 30, 1948.

———. "Distinction of Pennsylvania Village." *The Philadelphia Inquirer (Parade Magazine),* May 25, 1947.

Pennsylvania. A Guide to the Keystone State. Compiled by workers of the Writers' Program of the Works Progress Administration in the State of Pennsylvania. New York: Oxford University Press, 1957.

Sarge, Dick. "Boalsburg: Town That Is Happy with Its Past." *The Sunday Patriot-News* (Harrisburg), March 14, 1976.

Shurkin, Joel N. "Betsy Ross' Bones Believed Found." *The Philadelphia Inquirer,* December 17, 1975.

———. "Empty Grave. Betsy Ross's Body Missing." *The Philadelphia Inquirer,* December 16, 1975.

Stoudt, John Joseph. *Pennsylvania German Folk Art.* Allentown, Pennsylvania: Schlecter's for the Pennsylvania German Folklore Society, 1966.

Turner, Cal. "'Graves' Believed to Be Slaves.'" *The Evening News* (Harrisburg), April 17, 1976.

Windle, W. Stewart. "Lucretia Mott's Quiet Resting Place." *The Evening Bulletin* (Philadelphia), January 3, 1973.

PÈRE-LACHAISE CEMETERY

B_____, Madame de. *Memoirs of Rachel.* New York: Harper & Brothers, 1858.

Brown, Frederick. *Père Lachaise. Elysium as Real Estate.* New York: The Viking Press, 1973.

Cost, March. *Rachel. An Interpretation.* London: Collins, 1947.

Dansel, Michel. *Au Père-Lachaise. Son histoire, ses secrets, ses promenades.* Paris: Libraire Arthème Fayard, 1973.

Huddleston, Sisley. *In and About Paris.* London: Methuen & Company, Ltd., 1927.

Richardson, Joanna. *Rachel.* London: Max Reinhardt, 1956.

Simon, Kate. *Kate Simon's Paris: Places & Pleasures. An Uncommon Guide Book.* New York: G. P. Putnam's Sons, 1967.

Skinner, Cornelia Otis. *Madame Sarah.* Boston: Houghton Mifflin Company, 1967.

Woollcott, Alexander. *Enchanted Aisles.* New York: G. P. Putnam's Sons, 1924.

Wyndham, Violet. *The Sphinx and Her Circle. A Memoir of Ada Leverson by her Daughter.* New York: The Vanguard Press, 1964.

PROTESTANT CEMETERY, ROME

Beck-Friis, Johan. *The Protestant Cemetery in Rome.* Malmö, Sweden: Allhems Forlag, 1956.

Birkenhead, Sheila. *Illustrious Friends. The Story of Joseph Severn and His Son Arthur.* New York: Reynal & Company/William Morrow & Company, 1965.

Bowen, Elizabeth. *A Time in Rome.* New York: Alfred A. Knopf, 1960.

Clark, Eleanor. "Of Graves and Poets." *Commentary,* November 1974.

Crosland, Margaret, ed. *A Guide to Literary Europe.* Dimension/Chilton Books, 1966.

Curtis, Ludwig. *Rome.* New York: Pantheon Books, 1950.

Hare, Augustus J. C. *Walks in Rome.* Volume II. London: George Allen, 1897.

Venturi, E. *The Eternal City.* Rome: Lozzi Publishers, 1965.

RECOLETA CEMETERY, BUENOS AIRES

Montalbano, William D. "Life in the City of the Dead." *The Miami Herald (Tropic Magazine),* September 12, 1976.

REILIG ODHRAIN, IONA

Bolton, G. Douglas. *Scotland's Western Seaboard.* Edinburgh and London: Oliver and Boyd, 1953.

Finlay, Ian. *The Highlands.* London: B. T. Batsford, Ltd., 1963.

Freer, A. Goodrich. *The Outer Isles.* Westminster: Archibald Constable & Company, Ltd., 1902.

Iona. A Short Chronological Table. Edinburgh: The Church of Scotland Publications Department, 1932.

Leatham, Diana. *They Built on Rock.* Glasgow: The Celtic Art Society, 1948.

Murray, Ellen. *Peace and Adventure. The Story of Iona for Young Folk of All Ages.* London and Glasgow: Gowans & Gray, Ltd., 1936.

Ritchie, Alec. *Iona Past and Present.* Edinburgh: George Stewart & Company, Ltd., 1934.

Sharp, William. *Iona. Divine Adventure.* (In the Works of Fiona Macleod). London: William Heinemann, 1910.

Swire, Otta F. *The Outer Hebrides and Their Legends.* Edinburgh and London: Oliver and Boyd, 1966.

ROCK CREEK CEMETERY

Lash, Joseph P. *Eleanor and Franklin.* New York: W. W. Norton & Company, 1971.

Samuels, Ernest. *Henry Adams. The Major Phase.* Cambridge, Massachusetts: The Belknap Press of Harvard University Press, 1964.

Stevenson, Elizabeth. *Henry Adams.* New York: The Macmillan Company, 1956.

SHOCKOE CEMETERY, PETERSBURG

Zuckerman, Bob. "Marshall Marker Fading." *Richmond News-Leader,* September 5, 1975.

SLEEPY HOLLOW CEMETERY

French, Allen. *Old Concord.* Boston: Little, Brown and Company, 1915.

TRINITY CHURCHYARD

Churchyards of Trinity Parish in the City of New York, 1697–1969. New York: Corporation of Trinity Church, 1969.

VERMONT

Bearse, Ray, ed. *Vermont. A Guide to the Green Mountain State.* Third Edition. Revised. (The New American Guide Series.) Boston: Houghton Mifflin Company, 1968.

Hagerman, Robert L. "The Vermont Old Cemetery Association." *Vermont Life,* Summer 1973.

WOODLAWN CEMETERY

Kleinfield, N. R. "Inflation Can Create Grave Difficulties For Cemeteries, Too." *The Wall Street Journal,* January 9, 1975.

Reed, Henry Hope, Jr. "A Woodlawn Pilgrimage." *The New York Herald Tribune Sunday Magazine,* December 9, 1962.

Streeter, Edward. *The Story of The Woodlawn Cemetery.* New York: The Woodlawn Cemetery, n.d.

Index

274 INDEX